The Directorium Asceticum = or, Guide to the Spiritual Life

DIRECTORIUM ASCETICUM;

OR,

GUIDE TO THE SPIRITUAL LIFE.

THE

DIRECTORIUM ASCETICUM;

OR,

GUIDE TO THE SPIRITUAL LIFE.

BY

JOHN BAPTIST SCARAMELLI, S.J.

Originally Published in Italian. Translated and Edited at St. Beuno's College, North Wales.

WITH PREFACE

BY

HIS EMINENCE THE MOST REV.

CARDINAL ARCHBISHOP MANNING.

Fifth Edition.

IN FOUR VOLUMES.

VOL. II.

R. & T. WASHBOURNE,
4 PATERNOSTER ROW, LONDON.
BENZIGER BROS.: NEW YORK, CINCINNATI AND CHICAGO.
1902.

CONTENTS OF VOL. II.

TREATISE SECOND.

ON THE HINDRANCES TO BE MET WITH IN THE PATH OF CHRISTIAN PERFECTION, AND OF THE MEANS TO OVERCOME THEM.

PAGE

CHAPTER V.

CHAPTER VI.

ARTICLE III.

THE OBSTACLES TO CHRISTIAN PERFECTION WHICH ARISE FROM NOT GUARDING THE SENSE OF SIGHT.

CHAPTER I.

CHAPTER II.

CHAPTER III.

CHAPTER IV.

CHAPTER V.

PAGE

ARTICLE IV.

THE HINDRANCES TO PERFECTION ARISING FROM WANT OF DULY GUARDING THE SENSES OF HEARING AND OF SMELL.

CHAPTER I.

CHAPTER II.

CHAPTER III.

CHAPTER IV.

ARTICLE V.

THE HINDRANCE TO PERFECTION RESULTING FROM THE TONGUE CONSIDERED NOT AS ONE OF THE FIVE SENSES, BUT AS THE ORGAN OF SPEECH.

CHAPTER I.

CHAPTER II.

CHAPTER III.

CHAPTER IV.

PAGE

ARTICLE VI.

THE HINDRANCE TO CHRISTIAN PERFECTION CAUSED BY OUR ILL-REGULATED AND UNMORTIFIED PASSIONS.

ARTICLE VII.

HINDRANCES TO CHRISTIAN PERFECTION FROM THE LOVE OF WORLDLY GOODS AND RICHES.

ARTICLE XI.

THE HINDRANCES WHICH SCRUPLES SET TO CHRISTIAN PERFECTION.

GUIDE TO THE SPIRITUAL LIFE.

TREATISE SECOND.

ON THE HINDRANCES TO BE MET WITH IN THE PATH OF CHRISTIAN PERFECTION, AND OF THE MEANS TO OVERCOME THEM.

INTRODUCTION.

HAVING set forth in the foregoing Treatise the means which a devout soul must use in order to attain to Christian perfection, we now pass on to examine what are the obstacles which we have to overcome by the use of such means, in order to attain this perfection with the proper success. When a general wishes to take an important fortress, which is surrounded by strong ramparts, he begins by providing the means necessary for the fulfilment of his design —he collects a body of valiant soldiers, and provides arms, artillery, and the necessary provisions for the maintenance of his troops. After having thus equipped himself, he next sets about employing these means to overcome the obstacles which stand in the way of his success. And as these obstacles arise mostly from the forces of the enemy in the field, which withstand him and with all the might of their arms seek to impede his advance; or else from the garrison within—which is ever on the alert for the defence of the stronghold—and from the fortifications, both the outworks and main rampart; he makes every effort to overcome these obstacles, by employing for this purpose the soldiers, the artillery, and the stores he has provided: at one time routing the hostile squadrons, at another climbing the earthworks, now scaling the walls, now slaughtering the garrison. When all these difficulties are overcome, he enters triumphantly into the city, and makes himself master of the place. Thus, too, if any one have purpose to acquire that perfect love of God and of our neighbour in which, as we have shown with St. Thomas, true perfection consists, he must, without delay, embrace the means which lead to it. He must arm his heart with holy desires, choose for himself a trusty guide, apply himself to the practice of meditation and prayer, to the frequentation of the sacraments, and so on of other similar things which we discussed in the foregoing Treatise, and by help of these he must make every effort to overcome all the obstacles which the devil, the world, and the flesh oppose to the attainment of his holy purpose.

2. But that the reader may have a better insight into the order of the present Treatise, he must know that the impediments to perfection are twofold; some are within us, and others without. The former derive their origin from our bodily or outward senses, ever tending to licence and impatient of restraint; or from the inner senses, that is to say, the unruly passions that have their seat in the sensitive appetite, and which are contrary to our perfection, because, enticing the will by a delectation peculiar to themselves, they estrange it from God. The latter hinder our course, because, ridding themselves of the bridle of reason, they gain over the will, and drag it into complicity with their irregular motions, thus separating it from God and His holy love. The impediments also that are without us have two different sources, since some hinder our progress by allurements, others by direct opposition. As instances of the former we may take, 1. property and riches; 2. honour and dignities; 3. objects that amuse or distract our mind: since all these, by attaching the mind to the love of themselves, detach it from the love of God. Among the obstacles which hinder us by direct opposition may be numbered the demons, for by assailing us with their wicked suggestions, they prevail over us at times, and prevent us from conquering

divine love as we desire to do. To this we may add a further obstacle, which takes its rise partly within, partly without. I mean scruples; which may have their source in a temperament which is melancholy and gloomy, over-timid and self-conscious; or else may be inspired by the devil out of envy at our spiritual progress. For these also are great hindrances to perfection, since, putting the mind and soul into a state of struggle and agitation, they deprive it of that inward peace which is so needed for union with God in the bonds of holy love. Having stated this much, we intend in the present Treatise to set forth, one by one, each of the hindrances enumerated above, in the order already indicated, and to propose the most suitable means of overcoming them, so that the soul, having surmounted every obstacle, may repose at length in the bosom of God, and, as the Apostle says, become one spirit with Him by love.*

3. It must be borne in mind that my preceding Treatise concerns every devout person, in whatever state he may be, and hence is of practical use, not only to beginners, or to such as are running the race of perfection, but also to those who have well-nigh reached the goal. The present Treatise, however, is principally addressed to beginners, as they, according to the observation of St. Thomas, are usually the most beset with hindrances. With such the senses are ill trained, the passions as yet lively and very unruly. Beginners commonly experience a great attachment to wealth, or honours, or the other fascinating objects of this world. The devil usually wages a truceless war against beginners, because, having long had them in his clutches, he uses every stratagem to regain his lost dominion, and to entrap them once more in his snares. Experience shows that in these, as in a field which has long lain fallow, the thorns of scruples and the brambles of anxiety often spring up. Not that the proficient and the perfect are without many difficulties and hindrances in the path of perfection. For as long as we sojourn in this miserable world we are on a battle-field, hemmed in on all sides by raging foes; hence must we ever have our sword in hand awaiting the onslaught.†

* Qui adhæret Domino, unus spiritus est. 1 Cor. vj. 17.

† Militia est vita hominis super terram. Job vij. 1.

There is no one in the pilgrimage of this our life so full of woes but who meets with many obstacles to his progress in the path of virtue. All I would convey is, that such obstacles are less great with the proficient, and very much less great with those that are perfect. Hence I do not say that this Treatise is suited to beginners alone, but only that it concerns them chiefly.

ARTICLE I.

The hindrances to Christian perfection which may arise from not sufficiently watching over the sense of touch. Remedies against these hindrances.

CHAPTER I.

THE GRIEVOUS HARM WHICH THE SENSE OF TOUCH MAY CAUSE THE SOUL.

4. EVERY obstacle, not only to the acquirement of perfection, but to our eternal salvation, takes its first rise in our external senses—in the sight, hearing, taste, touch, and smell; because, as the soul derives from our deceitful senses the elements of all its knowledge, it imbibes, at the same time, the poison of all disorderly inclinations. The reason is clear. The senses, while supplying the soul with the elements of whatever it has to comprehend with the understanding, present outward objects in a form which is very different from the reality. They present, as estimable, what, in truth, is worthy only to be despised. They palm off on us, as agreeable, desirable, and suitable, what really deserves to be hated and rejected. Hence, it comes to pass that the poor soul is deluded, and becomes enamoured of these objects, conceiving a hankering for them, seeking after them eagerly, sometimes to the risk of eternal welfare, sometimes to the prejudice of perfection. Further, these senses of ours (no less than with the brutes) feed on nothing but a certain sensible delight, which is in full conformity with their own natural inclinations and tendencies, but which is, commonly speaking, quite out

of conformity with the dictates of reason and the laws of the Spirit. Thus, by entangling the will in the toils of this sensible delight, they withdraw it from virtue, and separate it from God. So that the primary source of all the obstacles which meet us, not only in the path of perfection, but even in that of salvation, is found in the deceits of our senses, which delude us by false appearances, and by their sensible delights. We have, then, first, to treat of the senses, and to point out the means which must be used to hold them in check, that they may not preponderate over reason, nor enslave the will, but rather remain in due subjection. And since, of all our exterior senses that of touch is—as it seems to me—the most dangerous, I intend to devote this present Article to its consideration, and briefly to show, in this opening Chapter, the great detriment which springs from it, inasmuch as it opposes all spiritual advancement of the soul, both as to salvation and perfection

5. We must first, however, premise the fertile observation of St. Augustine, that the pleasures of sense may be either lawful or unlawful. One may contemplate the deep azure vault of heaven spangled with bright stars, and laudably take pleasure in this spectacle. But, on the other hand, one may look at theatrical shows, at obscene sights, at vicious or dangerous objects, and, from the use of our eyes, derive an unlawful gratification. So, too, we may listen to a sacred chant, or we may fill our ears with songs of impure love. The former is lawful, the latter sinful. And the holy Doctor says the same of the sense of touch.*

6. But it is here precisely that the rock lies hidden on which so many heedless persons are shipwrecked. They are not content with lawful and moderate gratifications, sought after for a good and innocent purpose, which they might blamelessly enjoy

* Delectant enim, ut dixi, oculos et spectacula ista naturæ, sed delectant etiam oculos spectacula theatrorum: hæc illicita, illa licita Psalmus sacer suaviter cantatus delectat auditum: sed delectant etiam auditum cantica histrionum . hoc illicite, illud licite. . . . Delectant conjugales amplexus; delectant etiam meretricum; hoc illicite, illud licite. Videtis ergo, carissimi, etiam in istis corporis sensibus, licitas esse et illicitas delectationes. Serm. 17 De Verb. Ap., c. 2.

through the means of their senses; they go further, and seek out those unlawful and pernicious pleasures which defile the brightness of their souls, and realise the saying of the Prophet Jeremiah, that the death of sin finds its entrance through their senses, as by so many windows carelessly left open to the destruction of their souls. As St. Augustine observes: "Whatever delights the eyes by its beauty, whatever is pleasing to the taste, sweet to the smell, soft to the touch, tarnishes always—if we are incautious in taking such pleasure when forbidden, or if we take it not of any good motive, but merely to gratify the cravings of passion—the purity of our minds, and fulfils the saying of the Prophet, that death, the death of sin, enters by the windows of the senses to destroy our souls."* And the holy Doctor is right, for such gratifications, if unduly permitted, are either mortal sins, which, by their entry, slay the soul; or they are venial offences, which open the door to grievous sin and to the death of the soul. So, it holds good, that our bodily senses, unless they be carefully guarded, are so many openings whereby the death of sin makes its way into heedless souls.

7. But, if undue liberty being allowed to any sense prove so prejudicial to our spiritual life, we may assert that not only does the sense of touch—of which we are now treating—produce no ordinary harm when not properly guarded, but it even works ruin, destruction and complete perdition. First, because, unlike the other senses, this one is not confined to one or the other of our bodily organs, but extends over every part of our frame, so that it has greater power to win over the will, and, by a delectation peculiar to itself, to lead it into the captivity of sin. Sight resides in the eyes alone, hearing in the ears, smell in the nostrils, taste nowhere but in the tongue and palate; but touch is spread over the whole body; in every member does it lay snares for the will, spreading over all a certain poisonous

* Quidquid enim pulchrescit in visu, quidquid dulcescit gustu, quidquid blanditur auditu, quidquid lenocinatur odoratu, quidquid mollescit tactu, in his omnibus, si incauti fuerimus, surripientibus concupiscentiis malis, animæ virginitatem corrumpi permittimus, et impletur illud quod per prophetam dictum est: *Intravit mors per fenestras nostras.* Lib. Quinquag. Homiliar. Hom. 35.

pleasure. In a word, this sense is like a mighty enemy, who, being determined to take a fortress, confines not his attack to one or other of the outworks, but invests it on all sides, and from all quarters assaults and batters it, until he has reduced it under his power. Secondly, this is a vile and brutal sense, which hankers after the most pestilential and soul-destroying pleasure which can be conceived; it fattens on that impure and sensual delight which never misses giving death to the soul, and unfailingly puts it on the road to everlasting damnation.

8. I am not here going to enlarge on the excessive turpitude and deformity contained in the pleasure of which this vile sense is so greedy; for, as we are addressing spiritual persons who have emerged from this abominable filth, and have its depravity in horror, we should fear lest our remarks might sully their purity. I mean only, by way of serious warning, and to render all exceedingly careful in their guard over this sense, to set before them this great truth, that the slightest condescension on their part to the dangerous and empoisoned gratifications of the touch, will suffice to pluck from their souls all the buds of virtue which have been put forth in the course of their spiritual life. The pleasure which we experience in other sins may be likened to the axe which severs the branches of some one virtue, and causes it to wither. But the gratification peculiar to this sense—as St. Gregory asserts, on the authority of holy Job—is a raging fire, which, kindled in the soul, devours every virtue, reduces it to ashes, and wholly destroys it, so that it is seen no more. To such an extent, that the soul, which was hitherto like a delightful garden, adorned with the flowers of many virtues, becomes a frightful waste, barren of all spiritual good; since this sinful gratification stifles all good works, dries them up, and finally withers their very root, so that they can no longer put forth a single flower.*

* Beatus Job crimen luxuriæ definiens, ait: *Ignis est usque ad consummationem devorans:* quia nimirum reatus hujus facinoris, non solum usque ad inquinationem maculat, sed usque ad perditionem devorat. Et quia quælibet alia fuerint bona opera, si luxuriæ scelus non abluitur, immanitate hujus criminis obruuntur, secutus adjunxit, *Et omnia eradicans genimina.* Lib. xxj. Moral., cap. 9.

9. The reason of this is given by St. Thomas, who says that the deadly fascination of this unbridled sense overclouds the light of reason, distorts the understanding, perverts the will, and throws into disorder all the powers of the soul; wherefore it is no wonder that the unhappy person, however previously fruitful in good works, becomes unable to do anything that is good.*

10. To be convinced of this truth it will suffice to bring to mind the lamentable fall of Solomon. As we all know, he was in early youth full of wisdom, knowledge, prudence, justice, piety, religion, and tender devotion to God's service. But what did all these good qualities avail him, seeing that in his old age he slackened the reins which held this brutish sense in check, and allowed it to run after its own gratification? For being wholly corrupted by its excesses, he abandoned himself to such stretches of folly as to build temples to idols, and to offer to them abominable sacrifices. This reflection is taken from St. Basil.†

11. The motive which, in my judgment, will avail the most to persuade a devout person to guard with very watchful jealousy this wanton sense, and to keep it under by even the rigours of penance, is the reflection that but a slight indulgence shown to it, a small compliance with its tendencies, suffices for the overthrow of what it may have taken years of spiritual life to build up. Had you the wisdom of Solomon, did you vie with Moses in contemplation, with Abraham in faith, with Isaac in obedience, with David in meekness, with Job in patience, and had you all other virtues in the highest degree, if this unruly sense begin to prevail over you and to gain the mastery, all is lost. A wealthy merchant, if he knows, or has even the slightest suspicion, that there is within his

* Per vitium luxuriæ maxime appetitus concupiscibilis vehementer intendit suo objecto delectabili, propter vehementiam passionis, et delectationis. Et ideo consequens est, quod per luxuriam maxime superiores vires deordinentur, scilicet ratio, et voluntas. 2, 2, q 133, a. 5.

† Salomoni quid attulit commodæ frugis exuberans adeo opulentia infusæ sapientiæ et quæ vix dum adolescenti cœlitus de Deo cognitio indulta est; quando is demum per mulierculæ, quam ad insaniam usque deperibat, illicitos complexus, ex cordatissimo adolescente, per ætatem in senium devergentem, vecors factus, et in idololatriam prolapsus concidit. Epist. ad Chilonem. Anacoret.

house some one on the watch to rob him, how anxious will he not become! how he will make fast the door of his strong room, how carefully will he look to its bolts and bars, with what watchfulness will he not guard the chests which contain his store! He will pass sleepless nights, or if he close his eyes, he will watch even in his slumbers; every breath of wind will arouse him; he will awake at the slightest noise, raise his head, turn his eyes every way, scan and take note of everything: because he fears to lose in one short night the wealth which it has taken him years of toil to amass. Thus too, a spiritual man, who, by the practice of virtue, prayer, penance and mortification, has already laid up a certain treasure of merit in heaven, knowing full well that he has in his house, nay, even within himself, a traitor sense which, assaulting his will, and alluring it by the bait of its delectations, is able to strip it of all its spiritual wealth; with what jealousy ought he to keep guard over it; how sternly ought he to check its motions; how rigorously to keep it in subjection and restraint. But more of this in the following Chapters.

CHAPTER II.

FIRST REMEDY AGAINST EXCESSES IN THE USE OF TOUCH. CAUTION IN ITS USE.

12. THE first remedy against the depraved tendencies of the sense of touch is an extreme care never to lay hands on any one, especially of the opposite sex. A Christian should never allow himself to be led to do this on any conceivable pretence, whether of affability, friendliness, pleasantry, play, or politeness; because such liberties, though devoid of any evil intent, are an incitement to this frail sense, and always turn out fatal to the soul. Who is there that would play with fire, or touch flames when they are burning fiercely? There is no one but knows full well that the slightest touch is all that is needed in such case to cause a most

painful wound. Why, then, not take heed to ourselves of certain touches not over-modest or cautious—touches which are full of danger, in which lurks a poison that intoxicates the soul, and from which usually springs the fire whereby the soul is reduced to ashes? "Touch, young man," says St. Nilus, "touch fire rather than a person of the opposite sex, especially if she be one not yet advanced in years; for at the first touch of fire thou wilt quickly withdraw thy hand, forced by the pain; but thou wilt not shrink from being scorched by the touch or conversation of woman."*

13. Let the reader listen to what St. Gregory tells us in his Dialogues,† and he will be able to judge whether I have grounds for speaking thus. In the province of Nurcia there lived a venerable priest, whose name the Saint has omitted to tell, who was so far from allowing himself liberties or confidences with women, that he would not allow even the one that waited on him to come close to him.‡ Having blamelessly exercised the sacred ministry for the space of forty years, this great servant of God was seized with a violent fever, which soon brought him to extremities. He had already closed his eyes, lost all power of motion, and breathed with such difficulty that the bystanders thought him dead. In the meantime his housekeeper bent over him, and applied her ear to his nostrils, for the purpose of discovering whether or no he still breathed. The saintly old man perceiving this, gathered up his remaining strength, and began to exclaim, "Away, woman! there is yet in me a spark of life; you are straw, and I am fire.§ Begone! fire within me that is not wholly extinct may burst into flame, and reduce me to ashes."‖ Shortly after the holy Apostles Peter and Paul appeared to him, at the sight of whom he joyously exclaimed, "Welcome, dear Patrons! how have you

* Ad ignem potius ardentem quam ad mulierem juvenem, juvenis, appropinqua: nam si ad ignem accesseris, dolore affectus, resilies: at si feminæ verbis incensus fueris, haud ita facile recedes. Orat. 2, Adversus Vitia.

† Lib. iv. cap. 11.

‡ Eamque sibimet propinquare nullâ occasione permittens, ab eâ sibi communionem funditus familiaritatis absciderat.

§ Recede a me, mulier: adhuc igniculus vivit: paleam tolle.

‖ Recede a me, mulier, paleam tolle.

deigned to visit your unworthy servant? I give you thanks. Lo! I come."* And with these words he sweetly breathed his last in the arms of these two great Apostles.

14. What now will be said by certain persons—of piety sometimes, and even, at times, specially consecrated to God—who fancy it lawful to trifle with people of the other sex, to take unseemly liberties with them, and who pretend that there is no harm, and that all takes place with the greatest innocence? We have just heard of a saintly Priest found worthy to receive, on his death-bed, the visit of some of the most exalted members of the heavenly court, who, at an advanced age, with his spirit about to depart, and his body already chilled by the approach of death, yet, at the coming near of a pious woman (for anything that we know she did not touch him), fears, trembles, and cries out to her to withdraw without delay. And will men or women, with the hot blood of youth coursing through their veins, fancy that they can go as far as touches which, if not too free, are at least unbecoming, without any danger? I am amazed at them. Men and women are fire and fuel, as this saintly Priest so truly said; at the slightest contact they become heated; and if, at length, they burst not out into flame, it is a prodigy, a miracle. Let such as these listen to what St. Gregory of Tours relates of Bishop Nicetius, and then let them blush at their heedless freedom.† He tells us that not only did this holy prelate guard himself most carefully from all familiarity with women, but that he would not run the risk of touching with his hands the limbs of innocent babes; and when constrained to do so by reason of his office, he covered the part with his garment. With like care will one who wishes to preserve unblemished the brightness of his purity, guard his sense of touch.

15. Two reasons may be assigned for this guarded and watchful conduct of the saints in all their use of touch. First, the touch is so unruly a sense, that as soon as any liberty is allowed it, it

* Bene veniant, domini mei: bene veniant, domini mei. Quid ad tantillum servulum vestrum estis dignati convenire? Venio, venio: gratias ago, gratias ago.

† In Vitis Patrum, c. 8.

immediately attacks the will, and vanquishes it with the weapon of sensual pleasure, which being the most pleasant of all, is the surest to prevail. Secondly, because, as St. Thomas says, all the other senses have their foundation, as it were, on that of touch.* And as when the foundation of a building is weakened, the walls and the upper stories, and the roof which rests upon them, totter to their fall, so too, if the sense of touch be not carefully watched, it cannot be but that the other senses, which are stirred to action by it, should be spiritually weak. Hence a universal disorder pervades the whole man, and the spiritual fabric, supposing it to have already begun, must needs fall into ruin. It has been well said by St. Basil, that a person jealous of his purity will be as diligent as possible in guarding the sense of touch, as it is the most dangerous of all, the most alluring, and one which, by the bait of pleasure, draws all the other feelings and affections after it, and drags the whole man into crime and perdition.† St. Thomas's teaching, as we have seen, is substantially the same.

16. But as some of these thoughtless persons will be but little moved by the authority and examples of the saints (and would to God that they did not, at times, ascribe their caution in touching to a mistaken motive or a baseless fear), I will add to the foregoing instances the irrefragable authority, not of a saint merely, but of the Saint of Saints, of God Himself, who, from time to time, by wonders and prodigies, has given us to know how displeasing to Him is this incautious use of touch, even though it proceed not from an evil intent.‡ The Abbot Ghebard was tried by God with a long and most painful sickness, which deprived him of the use of all his limbs, so that he was unable to turn on his side, or even to put forth a hand to take the necessary refreshment. After a year of so tedious an illness, he recovered sufficiently to enable them to remove him from his bed and place him in a chair; yet, like a statue in its niche, he could stir neither hand nor foot,

* Omnes autem alii sensus fundantur supra tactum. I part. qu. 76, a. 5.

† Tactum vero, ut omnium sensuum perniciosissimum, et sævissime blandientem, sensusque reliquos in suas pellicentem illecebras, immaculatum quam maximâ poterit curâ servabit. Lib de Verâ Virginit.

‡ Chron. Hissangien. Jo. Trithem. Ad Ann. Dom. 1091.

nor any other limb. Meanwhile, he received a visit from Abbot William, a distinguished servant of God, who, touched with pity at his helpless state, exhorted him to beseech the Almighty to restore to him, at least, the use of his right hand, that he might employ it in some work. "No," replied the devout Ghebard; "never will I ask for bodily health. I rejoice that God thus tries me in this crucible of my infirmity, in order that, being wholly cleansed from every defilement, I may be made worthy to be united to Him." The tender heart of William could no longer brook seeing his friend in so wretched a plight; he seized his right hand, blessed and healed it, in the sight of all who were present. Some days after, a kinswoman of Ghebard came to visit him with all her family. The Abbot, thinking that civility required it, caused himself to be carried in his chair to the monastery gate, that so he might converse with her. While they were talking, Ghebard related the wonderful cure he had obtained of God, through the merits of William. On hearing this, the lady took hold of his hand, as of a sacred object, and kissed it. Were we to submit this fact to the judgment of people who are inclined to freedom in this point, they would see in it no shadow of evil, and would even approve it as an act of religion and piety. Yet at this touch, at this kiss, the Abbot's hand was benumbed, and became as helpless and as devoid of life as a stone. William, who had witnessed the scene in a vision, returned to visit Ghebard in his cell, and having reproved him for his heedlessness in allowing his hand to be kissed by the woman, he once more blessed it and restored its power. It is plain that, as this twofold cure was miraculous, the paralysis of the hand, resulting from the lady's touch, was no less the direct work of God. So, if the Almighty, by such a miracle, punished a servant of His with so great severity, it must needs follow that He is displeased with such touches, though they may be free from any evil intent; for of a truth such actions are always unbecoming, always unseemly, and always dangerous.

17. A further instance of God's displeasure in a like occasion, equally in a matter of touch, happened in the case of the Blessed Mary d'Oignies, and, to all seeming, this was most innocent: it is

related by the Cardinal de Vitry, in her life written by him. A friend of this servant of God, under an impulse of spiritual affection, took her hand and pressed it. At the very moment, the blessed woman heard within her the voice of the Spouse, whispering, *Noli me tangere.* Not understanding the meaning of these Latin words, she, in her single-mindedness, repeated them to her friend, that he might translate them for her. He, being fully aware of the import of the words, took to heart the rebuke God had addressed to him by the mouth of His servant, and the warning it implied to be on his guard against the like liberties; for they are always improper, and exceeding dangerous. It follows, then, that such precautions are not to be accounted as scruples, according to the view which some take of them; but are needed to keep a check on the sense of touch, which, like a wild horse, becomes our master, and hurries us to the precipice of deadly sin, if we but slacken the rein.

18. These same precautions are to be observed by devout persons with themselves. I am far from wishing to tarry on so delicate a matter. I will merely observe that the pious reader should be persuaded that, in the sense of touch, he bears about with him a domestic traitor, who, by sudden onslaughts, attacks the citadel of the heart, and but too frequently masters it. Now, as every one who can help it avoids dealing with traitors, or if compelled to do so proceeds with the utmost wariness, not to fall into their snares, so should every man who fears God avoid, with the greatest circumspection, all handling of his person that is not necessary, and proceed with caution even in such as necessity requires. I have known a holy soul, adorned with every virtue in a high degree, but especially with an angelic purity, who during the whole course of a life (which was not a short one) had never had experience of the least thought or emotion contrary to purity. This rare and almost miraculous privilege, in one dwelling in a frail body of flesh, had been earned by an unusual caution in dealing with herself. Without first asking leave of her Confessor, she never allowed herself to look at or touch any part of her person, even such as decency does not require us to veil, although

* Lib. ij. c. 5.

compelled to do so by the requirements of disease. And as she had to lie long in bed, under pressure of serious ailments, she asked her Director for leave to wear stockings, since she considered it unbecoming to touch one naked foot with another. This degree of caution in the guarding of the sense of touch, will, I am well aware, appear exaggerated and scrupulous to many, but yet God has willed that certain chosen souls should practise it, in order to teach others not to neglect the precautions which are absolutely necessary.

CHAPTER III.

ANOTHER REMEDY AGAINST THE DISORDERS OF THE SENSE OF TOUCH, WHICH IS TO KEEP IT UNDER PENITENTIAL INFLICTIONS.

19. St. Gregory says, that God, in His dealings with our spiritual infirmities, treats us as a physician when he is healing those of our bodily frames. Physicians cure contraries by contraries, and meet fever and inflammatory disease with cooling potions; and, on the other hand, for ailments which arise from a defect of vital heat, they prescribe drugs of a heating nature. So, too, does God heal our souls with remedies which are the exact opposite of our spiritual infirmities.* In order, then, to imitate the skill of our Divine Healer, let us examine what is the peccant humour, so to speak, of this unruly sense of touch, that we may discover a remedy suitable to its cure.

20. As was observed above, this brutal sense hankers after nothing but indulgence, delectations, pleasure; even unlawful:—such, when left to its natural tendencies, are its aliment; on such does it batten like an unclean animal. The Apostle St. Paul

* Cœlestis medicus singulis quibusque vitiis obviantia adhibet medicamenta Nam sicut arte medicinæ calida frigidis, et frigida calidis curantur; ita Dominus noster contraria opposuit medicamenta peccatis. Hom. 32 In Evang.

makes allusion to this when speaking of himself.* What is the law which he felt in his members, struggling against the law of his mind and reason, but the depraved tendency to pleasure found in this sense, in virtue of which it chafes under the yoke of reason, which would restrain it? This is what the Apostle meant when he said *that the flesh lusts against the spirit, and the spirit against the flesh*, whence arises between them a truceless war.†

Now what are these unruly rebellions of the flesh against the spirit, which it refuses to obey? what, but the deeply-rooted tendency of the touch to pleasures which set it in fierce opposition to the spirit, to which such gratifications are repugnant? Hence the lust that is within us has no other aim, with its evil desires and vile appetites, than the gratification of this unruly sense, and the satisfaction of its lawless requirements. It follows, then, in strictest consequence, that no one can enter upon and persevere in a devout and spiritual course, without mortifying this rebellious sense.

21. But by what means may we bring it under, so as to hinder its rebellious uprisings against the spirit, which it would withdraw from the way of perfection, and, what is far worse, from life everlasting? They are pointed out by St. Gregory, who prescribes the use of contrary remedies. The flesh hankers after indulgence, we will make it put up with rough and hard treatment; it clamours for pleasure, we will make it feel pain; it desires delectations, we will give it tortures instead; in a word, the body must be kept under by a continual practice of penance. It will thus be brought into subjection, and will allow the soul to live calmly and innocently in the practice of its devout exercises.

22. This is precisely the means taken by St. Paul, who, after having stated the rebellion of this sense, informs us of the remedy by which he overcame it. *I chastise*, says he, *my body, and bring it into subjection.*‡ And going into further detail, he shows that

* Video aliam legem in membris meis repugnantem legi mentis meæ. Rom. vij. 23.

† Caro enim concupiscit adversus spiritum, spiritus autem adversus carnem: hæc enim sibi invicem adversantur. Gal. v. 17.

‡ Castigo corpus meum, et in servitutem redigo. 1 Cor. ix. 27.

the means he employed were incessant labours, long night-watches, and rigorous fasts.* St. Augustine, commenting on these words, says, "Mark how the Apostle of the Gentiles dealt with his body as with a beast of burden; he tamed it by hunger, thirst, and fasting, and kept it as subject to the spirit as a slave. Learn hereby, thou who wouldst go to God by the path of perfection, how to bring thy body into subjection, lest it clog thy footsteps on this road; so that thou mayest draw nigh unto Him without hindrance, not indeed by thy footsteps, but by the affections of the heart."†

23. Let us now see how other saints dealt with the rebellion of this sense, when its disordered appetites rose up against the spirit. St. Jerome tells us of St. Hilarion, that whenever the holy solitary felt the assaults of the sense of touch, so greedy of pleasure, he would begin to strike his breast with clenched hand, and, indignant against his body, would say, "I will teach thee not to kick, unruly ass; I will give thee straw instead of corn, I will torment thee with hunger and thirst, I will crush thee with the burden of unceasing labour, I will ill-use thee and expose thee to the frost of winter and to the heat of summer; so that thou mayest be forced to think rather how to live than how to indulge thy lusts." Nor was he content with mere words, but came to deeds, for sometimes he withheld all food from his body for three or four days together, and then took only a little juice of herbs, as much as was sufficient to prevent him fainting through exhaustion and hunger. To this he added other hard usage, spending the whole day in digging the ground, exposed to all the inclemency of the weather; but, what was more, he armed himself against his own flesh with prayers and singing of psalms, imploring help from above in his arduous conflicts.‡ Such were the means of which

* In labore, in vigiliis, in jejuniis. 2 Cor. xj. 27.

† Vide eum gubernantem, eumdemque viatorem apostolum Paulum. Vide illum jumentum suum domantem. In fame, inquit, et siti, in jejuniis castigo corpus meum, et in servitutem redigo. Ita ergo tu, qui ambulare desideras, doma carnem tuam, et ambula. Ambulas enim, si domas; non enim ad Deum passibus, sed affectibus venimus. Tract de Divers. Capit., cap iij.

‡ Iratus sibi, et pectus pugnis verberans, quasi cogitationes percussione manûs posset excutere: Ego, inquit, aselle, faciam ut non calcitres, nec te hordeo alam, sed paleis: fame te conficiam, et siti: gravi onerabo pondere;

the saints made use for the purpose of bringing under the pride of the sense of touch, whenever it troubled the spirit with its unruly cravings for pleasure.

24. But let us listen to what St. Jerome tells us of himself. In the beginning of his life as a Solitary, not having yet overcome this unruly sense, he was disturbed by its rebellion, in the shape of swarms of unclean fancies, and the glowing fire of impurity which it kindled within his breast. He was not, however, disheartened, but, as a generous champion of the Crucified One, he bravely armed himself against this domestic foe, determined to overcome it, as may be seen in a letter written by him to the saintly virgin Eustochium, in which he relates the remedies that he employed against it.*

25. The holy Doctor tells us that, being in a desert which was

per æstus agitabo, et frigora, ut cibum potius, quam lasciviam cogites. Herbarum ergo succis per triduum, et quatriduum deficientem animam sublevabat; orans frequenter, et psallens, et rastro humum fodiens, ut jejuniorum laborem labor operis duplicaret. In Vitâ.

* Oh quoties ego ipse in eremo constitutus, et in illâ solitudine, quæ exusta solis ardoribus, horrendum monachis præparat habitaculum, putabam me romanis interesse deliciis! Sedebam solus, quia amaritudine plenus eram. Horrebant sacco membra deformia: et squallida cutis situm Æthiopicæ canis obduxerunt. Quotidie lacrymæ, quotidie gemitus: et si repugnantem somnus imminens oppressisset, nuda humo vix hærentia ossa collidebam. De cibis vero, et potu taceo: cum languentes monachi aquâ frigidâ utantur, et coctum aliquid comedisse luxuria sit. Ille igitur ego, qui ob gehennæ metum tali me carcere ipse damnaveram scorpionum tantum socius, et ferarum, sæpe choris intereram puellarum. Pallebant ora jejuniis, et ante hominem suâ jam carne præmortuum sola libidinum incendia bulliebant. Itaque omni auxilio destitutus ad Jesu jacebam pedes, irrigabam lacrymis, crine tergebam, et repugnantem carnem hebdomadarum mediâ subjugabam. Non erubesco confiteri infelicitatis meæ miseriam: quin potius plango, me non esse quod fuerim. Memini me clamantem dies junxisse cum noctibus, nec prius a pectoris cessasse verberibus, quam rediret, Domino increpante, tranquillitas. Ipsam quoque cellulam, quasi mearum cogitationum consciam pertimescebam, et mihimetipsi iratus, et rigidus, solus deserta penetrabam, sicubi concava vallium, aspera montium, rupium prærupta cernebam. Ibi meæ orationis locus; ibi illud miserrimæ carnis ergastulum: et ut ipse mihi testis est Dominus post multas lacrymas, post cœlo inhærentes oculos, nonnumquam videbar mihi interesse agminibus angelorum: et lætus, gaudensque canebam: *Post te in odorem unguentorum curremus.* Si autem hoc sustinent illi, qui exeso corpore, solis cogitationibus oppugnantur; quid patitur puella quæ deliciis fruitur? Nempe illud apostoli: *Vivens mortua est.* Epist. 22 ad Eustoch.

all parched by the burning rays of the sun, living in a frightful solitude, and wearing nothing but a garb of rough sackcloth, his fancy constantly suggested that he was in the midst of the pleasures of Rome, and in the company of Roman ladies, and he seemed to see the fire of lust blazing up before his eyes and in his heart. He, on his side, armed himself against these assaults of his senses by severe and prolonged fasts, going sometimes a whole week together, without taking so much as a mouthful of boiled herbs, or a drink of the tepid water of the place. He refused slumber to his eyelids, and when compelled by sheer fatigue to take a short interval of rest, he lay on the bare ground, and, to use his own words, his fleshless bones were pierced by the rugged rock on which he took his repose. He prostrated himself with loud cries and sobs at the feet of Jesus, bathed them with his tears, and wiped them with his hair. He struck his breast repeatedly with no light strokes. Indignant with his rebellious, unruly flesh, he wandered forth alone over the rugged mountain heights, through the hollows of the ravines, and there burst forth into loud lamentations and floods of tears, and, adding blows to his tears and groans, he spent in this manner whole days and nights. Through the rigour of his penance, his colour became like that of an Ethiopian; he was like a walking skeleton, as ghastly as a spectre. Such were the means employed by the saints to bring within bounds the rebellion of the sense of which we are treating. And, in truth, by these austerities, they succeeded at length so well, that they attained a most delightful calm, and seemed to themselves to be no longer on earth, but with the angelic choirs.*

26. Further, God's servants have, at times, found themselves compelled to recur to remedies still more violent than those related above, in order to overcome the assaults of this brutal sense; so unruly have its cravings occasionally become. There is a well-known instance in the lives of the Fathers of the desert, of the heroic act of a Solitary of Egypt, whose austere life had won for him in the neighbouring city a reputation of eminent sanctity.†

* Videbar mihi interesse agminibus angelorum.

† Ex Lib. Doctor. PP., De Fornic., c. 15.

A shameless and abandoned woman, mocking at the notion that he was better than others, said to certain dissolute youths, "How much will you give me if I induce him to fall into sin?" Upon this proposal, instead of being horrified at so great a crime, these young debauchees promised her a considerable sum of money if she could succeed in overthrowing this pillar of godliness. The infamous bargain having been struck, the wretched creature left the city, and arrived towards nightfall at the holy monk's cell. Here, pretending to be terrified at the desert into which she had wandered, having lost her way, and yet more terrified at the wild beasts that abounded there, she asked him for a night's lodging. The servant of God felt perplexed at her request, and was for a while at a loss how to act. Should he send her away? Charity forbade. Was he to give her shelter? He could not but see the danger to which he would be exposing himself. At length, after a brief deliberation with himself, he decided to admit her into the vestibule of his sleeping-place, and to retire into his inner apartment, and there lock himself in. Having done so, about the middle of the night the abandoned creature, feigning alarm, cried out piteously, "Open the door, Servant of God, I hear around the growls of bears and the roar of lions. For God's sake, open! they are coming, they are coming to tear me in pieces. Open to me, I beg, for love of Jesus; leave me not exposed to the attacks of these wild beasts." Overcome anew by his charity, he opened his cell and gave her admission, and, having locked her in, he lay him down to rest in the outer apartment. But, far from finding rest, he experienced in his senses a turmoil which allowed neither repose to his body nor calm to his mind. While struggling with this domestic foe, he bethought himself that diseases are cured by contraries, and that when an unruly sense craves with eagerness a certain pleasure, the surest remedy is to vanquish it with pain. What then did he do? He lit his lamp, and held first one finger and then another in the flame, continuing this torture without flinching during the remainder of the night, so that at dawn of day his whole hand was scorched. Thus did he, by dint of pain, overcome the sensual appetite that was urging him on to sinful pleasure.

27. We may hence infer the two following truths:—First; with what intensity the sense of touch hankers after the venomous delights of forbidden pleasure, and what pressure it puts on the will to force it to comply with its vile cravings, since it compelled these great servants of God to employ such violent and arduous means to keep it in check. Secondly; how great is the need we all have of bodily austerities if we wish to keep down this so formidable a foe, whom we ever bear about with us, and who forms a part of ourselves. This sense gains strength and vigour from the vivacity of the spirits and the heat of the blood; for which reason we all of us usually stand in need of mortifying the exuberance of the vital spirits by bodily inflictions, and of cooling the heat of the blood by abstinence and austerity, so as not to leave our domestic foe in such strength as to be able to do us harm.

28. This latter point applies more especially to beginners in the spiritual life. First; because with most of them this sense has never hitherto been mortified, but, on the contrary, is nearly always full of disorder through undue indulgence in past times. Secondly; because, as they themselves are the theatre of the intestine war to which this sense gives rise, they will not on any other condition enjoy that calm so needed by such as would give themselves to prayer and other spiritual exercises, and would make fitting progress in these holy practices. Lastly; beginners are still liable to God's justice for their past transgressions as regards the penalty, if not the guilt. It is therefore just that they should render to God the satisfaction due to Him by a fervent course of penance. If they be truly repentant of their past follies, the very repentance which has led them back to God will surely stir them up to great earnestness in this exercise. For this reason we now proceed to describe the various kinds of penance by which the saints have mortified their flesh, so that each one may adopt that which he judges to suit his case, or, to speak more accurately, that which his Director thinks most appropriate to his necessities.

CHAPTER IV.

THE DIVERS KINDS OF PENANCE PRACTISED BY THE SAINTS.

29. BEFORE entering upon the subject-matter of this Chapter, I would observe, that although the reason for which I am now speaking of bodily austerities be to show the effect they have in mortifying the sense of touch, and holding in check our disordered appetites, yet such is by no means the only valuable result produced in us by this virtue. It is one of the principal effects, I grant, but not the only effect. These austerities have the further property of mortifying the other senses, which, as we have already seen, so much depend upon that of touch; they weaken the body so as to prevent its rebellious uprisings against the spirit; they diminish self-love, and break its opposition to the spiritual efforts of the soul; and thus, by removing these divers obstacles, they make us more prompt and less hampered in running in the way of perfection. Besides, as was just now said, bodily austerities render to God satisfaction for past sins, blot out the remnants of former faults, and fit the soul for receiving at the hand of the Almighty a greater abundance of grace and help for advancing further in virtue. And experience shows, that after the practice of mortification a spiritual person is more recollected, more devout, and more earnest concerning the business of his perfection. I would infer from this, that though the mortification of this most dangerous sense of touch be a sufficient motive to engage us to apply ourselves to bodily austerities, the pious reader would do well to avail himself of these additional considerations as an encouragement to embrace them with greater fervour.

30. One of the bodily austerities most recommended by the saints is, beyond question, fasting; and doubtless it is one of the most effectual means of weakening the sense of touch, since, by depriving the body of food, this sense is deprived of the fuel that feeds it in its rebellions. But we shall treat of fasting in the following Article, where we shall speak more particularly of the sense of taste, the proper object of which is the savour of food. On this account we will now proceed to treat of other austerities.

31. The hair-shirt is certainly most suitable for mortifying the sense of touch, for, by its continual painful prickings, it blunts the untoward inclination of this sense for indulgence and delight, and has ever been in use among the saints. The sacred text tells us of the far-famed Judith, that she always girded her loins with a hair-shirt.* Holy David, that pattern of penitents, though clad in regal purple, disdained not, as he plainly acknowledges, to wear a hair-shirt under his royal robes.† And we read in the Book of Paralipomena, that when the plague was raging from house to house, and its victims were falling on every side, both King David and the elders of the nation prostrated themselves in the dust, clad in sackcloth.‡ And though the Divine Scriptures, by the word sackcloth, sometimes designate a garb of humiliation fashioned like a sack, it nevertheless, as in the case of Judith, bears the further meaning of an instrument of bodily mortification.

32. What took place in Samaria, during the siege of this city by the forces of Benadad, is most deserving of notice. The people were so sore afflicted with famine, that in some cases they were constrained to feed on human flesh. A mother came before King Joram, while he was walking on the ramparts superintending the defence of the city, and lifting up her voice, she cried for justice to be done on another woman with whom she had agreed to devour her own child, on the understanding that the child of the other was to furnish the second meal; and now that the complainant's child was eaten, the other refused to stand to the agreement. On hearing of this so terrible an event, the King tore his garments, and all the people could see that he wore sackcloth next to his skin.§

33. Nor should it astonish the reader to see the king of

* Et habens super lumbos suos, cilicium, jejunabat omnibus diebus vitæ suæ præter Sabbata. Judith. viij. 6.

† Cum mihi molesti essent, induebar cilicio. Ps. lxxxiv. 15, Posui vestimentum meum cilicium. Ps. lxviij. 14.

‡ Et ceciderunt tam ipse, quam majores natu, vestiti ciliciis, proni in terram. 1 Paralip. xxj.

§ Quod cum audisset rex, scidit vestimenta sua, et transibat per murum. Viditque omnis populus cilicium, quo vestitus erat ad carnem intrinsecus. 4 Reg. vj. 30.

Samaria clad in sackcloth, though standing on the ramparts of a beleaguered city and taken up with warlike cares, for it was the custom of the chosen people to practise such austerities in troublous times, in order to appease God's wrath. Thus we find in the inspired Volume, that when Holofernes, with a mighty host laid siege to Bethulia, the priests put on sackcloth.* So, too, in the time of the Macchabean wars, the combatants recommended themselves to God with their heads sprinkled with dust, and their loins girt about with sackcloth † Indeed, the Prophets themselves, while exhorting the people to repentance, often warned them to put on sackcloth as a fitting means for propitiating the wrath of the Most High. *Gird yourselves with sackcloth*, says Jeremiah, and with groans and loud cries implore the Lord to grant you pardon of your faults ‡

34. Under the New Covenant, this praiseworthy custom of using sackcloth as an instrument of penance has become far more general. The first to make use of it, after the birth of Christ, was he who first began to preach penance to the people, in order to prepare them to receive Him; it was the holy forerunner, John the Baptist, of whom St. Matthew says, *Now John himself wore a garment of camel's hair, and a girdle of leather round his loins* § Since his time the use of the hair-shirt has always been so common and familiar in the Church of God, that we can hardly find a single holy Confessor who has not adopted it. It may suffice to observe that the venerable Carthusian Order imposes on its members, as an inviolable precept, the rule of ever wearing the hair-shirt as an indispensable portion of their great mortification. So true is it that both under the New and the Old Covenant the hair-shirt has ever been taken to be an instrument most fitted to mortify the flesh, so as to appease God, to obtain forgiveness of sin, and, above all, to tame by its roughness the voluptuous sense of touch, which, by its love of indulgence, drags the great mass of mankind into everlasting ruin.

* Et induerunt se sacerdotes ciliciis. Judith. iv. 9.

† Caput terrâ aspergentes lumbosque ciliciis succinctos. 2 Machab. x. 24.

‡ Accingite vos ciliciis, plangite et ululate Jerem. iv. 8.

§ Ipse autem Joannes habebat vestimentum de pilis camelorum, et zonam pelliceam circa lumbos suos. Matth. iij. 4.

35. But here it should be observed that there are divers kinds of hair-shirts. Some are made of bristles, and such were in use in ancient times; others are made of brass or iron wire, in the shape of little chains, or in the form of bandages; invented some two centuries back by the piety of the faithful, who bind them round wrists and thighs. The roughness of the former is the more annoying, the pricking of the latter gives the more pain. The former kind, unless worn with due discretion, may be injurious to persons of a frail and delicate constitution; for, as they produce a certain local inflammation, they lessen the natural heat of the stomach, and weaken its powers. The latter sort are usually less prejudicial to health, especially if worn on the arms or wrists. I say this that each person may, with the counsel of his ghostly father, choose the description which may present the least danger to health of body, and be most advantageous for the progress of the soul.

36. Such are the hair-shirts in ordinary use, which almost every one may safely employ within the bounds of due discretion; for if we come to describe those used by many of the saints, we shall find that they were so severe and painful that the very thought of them makes us shrink. Some wore an iron girdle studded with sharp points; others wore continually next the skin an iron cuirass; some there are who have worn a shirt made of iron mail, or of some jagged metal; others a vest interwoven with sharp thorns. The blessed Henry Suso carried his penitential fervour to such an extent, that, besides a cross studded with nails, which he bore on his shoulders, he wore a pair of drawers set full of sharp needles, which tore his flesh to such a degree that swarms of worms bred in his flesh, and, so to say, devoured him alive; and, what is more wonderful, he kept his wrists handcuffed at night-time, that he might be prevented from relieving the painful itching caused by the vermin. Holy Church tells us of St. Rose of Lima, that she had scattered broadcast over the whole of her long hair-shirt very fine needles, in order to intensify the pain by the sharpness of their points.* I have seen a portion of the inner

* Oblongo, asperrimoque cilicio passim minusculus acus intexuit. In Festo S. Rosæ.

garment of the blessed Veronica, Capuchin nun of Città di Castello, into which were sewn the hooked thorns which are to be found on the stem of the rose-tree. She used to call it her embroidered garment, as if to imply that these thorns were to her as so many precious gems with which she delighted to adorn her penance. Hair-shirts of these kinds, being so far beyond the ordinary strength of our feeble nature, are certainly to be admired in those who wear them, but not to be adopted unless God vouchsafe a special inspiration to that effect. Nevertheless they should be for every one a great encouragement to undertake some sort of bodily mortification, and also should serve to refute a notion but too current among those who are over-careful of their bodies, that our penance should consist merely in contrition of heart; for if these holy persons afflicted so cruelly their innocent bodies, how ought we not to treat our guilty flesh? And if they mortified with such rigour the sense of touch, though in them it was not unruly, what should we not do, we, who so often experience its rebellion, and, it may be, feel its irregular motions so greatly to our cost?

37. Another very afflictive penance is night-watching, which deprives the body wholly, or in part, of the refreshment which it gains from sleep. This kind of bodily mortification was of old much in vogue amongst the servants of God, nor are there wanting instances nowadays of holy men who have signalised themselves by this practice. Cardinal Lauria tells of a remarkable expedient employed by St. Rose of Lima in order to pass the night without sleep. She was accustomed to fasten her hair to a nail fixed in the wall, so that if her head bent forward with sleep, the pain awakened her.* St. Peter of Alcantara, as may be seen in the bull of his canonisation, for the space of forty years never slept more than half an hour daily; and lest sleep should betray him by keeping him a longer time, he used to sleep with his head laid upon a piece of wood projecting from the wall.†

* Funiculo ex clavo pendente capillos de nocte ligabat, ut si quando gravatum pro somno caput deorsum declinaret, præ dolore excitaretur. l. 3 Sentent., tom. xij. art. 16.

† Per quadraginta annorum decursum sesquihoram tantum somno concessit.

38. It should, however, be observed, that, save under a special grace and call of God, such watchings as these neither should nor can be imitated; for the human body, except it be supported by an extraordinary assistance on the part of Almighty God, could not either continue alive or be fit for any useful work unless refreshed by a sufficient measure of sleep. Hence in this matter it is necessary to be guided by the rules of that discretion to which it belongs to give all good works their lustre and completeness. A rule suited to every one's case would perhaps be the following: A devout person should not allow himself all the sleep he desires, so that he may not become like to the brutes, which deny themselves nothing demanded from them by their bodies. He should mortify himself by taking off a portion. But yet this should not be so large as to incapacitate him in the discharge of his daily duties, or impede him in their performance. I make this remark, having known a man of uncommon virtue who mortified himself severely by not sleeping at night, but then he spent nearly the whole day in sleep, and thus found that almost all his employments were interrupted by sleep. This is by no means to be approved; for though God wills us to mortify our bodies, He also wills regularity in labour. As an instance in point, St. Charles Borromeo, seeing that, overcome by sleep, he frequently slumbered unawares during the public functions of the Church, thought it better to prolong his time of rest, so as to be able in the daytime to pay more attention to the duties of his pastoral charge. The body should, then, be mortified by the diminution of sleep, but with such moderation as not to injure health, nor prevent the discharge of our ordinary duties.

39. We may class under this head the practice of sleeping in a comfortless, or even painful manner, as was the common practice of holy persons, who lay down to rest on the bare ground, on planks, or on rough straw; or who strewed inside their bed pieces of wood, twigs, and pebbles, as was the custom of St. Aloysius, who thus managed to mortify himself while sleeping on a soft bed. But what is related on this point of St. Rose of Lima is truly wonderful, for the bed on which this tender maiden lay was formed of gnarled trunks of trees, the intervals between which

were filled up with pebbles, potsherds, and lumps of plaster, fitter to wound her body than to refresh it by repose. The pillow whereon she laid her head was a heap of chips. So that it was justly described by De Lauria, as "a bed of torture rather than a couch of rest."* Holy Church attests the same in the Breviary Lessons for the office of the Saint.† I am fully aware that we cannot be expected to practise austerities so far beyond our strength, but at least we should forbear to give encouragement to the deceitful sense of touch, by the conveniences and indulgences with which we are apt to wish our bed to be supplied; remembering that this domestic foe, like other traitors, often plots against us in the silence and darkness of the night.

40. Another infliction well suited to hold in check this sense, so eager after what is agreeable to its love of ease, is to suffer uncomplainingly the inclemencies of the season—heat, cold, and frost—and especially to seek no solace from the inconveniences of the weather; after the example of St. Aloysius, who in the midst of winter, which in Lombardy is usually very severe, would never go near the fire, how much soever his hands might suffer from the cold, nor could he at any time be induced, whatever the state of the weather, to cover with gloves his suffering hands. But far more heroic was the austerity of St. Peter of Alcantara, who made use of the elements as an instrument for the affliction of his flesh. He wore but one tunic, and when, from time to time, he washed it in cold water, he put it on again dripping wet. He went always barefoot over rocks, through thorny places, over ice and snow, with his head uncovered and exposed to the winds and rain, to hail and frost; nor did he ever, by hat or hood of his habit, protect his head from the rays of the sun. In mid-winter, while a cold north wind was blowing, he used to throw open the door and window of his narrow cell, and to remain unflinchingly exposed to the full blast of the wind. And, as if this were not enough, he would go and plunge naked into

* In lectulo extra cellulam, ex lignis, saxis, et textulis, constructo, et cervicali ex lignorum quisquiliis referto cubabat.

† Lectulum sibi e truncis nodosis composuit, horumque vacuas commissuras fragminibus testarum implevit.

frozen ponds, so that the cold might penetrate to his bones and to his very marrow. On account of this, and his other most rigid austerities, he seemed, as St. Teresa said of him, no longer to be made of flesh, but of the roots of trees, so thin was his face, so hollow his eyes, so dried up was he in all his members. Hence, he appeared to be, not a man, but a walking ghost of penance. All this is reported in the bull of his canonisation.* In bringing forward these well-authenticated facts, I do not wish to insinuate that my reader should, after the example of this illustrious penitent, make use of the weather, the wind, heat and cold, frost and sunshine, of heaven and earth, and of so many torturers to torment and disfigure his body, and, as it were, to annihilate it, as I know full well was done by this holy penitent. Our constitution could not stand it, nor does God require it of us. I but ask all that they should within the bounds of discretion seek to afflict their body by the inclemencies of the weather, or, at least, not to be so anxious as they are to guard against them. At the very least, all should bear willingly with such as cannot be warded off, as a means of mortifying the touch, and in satisfaction for sin.

* Itinera, quamvis longissima, atque asperrima, capite semper detecto, nudisque pedibus, per æstus, et frigora suscipiens, ita ut cum nudum caput imbribus exponeret, interdum capilli gelu deciderent, et æstate præfervidâ, exurentibus solis radiis vehementissime cruciaretur; respondere solitus interrogantibus, cur detecto capite semper incederet, nefas esse coram Deo, tecto capite ambulare. Cum vetus suum, et vile saccum abluebat, madidum corpori aptabat. Quin etiam in gelidam aquam, rigente hyeme, sese plerumque injiciebat. Præter hæc familiare illi erat, hyeme summâ, urgente nivis frigore, deposito pallio, fenestram, et januam reserare, ut frigidissimo recepto aere et gelu, acrius torqueretur caro, mox exurenda diris cruciatibus, cum fenestram clausisset, et januam. Eo devenit ob sævam macerationem membrorum, ut ex narratione S. Teresiæ, horrido, ex exangui corpore radicum arboris speciem exhibuerit. Oculi autem in cavum recedentibus, et sulcatis perpetuo lacrymarum imbre genis, miserabile pœnitentiæ simulacrum videretur, etc.

CHAPTER V.

ANOTHER DESCRIPTION OF AUSTERITY PRACTISED BY THE SAINTS, THAT OF SELF-FLAGELLATION.

41. To scourge ourselves with our own hands, or, as it is usually called, to take the discipline, was not in use in ancient times, nor do we find mention of this practice in any of the Holy Fathers. We sometimes meet with penitents who were scourged by their Confessors as a penance for their misdeeds; and it is well known that, according to the rules of some of the most ancient Orders of monks, certain faults were punished by the Religious receiving a scourging at the hands of their brethren.

42. It is very edifying to read what William de Nangis relates, on this point, of St. Louis, King of France, who was accustomed, after each Confession, to receive a severe discipline at the hands of his Confessor.* And what he further adds is not only a matter of edification, but greatly to be wondered at, namely, that one of the Confessors of the King, being destitute of common prudence, struck him so long, and with such severity, that the delicate frame of the Saint was quite exhausted by the immoderate blows. Yet, he bore all with the greatest humility and patience, without making the slightest complaint; only after the good man's death St. Louis mentioned it to his new Confessor, with a smile upon his face.†

43. The first who gave currency to the devout custom of self-flagellation, if he did not introduce it, was, according to Baronius, St. Peter Damian.‡ This pious custom has, since his day, been

* Post confessionem vero suam, semper disciplinam recipiebat a confessore suo. In Vitâ.

† Nec prætermittendum existimo de quodam confessario, quem habuit ante fratrem Gaufredum de Belloloco de Ordine Prædicatorum, qui solitus sibi erat dare disciplinas nimis immoderatas, et duras, sub quibus caro ejus tenera non modicum gravabatur. Quod gravamen numquam illi confessario, quamdiu viveret, voluit revelare. Sed post mortem dicti confessaris, quasi jocando, et ridendo, hoc alteri confessori suo humiliter revelavit.

‡ Eodem quoque tempore, etsi non eodem auctore Petro, tamen certe propagatore, atque adversus impugnantes propugnatore, introductus est in

adopted by the generality of devout Christians who are intent on the mortification of their bodies, and has been embraced by all Religious Orders of either sex, and it is, moreover, in many monasteries, practised on stated days prescribed by the rule. And St. Francis of Sales greatly recommends it, considering it a penance best suited for the mortification of the flesh, and for exciting devotion after it has become languid.

44. True it is that Clement VI. published a constitution against the Flagellants on account of the gross disorders, abuses, errors, and indecencies which accompanied some of their absurd public exhibitions. But this by no means proves that the practice of self-flagellation, whether in private, or even in public, if it be done properly, is condemned, or that it is not most commendable. The Flagellants were bands of men and women who came from Hungary, and went through Germany, Poland, Flanders, and other parts, scourging themselves to blood, with great indecency, twice a day, rather after the fashion of comedians and mountebanks, than of true penitents; and this apparent compunction served but to cloak the numerous errors with which they were infected, of which more than forty-four are recounted in history. But, as must be plain to all, it by no means follows from this, that we should discountenance private or even public self-flagellation, when performed in subordination to those set over us, in fitting time and manner, and with due order and compunction, as was the practice of St. Vincent Ferrer in his celebrated Missions; and as is even now customary on certain of the more solemn days of the year, in times of public calamity, or in Missions, when it is most just that we should appease God for our own and the sins of others. Such are the judicious observations of James Gretser in regard to the condemnation of the so-called Flagellants.*

ecclesiâ ille laudabilis usus, ut pœnitentiæ causâ fideles verberibus se ipsos afficerent, flagellis ad hoc paratis idoneis, exemplo B Dominici Loricati, sibi subditi sanctissimi eremitæ In Annal., Anno 1056, num. 7.

* Qui non damnati fuerunt propter flagella (neque enim ignoraverunt illius temporis orthodoxi sanctorum consuetudinem, qui flagellis sæpius in se animadvertunt); sed propter modum flagellationis, et circumstantias, crassosque errores, quibus incondita illa multitudo infecta erat (nam quadragintaquatuor

45. But to return to private self-flagellation; there is not one saint among those of recent times who has not made frequent and rigorous use of it for the mortification of the flesh, and of the sense of touch, from which sense originate all the rebellious motions of the flesh against reason. We read in the life of St. Francis of Sales, that he used to discipline himself to blood, and would frequently hand to his Confessor worn-out and blood-stained disciplines to have them repaired.* The Roman Rota says of St. Louis Bertrand, that he was accustomed to take the discipline so severely as not only to soak the instrument with blood, but even to sprinkle the walls with it.† Cardinal Lauria relates of St. Rose of Lima, that she scourged herself with such great cruelty as to make the blood flow in torrents, so that her back was always wounded and torn.‡ But I should never have done were I to tell of all the various kinds of severe disciplines with which the saints of God have tortured their bodies since the first introduction of this pious and wholesome custom; for there is scarce one but who, with his right hand armed with cruel scourges, has mangled his innocent flesh. I cannot, however, refrain from relating the request which St. Aloysius, when at the point of death, made to his Superior, for even were the examples of the other saints to fail us, this would suffice of itself to show how pleasing to the Spirit of the Lord is this description of penance.

46. This Saint, feeling that the end of his most innocent life was at hand, asked for the Holy Viaticum, and then begged the

articulos contra ecclesiam romanam ab illis traditos, defensosque fuisse testatur etiam hæreticus Munsterius), rejecti, damnatique fuere flagellantes. De Spont. Discipl., lib. ij., cap. 4.

* Nec ob eminentem episcopalem dignitatem indulgebat sibi, ut plerique solent: quinimmo jejunium observabat rigidissime, scuticâque carnem macerabat suam usque ad sanguinem: sanguinolentam enim scuticam suam sæpius confessario suo, viro integerrimo, reficiendam dedit. In Vitâ scrip. ab ejus Nepote, lib. v.

† Beatus Ludovicus adeo flagellis cædebat corpus suum, ut non solum ejus disciplina, sed etiam parietes conspersi sanguine viderentur. In Causâ B. Ludov. Bertrandi., Tit. de Temperantiâ.

‡ Disciplinis ad sanguinem ita dire se excarnificabat, ut dorsum lacerum semper, et plagatum restaret. Lib. iii., tom. 2, disp. 52, art. 6.

Provincial, who had come to pay him a visit, to have the bed-clothes removed, and to allow him to scourge himself to his heart's content; and if it was thought that his own arm was not equal to this rigorous infliction, at least to order some one of the community to beat him severely from head to foot. We draw this narrative from the Roman Rota.* Thus did this angelic youth yearn to mortify, even in death, that virginal flesh which had never risen against the spirit by the least rebellious motion. Let those then who bear a body stained with the guilt of many past falls, and which even now tends, by its evil inclinations, to relapse into the same transgressions, learn from this example how they are to treat their flesh in order to remedy past faults, and to guard against their future repetition.

47. To complete the doctrine of these two Chapters, I will set before the reader's eyes the description of a house of penitents—left on record by St. John Climacus, who saw it himself—which I trust may produce two salutary effects: first, confusion at beholding ourselves so different from those great servants of God whose penitential course is there related: secondly, a desire to imitate them, at least in some small degree, in the practice of this virtue.†

* A patre rectore petiit ut sibi Viaticum daret. Interim dum hæc agerentur, cum pater Jo. Baptista Carminata Provincialis Aloysium inviseret, rogavit illum præclarus adolescens, ut storeas supra lectum positas amoveri juberet, veniamque sibi daret, ut posset se verberibus afficere, aut saltem ut aliquis sese a vertice ad pedes flagellis cæderet, permitteretque se humi suo spiritum reddere Creatori. Titul De Felici ejus Obitu.

† Vidi quosdam ex illis innocentibus reis totas noctes usque ad mane sub diu immotis pedibus stantes, et miserabiliter cum somno, et naturâ luctantes, vique hujus pœnæ fractos, dum nullam sibi penitus quietem indulgerent, immo seipsos graviter objurgarent, et conviciis insuper, et contumeliis excitarent; alios cœlum intuentes, et illinc opem cum lacrymabili voce plerumque implorantes; alios item, qui in precibus perseverabant, manus post terga sceleratorum ritu revincti, vultus alto mœrore confusos humi defigebant, ut qui se indignos judicarent, qui cœlum aspicerent, etc Sedebant alii humi in pavimento super cinerem, et saccum, qui genibus vultum tegebant, frontibus humum ferientes. Alii assidue pectus tundebant; animæ suæ statum primum, vitamque pristinam, quam cum virtute traduxerunt, revocantes Ex his ergo pavialimentum lacrymis inundabant; alii lacrymarum fonte destituti seipsos diverberabant: alii tamquam in funere animas suas lamentabantur: nec mag-

48. St. John Climacus, alluding to these penitent monks, says, that he saw some standing immovable the whole night long in the open air until sunrise, struggling against sleep and against nature, which claimed some repose; stimulating themselves by reproaches and self-rebukes to remain without flinching; and he found them quite worn out and exhausted by their excessive watchings. He saw others with their eyes raised fixedly towards heaven, begging God's mercy with sobs and tearful accents; others, with their hands fastened behind their backs like criminals, were standing with heads bowed down, their eyes bent upon the ground, while, covered with shame and sorrow, they deemed themselves unworthy to lift up their faces to heaven; others sat in dust and ashes, holding their heads in their laps, and beating their foreheads against the ground: others were continually striking their breasts with hard blows; others watered the ground with their tears; others, finding that their tears refused to flow, struck themselves severely; others, unable to conceal the excessive grief that oppressed them, broke out into sobs and heart-rending lamentations, such as are heard at the death of those nearest and dearest to us; others tortured themselves by exposure to the direct rays of the sun, and to the most severe cold of winter; others would take a mouthful of water as though about to quench their thirst, and then leave off, it being enough for them if they did not die of thirst; others would take a morsel of bread and

nitudinem doloris pectore poterant continere, et alia hujusmodi. . . . Videre erat in illis linguas ardentes, et pro ritu canum ex ore promissas: alii in gravi solis æstu se cruciabant, alii frigore se torquebant: alii, cum modicum quid aquæ libâssent, desierunt, tantum ut ne siti necarentur: alii, cum panem gustâssent dumtaxat, illum rursus procul a se rejiciebant, se indignos dictitantes qui cibum humanum sumerent, qui bestiarum opera exercuissent, etc. Erat enim videre in illis genua quæ ex assiduâ geniculationum consuetudine callum obduxerant: oculos exesos, et debiles, aliosque in sinus capitis recedentes; genas habentes saucias, et ardore ferventium lacrymarum adustas, vultusque patientes, et emaciatas facies, nihil a mortuis, si conferres, differentes; pectora plagarum ictibus liventia, et ex crebris pugnorum verberibus cruenta sanguinis ex pectore rejecta sputa. Ubi illic lectus quieti positus? ubi munditiæ, et adversus frigora vestis munimentum? . . . Vidi, et feliciores existimavi, qui post lapsum ita lugent, quam qui numquam lapsi sunt, et seipsos non sic deflent.

throw it away again, saying that they were unworthy of human food after having behaved as beasts. It was a pitiable sight, continues the Saint, to see some with their parched tongues hanging out of their mouths like thirsty hounds, others whose knees had become hardened with continual kneeling, others with their cheeks scalded and furrowed by an incessant flow of tears, others with their eyes hollow and sunken within their sockets, others whose chest was raw with blows, others who spat blood from the violence with which they had beaten their breast. All were wan and wrinkled, so that, to all outward appearance, the only difference between them and corpses was that they still drew breath. He concludes by saying, that he esteemed that those who, having fallen, rose again by such heroic penance, were happier far than they who have never fallen, and who do no penance. Such as shrink from handling a discipline, from putting a hair-shirt round their loins, from fasting on a day not commanded by the Church, from taking an hour off their sleep, or from embittering it with some inconveniences, in order to restrain their flesh and to punish its past transgressions, would do well to consider this spectacle of penance, and, in presence of such rigours, to be ashamed of their excessive softness and their great tepidity.

CHAPTER VI.

CERTAIN RULES OF DISCRETION IN THE USE OF PENANCES WHICH MORTIFY THE TOUCH.

49. THE reader must not imagine that I have set before him the foregoing melancholy list of penances with the intention that he should straightway adopt them, and slaughter his body outright, still less would I have Directors give such advice to those under their guidance. So far am I from meaning this, that I repeat again, what I have already frequently said, that many of these penances are to be admired, not to be imitated. When God

wished for them from a few of His chosen servants, He vouchsafed special inspirations, and imparted extraordinary strength for the execution: hence, far from injuring their health, many holy persons were able, without injury to it, to live a longer life than they who spend their days in the lap of indulgence and luxury, and managed amid these rigours to attain to an age of more than a hundred years; as, for instance, St. Paul the Hermit, St. Romuald, and others. My object was only to imitate merchants in their dealings with customers. They open their drawers and unfold before them cloth of gold and silver, embroidered silks, brocades, and other expensive tissues; not with a view to a purchase being made of the whole by any one person, but in order to encourage their customers to buy what each feels that he stands in need of. And so have I set forth in detail a multitude of penances, many of which are extraordinary and unusual, not that every one should practise them all, but in order to enkindle, by the example of the saints, desires of mortifying themselves reasonably and discreetly, which may be in proportion to the mental and bodily strength of each one. This it is that is needed for the keeping under of the rebellious sense of which we are speaking, so that it may not hinder our progress in perfection.

50. St. Paul says: I beseech you to offer your bodies to God as a sacrifice of mortification and penance, but in such wise that this sacrifice may be holy and acceptable in His sight.* That it may become so, he adds, this painful sacrifice of mortification must be *reasonable*,† that is, made with discretion and without excess, which latter, as the Gloss observes, is ever prejudicial.‡ Theodoret makes a remark on these words, which agrees with my view. St. Paul, he says, exhorts us to offer our bodies to God, not as dead, but as living victims; because penance is meant to slay those lusts and perverse inclinations which tempt the body to sin, not the body itself.§

* Obsecro vos, ut exhibeatis corpora vestra hostiam viventem, sanctam, Deo placentem. Rome xij. 1.

† Rationabile obsequium vestrum.

‡ Sit cum discretione, ne quid nimis.

§ Hortatur ut nostra corpora fiant hostia, et appellat *hostiam viventem*, non enim jubet ut mactentur corpora sed ut sint peccato mortua.

51. However, to the effect that penance may be discreet and reasonable, conformably with the instruction left us by the Apostle of the Gentiles, it must fulfil two conditions, according to the rules which the Holy Fathers have prescribed for its practice. First, it should mortify the body, but not injure the health. Secondly, it must not hinder our fulfilment of the duties attached to our state of life. St. Basil expresses himself clearly in his Constitutions as to the former of these conditions; he will have penance taken in a measure proportioned to the strength of the body.* Notice that by continence the holy Doctor here means bodily austerities. We should imitate the camel, which kneels to receive its burden, but which, when sufficiently laden, rises to its feet, and refuses to take more. As St. Bernard says, the body must be afflicted by penance in such degree as to prevent its unruly turning against the spirit; but it is not to be disabled or annihilated, so as to hinder it contributing to the exercise of the inner virtues, which are by far the most useful † St. Gregory the Great is of the like mind, when he says that in the use of penance we should keep within these bounds: we should not slay the flesh, but only its unruly passions. ‡ And this coincides with the maxim of Theodoret.

52. St. Thomas gives the reason for this with the solidity that characterises his writings. He very properly distinguishes the end from the means. The end, he says, may be desired without any limit whatever, but moderation must be observed in the use of the means. Thus a physician called in to a patient will desire for him the most perfect health that can be enjoyed; but it does not follow from this that he prescribes every possible remedy: he will proceed cautiously, for his drugs are the means, and health is the end of his attendance. Making application of this comparison,

* Ita amplectenda a nobis continentia est, ut eam cum viribus corporis commetiamur. Cap. 3.

† Affligendum est corpus aliquando, sed non conterendum; nam exercitatio corporalis ad modicum quidem valet; et *pietas ad omnia utilis*. Ad. Frat de Monte Dei

‡ Sic necesse est ut arcem quisque continentiæ teneat, quatenus non carnem, sed vitia carnis occidat. Moral., lib. xxx., c. 14.

St. Thomas wisely observes, that the *end* and aim of spiritual life is the love of God, in which consists the whole essence of perfection. Bodily austerities are *means* which, by restraining the lust of the flesh, remove the hindrances by which it may impede our being united with God in the bonds of holy love. We may then aspire, without any restriction, to the perfect love of God, and long to burn, even as the Seraphim, in a furnace of charity; but we ought not to practise bodily mortification without measure; and while we adopt those mortifications which suffice to tame the flesh, and to keep within due bounds the unruly sensual appetites, we must not go further and ruin our constitution, prostrate our strength and destroy our health.* And this is plain common sense. No muleteer is so foolish as to load his beast to such an extent that it falls under its burden, and becomes lame on the road long before reaching its journey's end; no skipper would so load his ship as to make it sink before it comes into port. Why then should devout persons so overtask their strength with bodily mortification as to exhaust their body, and so ruin their health as to be unable to pursue the path in the spiritual life upon which they have so happily entered?

53. But the Angelic Doctor goes further, and hesitates not to assert that immoderate bodily austerities cannot be acceptable to God; and he assigns for this opinion a very solid and well-grounded reason. That any work of ours may be pleasing to

* Aliter est judicandum de fine; aliter de his, quæ sunt ad finem. Illud enim, quod quæritur tamquam finis, absque mensurâ quærendum est; in his autem, quæ sunt ad finem, est adhibenda mensura secundum proportionem ad finem; sicut medicus, qui sanitatem, quæ est finis ejus, faciat quantumcumque potest majorem; sed adhibet medicinam, secundum quod convenit ad sanitatem faciendam. Est ergo considerandum, quod in spirituali vitâ dilectio Dei sicut finis; jejunia autem, vigiliæ, et alia exercitia corporalia non quæruntur tanquam finis, quia, sicut dicitur ad Rom. xiv. *Non est regnum Dei esca, et potus*, sed adhibentur tamquam necessaria ad finem, primo ad domandas concupiscentias carnis, secundum illud Apostoli I. ad Cor. ix.: *Castigo corpus meum et in servitutem redigo.* Et ideo hujusmodi sunt adhibenda cum quâdam mensurâ rationis, ut scilicet concupiscentia dometur, et natura non extinguatur, juxta illud Apostoli Rom xij.: *Exhibeatis corpora vestra hostiam viventem;* et postea subdit: *Rationabile obsequium vestrum.* Quodlib. 5, art. 18.

God, it must be virtuously performed; now this lustre of virtue is not found in penance which is adopted without discretion; and, further, discretion requires that the flesh and its lusts should be kept in check, not that the body should be utterly prostrated.* The reason of this is, because discretion produces in virtue the effect which salt produces in meat; discretion is the seasoning of virtue, and makes it pleasing to the Most High. Now, as meat without salt is tasteless, so too is virtue which is wanting in discretion; it cannot be fully pleasing to God. Hence, to chastise our body in excess, is to go through a labour by which we lose rather than gain, and to produce a suffering which causes injury instead of profit.

54. The second condition required of bodily austerity that it may be discreet and virtuous is, that it hinder not the occupations, whether interior or exterior, in which each one is bound to employ his time, according to the station in which God has placed him. Every one has some duty which he is bound to fulfil. Some apply to prayer, others to study; some are called upon to preach, others to teach, or to hear Confessions. Several are engaged in manual labour, some in domestic work, others in trade, others in mechanical arts, or in administering justice, or in government. Now, it happens not seldom, says St. Gregory, that a person in a fit of indiscreet fervour, in order to extinguish the fire of the lusts that prevail in his flesh, will undertake an excessive penance, and so weaken his body as to render it incapable of discharging its duty, or at least make it ill-fitted for the purpose. This is to forget that although the body be a domestic enemy, which lures us to sin, it must nevertheless be our partner in good works; we cannot perform these without its aid; and though it justly incurs our hate, as an obstacle to perfection, it claims our love as a colleague and companion, with whom we are inseparably bound in well-doing.†

* Maceratio proprii corporis, puta per vigilias et jejunia, non est Deo accepta, nisi in quantum est opus virtutis; quod quidem est, in quantum cum debitâ discretione fit, ut scilicet concupiscentia refrænetur, et natura non nimis gravetur. 2, 2, qu. 88, art. 2 ad 3.

† Plerumque cum plus justo caro restringitur, etiam ab exercitatione boni operis enervatur, ut adorationem quoque, vel prædicationem non sufficiat,

55. To act thus, says the Angelic Doctor, cannot but be sinful, as every one is bound to fulfil the duties of his state of life; and hence too, is bound also not to incapacitate himself for their discharge. A preacher, he adds, who would so exhaust his strength as to be unable to announce the Word of God to the people, would be surely guilty of sin; so, too, a professor who, by the austerity of his life, should so weaken his body as to disable himself from applying to his studies, and imparting to his hearers the knowledge he has gained. The same applies to the whole range of human occupations.*

56. And in fact St. Bernard acknowledged the sinfulness of the early excesses of his fervent penance, which had ruined his health and rendered him incapable of common observance, as is remarked by St. Thomas himself.† What with hair shirts, watchings, and rigorous fasts, he had so weakened his stomach and destroyed its tone, that when in choir he was continually expectorating, to the intense disgust of his monks. He sought at first to obviate this by making a hole close by his stall, wherein these evacuations might be concealed from sight; but as even this plan gave annoyance to those near him, he resolved to exempt himself from attendance in choir in order not to inconvenience his brethren. For the same reason he felt himself compelled to withdraw from many of the charges and burdens of monastic life; and being fully aware that this inability to fulfil the duties of his state had been caused by his own indiscreet fervour, he accused himself of his fault as of a

dum incentiva vitiorum in se funditus suffocare festinat. Adjutorem quippe habemus intentionis internæ hunc hominem, quem exterius gestamus: et ipsi insunt motus lasciviæ, ipsi effectus suppetunt operationis bonæ. Sæpe vero dum in illo hostem insequimur, etiam civem, quem diligimus, trucidamus. Moral., lib. xxx., c. 14.

* Si vero aliquis in tantum vires naturæ debilitaret per jejunia, et vigilias, et alia hujusmodi, ut non sufficiat debita opera exequi, puta prædicator prædicare, doctor docere, cantor cantare, et sic de aliis; absque dubio peccat: sicut peccat vir, qui nimiâ abstinentiâ se impotentem redderet ad debitum uxori reddendum. Unde Hieronymus dicit: De rapinâ holocaustum offert, qui vel ciborum nimiâ egestate, vel somni penuriâ immoderate corpus affligit. Quodlib 5, art. 18.

† S. Bernardus confitebatur se peccâsse in hoc, quod nimis corpus suum jejunio, et vigiliis debilitâsset. Loco citato.

sacrilege. This fact we learn from his biographer, who strives to excuse him, though the Saint was far from wishing to excuse himself.*

57. To complete this instruction we may observe, with the same St. Bernard (who had purchased experience by his own errors), that the devil himself not unfrequently inspires certain devout people, especially beginners, with a fervour of his own—urging them to prolong their watchings, to multiply fasts, to observe no measure in the use of hair-shirts and disciplines, to undertake excessive labours—in order that they may weaken themselves, and be disabled from the discharge of the duties of their state of life.† The demon makes use of this stratagem, for he is well aware that by undertaking such austerities as are wholly beyond their strength, they get weary at last; and, unable to bear up under so excessive a burden, they lose heart, and abandon everything. But even if this be not the case, they gradually ruin their health, or seriously injure it, and then, being wholly intent on recruiting their shattered powers, they leave off their spiritual exercises, give themselves up to dainties, to delicacies, to all manner of luxuries; as St. Bernard very fitly warns his monks: "You know by your own experience how several, unable to control themselves when transported by the vehemence of their first fervour, and having embraced every description of mortification, have since become imperfect and carnal, and have concluded a shameful truce with their bodies, against which they once waged so fierce a war."‡ It is therefore more expedient and better every way, says St. Basil, to

* Etsi nimietate forsitan excessit (quid eum excusare nitimur, in quo non confunditur accusare se ipsum?) quod servituti Dei, et fratrum suorum abstulerit corpus suum, dum indiscreto fervore imbecille illud reddiderit et pene inutile. In Vitâ S Bern., lib. I., cap. 8.

† Quoties suggessit satanas anticipare vigilias, quod ad solemnia fratrum illuderet dormienti? Quoties produci jejunia, ut divinis obsequiis eo inutilem redderet, quo imbecillem? . . . Quoties ad opus manuum plus quam opus fuerat incitavit, et fractum viribus, ceteris regularibus exercitiis invalidum reddidit? Serm. in Cant. 33

‡ Exsperti estis, quomodo quidam, qui antea inhiberi non poterant (ita in spiritu vehementi ferebantur ad omnia), cum spiritu cœperint, nunc carne consummentur; quam turpe nunc ineant fœdus cum suis corporibus, quibus crudele ante indixerunt bellum. Loc. cit.

preserve our strength for God's service than to destroy it; and to keep the body in fitting strength for that service, than to ruin it by excessive macerations.*

58. The reader, especially if he have charge of souls, may hereby perceive the great necessity there is of keeping to the middle path in the practice of penance, if this is to be meritorious and pleasing to God, and to serve as a spur, not as an obstacle, to devout persons desirous of making progress in the way of perfection. On the one hand, penance is necessary in order to keep down the sense of touch, which renders the flesh inclined to sensual pleasure, stirs it up to rebel against reason, and makes it opposed to the practice of virtue; but, on the other hand, penance requires discretion; it must not be prejudicial to bodily health, or so weaken our strength as to disable us from the proper discharge of our common duties. It must mortify, not kill, the body, must take away its unruliness, but not the strength and vigour needed for well-doing. What, then, are we to do to keep so just a measure as not to fall by an excess of self-love into the error of pampering our bodies, and, at the same time, to avoid the opposite excess of an indiscreet vigour? The rule is simple. Let each one be guided in the matter by the advice of his ghostly father, and perform no mortification without his direction. This is the rule laid down by the saints, and it is the safest that can be given on so delicate a subject. Should any one, says Cassian, deem himself to stand in need of rigorous fasts, of lengthened watchings, or other bodily mortifications, he must lay before his Superiors the motives which make him desire these austerities, and fulfil in all humility whatever they may determine.†

59. St. Bernard, in his discourse at the funeral of the saintly youth Urbanus, awarded the praise that he so well deserved on

* Et honestius, et utilius esse, confirmando corpori suggerere, quam adimere, vires; idque strenuum reddere obeundæ bonæ actioni, quam ultroneâ quâpiam maceratione exoletum. Const. Mon., cap. 5.

† Si sit, qui necessario acriore vel jejunio, vel vigiliâ vel aliâ quâvis re opus esse arbitretur; rationem is, quare id sic æstimet, iis aperito, quibus credita est communis disciplinæ procuratio; et quod illi statuerint, id observato. Coll. ij. cap. 10.

account of the fervour of his life, with this reserve, that he considered the young man blameworthy on account of his excessive abstemiousness, and for having failed to conform fully on this point with the counsels of his Abbot.*

St. Jerome, in his Life of St. Paula, writes a magnificent panegyric on her numerous and heroic virtues, but disapproves of a certain tenacity in persisting, contrary to advice, in some of her penitential practices. This saintly lady had recovered from an all but fatal fever, and her physicians counselled her to mix a little wine with the water which she always drank pure; thinking to obviate the tendency to dropsy to which they had reason to fear she was liable. Still she would not be persuaded, either by St. Jerome, or by St. Epiphanius, the Bishop, to relax anything of her early fervour.† All, therefore, who are aiming at the spiritual life, should discover to their Director every practice which they feel inspired to adopt for the chastisement of the body, and should regulate such exercise by his advice. They will thus proceed in an orderly manner, without danger of delusion in the mortifications they may undertake, and will receive from God the reward of the penances which they shall have performed, and also of those which they shall have omitted by the advice of their Confessor, but which they had the will to do.

CHAPTER VII.

PRACTICAL HINTS TO DIRECTORS ON THE PRESENT ARTICLE.

60. FIRST suggestion. The Director must be prudent in allowing his penitents to afflict their flesh, but he must not be altogether averse to the practice. I say this, because I have often met with Directors who seemed to set their faces entirely against any such

* Quia si quid triste sensit, propter hoc sensit quod minus nobis consensit de necessitate corporis.

† Fateor, in hâc re pertinacior fuit, ut sibi non parceret, et nulli cederet admonenti. Hæc refero; non quod inconsideranter et ultra vires sumpta opera probem.

practice. I have found Confessors of nuns, even of those who live in convents where the rule was not so austere as to impose upon the Religious such a measure of penance as could not prudently be executed, who would never allow any nun the slightest bodily mortification. So that none of the community ever took the trouble to ask for anything of the kind, knowing full well beforehand that all such requests were useless. I cannot understand how any Director can justly deprive the souls committed to his care of so useful a means of perfection, and one so constantly practised by the saints, thus debarring them from all the spiritual good which is its usual effect; especially when his penitents are still young, and stand much in need of this kind of remedy, on account of the abundance of their animal spirits, and the effervescence of their blood. These Directors may plead that they must have a care for health. I praise such care, but this only means that penances are to be disallowed to such as are infirm, or of a weak constitution; it by no means proves they ought not to be permitted in moderation to those who enjoy good health. To this it will be replied, that the chief stress is laid on interior virtues, and on the observance of rule, which is the very life-blood of religious perfection; that these outward practices are but of slight importance; that a Religious may be sanctified without them. I am far from disputing that Christian and religious perfection consist mainly in the interior dispositions. But we must not be misled. In order to attain this perfection, the mortification of the bodily senses is necessary; for if the body be unruly, it will be more than a match for the spirit, nor will it be possible to practise in peace those virtues, of which these Directors have justly so great an esteem. The truth of this is seen the more clearly if we consider that, by bodily mortification, we earn at God's hands an abundance of grace and of effectual helps, enabling us to practise those inner virtues which are of such importance. In a word, the Director must bear in mind what St. Gregory of Nazianzus says, that to pamper the body is nothing else but to heap fuel on burning embers, to feed a wild beast so as to make it more unmanageable, and enable it to contend with greater power against the spirit, which it drags after it to make it work its lusts * He should not, therefore, if he wish to see his penitents full of vigour of mind and will, be too averse to allow them to curb their bodily appetites by a moderate use of penance.

61. Second suggestion. That a Director, in prescribing penitential practices, may keep within those limits of discretion which we have laid down in the foregoing Chapter, he must take account of two things :—first, of the condition of his penitent, second, of the nature and degree of the penances which he appoints. As regards the first, it is certain that young people of tender years, and also those who are advanced in life, are little fitted to do penance, as it is necessary for them to husband their bodily strength, rather than diminish it. Youths and maidens should be allowed some exercise of penance as a remedy suitable to the vivacity of the animal spirits and the effervescence of the blood; and that too in a larger measure than is allowed to married people. The Director may here call to mind the words which we have quoted in the previous Chapter from St. Thomas, when the Saint is treating of such as are married.† With Religious we should be more open-handed; for, as they are more strictly bound to perfection than others, they are under greater obligation to employ a means which contributes so effectually to its attainment. Still, account must be taken of their constitution and strength of body, and the allowance of penance must be proportioned to the degree of their vigour.

62. With regard to the quality or description of the penance, I believe that the discipline discreetly applied cannot be injurious to the health, for the pain which it causes has its seat in the skin, and ceases as soon as the stripes themselves cease; especially when the strokes do not fall upon the spine, but on parts more distant from the stomach, since thus it interferes less with digestion. On the other hand, it is a penance most suited to mortify the flesh by the feeling of pain, the exact contrary of the pleasure which it so greedily hankers after; and, further, it is a great help to devotion, as we observed above, on the authority of St. Francis

* Sufficit corpori malitia sua. Quid flammæ ampliori materiâ opus est? aut belluæ copiosiori alimento, ut efferatior, et violentior reddatur. Orat. 44.

† Cap. 6, num. 55.

of Sales. So that the Director may safely be at his ease when permitting its use. I do not, however, mean that he should be ready to permit disciplines which bring blood; on the contrary, with regard to this point, I should wish him to exercise great reserve: first, because the same mortification of the flesh can easily be obtained without any loss of blood, which is a loss not unfrequently injurious to the health; and secondly, to avoid a certain vanity which is often excited in some who, after one of these bloody scourgings, think that they have done some great thing, and, as the saying is, that they have already put their hand upon the door of heaven.

63. The chain, *catenella* as it is called, is usually less prejudicial to health than the hair-shirt, as we have already remarked; for the latter, by causing local irritation, weakens the stomach: hence the Director will be more in favour of the former. However, even the small chain should not be worn round the loins by persons of weak chest or feeble constitution, but rather on the arms or elsewhere. As regards the length of time, and the frequency of the use of such instruments, these are to be measured by the bodily strength and spiritual fervour of penitents. Care must be taken not to allow the use of the chain during the night, lest sleep be broken; nor immediately after meals, to prevent interfering with digestion. The best time is in the morning, for a period proportioned to the penitent's constitution and state of health.

64. Persons of a robust constitution may be allowed to sleep on the bare floor, those who have less strength may sleep on straw mattresses, or with some other discomfort; and the measure is to be sought in the degree of each one's bodily vigour and in the greater or less soundness of sleep, which allows them to take their rest without break or interruption, despite such inconveniences. Care, however, should be taken that those who sleep thus be sufficiently covered, lest the chill should damage their health. No one should be allowed to lie on the bare ground, as the cold and damp might do serious injury. With regard to watching, great heed must be taken, as experience proves that many who watch the night through are unfit for work in the day-time. It is true that certain saints passed whole nights without ever closing

their eyes, or allowed themselves only a very brief interval of rest, as we have seen in the fourth Chapter; but this they did by means of an extraordinary help of God's providence, Who, as such austerities were required from them, supported them independently of the necessary refreshment of sleep. It must be further observed, that God compensated these saintly souls for the sleep which they sacrificed in their night-watching, by keeping them the whole night long absorbed in lofty contemplation; which, by imparting to their spirit a great sweetness, helped to invigorate their bodily frames, and served as a stay to enable them to support these excessive rigours. But they who are not thus favoured by God, and cannot expect such extraordinary assistance, must be content to allow their body sufficient rest, in order that, being fitted for the burden of the day, it may render the spirit due service. It will hence be enough for them to mortify themselves by curtailing somewhat of their sleep; in other words, by lessening that full allowance of sleep which is not necessary for life and work, but serves merely to indulge the senses, always too much inclined, to seek repose. They should, moreover, declare before God that they allow their bodies this limited and reasonable refreshment, not out of compliance with the tendencies of nature, but only in order to do His will, to perform what He requires of them, and to be better able to do Him some service. Fasting will be treated of in the following Article.

65. Third suggestion. The rules heretofore laid down apply to the ordinary direction of souls, but admit of exceptions in the extraordinary cases which may from time to time present themselves. In all past ages, God has willed that there should be in His Church persons signalised by the rigours of an extraordinary penance; in other words, He has been pleased to sanctify some by an austerity which transcends the powers of human nature; and we meet with and admire instances of the kind in almost every page of the Church's annals. It follows from this, that it is by no means likely that nowadays there are no souls whom God designs to lead to perfection by these unfrequented paths. Should, then, a Director chance to have the guidance of any such

persons, he would most surely not be at liberty to withdraw them from the path by which God calls them to seek perfection; for, as we have before observed, properly speaking, we are not the guides of souls, but God. We are but the ministers of this Supreme Director, whose indications we must diligently watch for, in order that these traces may be followed by our penitents with fidelity and constancy.

66. But here, a Director may reply, lies the whole difficulty. How are we to discover the will of God in so extraordinary a matter, and how escape the danger of seriously damaging our penitents in body and soul? I answer, We must not lose heart; for, guiding our course by the dictates of prudence, by the light of that discernment which should ever be sought for from above, we shall attain to a moral certainty of what is God's pleasure. We will lay down two rules:—First, We must observe whether the penitent have frequent and powerful inspiration to practise great austerities; but that will not suffice of itself, as Satan can transform himself into an angel of light, and urge on the penitent for the purpose of ruining his health, and rendering his mind incapable of anything that might promote his perfection. Secondly, The ford, so to speak, must be tried step by step. The penitent may be allowed some uncommon mortification, and we should carefully watch how he endures the weight of such austerity. If his health keep up, nay, even improve—as was the case with the three Holy Children of Babylon, who, living on pulse and water alone, were more full of flesh, stronger, and healthier than their companions, who were fed from the king's table;—and still more, if, on giving up these practices, the penitent fall, as sometimes happens, into some sickness or bodily ailment; it will be a clear indication that God wills him to walk in this thorny path. For, on the one hand, the Almighty has made known His will by inward inspiration; on the other hand, He supplies an authentic proof by the special assistance He affords to enable the penitent to bear up under so great a burden. At times God notifies His good pleasure by prodigies, as happened in the case of St. Mary Magdalen de' Pazzi, with whom His will was that she should go barefoot, in a convent where all the others wore shoes, and He made her feet

swell every time she put on shoes, while the swelling went down as soon as she took them off. We have also the instance of the Venerable Sister Veronica, of Città di Castello. God Almighty wished her to observe for several years together a rigorous fast on bread and water, and caused her immediately to throw up every description of food except plain bread and pure water. Should God declare His purposes by signs so manifest as these, the Director may proceed without misgivings, and allow, without stint, the special penances to which some feel themselves impelled by the Spirit of the Lord. But he should never permit them to do any penance at their own whim and fancy, and without previous leave; thus keeping the spirit, as well as the body, in subjection; and if he discover, in course of time, any notable decline in the penitent's health, let him at once change his conduct, and withdraw the permission which he had previously given, lest the evil increase and at length disable the person from performing the exercises proper to the spiritual life.

67. Fourth suggestion. But the Director must, before all else, take notice whether these penances be performed with an interior spirit, otherwise they will torture the body with little or no profit to the soul; for if they are done with sentiments of vanity and self-satisfaction, they will do more harm than good. The Flagellants mentioned above scourged themselves to blood twice a day, yet they were wicked wretches, infected with heresy, and addicted to abominable sins. In Turkey, and in many heathen countries, there are penitents whose lives are most austere, and yet they are by no means saints, because their penance does not spring from a right principle. Wherefore the Director must strive that his penitents mortify their bodies with a right intention, with compunction and humility of heart, so that their penance may be both profitable to themselves and acceptable to God. As regards the intention, they should have none other than that of subjecting the flesh to the spirit, of making satisfaction for their faults, of being agreeable to God, and of obtaining plenteous graces for the amendment of their failings and the acquisition of solid virtues. As to compunction, before beginning their penitential inflictions, let them set before their eyes their sins, both past and present, conceiving a

lively sorrow for them, and a holy zeal to give God some satisfaction for them by the endurance of some punishment. With respect to humility, their bodily afflictions should ever be united to our dear Lord's sufferings, and His most Precious Blood; in the firm conviction that of themselves their penances are of no avail, but derive whatever merit they may possess from the infinite merits of Jesus Christ, to Whom all the honour is due. Thus shall they offer their bodies to God as a perfect sacrifice on the altar of penance.

ARTICLE II.

The hindrances to perfection arising from the sense of taste, and remedies against such hindrances.

CHAPTER I.

DESCRIPTION OF THE SENSE OF TASTE, IN CONNECTION WITH THE VICE OF GLUTTONY; THE SEVERAL WAYS OF COMMITTING SIN BY THIS VICE, AND THE HINDRANCES WHICH IT OFFERS TO PERFECTION.

68. THE sense of taste is that by which we discern the savour of food and drink. As Aristotle remarks, it abhors what is unsavoury, and craves for what is agreeable to it.* Its sole tendency, therefore, is to the pleasure of eating and drinking—a merely brutal gratification, as it is common to us with the lower animals. This sense, as we learn from Aristotle,† resides in the tongue; and, in animals that are without tongues, in some organ fitted to receive the same sensations as the tongue. Whence it follows, that though

* Gustus salutarem cibum a pestifero ita discernit, ut insuave, et ingratum fugiat: salutare, gratumque appetat. Lib. Sens.

† Organum gustûs, sive ipsius instrumentum, est lingua, aut quidquid linguæ proportione respondens in his, qui linguâ carent.

this sense be distinct from the vice of gluttony, which resides in the sensual appetite, yet it is closely connected with it, supplies it with a stimulus; strengthens, nay, is the sole object of, its disordered cravings and evil motions: for, as St. Thomas says, the vice of gluttony consists in an inordinate desire of the pleasure which arises from eating and drinking, a pleasure which is the only object of the craving of the sense of taste.* Thus the same animal gratification is the object of these two brutal senses—the one internal, which is gluttony; the other external, that is to say, the sense of taste: and the mortification of the one is therefore equivalent to the subjugation of the other; as, on the other hand, the gratification of the taste by taking savoury food, is a pampering of the inner appetite. So that we may speak of both as of two enemies leagued together, not only against our perfection, but against our eternal salvation, should they be allowed to make their unruly cravings prevail, to the prejudice of reason.

69. St. Gregory the Great says, that we are tempted to gluttony in five ways, and that this vice opposes five hindrances to our perfection. We are tempted when, for the purpose of gratifying our palate, we forestall the regular time of meals, or, without anticipating the time, when we seek delicacies wherewith to gratify this vile sense. It may further happen that, although content with ordinary food, we may seek sauces and seasoning for the gratification of our taste. We may also, without exceeding in the quality of our food, or in its accompaniments, exceed in quantity, so as to partake of common dishes beyond what we really need. Lastly, the food we eat may be coarse in quality, yet we may partake of it with too great eagerness. This last fault is worse than all the others, as it is a clearer sign of our attachment to the gratification which eating affords to the palate.†

* Gula proprie consistit circa immoderatam delectationem, quæ est in cibis, et potibus. 2, 2, quæst. 188, art. 6.

† Quinque nos modis gulæ vitium tentat. Aliquando namque indigentiæ tempora prævenit. Aliquando vero tempus non prævenit, sed cibos lautiores quærit. Aliquando quælibet, quæ sumenda sint, præparari accuratius expetit. Aliquando autem et qualitati ciborum et tempori congruit; sed in ipsâ quantitate sumendi mensuram moderatæ refectionis excedit. Nonumquam vero

70. Having thus enumerated the five evil inclinations which tempt us to pamper the sense of taste—termed by St. Thomas the five species into which the vice of gluttony may be divided*—St. Gregory proceeds to illustrate from Holy Writ their peculiar deformity. With regard to anticipating the time of meals, he brings forward the example of Jonathan, who, having tasted wild honey before the close of the day on which it was strictly forbidden to any to taste food, incurred the sentence of death pronounced against him by his father's lips.† To deter us from daintiness, he instances the gluttony of the children of Israel, who, despising the manna, hankered after the flesh-pots of Egypt, dwelling on the thought that, in the land of their captivity, they had fared more sumptuously; for which cause many of them were struck by God with death.‡ With regard to superfluous seasoning of food, he relates the gluttony of the sons of Heli, the high priest, who sought the meat of the sacrifices before it was cooked, contrary to the ancient usage, in order that they might prepare and season it to their own liking, whence both they and their father were visited by God with the severest punishments.§ Against excess in quantity, he alleges the saying of Ezechiel, whereby the prophet clearly implies that the ruin of Sodom had its origin in excess of eating and in drunkenness.|| As a warning against over-eagerness in eating even coarse and common food, he adduces the case of Esau, whose greediness in partaking of a dish of lentils is sufficiently apparent from the fact of his having sold his

et abjectius est, quod desiderat; et tamen ipso æstu immersi desiderii deterius peccat. Mor., lib. xiij., cap. 30.

* 2, 2, quæst. 148, art 4.

† Mortis quippe sententiam patris ore Jonathas meruit; quia in gustu mellis constitutum edendi tempus antecessit.

‡ Et ex Ægypto populus eductus in eremo occubuit; quia despectâ mannâ, cibos carnium petiit, quos lautiores putavit.

§ Et prima filiorum Heli culpa suborta est, quod ex eorum voto sacerdotis puer, non antiquo more coctas vellet de sacrificio carnes accipere; sed crudas quæreret, quas accuratius exhiberet.

|| Et cum ad Hierusalem dicitur: *Hæc fuit iniquitas Sodomæ sororis tuæ, superbia, saturitas panis, et abundantia;* aperte ostenditur, quod idcirco salutem perdidit, quia cum superbiæ vitio mensuram moderatæ refectionis excessit.

birthright for so mean a price. The misfortunes that this vice brings upon us are, then, sufficiently known.*

71. We may here remark, that the deformity of these five species of the vice of gluttony may be reduced to the search after gratification of the palate, and to the pleasure which accompanies eating. If the reader will but reflect on each of these, he will be convinced of the truth of this view. Why is it an imperfection to forestall the hour of meals, but that this argues an impatience to gratify the palate? Why is it blameworthy to seek out costly dishes and savoury sauces, except that this arises from a desire to give pleasure to the taste? Why is it sinful to eat to excess? Surely because it is a sign that we eat not out of necessity, but for pleasure's sake. The same may be said when we eat greedily, or with too much eagerness. That it is sinful is certain, for whoever should assert the contrary, maintaining that to eat and drink to satiety for mere pleasure is no sin, would be thereby upholding a proposition condemned by Innocent XI., and would incur the condemnation pronounced on all who should maintain this error. The condemned proposition may be thus stated, word for word: "Eating and drinking to repletion for the sole gratification of the palate is no sin, provided it be done without prejudice to the health, as the natural appetite may lawfully take pleasure in its acts."†

72. But I must not be misunderstood as saying that it is sinful to feel pleasure in eating, for it is impossible for man, when partaking of food, not to experience in the organs of taste a gratification depending upon the quality of what is taken. I mean only to say, that it is wrong and greatly prejudicial to perfection, to eat with a view of procuring this gratification for ourselves, as do the brutes, which eat merely for pleasure, without determining for themselves any lawful or reasonable purpose. St. Gregory proves this by a most convincing argument. At times we may par-

* Et primogenitorum gloriam Esau amisit, quia magno æstu desiderii vilem cibum, scilicet lenticulum concupivit, quam dum venditis etiam primogenitis prætulit, quo in illam appetitu anhelaret, indicavit

† Comedere, et bibere usque ad satietatem ob solam voluptatem, non est peccatum, modo non obsit valetudini, quia licite potest appetitus naturalis suis actibus frui. Prop. viij. inter damn. ab Innoc XI.

take of dainties, he says, without any fault, while at other times we do not eat even the plainest food without sin of gluttony. The reason is, that in the former case, though the flavour be more attractive, we do not seek our gratification, while we do seek it in the latter, though the attraction of the food be less. Thus did Esau part with his birthright for a coarse and unpalatable mess, but Elias received no hurt from eating flesh meat in the wilderness; for the Prophet partook of food with great detachment, while Esau devoured his unsavoury portion with an eager desire of gratifying his taste.* The holy Doctor pursues this argument by adding, that the devil—being well aware that, for most, not the food itself, but their attachment to the pleasure of eating, is the occasion of their damnation—tempted neither the first man, Adam, nor the Second Man, who is the Redeemer, by setting before them a steaming joint, but entrapped the former by an apple, and sought to ensnare the latter with plain dry bread.† We may hence infer that the vice of gluttony may be reduced to the unruly inclination which prompts us to gratify the sense of taste, and to seek the pleasure we experience in partaking of food and drink. Indulgence in the pleasure proper to this sense is so formidable a hindrance to perfection, that unless we overcome it we can never make any progress worthy of the name. Hence we must needs withhold from it all such gratification, or at least grant it sparingly, and, when necessity requires it, with that uprightness of intention which may prevent any harm being done to the spirit; as will be more fully developed in the course of this Article.

73. How much God is displeased at every unreasonable indulgence granted to this brutish sense may be briefly shown by the serious prejudice which often results to the soul. For the present it will suffice to prove this by certain occurrences which St. Gregory

* Neque enim cibus, seu appetitus in vitio est; unde lautiores cibos plerumque sine culpâ sumimus, et abjectiores non sine reatu conscientiæ degustamus. Hic quippe, quem diximus, Esau primatum per lenticulum perdidit, et Helias in eremo virtutem spiritûs carnes edendo servavit. Loco supra c.

† Unde et antiquus hostis, quia non cibum, sed cibi concupiscentiam esse causam damnationis intelligit; et primum sibi hominem non carne, sed pomo subdidit; et secundum non carne, sed pane tentavit.

relates.* For as we have begun this Chapter by alleging his authority, we will end in the same way. A nun was walking in the garden of her convent, and seeing a fine lettuce, was tempted to gluttony, and plucking it up, began to eat it greedily.† But it proved fatal to her, for while she was devouring it a devil entered into her, immediately threw her to the ground, and began to torment her in a thousand ways. Her companions, alarmed by her struggles, screams, cries for help, and contortions, sent at once for the holy Abbot Equitius, in order that he might restrain, by his authority, the rage of the infernal spirit, who was so cruelly torturing their unhappy Sister. The holy man came at once, and no sooner had he set foot in the garden than the fiend began to cry by the mouth of the possessed nun, "What have I done? what have I done? I was resting on a lettuce; she came and swallowed me up greedily, and I have taken possession of her."‡ The Servant of God commanded the devil to depart forthwith; and by the authority of his adjuration, and the merit of his holy life, the demon was expelled so effectually that he never returned to molest her. Thus, for a mouthful of lettuce, eaten in satisfaction of gluttony, a person consecrated to God fell under the power of the devil! The reader should reflect on the severity of this chastisement, and learn how hateful to God is the irregular gratification of the palate, especially in spiritual and devout persons who make profession of perfection.

74. But the same holy Doctor relates a far more fearful chastisement which befell a monk, who, on account of this vice, remained, not for a time only, but for ever, the prey of the infernal dragon. This hapless man lived in a monastery of Lycaonia, and was held in great esteem and veneration by all his brethren for his excellent behaviour, and the exactness wherewith he performed, at least to outward appearance, all his duties. But the poor wretch was a slave to gluttony, so that, while the others

* Dial., lib. i., cap. 4.

† Lactucam conspiciens concupivit, avide momordit.

‡ Ego quid feci? ego quid feci? Sedebam super lactucam: venit illa, et momordit me.

fasted, he took secret opportunities of eating. At length he was overtaken by serious illness, which soon brought him to extremity. As the hour of his departure drew nigh, the monks flocked round his bed, thinking to behold and to hear, at the death of so holy a man, something for their edification and comfort. What they did hear was this: "Brethren, when you fasted I feasted in secret, for which cause am I given over to the infernal dragon, who is already coiling himself round my feet and knees, and even now is putting his head into my mouth to drag out my soul." With these words he expired in the devil's clutches.* Devout persons and religious may hence take a lesson; they who have surmounted the obstacles which the world, flesh and blood, and the devil, put in the way of their salvation and perfection, but have failed as yet to overcome their sensuality and greediness, in that they seek for dainties, desire them eagerly, take great pains to procure them, complain when they have to forego them, and devour them without the least restraint,—they may learn, I say, from this how displeasing their sin is in God's sight, since even in this life He gives such tokens of His displeasure.

CHAPTER II.

EVIL EFFECTS, AND THE PREJUDICE TO THE SOUL, WHICH SPRING FROM PAMPERING THE TASTE, AND INDULGING IN HABITS OF GLUTTONY.

75. THERE are, St. Thomas teaches, five sisters all born of gluttony, the vile mother of a prolific family; in other words—according to the explanation which he himself gives—five most baneful results spring from an immoderate indulgence in the pleasures of eating and drinking, which are opposed, not only to perfection, but even to the fundamental conditions of a Christian

* Ecce ad devorandum draconi datus sum, qui caudâ suâ genua mea, pedesque colligavit. Caput vero suum intra os meum mittens, spiritum meum ebibens abstrahit. Quibus dictis, statim defunctus est Dial., lib. iv, c. 38.

life.* Four of the children of this brutish mother are begotten in the soul; the fifth, continues the Saint, is brought forth in the body. All five are in league to injure our soul, and to compass its ruin.† Now, of these five perverse daughters (or, to sink all further metaphor), of these five evil effects of gluttony, which invariably originate in the indulgence of the palate, we will treat in the present Chapter, and will ponder with St. Thomas their moral deformity, and the prejudice they occasion to the souls of devout persons who have yet to overcome this animal vice.

76. The first effect of gluttony assigned by St. Thomas, and one which is most injurious to all spiritual advancement, is the darkening of the mind by the superabundance of meat and drink, whereby the soul becomes incapable of prayer and of understanding divine truths. On the other hand, nothing better fits the mind for the contemplation of supernatural and heavenly things than fasting and abstinence.‡ In what manner did Moses prepare himself when summoned to speak to God face to face on the summit of Mount Sinai? By a fast which was kept up for full forty days. How did Elias dispose himself for the vision of God in the cave of Horeb? By the like rigorous fast continued for forty days.§ And how did Daniel fit himself for those mysterious revelations and hidden secrets of which we read in his prophecy, but by a three weeks' fast.‖ On the other hand, what led the Israelites to forget God and His claims to their veneration, homage, and worship, but the excess of gluttony into which they fell by immoderate feasting? Holy Writ tells us, that while being encamped and taking their rest at the foot of Sinai, they devoted themselves to eating and drinking.¶ But what came of

* Illa vitia inter filias gulæ computantur, quæ ex immoderatâ delectatione cibi et potûs consequuntur. 2, 2, quæst 148, art 6.

† Quæ quidem (scilicet filiæ gulæ) possunt accipi ex parte animæ et ex parte corporis Ex parte animæ quadrupliciter, etc.

‡ Primo quidem quantum ad rationem, cujus acies hebetatur ex immoderantiâ cibi et potûs. Et quantum ad hoc ponitur filia gulæ hebetudo sensûs circa intelligentiam, propter fumositates ciborum perturbantes caput. Sicut e contrario abstinentia confert ad sapientiæ perceptionem.

§ III. Reg. xxix.

‖ Daniel x.

¶ Sedit populus manducare, et bibere. Exodi xxxij. 6.

this excess? They lost the light of God's knowledge, and made a golden calf, which they adored in their insolent folly.

77. St. John Chrysostom handles this subject admirably. Look, he says, at a ship that has just discharged her cargo: how lightly she skims over the waves; how, borne, as it were, on the wings of the winds, she vies with them in speed; how swiftly she leaves the shore and disappears on the main, far from the gaze of all beholders. On the contrary, a ship that is laden with merchandise moves slowly, and yields but little to the impulse of the winds, because she is weighted by the charge she carries, which at times even causes her to sink. Thus, too, a man with his body not laden with food, rises unchecked and speedily to the contemplation of heavenly things. But when the belly is full of meat, and the mind overclouded with the fumes of wine, he cannot rise to God, being borne down by the weight of his intemperance.* So too a spiritual person must not expect to make progress in prayer and familiarity with God, if he bridle not his appetite, by refusing his palate the gratification after which it hankers.

78. The second pernicious effect of gluttony—as we learn from the same holy Doctor—is, that when the reason is troubled, and the sensitive appetite affected by excess of meat or drink, we must needs show by outward behaviour a certain unmeaning boisterous merriment.† And this was just what happened to the Israelites at the foot of Mount Sinai. While Moses was fasting, and had entered into the mystic cloud of the loftiest contemplation, they fell, through excess of eating and drinking, into immoderate rejoicings.‡ Being filled with meat, and their heads made giddy with the fumes of wine, they gave themselves up to dissolute gambols, to dancing, music, singing, and sports of all kinds. The result we have seen above. They bent their knees to the image of a

* Quemadmodum leviores naves maria velocius transeunt; contra multo onere gravatæ submerguntur, ita jejunium leviorem reddens mentem efficit ut facilius hujus vitæ pelagus transmittat, ac ea quæ in cœlis sunt, respiciat; et nihili faciat præsentia. In Genes Hom. 1.

† Secundo, quantum ad appetitum, qui multipliciter deordinatur per immoderantiam cibi, et potûs, quasi sopito tabernaculo rationis. Et quantum ad hoc ponitur inepta lætitia

‡ Sedit populus manducare, et bibere, et surrexerunt ludere.

calf, fashioned by their own hands; they offered it profane incense and abominable sacrifices. See the results of intemperance, a foolish joy which, blinding the reason, draws us into grievous excesses: as St. Jerome wisely observes in his Commentary on this passage.* They, then, who wish to serve God, must take heed not to indulge all the cravings of their appetite and palate, for, losing thereby the inner light which regulates their behaviour and bearing, and casting aside all modesty, both inward and outward, in the transports of a boisterous gladsomeness, it must needs happen, not that they should turn their backs upon God by grievous sin, as was the case with the Israelites (for I cannot bring myself to augur so dreadful a misfortune), but that they will offend Him in countless manners, cease from their accustomed virtuous practices, and lose devout recollection.

79. The third effect of gluttony is talkativeness.† For meat and drink, when taken to excess, with their fumes and vapours, set in motion the phantasms of the brain, whence arises an abundance of thoughts and words, but of thoughts which are not to the purpose, of foolish, ay, and often sinful, words, as may be frequently seen in such as have allowed themselves to be overcome by want of moderation in eating and drinking.

80. The rich glutton, when buried in hell, sought only to cool his burning tongue.‡ But wherefore, St. Gregory asks, does he seek relief rather for his tongue than for any other part of his body, which was wholly plunged in a sea of devouring flames? On account of the great talkativeness, replies the Saint, which arose from his excesses; on this account he was more cruelly tormented in the tongue. The holy Doctor infers from this that gluttons are usually reckless talkers.§ To the end, then, that the

* Moyses quadraginta diebus et noctibus jejunus in monte Sinâ . . . cum Domino loquitur; populus autem satur idola fabricatur. Ille vacuo ventre legem accipit scriptam digito Dei: iste manducans, et bibens, consurgensque ludere, aurum conflat in vitulum. In Jovinian.

† Tertio quantum ad inordinatum verbum: et sic ponitur multiloquium.

‡ Mitte Lazarum, ut intingat extremum digiti sui in aquam, et refrigeret linguam meam. Lucæ xvj. 24.

§ Nisi gulæ deditos immoderata loquacitas raperet, dives ille, qui epulatus quotidie splendide dicitur, in linguâ gravius non arderet. Pastor., part iii., damon. 20.

tongue may not transgress by unmeasured talk, or by improper and unseemly expressions, it must be kept in moderation as regards the pleasures arising from eating and drinking, which it naturally seeks after.

81. The fourth effect of gluttony is scurrility, and want of due restraint in our outward bearing. For, as St. Thomas truly observes, when excess of meat and drink has clouded, not only reason, but still more the supernatural light of grace, and the appetite of the inner sense is stimulated, we must needs break out into foolish sayings, and into unbecoming gestures: unseemliness that scandalises, and buffooneries which move the bystanders to laughter, are sure to follow.* It must be plain to every one how misplaced such things are in those who make profession of piety.

82. The fifth, and by far the most pernicious, effect of gluttony, is impurity. This, says St. Thomas, mainly concerns the body; nevertheless it inflicts on the soul a far more fatal blow than the other four, and causes its death.† It was mainly on account of this shameful result that the Holy Fathers are so emphatic in their denunciations of intemperance in eating, and still more in the use of wine, especially when carried to excess, that they unanimously inculcate the mortification of the palate by means of temperance, fasting, and abstinence from eating or from abundance and variety of numerous dishes. "Meat and wine, and a full stomach," says St. Jerome, "are the seed-plot of incontinency."‡ This Saint is ever repeating the same in his letters to those whom he directed in the spiritual path; on all of whom he imposes a rigid abstinence from dainties and from wine, lest these supply fuel to the treacherous vice of impurity. St Basil says that whosoever will remain a virgin (and the same may be said of all who would keep themselves untainted and pure) must strive courageously against the cravings of the palate, this being the fountain-head and well

* Quarto, quantum ad inordinatum motum. Et sic ponitur scurrilitas, idest jocularitas quædam, proveniens ex defectu rationis: quâ sicut non potest cohibere verba, ita non potest cohibere exteriores gestus.

† Ex parte autem corporis ponitur immunditia.

‡ Esus carnium, et potus vini, ventrisque saturitas seminarium libidinis est. In Jovinian.

spring of all sensual pleasures, and the stimulus of all uncleanness.* Cassian asserts that it is impossible, with a full stomach, not to feel rebellious motions.† From this, in the following Chapter, he infers that the intemperate man, being unable to restrain his appetite, will have still smaller success with the temptations of the flesh; these being more violent.

83. Such, then, are the five evil effects which, according to St. Thomas, arise from the indulgence of the sense of taste by gluttony; and, summing up this teaching, we may say, in a few words, with St. Gregory, that gluttony gives birth to an obtuseness of mind with regard to the understanding of heavenly things, to foolish joy, buffoonery, loquacity, and impurity.‡ This last effect is, beyond question, the most to be dreaded, and of itself, even were there none other, ought to suffice to engage a Christian to wage a truceless war with gluttony and the palate. For all must be well aware that both these are in close league with impurity, not only to drive us from the degree we may have already reached in the path of perfection, but to make us stray from the road that leads to life everlasting; since there is no other vice which drags men so powerfully into eternal damnation.

84. The reader will not then be astonished if, in reading the works of the saints, he finds that the first maxim they inculcate on devout persons who are resolved to aim at real perfection, is to resist the cravings of taste, and to trample under foot the tendency which gluttony has to gratify this dangerous sense; for, as every one must see, it is absurd to talk of perfection amid the gross, glaring, and disgraceful faults which swarm from this swinish vice. But should it be the case that he has never met with such teachings and lessons of the saints, let him listen at

* Ante omnia adversus gustum virgo totâ intentione pugnabit, fontesque voluptatum ventris, et impudicitiæ fomitum inde manantium, a principio, castitatis studio, et ardore siccabit. . . . Ventre enim distento epulis, necesse est ea, quæ sub ipso sunt membra, ex humoris redundantiâ, ad propria, et naturalia officia moveri. De Vera Virginitate.

† Impossible est saturum ventrem pugnas interioris hominis non experiri. Instit., lib. ix., cap. 13.

‡ De ventris ingluvie inepta lætitia, immunditia, multiloquium, hebetudo mentis circa intelligentiam propagantur.

least to the maxim laid down by St. Gregory on this very point: "No one should venture to think of undertaking the spiritual life who has not yet overcome the great domestic foe he carries within him, which is the appetite of gluttony."* And elsewhere, he more than once repeats, that none should flatter themselves with the hope of winning laurels in the spiritual warfare, or attaining to perfection, unless the allurements of the flesh have been first overcome by the mortification of the appetite and of gluttony.†

85. Cassian alleges a further reason for this, saying, that all are incapable of resisting greater vices who have not yet prevailed over the lesser.‡ He who has been vanquished by a pigmy will certainly be unable to conquer a giant; nor can he expect to throw a robust soldier who has been cast to the ground by a feeble woman. So, also, is it idle to expect to overcome the greater vices and the more violent passions which sway our hearts, and thus to attain the glory of a certain progress in perfection, if we are unable to withstand our natural inclination for the relish of food, a lesser vice and one easier to overcome. I might prove this truth by several instances, but will confine myself to one which is connected with the life of St. Bernard, and is recorded in the annals of the Cistercian Order §

86. The holy Abbot went one day to visit his novices, as was his frequent custom, according to the duty of a good shepherd concerned for the well-being of his flock; and after having consoled them with a spiritual discourse, admirably suited to their needs and capacity, he called aside Achard and two others, and pointing out to them another novice who was present, told them that the unfortunate man would that very day leave the monastery.

* Neque ad conflictum spiritualis agonis assumitur, si non prius intra nosmetipsos hostis positus, gulæ videlicet appetitus, edometur. Moral., lib. iij, cap. 13.

† Nullus palmam spiritualis certaminis apprehendit, qui non in semetipso prius, per afflictam ventris concupiscentiam, carnis incentiva devicerit. Ibid., cap. 26.

‡ Numquam robustioribus æmulis colluctari posse confidas eum, quem in leviori conflictu conspexeris ab inferioribus, pravisque superari. Instit., lib. vj., cap. 11.

§ Vincent., Specul. Hist., lib. vij., cap. 108.

He therefore ordered them to keep an eye upon him, to follow him, and to stop him in his flight. Achard remained on the watch the whole night, anxiously awaiting the fulfilment of the holy Abbot's words. About the time that the signal for rising and going to the choir was given, he beheld two men of gigantic stature enter the dormitory; their features were repulsive, their looks sinister, and both were clad in dark raiment; one of them carried a roast fowl, spitted on a stick, and around it was coiled a hideous frightful serpent. They drew near to the couch of this unhappy novice, and holding to his nose the smoking dainty, repeatedly strove to lure him by the odour of the savoury dish. The reader will perceive that God's purpose in this vision was to show that the devil tempted this poor wretch by gluttony, and lured him by the relish of food. Meanwhile the poor novice awoke, and, dressing hastily, looked around with a suspicious eye, to make sure of not being watched; he then rushed like a madman to the monastery gate, in order to run away: thus fulfilling the prophecy of St. Bernard. Then Achard, who had attentively taken note of everything, called the community, told them what had happened, and begged them to make haste. They all together started after the fugitive, came up to him, and stopped him; but to no purpose, for, overcome by his gluttony, he was deaf to argument, to entreaty, and to threats. He was firmly and basely resolved to leave without bidding his saintly Abbot farewell. He returned to the world, where he made a miserable end. Now this young man had started with great fervour on the way of perfection, and, what makes the greatest impression on me, he began his course in the holiest place that was then to be found in the world, in the Abbey of Clairvaux itself, and under the ablest master of the age, the great St. Bernard. But to what purpose were all his generous resolves? They were of no avail, for he had not succeeded in overcoming his natural cravings for the pleasures of the taste. So true is it that the first steps which a person must take in the path of perfection are to mortify the palate, and to subdue the vice of gluttony, that seeks only to gratify the taste with the abundance, the quality, and the savour of the food which it finds most pleasing.

CHAPTER III.

FIRST MEANS TO KEEP IN CHECK THE SENSE OF TASTE, AND ITS COMPANION THE VICE OF GLUTTONY.

87. It is not easy to keep the sense of taste within the bounds of due moderation, for, on the one hand, we must necessarily allow ourselves food enough to support bodily strength and to maintain ourselves in health; and, on the other hand, it is not lawful to go beyond the limits of reasonable sustenance, so as to prevent the brutal vice of gluttony having any opportunity of exercise. But how difficult it is to hit upon a medium between these two extremes! St. Augustine owns candidly of himself, that he had a daily struggle with his appetite for food and drink, and could hardly bring himself to the just medium between too large and too small an amount. "For," he says in his Confessions,* "this is not a vice like the others, which may be cut off at one stroke, by withdrawing from them everything on which they could feed, as I did with regard to incontinency at the beginning of my conversion: I am forced to take food, and yet am bound to restrain myself. But, on the other hand, O God, who is there that, in the refreshment of the body, does not overstep somewhat the limits of necessity? If there be one, he is in truth a great man; let him, O Lord, magnify Thy Name, for he has indeed good cause. For my part, I am not such an one, nor can I hope to receive so great a grace, for I am a sinful man."† The reader may hence infer how difficult it is to afford the body due refreshment without indulgence of the sense of taste, and yielding to the cravings of gluttony by some excess. So that it is necessary to prescribe certain remedies, by means of which (at

* Lib. x., cap. 34.

† Certo quotidie adversus concupiscentiam manducandi et bibendi. Non est, quod semel præcidere, et ulterius non attingere decernam; sicuti de concubitu potui. Itaque fræna gutturis temperatâ relaxatione, et constrictione tenenda sunt. Et quis est, Domine, qui non rapiatur aliquantulum extra metas necessitatis? Quisquis est, magnus est: magnificet nomen tuum. Ego autem non sum, quia peccator homo sum.

least as far as it is morally possible) a devout person may hit that just medium in which the virtue of temperance in eating may be said to consist.

88. The first remedy employed by the saints against this deceitful sense, and the unruly lust of gluttony, has always been fasting; for by denying their palate a part of its daily food, they made sure of not falling into the extreme of over-indulgence. Some of God's servants were so rigorous on this point, that they would lie open to some suspicion of excess, were it not that the extraordinary assistance God vouchsafed to their fasts not only justifies them against all gainsayers, but even proclaims them to have been saints. St. John the Baptist fasted continually, living on locusts and wild honey, without ever touching meat-flesh, and much less such dainties as birds, as we learn from St. Augustine.* St. Gregory of Nazianzus says of the Prince of the Apostles, St. Peter, that he observed an almost continued fast, taking merely a few lupines, and in such quantities only as sufficed to stave off death.† Clement of Alexandria relates of St. Matthew, that he never tasted flesh, but lived only on herbs‡ Eusebius says as much of St. James, who, he tells us, kept a perpetual abstinence from flesh-meat.§

89. What wonder if the great saints, the chosen pillars of the Church, practised such rigorous fasts, if among the laity, in those happy early centuries, it was usual to abstain from flesh-meat, as St. Epiphanius relates.|| He specially records this of the Christians of Alexandria, who were the disciples of St. Mark. And Philo the Jew himself attests this fact, to the honour of our religion. It was the custom of all the faithful, in those primitive times, to fast every Wednesday and Friday of the year, besides Lent and the Ember-Days, as appears from the Epistle of St. Ignatius Martyr to the Philippians;¶ from Origen;** and especially from a canon

* Joannes præcursor Domini locustis in eremo, et agresti melle nutritur; non animalium carnibus, non volucrum suavitatibus pascitur. Serm. de Temp. 65.

† De Paup Amore. ‡ Lib. ij., Præd., cap. 2.

§ Lib. ij. Hist. Eccl, cap. 2. || In fine Peiæn.

¶ Quartâ et sextâ feriâ jejunare, reliquias pauperibus porrigentes.

** Habemus quartam et sextam septimanæ diem, quibus solemniter jejunamus. Homil. 10 in Levitic.

of St. Clement of Rome.* Nor were their fasts like ours; for we are satisfied if we abstain from flesh and white meats, and are allowed a collation. But these fervent Christians, besides taking food only once a day, abstained even from fish, as may be seen in a homily of St. John Chrysostom. "To what purpose will it be," says the Saint, while preaching to his people, "if while we abstain from flesh and fish in our fasts, we backbite our brethren, and devour them, as it were, with insulting words?"† And, further, they denied themselves the use of wine, as St. Basil assures us: "On fast-days you will not eat flesh, but you devour your brother by irritating words; you drink no wine, but cannot refrain from railing."‡ Thus does the Saint, while rebuking the faults of some, discover to us how rigid was the abstinence observed by all.

90. If, however, we wish to form a correct notion of the severity of the fasts which were observed by the faithful in those early ages, it will suffice to read a letter of St. Jerome to Nepotian, in which he blames the fasts which were, in his days, observed at Rome. We shall see that many of the shortcomings, against which the holy Doctor protests with such vehemence, would, in our fasts, be considered as extreme rigours. I will give his own words: "Fix for yourself such a measure of fasting as you are able to bear. Let your fasts be pure, simple, moderate, and not superstitious. What use is there in abstaining from oil, and yet being anxious to get together a variety of food: dried figs, nuts, spices, dates, honey, and sweet pastry? The gardens are furrowed with ceaseless cultivation, because people will not be content with bread alone, and, by seeking gratification, put themselves far from the Kingdom of Heaven. I hear, too, that some, departing from common usage, refuse to drink water, or to eat bread, but take certain delicious beverages, flavoured with pounded herbs, and the sweet juice of the beet-root; nor do they care to

* Post hebdomadam jejunii; in omni quartâ feriâ, et Parasceve, præcipimus vobis, ut jejunetis. V. Constit., cap. ult.

† Quæ utilitas, cum ab avibus quidem, et piscibus abstineamus, fratres vero mordeamus, et comedamus? Hom 3 ad Popul.

‡ Carnes non edis, sed comedis fratrem tuum. A vino abstines, sed ab injuriis tibi non temperas. Homil. 1 de Jejunio.

take these even from any common cups, but must have a peculiar drinking-vessel. For shame! We ought to blush at such trifling! Mortifications so unusual and so full of superstition ought to fill us with disgust. We are come to this, that amid dainties we take to ourselves credit for our abstinence. The best fast is on bread and pure water. But because such a fast has nothing remarkable about it, as every one takes bread and water, it is considered by some too vulgar a mode of fasting."* Now, who can read these observations without a blush at seeing how far we fall short of those really good Christians? for what was reckoned a defect in their fasts, would, in these dainty times of ours, be looked upon as the height of austerity.

91. But if in those ages such was the rigour of the fasts observed by mere laymen living in the world, what must it have been with the monks who dwelt in the deserts, and who treated themselves with so much austerity? Their fasts were continual, and their meals were so frugal and so scanty, that the very narrative of the trustworthy authors who describe them, strikes one with astonishment. St. Jerome tells us that in the wilderness to which he retired, on his first departure for Rome, to lead therein a penitential and eremitic life, it was deemed a sort of luxury to take anything that had been cooked at the fire, even were it only a mere mouthful of warm water.† Cassian relates, that it was with the monks an inviolable law, established by the Fathers, that their daily nourishment should not exceed two little cakes—that is, two small rolls, which, taken together, would scarce weigh a pound.‡

* Tantum tibi jejuniorum modum impone, quantum ferre potes: sint tibi pura, casta, simplicia, moderata, et non superstitiosa jejunia. Quid prodest oleo non vesci, et molestias quasdam, difficultatesque ciborum quærere, carycas, piper, nuces, palmarum fructus, similam, mel, pystaciæ? Tota hortorum cultura vexatur, ut cibario non vescamur pane: et dum delicias sectamur, a regno cœlorum retrahimur. Audio præterea quosdam, contra rerum hominumque naturam, aquam non bibere, nec vesci pane: sed sorbitiunculas delicias, et contrita olera, betarumque succum, non calice sorbere, sed conchâ. Proh pudor! Non erubescimus hujusmodi ineptiis, nec tædet superstitionis. Insuper etiam famam abstinentiæ in deliciis quærimus. Fortissimum jejunium est aquæ, et panis. Sed quia gloriam non habet, et omnes pane, et aquâ vivimus, quasi publicum, et commune jejunium non putatur.

† Aliquid coctum comedisse, luxuria est. Ad Eustoch.

‡ Vix libræ unius pondus habere certissimum est.

Many of their number would spend two, three, and even four days, without tasting a mouthful. And St. Jerome tells of St. Hilarion,* that he would never intermit his rigid fast, even on festivals, or when attacked by grievous ailments. But far more wondrous is what St. Augustine relates that he had seen in Rome—namely, that not only men, but women living in community, despite the weakness of their sex and constitution, would frequently fast for three or four days without taking a crumb of bread or a drop of water, as if, divested of the body, they no longer stood in need of necessary sustenance.†

92. Thus did our Christian forefathers mortify the sense of taste, bringing into subjection the vice of gluttony, afflicting their flesh, and making it obedient to the spirit. Thus did they dispose themselves to prayer, and to receive therein the abundance of heavenly gifts. "And we, shame upon us!" exclaims St. Laurence Justinian, inflamed with a holy indignation, "we cannot resolve to deny ourselves even delicacies, to forego some favourite dish, or to undertake a fast—I do not say on bread and water, but even of the ordinary severity—unless it be imposed upon us of strict precept; a sure sign that our charity has waxed cold, and that the primitive spirit of fervour is quenched within us."‡

* In Vitâ.

† Jejunia etiam prorsus incredibilia multos exercere didici non quotidie semel sub noctem reficiendo corpus (quod est usquequaque usitatissimum); sed continuum triduum, vel amplius sæpissime sine cibo, et potu ducere. Neque hoc in viris tantum, sed etiam in fœminis, quibus item multis viduis et virginibus simul habitantibus, et lanâ, et telâ victum quærentibus, præsunt singulæ gravissimæ, probatissimæque, non tantum in instituendis, componendisque moribus, sed in instruendis mentibus peritæ, ac paratæ. De Mor. Eccl., lib. i., cap. 33.

‡ Ipsi vero, tamquam milites strenui, et zelatores Dei, jejuniis corpora macerabant, et carnem prolixâ inediâ subjugabant; ita ut quasi vitâ deficerent præ lassitudine, leguminibus namque, oleribus, pane, et aquâ parce utebantur; et his contenti, quibus natura sustentabatur; spiritualibus potius, quam corporalibus nutriebantur alimoniis. Sed, heu! temporibus nostris, frigescente caritate, et deficiente calore spiritûs, non est qui saltem delectabilibus privari velit. De Discipl. Monast. Conver., cap. 20.

CHAPTER IV.

CERTAIN RULES OF DISCRETION CONCERNING THE REMEDY PRESCRIBED IN THE FOREGOING CHAPTER AGAINST THE SENSE OF TASTE AND THE TENDENCY TO GLUTTONY.

93. It is by no means uncommon for remedies to turn out more injurious than the diseases themselves, and for them to hasten, instead of keeping off death, if not applied in a measure discreet and suited to the needs of the patient who has to take them. I have set forth fasting as a specific remedy for keeping under the sense of taste, and for freeing the devout person from the vice of gluttony, which is so fatal to all progress in spirit. I have proved the efficacy of this remedy by the example of the saints and of the faithful who lived in the first ages of the primitive Church. But that it may prove of use, it must be applied with befitting moderation, else, far from being advantageous, it would be prejudicial to perfection. Hence it is requisite that certain rules of discretion be laid down, of much the same nature as those given in the foregoing Article, when we were treating of bodily austerities.

94. But that these rules may be free from all suspicion of laxity, I will take them from one of the most austere, and, at the same time, one of the most trustworthy, of the Doctors that Almighty God has vouchsafed to His Church: it shall be St. Jerome. Every one knows how great a value he set upon fasting, and how rigid was his own practice in this regard. His letters show how he inculcated it upon his spiritual children, and the zeal wherewith he rebuked any omission on this point. Yet as he was not wanting in the light of discretion, which is the seasoning of every virtue, he wished every one to proceed in this matter with due moderation; and he laid down for his disciples very prudent rules, which we will now proceed to detail.

95. The first rule is, that fasting should not be so prolonged or so severe as, by withholding nourishment, to weaken the stomach and disable it from its natural functions, with detriment to the health, so as to make ourselves almost, if not entirely, unable to

continue in the path of perfection. St. Jerome gives this rule to Demetrias: "I do not require of you immoderate fasts, nor an unmeasured abstinence from food, by which delicate constitutions soon lose their vigour, and men begin to fail in health before even the first foundations of perfection have been laid."* This is at times the case with beginners, who, transported by that sensible ardour which God commonly imparts to such, to spur them on to virtue, will neither eat nor drink. But what is the result? They fall beneath the burden of immoderate abstinence, and ruin their health ere they have laid the foundations of perfection, so that they are hampered by their indispositions, and hindered from carrying on the building which they projected. And further—as St. Jerome writes to the monk Rusticus—the stomach becoming weak and relaxed, throws off certain crudities which produce those most irregular motions which we seek to prevent by the rigour of fasting; and hence the Saint advises his friend to moderate both the length and severity of his fasts.†

96. The second rule is, that our fasts should neither be so long nor so rigid as to hinder reading, study, prayer, watchings, labour, business, and other usual occupations The same saint lays down this rule for Celantia ‡ We have already given this very rule, quoting St. Thomas, and it is a point of the greatest importance in all bodily austerity; for, as we have already said, God demands the sacrifice of our bodies to His service · and our bodies must not be dead, but living. God would have our bodies fit to do Him service, and to work for His glory. And further, how can mortification be an act of virtue when it hinders the practice of those other virtues which are required of us by the duties of our condition? All the virtues are sisters; they all walk hand in

* Neque vero immoderata tibi imperamus jejunia, et enormem ciborum abstinentiam, quibus statim corpora delicata franguntur; et ante ægrotare incipiunt, quam sanctæ conversationis jacere fundamenta.

† Balneorum fomenta non quærat, qui calorem corporis jejuniorum cupit frigore extinguere; quæ et ipsa moderata sint, ne nimia debilitent stomachum, et majorem refectionem poscentia erumpant in cruditatem, quæ parens libidinum est.

‡ Sic debes jejunare, ut non palpites, et respirare vix possis, et comitum tuarum vel porteris, vel traharis manibus; sed ut fracto corporis appetitu, nec in lectione, nec in psalmis, nec in vigiliis solito quid minus facias

hand, and give each other mutual assistance. Abstinence, then, which is so rigid as to eject other virtues from the soul, and drive them far from the person who is bound to their practice, is by no means a virtue.

97. The third rule is, that fasts should not be so long and severe as to exhaust us, or to overtask and disgust us with the spiritual life. This warning was addressed by St. Jerome to Leta: "I do not approve, especially in those of tender years, of long and immoderate fastings continued for weeks together, with abstinence from oil and fruit; for I have learned by experience, that the ass, when it wearies on the road, will not only refuse to go forward, but will turn back, or stray from the road at the first opening."* So too, human nature, if overtasked by excessive abstinence, will seek diversion, amusements, and solace, and will wander from the straight path of virtue. If then, a devout person wishes constantly to go forward in the way of perfection, it behoves him to observe a prudent moderation in his fasts.

98. Lastly, this holy Doctor, with a view of convincing Demetrias of the paramount importance of discretion in the practice of fasting, alleges the examples of several persons well known to him, who, by excessive and ill-regulated abstinence, had incapacitated themselves for God's service. He writes: "I have known persons of either sex who through immoderate abstinence have done injury to their brain, especially some whose cells were in damp situations, so that eventually they did not know what they were doing or what they were saying, and thus became as stupid and senseless as so many blocks of wood."† To avoid foundering upon either of these rocks, we must avail ourselves of the rules just laid down. Fasting is a most effectual remedy against the excesses of the palate and the vice of gluttony, which, by its inward cravings, powerfully inclines us to gratify it. But it must

* Displicent mihi, in teneris maxime ætatibus, longa et immoderata jejunia, in quibus junguntur hebdomades, dum oleum in cibo, et poma vetantur. Experimento didici, asellum, in viâ, cum lassus fuerit, diverticula quærere.

† Novi ego in utroque sexu per nimiam abstinentiam, cerebri sanitatem in quibusdam fuisse vexatam, præcipue in his, qui in humectis, et frigidis habitavere cellulis, ita ut nescirent quid agerent, quove se verterent, quid loqui, quid tacere deberent.

be employed with prudence and discretion, lest, instead of being a help, it serves as a hindrance, to our advance in perfection.

99. Should the reader ask, What, then, is the measure to be kept by each one in fasting? should he abstain from flesh and white meats? should he at times fast on bread and water, or spend whole days without food? I reply, that when we come to such particulars, it is impossible to lay down a general rule suitable to every case, as the length and the severity of fasting must be measured by the spiritual and bodily strength of each individual, who therefore must regulate it by his experience of the prejudice or advantage resulting from the abstinence already practised. As a general rule, applicable to every case, and to be inviolably kept by all who wish not to go astray, we may give the prescription suggested by St. Benedict to his monks, whom he exhorts to some moderate abstinence, while he commands them to obtain leave for this from their Abbot; assuring them that every mortification they practise without the sanction of their spiritual father will be set down by God to the account of their vanity and self-will, and will not be reckoned as a matter of merit.*

CHAPTER V.

ANOTHER REMEDY AGAINST THE SENSE OF TASTE AND THE VICE OF GLUTTONY, SUITED TO ALL, EVEN TO THOSE WHO ARE UNABLE TO FAST.

100. THE remedy which we have indicated above for rooting out faults of gluttony will not suit every one. Persons of a weak stomach, of a slender build, or of attenuated strength, cannot prudently undertake severe fasts; and still less those who have to undergo great fatigues requiring a large expenditure of the vital

* Hoc ipsum tamen, quod unusquisque offert, abbati suo suggerat, et cum ejus fiet oratione, et voluntate: quia quod sine permissione patris spiritualis fit, præsumptioni deputabitur, et vanæ gloriæ, non mercedi. In Regulâ. Cap. 49.

force, which must needs be restored by food so that the body may be enabled to persevere in its laborious occupation. Hence, Holy Church herself, as a prudent mother, dispenses such from the practice of penances, even when she imposes them upon others by rigorous precept. Yet, on the other hand, this class of people are not exempt from the necessity of checking the vicious propensities of the taste and their appetites, which strive so powerfully against their salvation and perfection; so that even to them we must prescribe some suitable remedy by which they may withstand the allurements of these two great enemies. This will be temperance in eating and drinking; a remedy which, if less effectual than fasting, is yet able to keep the taste within due bounds, and to restrain gluttony. All have need to do this, whether capable of fasting, or not. This temperance is nothing else but guarding one's self with great care against falling into any one of those five defects or species of gluttony which we enumerated with St. Thomas in our second Chapter; in other words, to take heed not to commit any one of those five excesses which well up from the brutal vice of gluttony, as from a turbid source, to defile our souls. This being done, temperance is perfect, for these defects being carefully avoided, eating and drinking will be no longer a merely animal function, but a human act; since thus it will be regulated by reason, and accompanied with virtue: as will be seen when we treat of each in particular.

101. A devout person will arm himself against the first species of gluttony by not allowing his appetite to lead him to forestall the usual times of refreshment; for to do so would be to act by passion, not by our reason. A monk, says Cassian, (and this applies to every one who would live temperately,) must, in the first place, lay down for himself as a rule which he must always observe, never to allow himself to be prevailed upon by the longing of the palate to take even a drop of water, or a mouthful of bread before the accustomed hour of meals.* He lays the greatest stress on

* Monachus hanc in primis cautionem sibi indicat, ut non potus quisquam, non esus ullâ oblectatione devictus, ante stationem legitimam, communemque refectionis horam extra mensam percipere sibimet prorsus indulgeat. Lib. V. Inst., cap 20

this point of self-control, for, in reality, this forestalling of the usual meal-time is (except in the case of real necessity) a compliance with sensual appetite.

102. We read in the lives of the Fathers of the Desert, that a certain monk was tempted by the devil to break his fast, even at the very beginning of the day. Being fully aware of the quarter whence this suggestion came, he conquered it in the following manner: "Let us wait," said he to himself, "to the end of Tierce, and then we will take something." After Tierce, he would say, "We might as well wait until Sext." When this had passed, he would say, "As we have already gone so far, we may await in patience the hour of Nones," which was the regular hour of meals, for the monks. Thus did he proceed for two or three days, at the end of which, the devil, seeing himself outwitted, withdrew, and with him vanished all cravings of fictitious appetite. Such means as these should be made use of by every one, in order to cheat his appetite, unless he wants to become the slave of gluttony. *Woe to the land*, says the Spirit of God, *whose princes eat at early morn! Happy the land whose princes eat at due times.** And with good reason, because, from the efforts made to restrain the cravings of appetite for meat and drink, we may estimate a person's good or evil qualities.

103. As regards the second and third description of gluttony, St. Basil observes: "We may seek the food needed to support life and health, but must reject dainties and exquisite sauces and seasonings; for it is plain that we seek these only for the gratification of the palate, and to comply with the cravings of gluttony, since such things are by no means necessary for life, or to maintain health and strength, but, on the contrary, are frequently prejudicial.† If, then, we be so circumstanced as to have the choice of food, we should forego these delicacies, as being inconsistent with the virtue of temperance. If we have to leave the choice to

* Væ tibi terra, cujus principes mane comedunt. Beata terra, cujus principes vescuntur tempore suo. Eccl. x. 16.

† Omnibus locis cibus, qui sit ad victum necessarius, solerti ratione inquirendus; condimentorumque elaboratæ blanditiæ, ut voluptatis illecebræ, repudiandæ. De Verâ Virginitate

others, let us practise the advice which St. Bernard gave to his monks, and make to God, at each meal, the sacrifice of what is most pleasing to the palate.* Thus, besides the reward which we shall receive from God for our abstinence, we shall avoid all guilt in eating what is set before us, even though it be costly, and daintily seasoned; for it will be regarded as necessary sustenance, since we have none other for our stay and support.

104. Under this head we may consider moderation in the use of wine. St. Jerome proves himself very averse to this exciting drink, and in fact almost its sworn enemy: and he gives his disciples very rigorous advice about its use, for he looks upon it as the inseparable accomplice of lust, leagued with it to compass the ruin of youth. In his letter to Eustochium, he expresses himself as follows:—"If I am able to give any good advice, if I may rely on my own experience, I first warn thee, and conjure thee as a bride of Christ, to shun wine like poison. Wine is the chief weapon of which the devil makes use against young people. He cannot seduce them by greed of gain, or puff them up with pride, or lure them by ambitious dreams, so surely as he can overcome them by this potent drink. Wine and youth are the two torches that kindle the fires of forbidden pleasure. Wherefore, then, cast oil on the flames, or apply a flaming brand to a young frame that is already on fire?"† In his letter to Leta he warns her to habituate her daughter from her tenderest years to abstain from wine, wherein is lust ‡

105. But if you have not self-command enough to keep to pure water, or if so plain a beverage be unsuited to you, as it was to Timothy, you should apply to yourself the advice which was given

* Unusquisque super mensam sibi indictam aliquid propriâ voluntate cum gaudio Spiritûs Sancti offerat Deo, idest subtrahat corpori suo de cibo, et de potu In Regul, cap 49.

† Si quid itaque in me potest esse consilii, si experto creditur, hoc primum moneo, hoc obtestor, ut sponsa Christi vinum fugiat pro veneno. Hæc adversus adolescentiam prima arma sunt dæmonum. Non sic avaritia quærit, superbia inflat, delectat ambitio. Vinum, et adolescentia duplex incendium voluptatis Quid oleum flammæ adjicimus? quid ardenti corpusculo fomenta ignium ministramus? Epist. 22.

‡ Discat jam vinum non bibere, in quo est luxuria.

him by St. Paul: *Drink a little wine for thy stomach's sake and thy frequent infirmities.*[*] You can do likewise, but mind you take little, as the Apostle prescribes, and that it be duly tempered, so that it may prevent the crudities of the stomach and other bodily ailments. To act otherwise is manifest self-indulgence, which can be accounted for only by a disorderly inclination of gratifying the palate, and of sating the appetite with this pleasing drink, without any concern for how much fuel is heaped on the impure fires of lust.

106. With regard to the fourth kind of gluttony, that is, to the excessive quantity of food taken, each one must keep a tight hand over his palate and his appetite, in order not to exceed. The advice which St. Jerome gives to his disciples on this point is, that they should never eat to repletion, but leave the table with some remnant of appetite[†] He writes to Rusticus, that food taken sparingly and in moderation is profitable both to soul and body.[‡] And in very deed it is from excessive eating that indigestion, catarrhs, dysenteries, fevers, and in general almost all the ailments to which we are liable, take their rise. But far more noteworthy is what he tells the widow Furia; saying, that a spare meal which leaves the stomach somewhat to desire, is preferable to a three-days' fast: as it is better to eat little habitually than to spend whole days without sustenance, and then to make up for the privations of the stomach by an immoderate repast, which has the effect of overloading it, and of clogging the spirit. He illustrates his meaning by the example of the rain, which does far more good when it falls lightly than when it pours in torrents, for, in the former case it refreshes the fields, in the latter it ruins them. And as a means of keeping herself within the bounds of this moderation, he gives her the rule that she should eat so as to be able to apply immediately after to prayer or to the reading of the Holy Scriptures.[§]

* Sed modico vino utere, propter stomachum tuum, et frequentes tuas infirmitates. 1 Tim. v. 23.

† Sit tibi moderatus cibus, et nunquam venter expletus. Epist. 22.

‡ Modicus, et moderatus cibus, carni et animæ utilis est.

§ Parcus cibus, et venter semper esuriens, triduanis jejuniis præferendus: et multo melius est quotidie parum, quam raro satis sumere. Pluvia illa optima

107. Further, it may be shown, by the example of great servants of God, that the virtue of temperance mainly consists in eating thus sparingly and soberly, with a view to support bodily strength, and not to gratify the appetite by overloading the stomach. Palladius relates* that a priest named Isidore, who took his meals every day so sparingly that he had never in all his life risen from table fully satisfied, had acquired great reputation for self-control, though he never practised the extraordinary fasts customary with the other solitaries And Cassian speaks highly of an aged monk, who had been at table no less than six times in one day, for the entertainment of strangers, and had on each occasion taken something to encourage them by his example, yet did this so sparingly and so dexterously, that at the sixth time, he was not yet fully satisfied, but still felt the need of more food.† This is a kind of temperance which every one may make his own, even such persons as through weakness of stomach, or need of food, cannot fast without danger. And further, it is a most excellent way of mortifying the palate and the appetite; for, as the same writer truly says, it is more difficult to control ourselves when food is set before the eyes, than when—as in the case of fasters—it is not near at hand.‡

108. Wherefore, they who wish to attain this degree of abstinence would do well to avail themselves of the practice employed by St. Dorotheus with his disciple St. Dositheus § The latter was of noble birth and delicate constitution, and had been brought up in luxury in his father's house. Dorotheus, wishing to train him to the perfection of temperance, followed this plan:—At the outset he allowed him to eat as much as he liked. Next, he diminished the meal by a small portion, withdrawing, for instance, a single ounce for each pound of food; and then asked him whether he felt hungry. The other would reply that he felt slightly so. Then the able master would leave him till he was accustomed to this reduced quantity. When he found that the novice's stomach had

est, quæ sensim descendit in terram. Subitus, et nimius imber in præceps arva subvertit. Quando comedis, cogita, quod statim tibi orandum, illico et legendum est.

* Hist. Lausiac., cap. 1.

† Instit. lib. v. cap. 25.

‡ Difficile esuriens positâ retinere mensâ.

§ In ejus Vitâ

grown accustomed to the reduction, and that he no longer felt any inconvenience from it, he would diminish the allowance by another ounce, and so brought him at length to live most sparingly without feeling the least incommoded by it. The reader may employ the like stratagem with himself. But it must be borne in mind, that this abstinence is to be observed even with coarse food; since satiety, or the filling of the stomach, is, according to St. Jerome, always to be blamed.*

109. With regard to over-eagerness in eating, one needs to be very careful and circumspect; for (as was observed in the first Chapter) the sin of gluttony consisting mainly in seeking pleasure in food, that person is surely not guiltless of the vice who devours his meat greedily. St. Basil says that the vice of gluttony depends not on the multitude of dishes, otherwise Kings and Emperors, and other great personages of the earth, would be in a miserable condition, because they are forced to have their table loaded with a multitude of choice dishes, and would thus be actually obliged to gluttony. The vice consists, says the Saint, in the relish and gratification which many seek in eating even coarse and cheap food.† Hence St. Augustine affirms, that it may happen that a wise man will partake of a great delicacy without imperfection, while one less wise will not eat even of the coarsest food without sinning by gluttony.‡ "Who would not," continues he, "prefer to eat fish with Christ, to sharing in Esau's coarse lentils?§ Are we to say that beasts of burden are more temperate than ourselves, for they live only on hay, barley, straw, and other most plain food?"||

* Sed et in vilissimis cibis vitanda satietas est. Nihil enim ita obruit animum ut plenus venter, et exæstuans, et huc illucque se vertens, et in ructus vel crepitus, ventorum efflatione respirans. In Jovinian., lib. ij.

† Gulæ vitium, non in escarum copiâ naturæ suæ vim exercere novit; sed in voluptate, atque gustu, licet modicis admodum utare. Serm. de Abdicatione.

‡ Fieri potest, ut sapiens pretiosissimo utatur cibo sine vitio cupidinis, et voracitatis; insipiens autem fœdissima gulæ flamma in vilissimum ardescat. Lib. iij De Doct. Christ., cap. 12.

§ Sanius quisque voluerit more Domini pisce vesci, quam lenticulâ more Esau nepotis Abraham.

|| Non enim propterea continentiores nobis sunt pleræque bestiæ, quia vilioribus utuntur escis.

So that temperance depends no less on the quality of what we eat, than on the end for which we eat, and on the manner and degree of detachment with which we eat.*

110. Wherefore let no one sit down to table without first proposing to himself a holy, or at least a lawful end, in this animal act; protesting to God that he has no other purpose in taking his food than to support life, health, and strength, in order to do Him some service, or to fulfil His most holy will, which, as St. Paul teaches, requires that we sustain this mortal existence by means of food.† If afterwards, in the course of the meal, we find that a feeling of gratification is creeping over us, we must repeat the raising up of our mind to God, renew our intention and protestations, declaring to the Lord our readiness to break off this animal act as soon as the purposes which compel its performance shall have been fulfilled. A saintly old monk, as may be seen in the lives of the Fathers of the Desert,‡ while sitting at table with the other monks, had an interior vision, in which he saw that some of them were eating honey, others bread, and others offal. Astonished at this vision, as he was well aware that the same food had been provided for all, he besought God to enlighten him as to its meaning. The Lord granted his prayer, and told him that they who fed on honey were those who were eating in fear of transgressing against temperance, and hence had their minds uplifted to God, and joined prayer with eating; that those who were eating bread were they who were taking their meal with thankfulness, and were acknowledging their food as God's gift; that the remainder, who were feeding on filth, were those who said to themselves, "How good this is, how bad that;" in a word, those who were eating for the sake of eating. The vision set forth the divers effects of eating on the souls of the monks, according to the end and intention which they proposed to themselves in an action of its own nature so vile and degrading.

* Nam in omnibus hujusmodi rebus, non ex earum rerum naturâ, quibus utimur, sed ex causâ utendi, et modo appetendi, vel probandum est, vel improbandum quod facimus.

† Sive manducatis, sive bibitis, sive quid aliud facitis, omnia in gloriam Dei facite. 1 Cor. x. 31.

‡ Lib. De Provid., cap. 25.

To those who were eating for a holy purpose, their nourishment was as bread and honey; while to the souls of those who were eating for the brutish end of gratifying their palate, it was changed into filth, defiling them with numerous faults. If then, we wish our food to be profitable to the body without prejudice to the soul, let us set before ourselves a right intention, and perform this action without eagerness, and with an inward renouncement of all gratification.

111. Another means of distracting the mind from all sensuality in eating is to listen in time of meals to some devout reading, as is the practice of religious communities; or to engage in some spiritual or learned conversation, as was the custom of St. Augustine at his table:* for then the mind, being intent on devout thoughts, feeds on them, and is not absorbed in the mean function which the outer senses are fulfilling; or, at least, it does not wholly give itself up to the action. Our own personal experience teaches all of us how very true is the observation of Cassian, that we cannot but yield to a grateful feeling whenever food is taken, unless the soul, seeking distraction in good and virtuous objects, find in such a more befitting pleasure.† In connection with this, we read in the Annals of the Friars Minor,‡ that St. Clare, who had long desired and earnestly entreated to have the company at table of her holy Father, Francis, at length obtained her request. The appointed day for this holy repast having come, the two Saints met, and sat down on the bare ground, in a spot where a frugal meal had been prepared At the beginning of the repast St. Francis spoke of God with such depth and fervour that St. Clare, and the friars with her, losing all relish for the food set before them, remained absorbed in great inward spiritual sweetness. Meanwhile God, in order to make known to the world the pleasure that He takes in repasts which are seasoned with devout converse or reading, made the inhabitants of the surrounding

* Possidon In ejus Vitâ.

† Pluribus intentus minor est ad singula sensus: nequaquam enim poterimus escarum præsentium spernere voluptates, nisi mens contemplationi divinæ defixa, amore virtutum potius, et pulchritudine rerum cœlestium delectetur. Inst. Lib. v., cap. 15.

‡ Lib. x., cap. 3.

country behold an immense flame, which settled over the Church of St. Mary of the Angels in the wood where this holy band was seated together at their meal. Every one hastened to the spot to extinguish the fire, but, on arriving, they found that nothing was injured; and when they entered the place, they saw with their own eyes that St. Francis and St. Clare, with all the other Religious, were rapt in ecstasy. From this they understood that the flames which had been noticed, were a symbol of the fire of that divine love which was burning within their breasts. Thus does the nourishment given to the soul during time of meals by holy converse or by devout reading, moderate the pleasure afforded by food to the palate, so that we are enabled to go through an animal action with due detachment.

CHAPTER VI.

PRACTICAL HINTS TO DIRECTORS ON THE SUBJECT OF THE PRESENT ARTICLE.

112. First suggestion. A Director should not be too easy in allowing frequent fasts, much less fasts on bread and water, especially to young people of either sex; as food in moderation is the mainstay of human life. On it depend the formation of our vital spirits, the establishment of our strength, the equilibrium of our health. As a plant deprived for a long time of its aliment withers and dies, so the human body unless it receive the necessary food languishes, and even if it lose not life will, little by little, fail in health and strength. I do not imply that fasting should not be allowed, especially when there is a divine call to a particular austerity of life. I only say, that while it behoves us not to be close-handed, it were better to be more liberal in regard to the bodily inflictions treated of in the foregoing Article, at least when experience shows them to be free from danger.

113. What a Director must strive, by all means, to obtain from his penitents is, that while taking their necessary sustenance,

they mortify themselves in many of those things which are agreeable to the palate, but which are not needed for the preservation of health; that they be sparing in their diet; that this sparingness be with them a settled habit: for, as St. Jerome says, "Far more preferable is continual sobriety than frequent fasting alternating with heavy meals"* Again, that they take their food with an upright intention, and with inward disengagement; and especially that they never complain when the dishes are not agreeable, or are unpalatable and badly seasoned; and also never praise them, nor show their appreciation of them, when well and daintily prepared, but eat simply, and without comment, of what is set before them; for in good truth nothing is so sure a token of a mind disengaged from sensual indulgence, as this indifference in partaking of food, whether it be good or bad. We read of St. Thomas Aquinas that he never asked for any dish in particular, but was content with what fell to his lot, and partook of it with great moderation.† Father Maffei relates of St. Ignatius Loyola, that he never refused any dish, however disagreeable to his taste; that he never complained of the food being insufficiently or badly cooked or prepared, nor of the wine being bad and sour; and that he never would permit himself any exemption in his meals. It once happened that the Father Minister set before him a bunch of grapes as an extra dish; but so little was he pleased with it, that, as a reward for the delicacy, he gave the Minister a severe penance.‡ The Director will strive to train his penitents to the like sobriety, and if he succeed, he may be persuaded that it will suffice to keep in check the sense of taste and the passion of gluttony. But he will have to labour much and long, as it is easier

* Multo melius est quotidie parum, quam raro satis sumere.

† Fuit magnæ honestatis, et magnæ sobrietatis, numquam petens speciales cibos; sed contentus erat iis quæ apponebantur sibi, et illis temperate, et sobrie utebatur. In cibo et potu fuit tantæ sobrietatis, quod singularitates ciborum non petebat. Apud Bolland., tom. 1, Die 7 Martii, cap. 5, n. 42.

‡ Nullum edulii, vel condimenti genus cuiquam indixit: nihil unquam inter edendum est questus, licet per adjutorum inscitiam incuriamque, cibaria male cocta, conditaque, vinum etiam fugiens, aciduumque præberetur: nihil denique sibi proprie apponi voluit unquam; et graviter administrum aliquando puniit, quod uvæ racemum uni sibi apponi voluit. In Vitâ, Lib. iij, cap. 12.

to get people to fast often, than to practise temperance perseveringly and in perfection.

114. Second suggestion. The Director will be still more careful in allowing fasts to those who take their meals at a public table, as is done by Religious of either sex; since these extraordinary penances are an occasion of vanity on the part of such as perform them, and are exposed to the gainsaying and remarks of those who may witness them. St. Bernardine, speaking of such as practise extraordinary abstinence, says, that they who live in community frequently take more pride in a fast which they perform alone, than in seven which they keep with their brethren.* Cassian teaches, that whatever in a community is not consonant with common usage, is to be shunned as an occasion of vanity and self-boasting.† This fits in well with what St. Philip Neri used to say, namely, that when at table in company with others, we ought to eat of everything; words which must of course be taken in the sense that was intended. And he was most earnest in exhorting all to avoid the slightest singularity, as being the source of pride of spirit and of all kinds of pride, and the fuel which feeds their fire.‡ If the person who wishes to do penance by lessening the quantity of his food, be truly moved by the Spirit of God, he will find means of denying his appetite without attracting the attention of those who are at the same table with him; for the Holy Spirit renders us both cautious to conceal our virtuous actions, and expert in discovering means to conceal them. This was the conduct of St. John Climacus, of whom his biographer, the monk Daniel, tells us, that at table he partook of whatever was set before him, but so sparingly, that he seemed rather to taste than to eat of the various dishes. He thus effectually mortified his taste and appetite without running the risk of any temptation to vanity.§

* Plus sibi blanditur de uno jejunio quod ceteris prandentibus facit, quam si cum ceteris septem dies jejunaverit. De Grad. Hum.—Grad. 5.

† Quidquid in conversatione fratrum minime communis usus recipit, vel exercet, omni studio, ut jactantiæ deditum, declinemus. Instit., lib. xj., cap. 18.

‡ In Vitâ, lib. ij., cap. 14, num. 6: et cap. 17, num. 26.

§ In mensâ nihil rejiciebat, quod a religiosæ vitæ instituto, legibusque non

115. But let us hearken to the Angelic Doctor, who, discussing this very point in his usual accurate style, settles it with his customary depth and solidity. He says that there are two courses of life which we may lead—the one private, in the exercise of rigid abstinence; the other, in community, adapting itself to common usage. Both, in his view, are praiseworthy, as our most loving Redeemer has set us the example of both; at one time retiring to the wilderness and observing an unbroken fast, at others sitting at table with His disciples, and taking, even in company of strangers, the same food as the rest.* The Director, then, must induce such as live in community to be exact in observing temperance; to deny themselves in the use of food; yet so as not to attract the notice of those at table. This, however, does not imply that he must never allow a rigorous fast, especially at holy seasons, or on the vigil of some Patron Saint. But before allowing this, the Director will take notice whether the penitent be one of those who would gain nothing from the mortification of the body beyond the spiritual detriment of vain self-complacency; for in such case the damage would be greater than the gain.

116. Third suggestion. The Director will bear in mind that certain ill-instructed persons make all their perfection consist in fasting and the mortification of the appetite; and though these are easily moved to anger, are impatient, vain, haughty, and uncharitable, they think that they have nothing more to do. People of this description must be warned, for they are wofully in the dark as to the due regulation of their spiritual life. What is more, it may easily happen that it is the devil who inwardly instigates them to fast, in order to keep up so pernicious a delusion. Such must be told, as St. Jerome wrote to Demetrias, that "fasting is not the

abhorrebat; sed cibum ita modice sobrieque sumpsit, ut gustare potius, quam edere videretur. Atque ita, fracto cornu superbiæ, per sobrietatem quidem, sed parcitate prandii et cœnæ, dominam voluptatem multis exitiosam elisit. In Biblioth. Patrum, tom. x.

* Utraque enim vita est licita, et laudabilis, ut scilicet aliquis a consortio hominum segregatus abstinentiam servet, et ut societate aliorum positus communi vitâ utatur: et ideo Dominus voluit utriusque vitæ exemplum dare hominibus. 3 p. q. 40, art. 2, ad primum.

all in all of Christian perfection, but only its foundation, and a ladder by which it may be reached, a disposition to acquire it. It is not the substance of perfection, but only a help to attain it. Hence," as the holy Doctor continues, "if one were never to cease from fasting, even though he were a pure and spotless virgin, he would not on that account have won the bright crown of perfection."*

117. In a letter to Celantia the same Saint writes: "It avails little to reduce the body by fasting, and to puff up the soul with pride; to make the cheeks wan with privation, but the heart livid with envy; to fast from bodily food, but not to fast from the vices of the soul; to forswear wine, and yet to become intoxicated, as it were, with anger, hatred and ill-will. Such abstinence is mere foolery. Abstinence worthy of the name is that which is directed to the uprooting of vicious passions and to the acquirement of solid virtues. Those may be truly said to abstain who afflict the flesh by fasting in order to humble the spirit, so that it may despise self in all things and be subject to the divine will.† The director will let these views sink deeply within him, and thus dispel the delusion of those who mistake fasting for the end instead of the means of perfection; who, while fasting, trouble the quiet of their homes; who cannot put up with an injury, are keen after gain, unrestrained in their speech, full of vanity, proud and haughty in their behaviour; and, as if they had done everything by mortifying their palate, take little or no heed to amend their lives.

* Jejunium non perfecta virtus, sed ceterarum virtutum fundamentum est, ut satisfactio, atque pudicitia, sine quâ nemo videbit Deum Gradum præbet ad summa scandentibus, nec tamen, si sola fuerit, virginem poterit coronare.

† Quidquid supra justitiam offertur Deo, non debet impedire justitiam, sed adjuvare. Quid enim tenuatur abstinentiâ corpus, si animus intumescat superbiâ? quam laudem merebimur de pallore jejunii, si invidiâ lividi sumus! Quid virtutis habet vinum non bibere, et irâ, et odio inebriari? Tunc, inquam, præclara est abstinentia, tunc pulchra atque magnifica castigatio corporis, cum esset animus jejunus a vitiis. Immo qui probabiliter, et scienter virtutem abstinentiæ tenent, eo affligunt carnem suam, quo animæ frangant superbiam; ut quasi de quodam fastigio contemptûs sui, atque arrogantiæ, descendant ad implendam Dei voluntatem, quæ maxime humilitate perficitur. Idcirco a variis ciborum desideriis mentem retrahunt, ut totam ejus vim occupent in cupiditate virtutum.

ARTICLE III.

The obstacles to Christian perfection which arise from not guarding the sense of sight.

CHAPTER I.

THE FIRST REASON WHY THE IRREGULARITIES OF THE EYES MAY PROVE A HINDRANCE, NOT ONLY TO PERFECTION, BUT TO SALVATION. HOW CAREFULLY THEY SHOULD BE KEPT IN CHECK.

118. ONE of the noblest of the senses with which our Creator has endowed the human body is doubtless the sense of sight, on account of its lively and far-reaching character, and the readiness with which it performs the actions proper to it; but this sense is the more to be esteemed, because, more than the others, it furnishes the mind with those phantasms out of which are formed the ideas whereon its judgments are grounded, its reasonings are framed, and by which all its rational acts are performed. But on this very account is this same sense a greater source of danger when not guarded; for then it supplies the soul with images prejudicial, not only to its perfection, but also to its salvation.

119. To make this most important truth intelligible, we must lay down, according to the teaching of philosophers, that every one of our passions is in strict dependence on the imagination, which they all of them serve, and to which they are wholly subject, so that they cannot act but by the impulse of the fancies which are conceived in the imagination. Thus, for instance, the imagination presents to the appetite the image of some delectable object, the sensitive appetite is at once excited, and the passion of love awakened; if, on the other hand, a hateful image be presented, the appetite is at once inflamed with hatred and horror. Whenever an object is presented as suited to our nature, the appetite is

at once stimulated to desire its possession. The same holds good of all the other sensible emotions of the soul which go by the name of passions. On the other hand, it is certain that the greater part of the images in our mind depend for their formation on the eyes, which transmit to the imagination the elements whereof it forms its images. According to that trite old adage, "Nothing is in the mind but what has first passed through the senses"—a saying applied to the eyes and the other senses alike. We may hence infer that the unruly motions of the passions, which give the soul so much trouble, take their rise in the careless use of the sense of sight, which sends on to the imagination the images of the objects whereby the disorderly motions of the passion are stirred up. Thus, if there are excited in man the passions of sensual love, of unlawful desire, of impure affection, the blame lies at the door of the sight; for, when this is not kept in due check, objects are represented to the imagination by means of the visual species, as pleasing, lovable, and worthy to be possessed, while they are in reality to be shunned and abhorred.

120. It was in the conviction of this great truth that holy Job made a covenant with his eyes not to fix them on the countenance of a woman, knowing full well that heedless looks are followed by dangerous images, which excite unclean emotions; these in their turn solicit the free consent of the will, and this consent entails sin, the ruin and perdition of the soul. The holy man says that he had *made a covenant with his eyes never to think of a virgin.** It would seem that he ought to have said, *not to look at a virgin*, because looking, not thought, is the natural function of the eye But he was quite correct in this expression, as to look at and to think on an object are so inseparably connected, that they appear to be one and the same act. Hence, having settled with himself not to think on dangerous objects, such as young women undoubtedly are, he resolved not to look at them, considering one the same thing as the other. The Holy Ghost says, with still greater emphasis, *Turn away thy face from a woman dressed up, and gaze not about upon another's beauty, for many have*

* Pepigi fœdus cum oculis meis, ut ne cogitarem quidem de virgine. Job xxx. 1.

*perished by the beauty of a woman.** But, wherefore, may it be said, should we fear such dreadful consequences from a simple look? For this reason: the look is inseparably connected with the unclean images which excite lust, and kindle the fires of impurity.† Close, then, thine eyes, or guard them with care, if thou desire not to fall into the like perdition, if thou wilt not have to shed bitter tears, and to say with the Prophet Jeremiah, "*Mine eyes have pillaged my soul,* by the thoughts, the affections, the unclean passions they have stirred up within me."‡

121. So true is the view here taken, that profane poets, in their empty songs, commonly attribute to the eyes the origin of their amorous transports, so that one of them might truly say, "Know well, if thou knowest it not already, that the eyes are the guides of love, introducing it into the soul by means of their glances."§ But this sentiment is still more pithily expressed by the author of Ecclesiasticus, in these two brief words, *I saw, and I perished.* Scarce had I glanced at the forbidden object but I was undone. The same truth was also well expressed by a sculptor in a line which he engraved at the foot of his statue. It was a sleeping Venus, and these were the words: "Passer-by, take care not to awaken the goddess; for if she open her eyes, she will cause thine to close."‖ As much as to say, that by unwary glances of the bodily eye at dangerous objects, we close the eyes of the understanding, which is blinded by the emotions of sensual passion.

122. But wherefore seek authorities among profane authors? Are there not in Holy Writ notable examples of persons famed even for great virtue, who, through a single glance, have been consumed by the fire of impure love? How came David, that man according to God's own heart, the chosen ancestor and Prophet of the

* Averte faciem tuam a muliere comptâ, et ne circumspicias speciem alienam. Propter speciem mulieris multi perierunt: et ex hoc concupiscentia quasi ignis exardescit Ecclus. ix. 8, 9.

† Ex hoc concupiscentia quasi ignis exardescit.

‡ Oculus meus deprædatus est animam meam. Thren. iij. 51.

§ Si nescis, oculi sunt in amore duces.

‖ Cave, viator, excites a somno deam. Sua adaperiens, tua namque claudet lumina.

Messiah that was to come, who in his lofty contemplations was so highly honoured by the familiar intercourse of God,—how came he to fall into adultery, save by a heedless glance which he cast at Bersabee from the roof of his palace?* What made the two elders, in a ripe old age, with gray hair and mature mind, judges too of the people, tempt the virtue of the chaste Susanna? What, but their looking at her walking in her garden? They gazed at her, and returned to gaze, and thereby kindled in their chilled hearts the flames of impure desire.† Every one knows with what unbridled passion the wife of Putiphar solicited the chaste Joseph, and what violence she made use of to overcome his constancy. But whence this violence in a woman, who by nature is timid and modest? She cast her eyes upon him, as the inspired text tells us, and by this look was quickly undone.‡ What robbed Dinah, the modest daughter of Jacob, of her virginity and her honour? What, but the lust of looking curiously about her?§ But what were the results of this license in gazing upon all that was going on? Listen to what the Spirit of God tells us. The prince of the land carried her off and ravished her.‖ What enslaved Holofernes, that formidable foe to the people of Israel, and made him the prey of a feeble woman? The Sacred Volume says that the toils, the chains which bound his heart, and which laid him, conqueror as he was, at the feet of her who had led his heart captive, were her sandals, which ravished his eyes, and her beauty, which made him a slave.¶

123. But there is no end to the evils caused by freedom of the eyes. We might as well pretend to number the stars of heaven,

* Vidit mulierem se lavantem ex adverso supra solarium suum. . . . Missis itaque nuntiis tulit eam. II. Reg. xj. 2. 4.

† Et videbant eam senes quotidie ingredientem, et deambulantem; et exarserunt in concupiscentiam ejus. Daniel xiij. 8.

‡ Injecit domina oculos suos in Joseph, et ait: dormi mecum. Gen. xxxix. 7.

§ Egressa est autem Dina filia Liæ, ut videret mulieres regionis illius. Genes. xxxiv. 1.

‖ Princeps terræ illius adamavit eam; et rapuit, et dormivit cum illâ, vi opprimens virginem.

¶ Sandalia ejus rapuerunt oculos ejus: pulchritudo ejus captivam fecit animam ejus. Judith xvj. 11.

or the grains of sand on the sea-shore. Suffice it to say, that the wholesale destruction of the world at the Flood took its rise from license in the use of sight, as Holy Writ witnesses. The proximate and immediate cause of this universal ruin was indeed sin of the flesh,* or, as the Gloss has it, man was too much given to carnal sins. But the origin of this corruption, as plainly stated in the inspired writings, was the too great liberty men allowed their eyes in looking at women.† Then it was that God thundered forth the dreadful sentence. By looking they had become carnal, and because they were carnal they were hateful to Him, and were punished by that mighty flood that swept them all away.‡ Let him, then, who makes profession of a devout life shut down his eyes, let him bolt the windows by which death makes its way into the soul; nor let him rely upon his virtue, or upon his former experience: for, as St. Gregory says, "He who through these windows of the body, recklessly looks abroad, very often falls, even against his will, into the sweetnesses of sin, and being fast fettered by desires, begins to will what before he had never willed."§

124. Granting, however, that it might happen to some one individual not to fall into grievous sin by allowing his eyes this unbecoming freedom, certain it is that, in the words of St. Gregory, unholy thoughts and unchaste emotions must, whether he will it or not, enter the mind after such looks. And even though they be rejected, they usually leave after them some stain on the conscience, or at least overcloud the serenity of the mind, and disturb the peace of heart so essential to the practice of virtue and holy prayer. * Hence, if we would keep our minds free from these wanton thoughts, which, if not morally sinful, are ever full of deep

* Non permanebit spiritus meus in homine, quia caro est. Genes. vj. 3.

† Videntes filii Dei filias hominum, quod essent pulchræ, acceperunt sibi uxores ex omnibus, quas elegerant.

‡ Dixitque Deus. non permanebit spiritus meus in homine in æternum, quia caro est.

§ Deprimendi sunt oculi, quasi raptores ad culpam. . . . Quisquis enim per has corporis fenestras incaute exterius respicit, plerumque in delectationem peccati etiam nolens cadit; atque obligatus desideriis, incipit velle quod noluit. Moral., lib xxj, cap. 2.

peril, we must, concludes St. Gregory, keep a strict watch over this excitable sense, in the conviction that it is not lawful to look at what we may not desire.*

125. And here it will not be out of place to relate a circumstance mentioned by St. Augustine in the Sixth Book of his Confessions concerning his friend Alypius, for it throws a peculiar light upon the influence exercised by the eyes over the affections of the heart, nor over such only as are mild and gentle—of which we have so far been speaking—but even over the fiercer passions; all which is well suited to our present purpose. Alypius, a bosom friend of St. Augustine, happened to be staying in Rome at the time of the gladiatorial games, to which bloody spectacle the people flocked in crowds. He was invited by some friends to go there with them, but abhorring those cruel diversions, which borrowed their attractions from wounds and bloodshed, he refused the invitation. Being however dragged thither, as it were, by his acquaintances, he yielded to their violence, but with a full determination to be present at the show in body only and to be absent in mind, and not to cast even so much as a single glance at the inhuman scene. He went, and taking his seat with the others in the public amphitheatre, he closed his eyes, and diverted his attention to objects more worthy of an intellectual being. On a sudden, at a dexterous home-thrust given by one of the gladiators to his adversary, the theatre echoed with shouts of applause and acclamations. At this sound, Alypius could not refrain from opening his eyes and looking. At this glance he was, as St. Augustine says, wounded in spirit far more fatally than the gladiator was wounded in body, and fell more miserably than the man who was stricken to the ground.† On opening his eyes, he began to look with interest at the fierce struggle of the gladiators, to delight in their cruel conflicts, and to become, as it were, intoxicated with this bloodthirsty pastime. Further, this barbarous taste got such

* Ne ergo quædam lubrica in cogitatione versemus, providendum nobis est: quia intueri non licet, quod non licet concupiscere. Ibid.

† Aperuit oculos, et percussus est graviori vulnere in animâ, quam ille in corpore, quem cernere concupivit: ceciditque miserabilius, quam ille, quo cadente factus est clamor. Conf., lib. vi, cap. 8.

hold of him that he began to shout and applaud, mingling his voice with the cries of the people.* Things came to such a pass, says the Saint, that, far from needing that any one should invite him to go, or show him the way, in order to return to such scenes, he not only went thither by himself, but induced others to go with him. So much had this inhuman and barbarous diversion won the mastery over his heart at one single look. Now, if a sudden glance could have power enough to change a well-regulated and cultured mind like that of Alypius, and to transform its tendencies into inclinations so cruel and foreign to our nature, as to take delight in the wounds and death of a fellow-creature; what will not be the power of an unguarded look when its object is a person of another sex, agreeable to the eye, of graceful and charming manners, fitted in all respects to excite in the heart an agreeable emotion, which it will greedily drink in, and which will prove at length a mortal draught of deadly poison?

126. Our eyes must then be duly and modestly guarded, as, failing this, not only can there be no spirituality, but not even every-day virtue. "Would we remain with our souls uplifted to heaven, let us," says St. Augustine, "keep our eyes fixed upon the earth."† We have already remarked, in speaking of our other senses, that the eyes are the soul's windows. St. Augustine goes further, and says that they are the door of the soul. People, save with rare exceptions, enter a house by the door; few by the windows, as the former is by far the easier mode of ingress. And, moreover, to enter into a house by the door, it suffices that it be open, not so with the windows. So that, according to St. Augustine, if the other senses are the windows whereby sin enters, and the eyes are the door, these have but to be left open for sin to make its way into our souls.‡

* Sed fixit aspectum, et hauriebat furias, et nesciebat: et delectabatur scelere certaminis, et cruentâ voluptate inebriabatur. . . . Spectavit, clamavit, exarsit; abstulit inde secum insaniam. Ibid.

† Summe custodiendus est oculus, quia janua cordis est. Serm. 31. Ad Fratres in Eremo.

‡ Summe custodiendus est oculus, quia janua cordis est.

CHAPTER II.

FURTHER REASONS TO SHOW THE SERIOUS HARM WHICH MAY ARISE FROM WANT OF STRICTNESS IN CUSTODY OF THE EYES.

127. ALTHOUGH it would seem that the close connection which has been shown to exist between the sense of sight and the interior passions, would be sufficient to engage all Christians (not to speak of devout persons) to guard their eyes rigidly, and to deny them full liberty of roving hither and thither; yet, as we are now treating of so dangerous a sense, it will perhaps be well to ponder other motives which may quite convince us of the great necessity there is of holding our eyes in check. One great motive, to my mind, for always keeping the sense of sight in check, is the great natural freedom of the eyes: that is to say, the ease with which they take in objects, even though these be dangerous: to such an extent, indeed, that their quickness of perception constantly anticipates our reason. It is not thus with the two other senses of which we have spoken. These are more under the command of the will, without whose orders they cannot stir. Certain it is that unless my will consent, my hand will not get so far as to touch food, nor can my palate taste it without the consent of this same will. But not so the eyes, which forestall the command of the will and freely turn to gaze at objects which it would not wish them to look at; and so boldly kindle a fire in the house by which, in the end, it may be reduced to ashes.

128. Now if the will give the eyes a little liberty, they will certainly escape from all control, and will force it, in its own despite, to take pleasure in the objects wherein they find gratification. St. John Chrysostom likens our eyes to those spirited horses which cannot be reined in without much difficulty; and if the driver once slackens his hold of them, they dash along so impetuously as to cast themselves, with the chariot and all within it, down some precipice. Thus the eyes, being so full of activity in the glances they cast about them, are with difficulty controlled by reason. But if one cease to keep a tight rein over them, or allow them a little freedom, they get the upper hand of the will,

and by the agreeable images which they present, they lead us to our ruin.*

129. As may often be seen when some one is mounted on an obedient, tractable horse, the rider slackens the reins, and pursues his course without thought or care. It is only when he comes to some difficult or dangerous pass that he tightens the rein and goes cautiously, taking notice of every step and motion of the animal. But should he have to ride on a spirited, impetuous, hard-mouthed charger, he keeps a tight hand upon the rein, is ever on the watch, and goes carefully, even on a broad and level road, as his beast may at any moment play him a trick, obtain the mastery, throw him off, and leave him to die amid rocks and precipices. In like manner, with the other senses it is enough for us to be on our guard only on certain occasions; for instance, with the sense of taste we have to look to ourselves only at meal times; with that of touch when we meet with perilous occasions. But with the sense of sight—which, as St. John Chrysostom says, is like a fiery horse, shakes off the yoke of reason, and at all times is busied with rash and inconsiderate glances—we have ever to be on our guard, keeping our eyes downcast, both in our walks abroad, and in houses, when obliged to converse with persons of the opposite sex, though their character be above all suspicion. For the sight is an unruly sense, which may, in one instant, betray us to our undoing. St. Eusebius of Emesa is of the same mind as St. John Chrysostom, when he says, the greater the rapidity with which the eye can turn from one object to another, the more careful should we be in guarding the sight; keeping our eyes, by a modest and almost habitual caution, cast downwards to the ground.†

130. The reader may now understand the great care taken by the saints to keep their eyes from fixing on persons, especially those of the other sex; a caution which may, in some cases, appear to have been excessive. It is told of St. Clare that she had

* Oculi est videre, male autem videre a mente est. . . . . Postquam autem hæc negligens esse et habenas laxare cœperit; quemadmodum auriga, nesciens indomitorum equorum ferociam compescere, et equos currum trahentes et semetipsum in præceps ire facit: sic et voluntas nostra. Hom. 22 in Genes.

† Quam facile potest in puncto temporis vagari velocitas oculi, tam solicite præcavenda est irruentis noxa delicti. Homil. 4.

never seen the countenance of a man, until she once, on raising her eyes to the Sacred Host in the Priest's hands, chanced to see his face; and she bitterly deplored the involuntary fault of this casual look. Of St. Francis we read, that obliged as he was by his duties to deal constantly with women, he knew not one of them by sight, but only by the tone of their voice. Of St. Peter of Alcantara we read, that though he had walked for full three years in the streets of the city with the Religious his companions, he had never beheld the face of any woman, nor even as much as looked at the roof of the church where he so frequently prayed; so confirmed a habit had he contracted of keeping his eyes downcast. Of the Bishop St. Hugh it is said, that though compelled by his pastoral charge to deal with women, he had never for forty years looked one in the face. And of St. Aloysius we are informed that he never fixed his eyes on the countenance of any woman, not even of his own mother. These great saints knew full well how quick and how pleasure-seeking is the sense of sight, and how dangerous its liberty may prove to the soul, and hence they never trusted it on any occasion, nor in presence of any object, but ever held it in check like a hard-mouthed horse.

131. In connection with this point we read of the holy Abbot Arsenius, that when a noble lady went to call upon him, no sooner had she made her appearance than, without saying a word, he turned his back upon her. On being treated with such apparent incivility, the lady said, "Do not take it ill that I have come to see you, for I am here simply for the purpose of recommending myself to your prayers. Pardon me then, and pray to God for me." "Yes," replied the servant of God; "I will beg the Lord to blot the remembrance of you out of my mind." It is related of another monk, called Pionius, that having been commanded by St. Antony to visit his widowed sister, who for thirty years had longed to see him, he obeyed to the letter; went quickly, and on reaching her abode, without setting foot within, stood on the threshold, and there addressed her a few words, but always, as long as he was in her presence, keeping his eyes shut. This manner of behaviour will, I am

aware, appear rude, unseemly and uncivil. But the fear which the servants of God felt of being entrapped by this excitable sense, and their dread of being vanquished by it on occasion of some sudden surprise, induced them to act thus. Much more ought we to fear, since our virtue is not so tried as theirs, nor do we receive such powerful helps of divine grace. Far more than they, should we guard our eyes with a modesty, which, if not as rigid, is at least circumspect, exact and reasonable; not allowing the sight to wander upon every object, and not fixing our gaze upon the face of one of the opposite sex, when we meet, or are forced to converse, with such.

132. A further reason for keeping a strict guard over our eyes, and not allowing them to fix themselves on pleasing objects, is, that by this means we may obtain of God a special aid either to be free from thoughts and temptations contrary to holy purity, or, if not so privileged, that we may be enabled to resist them readily, so that, instead of being to us a snare and occasion of falling, they may contribute to our merit and our crown. Certain distressing temptations which disturb the peace of God's servants are, at times, allowed by the Almighty in punishment of some indiscreet glances. The Abbot Pastor, in punishment of having curiously looked at a girl as she was gleaning, was for forty years troubled with violent sensual temptations. And the famous temptation which forced St. Benedict to roll himself naked in the thorns, was, as we learn from St. Gregory, occasioned by his having once incautiously glanced at a woman.* God has also permitted persons at times to fall into grievous sin, in chastisement of some heedless look, as befell David and others, whose sad examples are chronicled in ecclesiastical history.

133. So that if a person will but proceed with due modesty and caution in the use of his eyes, God will surely impart to him some special help; for it is a never-failing maxim, that when a man does what he can on his side to guard himself, God will not withhold His singular protection, with the aid of which all may live free from every sin.† Roger, who, by his stainless purity, was

* Dial., lib. ij., cap. 20.

† Facienti quantum in se est, Deus non denegat gratiam.

worthy to be a son of St. Francis, was so careful in guarding his eyes that he never looked a woman in the face, even though, on account of the closeness of relationship with him, she were above suspicion, and there might well have seemed to be neither danger nor ground of suspicion. Being asked one day by his ghostly father the reason why, endowed as he was with the gift of a singular purity, he was so careful not to look at women, and avoided meeting them, he replied, "When a man does what in him lies and guards against danger, God will do His part and help and defend us from all dangerous temptations. But if we allow our eyes full freedom, and conversing with every one expose ourselves to temptation, we are justly forsaken of God; and being left with no other stay than our own frailty, must needs fall into the pit of some grievous crime."* Words well worthy of being written in letters of gold. We must then keep custody of our eyes, and behave with great modesty in our looks, if we wish God to preserve our heart and mind free from defilement.

134. But apart from chastity to which, as we have seen, modesty of the eyes is so necessary, how is it possible, may I ask, that a person can be truly spiritual who allows an excessive liberty to the sense of sight, when the custody of the heart, so important for a devout life, depends upon that of the eyes? Show me one who goes about casting his eyes on every object that may come before him, and I will show you one who will never have any recollection in prayer; for while he is engaged in this exercise, the images of the worldly trifles at which he has been looking throughout the day will pass through his mind, and though his body be in God's presence, his soul will be constantly wandering hither and thither. But supposing that God, despite of the demerits of such a one, favour him with some feeling of devotion, this can have no permanent abode in his heart; for, relapsing after prayer into his former habit of unrestrained use of the eyes,

* Pater, quando homo facit quod in se est, et occasiones peccandi fugit; tunc vicissim Deus facit quod in se est, et hominem tuetur, et custodit. At quando homo se temere conjicit in discrimen, tunc etiam juste a Deo deseritur: et ita fit, quod facile ob naturæ corruptionem in peccatum aliquod grave dilabatur. Lib. I. Conformit. S. Franc.

the affections will at once escape through these outlets. Because the Spirit of the Lord resembles, in this, certain essences which soon evaporate unless kept in a close vessel; and thus the unhappy person is left as before, and perhaps a prey to still greater dissipation. But one who lives thus in continual distractions cannot be expected to pay serious attention during the day to the practice of mortification, charity, humility, patience and other Christian virtues, devoid as he is of thoughts and affections calculated to incite him to their practice; and consequently he will neither lead a religious life, if in the cloister, nor live devoutly, if in the world.

135. And this is why St. Laurence Justinian not only kept his eyes shut against the dangerous objects he might meet with in the city, but, even when he might blamelessly have used his eyes, abstained from contemplating the beauty of the country, and the foliage of the trees which grew in his private garden. This is why, in a monastery of Scythia, a holy nun called Sara, having dwelt for forty years close to the waters of a limpid fountain, had never cast one single look at it. This is why the ancient solitaries, while working in each other's company, never raised their eyes to look each other in the face. They bore in mind how much the custody of the heart depends upon the custody of the eyes; denying to their sight every solace, in order that their hearts might find their comfort and repose in God. Hence, the above-mentioned St. Laurence Justinian often remarked, that the heart of a wise man loses its strength by the disorderly looks of the eyes; for unchecked freedom of the sight fills the soul with the images of earthly objects, and of such things as lust hankers after. These, by their importunity, dissipate godly thoughts, and weaken spiritual strength, so that the soul is made incapable of virtuous action.* This doctrine is exactly the same as that which we laid down above. He, then, who would cultivate inward recollection, must

* Ex inordinato oculorum aspectu imprudentis transfigitur cor. Transmittunt utique effrenati intuitus ad animam corporearum rerum formas, atque concupiscibilium qualitates imaginum, suâque importunitate internam dividunt virtutem, sanctos dissipant cogitatus, animi vigorem debilitant. De Vitâ Felici, cap. 7.

strive to acquire a great modesty in his looks, and to keep his eyes closed against the vain sights of earth, if he would have the eye of the mind constantly open to things of heaven.

CHAPTER III.

TO ACQUIRE THE VIRTUE OF MODESTY, NOT ONLY CUSTODY OF THE EYES IS REQUISITE, BUT ALSO OUTWARD COMPOSURE OF THE WHOLE PERSON.

136. I AM far from denying that the due regulation of the eyes and the sight is a main part of the virtue of modesty, as well as the most important and the most arduous to secure. Arduous, on account of our natural inclination to allow our eyes to wander upon every object that may present itself: necessary, on account of the hindrances which, as was shown above, the unrestricted liberty of the eyes places in the way of Christian perfection. I only affirm that the virtue of modesty consists not in this alone, but in the orderly bearing of the whole outer man. And if we want to speak with rigorous accuracy, even this does not constitute the virtue of modesty, but it is the effect and act of the virtue. Because, as St. Thomas has it, modesty resides in the soul as in its proper subject, but is made manifest in the outward motions of the body. In fact, modesty is a habit regulating certain minor passions of the soul, which move men to outer actions of an immoderate and ill-balanced nature;* and in this modesty differs from temperance, which is concerned with those passions of the sensitive appetite which are of a more violent nature. And as modesty regulates the minor passions which incline us to the neglect of outward composure, it gives rules in detail for the eyes, concerning the use of sight; for the tongue, concerning the manner of speaking and laughing; and for the whole exterior man, laying down the law of the movement of every limb, and the proper use of the dress which we have to wear.

137. St. Gregory is of the same mind with St. Thomas, where he

* Quæ in rebus mediocribus, ac minimis modum ponit. 2, 2, q. 160, art. 1.

says, that the virtue which regulates our exterior resides in the interior.* And he further adds, that every one who behaves outwardly with disorder and levity, gives clear proof that this virtue, the guide of his affections, has no root within his soul.† St. Basil agrees with the two last-named writers, as he is of opinion that to burst out into loud laughter, to shake the whole frame with merriment, and the like breaches of good manners, are the marks of an ill-regulated soul, which is not master of itself and of its motions.‡ The virtue of modesty being thus, according to these holy Doctors, implanted in the mind, while the outer bearing is nothing but its manifestation, we may say that it is a habit which moderates certain of our minor passions and inward affections, so as to prevent us from breaking out into ill-regulated actions of our members or our senses.

138. But if the virtue of modesty spring from the interior of the soul as from its source, and diffuse itself through the senses and members of the body, as through so many channels, in order to give decorum to our whole outward bearing, the reader may easily infer its necessity for every devout person, especially a Religious, for the maintaining a decent comportment, and affording due edification to our neighbours. For being unable to see the order and composure which may be lying hid within our souls, they may fairly claim to judge us by the motions and postures of our bodies. If, in your walks through the streets, you chance to see smoke coming out of the roof of a house, and rolling upwards in dense masses, you will surely say that a fire is burning within that house. So, too, if one sees that you are careless in looking about you, not well-regulated in your language and conversation, laughter, gestures, gait and manner of dress, they may gather with full certainty that your mind is not under proper control; for these outward tokens are plain indications of the disorder which reigns within.

* Intus est custodia, quæ composita servat exterius membra.

† Qui ergo statum mentis perdidit, subsequenter foras in inconstantiâ motionis fluit; atque exteriori mobilitate indicat, quod nullâ interius radice subsistat. Pastoral., Part. iij., Admonit. 24.

‡ In immanes cachinnos prorumpere, et corpore contra animi voluntatem subsultare, nequaquam est ejus, qui animo composito sit, aut plane probo, et compote sui ipsius. In Regul. Fusius Disput., q 17.

139. In proof of this, I will allege a most unimpeachable authority, and relate two events which are vouched for by St. Ambrose, as having occurred to himself. He tells us that he had conceived a very unfavourable opinion of two persons: one of whom he would never admit to the clerical state; the other he found already promoted to holy orders, but being unable to bear the sight of him, he gave orders that the man should keep behind him, never going in front in the course of the sacred functions, or at other times when necessarily in attendance on the Bishop. He owns plainly that the sole reason he had for this unfavourable opinion was the disorderly bearing he perceived in each. Nor was he deceived: for both, in the end, apostatised from Holy Church: one fell into the Arian heresy; the other brought disgrace upon his vocation by renouncing the priesthood in order to escape the jurisdiction of the ecclesiastical court.*

140. We may compare this with the presentiment of St. Gregory of Nazianzus concerning the future course of Julian the Apostate. His judgment was founded on the disorder and want of modesty which the young prince showed in his outward deportment; except that, in the event, the prognostic of the Saint proved too little disastrous, since the expectation was more than verified when Julian became an unbelieving idolater and a ruthless persecutor of the Church. The holy Doctor says, that when they were dwelling together as young students at Athens, he augured that, from the mere sight of the levity of Julian's behaviour, he would certainly turn out a master of wickedness in the course of years. "Of evil omen to me," says the Saint, "were the tossings of his head, the shrugging up of his shoulders, the rolling about and wandering of his eyes, the fierceness of his looks, his unsteady and shuffling feet, his nose elevated so as to express disdain and contumely, the ridiculous contortions of his features (a mark of the same passions), his loud and unseasonable laughter, his unmeaning gestures, his broken and incoherent way of talking, his precipitate and silly

* Nec fefellit sententia. Uterque enim ab ecclesiâ recessit, ut qualis incessu prodebatur, talis perfidiâ animi demonstraretur. Namque alter Arianæ infectionis tempore fidem deseruit alter pecuniæ studio, ne judicium subiret, sacerdotem se nostrum negavit. Lucebat in eorum incessu imago levitatis, species quædam scurrarum percursantium.

questions, and his answers as foolish as the questions themselves."* Now from all these tokens of disorder, and from the want of control in his carriage and bearing, the Saint was able to foretell that he would be one day the miscreant and the impious wretch that in very deed he afterwards showed himself.† The Saint makes use of these very remarkable words: "If any were now present of those who were my companions at that time and who heard what I then said, they would bear me out, that scarce had I beheld this strangeness of demeanour in him but I at once exclaimed, 'What a fearful monster Rome is nourishing at her breast!' And I went on—'God grant I may be a false prophet.'"‡ So true is it that nothing more surely indicates an ill-regulated mind than outward disorder in the deportment and whole behaviour. No motive, as it seems to me, should avail so much as this one to induce us to cultivate the virtue of modesty in persons who have good will, who wish to give edification, and who would not willingly cause surprise or give bad example to any neighbour.

141. To come to particulars: in the first place—as we began by saying—modesty must be practised by custody of the eyes, which should usually be kept downcast, to avoid the inconveniences to which we have alluded above. I say *usually*, as I do not mean that a devout person should never raise his eyes, or give a single glance at anything, though for the purpose of lawful distraction, as we know was done even by those illustrious servants of God whose singular modesty we have already taken occasion to admire. It will be enough to keep the eyes generally cast down, this being a sure token of the inner peace and recol-

* Neque enim quidquam boni ominari videbatur cervix non stata; humeri subsaltantes, et ad æquilibrium subinde agitati; oculus insolens et vagus, furiioseque intuens; pedes instabiles et titubantes; nasus contumeliam et contemptum spirans; vultus lineamenta ridicula idem significantia; risus petulantes et effrenati; nutus et renutus temerarii, sermo hærens, spiritusque concisus; interrogationes stultæ et præcipites, responsionesque his nihilo meliores. Orat. Prima in Julian.

† Talem ante opera suspicatus sum, qualem in operibus postea cognovi.

‡ Quod si quidam ex iis, qui tunc mecum erant, quidquid dixerim audierunt nunc mihi præsto essent, haud ægre testarentur, quibus, ut hæc constitui, statim prolocutus sum: Quale monstrum Romanorum terra nutrit! præfatus licet hæc, mihi, ut falsus essem vates, deprecatus.

lection of the soul; and especially in the public streets, where we are made a spectacle to every one, and where dangerous objects are more frequently to be met with, edification requires a greater guard over our eyes. Above all, in conversing with persons of the opposite sex, we should avoid looking them full in the face, but rather fix our eyes somewhat lower, or else, without apparent constraint, direct them to some other object; for in these cases the danger is greater, and there is more risk of suspicion arising through an excessive freedom of our sight. In a word, we must bear in mind that the eyes are a mirror which reflect all the affections of the heart.* Now as nothing represents objects more clearly and faithfully than a mirror, so nothing more vividly images forth the good or bad qualities of the soul than the greater or less control that we exert over our eyes.

142. Modesty must further be observed in our conversation. It is St. Ambrose who lays down for us these special rules.† "We must be moderate in conversation, taking heed not to speak too much, nor to interrupt others, nor overwhelm them with talk, without giving them a chance of having their say; for otherwise we become burdensome to our friends, and betray a want of humility by showing an intention of silencing them with our wisdom. Take heed," continues the holy Doctor, "never to utter unbecoming words,‡ for this would be a clear sign that thy own heart is defiled with unbecoming thoughts." It should also be borne in mind that we must avoid raising our voices to a loud key, lest we weary the ears of the bystanders § For modesty must regulate even our tone of voice, that its very sound may show it to be under control, especially as this is the token of a mind which is itself humble and under control.

143. Modesty has also to regulate our laughter. We may borrow a rule on this point from St. Basil. "Whoso," says this Saint, "makes profession of piety, should take great care not to burst out into immoderate laughter, this being a sign of an ill-

* Speculum sunt lumina cordis.

† Ne modum progrediaris loquendi. Lib. i. Offic., cap. 18.

‡ Ne quid indecorum sermo resonet tuus.

§ Ipsum vocis sonum libret modestia, ne cujusquam offendat aurem vox fortior.

regulated disposition, where the movements of the soul are not under due control."* Not, he continues, that a merry laugh, showing our cheerfulness to bystanders, is contrary to decorum.† Hence that laugh alone is opposed to modesty, which is loud, immoderate, and unseemly.

144. Modesty, moreover, should be shown in our gait and carriage. We return to St. Basil for the suggestions that are to be followed concerning our manner of walking. "Let your step," he says, "be neither too slow nor too quick; the former betrays a sluggish disposition, the latter a hasty and impetuous character."‡ Hence our gait, to be such as modesty demands, should be moderated with due, but not affected gravity. Above all, should we avoid any swaying of the head and body, but walk demurely; shun all useless swinging about of the arms and hands, which should be kept becomingly occupied in holding either our garments, or whatever else persons of our condition usually carry in their hands. In our clothes all indecency and disorder are to be guarded against, for, as we read in Ecclesiasticus, *The attire of the body, and the laughter of the teeth, and the gait of the man, show what he is.*§ In a word, we should take heed not to give any indication of levity in our deportment, lest that apply which St. Ambrose spoke of the two clerics, in whose outward bearing the levity of their character was clearly manifested. If any one should object, that several of the defects noted above are natural rather than wilful, and hence not easy to correct; we may reply, after St. Ambrose, that even granting that such faults spring from untrained nature, they may, and should, be amended by assiduous care.‖

* Illud etiam non mediocriter cavendum est ab iis, qui colendæ pietati student, ne in risum præter modum effusi sint, quia intemperantiam non abesse a se significat is, ubi profuso nimis, petulantique risu teneatur, et animi motus nequaquam sedatos declarat. In Regul. Fus. Exp., Quæst. 17

† At modicum risum deducere, eoque animi sui hilaritatem significare, non esse contra decorum.

‡ Incessus esto nec segnis, ne animum dissolutum declaret, nec cursus vehemens insolenterque incitatus, ne consternatos impetus animi significet. Epist. ad Greg. Theol.

§ Amictus corporis et risus dentium et ingressus hominis enuntiat de illo. Ecclus. xix. 27.

‖ Si quid sane in naturâ vitii est, industria emendet. Lib. i. Offic., cap. 18.

145. The reader must, however, be warned that these acts of modesty are not to be practised to keep up appearances, nor out of the hypocritical wish of being accounted good by others, else they would be neither virtuous nor meritorious, but deserving indeed of nothing but chastisement. They must be the natural result of the interior virtue of modesty, which, regulating for a fitting purpose—as we have seen above—certain minor passions, so controls the outward motions of the body that they may not be unbecoming. For instance, modesty teaches us to check certain movements of curiosity, and hence mounts guard over our eyes; to restrain foolish and excessive merriment, and so checks immoderate laughter; it holds within bounds our desire to shine in our conversation with our fellows, and thus teaches us to be sparing of our words; to avoid a loud or quarrelsome tone of voice:—and thus we might go on enumerating the other acts which all spring from this virtue. Each one should therefore control himself from a motive of virtue, if he desire that his outward indications of modesty be truly virtuous.

CHAPTER IV.

TWO PATTERNS OF MODESTY WHICH MAY ENCOURAGE US TO STRIVE AFTER THIS VIRTUE..

146. THE two examples of modesty which we should do well to take as the rule and standard of our outward bearing, come to us with the highest sanction, as they are the two noblest Beings Who have ever lived here below, and Who are now reigning in Heaven. The first is our most loving Redeemer; the other, His own most tender Mother, the Virgin Mary, who is also our Mother. The Apostle St. Paul speaks in most expressive terms of our Saviour's modesty: *I Paul, myself beseech you by the mildness and modesty of Christ.** Here the Apostle couples together the modesty of Christ and that meekness which was His peculiar and distinguishing

* Ipse autem ego Paulus obsecro vos per mansuetudinem et modestiam Christi. II. Cor. x. 1

virtue; for no distinction is made when he conjures the Corinthians by these two qualities of our Blessed Lord. We may hence infer, that the modesty of Jesus was as singular as His meekness was unparalleled. This will be made plainer if we consider the acts of this virtue.

147. St. John, making mention of the conversation of Jesus Christ,* says, *that never had man spoken as this man.* St. Luke relates, that the inhabitants of Nazareth wondered at the words of grace which came forth so sweetly from His sacred mouth.† St. Matthew tells us, that in Christ the grace of speech was accompanied by a certain winning air of authority, which had never been met with in the discourse of the Scribes and Pharisees.‡ As to laughter (especially loud and unbecoming laughter), St. Basil says, "that as far as we can gather from the inspired text, it never found place on the most modest countenance of Jesus; and that though He had, of His own free choice, taken upon Himself the infirmities to which human nature is of necessity liable, laughter, at times so unavoidable to us, is the only weakness to which He would not subject Himself."§ St. John Chrysostom, speaking of our Saviour's countenance, says, "that it shone with a gentle majesty, full of power to ravish all hearts with a single look, as amber attracts straw, and the magnet iron."|| His eyes, as the same holy Doctor tells us in another place, "beamed like two bright stars, so that on his face there appeared something godlike."¶ His caution in treating with women was so great, that His Apostles were surprised at finding Him

* Nunquam locutus est homo, sicut hic homo. Jo. vij. 46.

† Mirabantur de verbis gratiæ, quæ procedebant de ore ejus. Luc. iv. 22.

‡ Erat docens eos sicut potestatem habens, et non sicut scribæ et pharisaei. Matth. vij. 29.

§ Hoc ipsum ita esse Dominus ostendit, qui susceptis ceteris, quæ necessario corpus sequuntur, affectionibus. . . risu, quantum ex Evangeliorum historià dignosci potest, usus nunquam fuit. In Regul. Fusius Explic., Quæst. 17.

|| Certe fulgor ipse et majestas divinitatis occultæ, quæ etiam in humanâ Christi facie relucebat, ex primo ad se videntes trahere poterat aspectu. Si enim in magnete lapide et succinis hæc esse vis dicitur, ut annulos et stipulam et festucas sibi copulent: quanto magis Dominus omnium creaturarum ad se trahere poterat, quos volebat? Homil. in cap. 9 Matth.

¶ Igneum quiddam, atque sidereum radiabat in oculis ejus, et divinitatis majestas lucebat in facie. Homil. in cap. 21 Matth.

speaking alone with the woman of Samaria at the well of Jacob.* Let every virtuous and devout person set this divine model before the eyes of his mind, and fashion all his outward actions on this so perfect a pattern. Let him imagine he beholds before him a lovely and majestic presence, a carriage marked by pleasing self-restraint, a manner of speaking that attracts and yet possesses authority, a calm serenity of countenance, a great degree of caution, regulating the features and every movement of the body. Let him figure to himself the composed and gentle expression of face, which drew whole crowds after our Lord, brought them out of cities and villages, led them into woods and deserts and to the solitude of the sea-shore, unmindful of food and drink, and of household cares. Let him strive earnestly to reproduce in his bearing this modesty and self-control; and to render himself, as far as may be, like unto this great example.

148. Abimelech, after having taken the town of Sichem, wishing to make himself master of the fortress, determined to reduce it by fire. But as his plan required him to heap up at the foot of this citadel a whole forest of trees, he led his army to the top of Mount Selmon, where a large wood was growing. Then he took an axe in his hand, and cutting down a bough from one of the trees, laid it on his shoulder, and walking towards the city, kept crying out as he went, *What you see me do, make haste and do likewise.*† At so noble an example, you might have seen not only the common soldiers but the captains and the highest officers, with axe in hand, cutting down every man his bough, vying with each other who should carry most, that one believing his glory to be the greatest whose burden was the heaviest. Thus did that wood of trees pass in a short time from the summit of Selmon to the foot of the tower of Sichem. In like manner do you, after having contemplated your Saviour under these comely, modest, and amiable appearances, imagine to yourself that you hear Him say to His followers, " Perform your outward actions after the manner in which I performed all of them; behave with that composure, modesty, decency, caution, with that fitness and gentleness where-

* Mirabantur, quod cum muliere loquebatur. Joan. iv. 27.

† Quod me videtis facere, cito facite. Judic. ix. 48.

with I behaved on earth."* By frequently setting before us this devout representation, both in and out of time of prayer, we may surely hope to regulate our carriage and behaviour, and to produce in ourselves some resemblance to the bearing of our Divine Master.

149. The second great example you should strive to copy is the Blessed Virgin, whose modesty is set forth in a beautiful description given by St. Ambrose.† The main features of the portrait he has drawn are the following :—" Mary was lowly of heart, considerate in her words, prudent in her resolutions, sparing of her speech, assiduous in reading, intent on her work, modest in her discourse ; repelling none, kind to all, respectful to her elders. Never could an angry look be discovered in her eyes, nor a rash word be heard to escape her lips, nor did any one ever witness in her an act which was wanting in perfect modesty, or a gesture too free, or a mode of behaviour too little restrained, or a tone of voice showing the slightest petulance. When did she ever offend her parents by a look ? or repel her acquaintance ? or cast a reproachful glance at those beneath her ? or mock the weak and disabled ? or show herself above dealing with the poor ? In a word, her whole exterior was a lively image of the perfect inward order that reigned in her soul, a most vivid expression of her peerless sanctity."‡

150. But these colours, brilliant as they are, do not sufficiently set forth the angelic modesty of the Blessed Virgin. I will, therefore, relate what Denys the Carthusian borrows from Denys the Areopagite,§ as a more faithful rendering of this great subject. He tells us, that the Areopagite having left

* Quod videtis facere, cito facite.

† Sit vobis in imagine descripta virginitas vitaque Mariæ. De Virginibus, lib. ij., post initium.

‡ Corde humilis, verbis gravis, animi prudens, loquendi parcior, legendi studiosior, intenta operi, verecunda sermone, arbitrum mentis solita non hominem, sed Deum quærere ; nullum lædere, bene velle omnibus, assurgere majoribus natu. . . . Quando ista vel vultu læsit parentes ? quando discessit a propinquis ? quando fastidivit humilem ? quando derisit debilem ? quando vitavit inopem ? Nihil torvum in oculis, nihil in verbis procax, nihil in actu inverecundum : non gestus fractior, non incessus solutior, non vox petulantior ; ut ipsa corporis species simulacrum fuerit mentis, figura probitatis.

§ De Divin. Nomin., cap. 3.

Greece for Judea, wanted to visit that great Lady who had borne the Saviour of the world. On coming into her presence, he was so struck in beholding her singular modesty, mingled with a certain gentle majesty and more than earthly beauty, that he fell prostrate on the ground; and if faith and reason had not taught him there was but one God, he would have worshipped her as a goddess. Such is the picture which I would have all, especially maidens and innocent youths, continually keep before their minds, as St. Ambrose advises in the passage above quoted: in order to copy in our own bearing its main features, and to reflect, when performing our outward actions, what was the Blessed Virgin's deportment, her manner of walking, speaking, conversing and using her eyes; endeavouring thus to make ourselves like her. When the queens of this world adopt some new fashion of dress, whatever it may be, whether of clothing, or jewellery, all the women in the kingdom glory in following their example, and take them as their models in the adornment of their persons. Why then should we, too, not deem it a glory to imitate the Queen of Heaven in our behaviour?

CHAPTER V.

PRACTICAL SUGGESTIONS TO DIRECTORS ON THE PRESENT ARTICLE.

151. FIRST suggestion. Although the Director must strive to train all his penitents to keep guard over their eyes, he must insist upon the point chiefly with young people, as this virtue is specially suitable to them, and because too much freedom in the use of the eyes is for them fraught with more dangerous results. In youths and young maidens the passions are by so much the more lively as reason is less mature. Hence, a single look will, at times, suffice to inflame them with love, or to awaken thoughts and desires contrary to purity; so that they lose in a day what they had acquired by the devout exercises of months and entire

years. Should the Director be hard to convince, he will soon discover by his own experience how true this is. He may chance to have among his penitents a young girl who once afforded great ground of hope of future perfection, because she was wholly devoted to piety, given to prayer, fond of mortification, docile, ready to comply with all advice; and then, all of a sudden, he may see her quite change, and become, within a brief space, undevout, unmortified, taking offence at, and putting an ill construction upon, his prudent warnings; and in the end turning her back upon him and leaving him altogether. If he seek the cause of this deplorable alteration, he will discover that it arose from unguarded freedom of the eyes. For she began to look fixedly upon some attractive object, and to take delight in it: and this earthly affection—as usually happens with persons of this disposition—suddenly quenches every feeling of piety. The Director must insist, with the utmost vigilance, that the young people under his charge go with downcast eyes, especially in the public streets. But this should not be done with affectation: it must be natural. And when such are forced to deal with persons of the opposite sex, they must be warned (as we have already observed) not to look them full in the face: for this precaution, which modesty suggests, will give proof to others of a deep-seated purity, and will secure them against any untoward results happening either to themselves or to those with whom they converse. We read of St. Ignatius Loyola, that on the occasion of his taking leave of Father Oliver Manareus, who was about to change his place of residence, this Father fixed his eyes on the face of the Saint: probably because he felt pained at parting. St. Ignatius gave him to understand, by Father Polancus, that he was to examine himself daily on this failing, and that when writing to him on business, or for any other reason, he was to give an account of his exactitude in performing this penance.* If a Saint of such consummate prudence, deemed it so great a fault in a religious subject to look his Superior full in the face, even when taking leave of him, how far more blameworthy would it be in a young man, or in a girl (especially if she were not married) to do the

* Lancis. Opusc. 2, n. 304.

same with one of the other sex, and, by the eyes, to be constantly drinking in wickedness of heart!

152. Second suggestion. If penitents, of either sex, be persons in any degree concerned about perfection, the Director will endeavour to rid them of other breaches of modesty, and of the marks of levity so frequently to be witnessed in talking and laughing, as well as in their style of walking and social converse: all which we have detailed in the foregoing Chapter. He should take care not to look upon these things as of little or no importance, and as mere trifles; for such failings are a hindrance to Christian perfection. It should be evident that one who cannot overcome himself in these little things will surely fail to do so in matters more weighty. In order to be persuaded of this, the Director need only to call to mind what St. Gregory relates of a young lady, by name Musa. One night there appeared to her the Queen of Heaven, with a suite of glorious virgins, all clad in white, and crowned with lilies; and the damsel was asked if she would like to come and live with the glorious Mother of God, and in company with these bright and beautiful virgins. Musa, already enchanted at the sight of them, replied, "Yes, I do wish it, and beseech you to grant me this favour." Our Lady then answered, "If you would join our company, you must leave off laughter, and all that savours of levity and childishness. You have only to do this, and in thirty days you shall be with us." When the vision had disappeared, the young lady was wholly changed; she became modest in her looks, serious of countenance, sparing of her words, well regulated in all her person. Her family, astonished at this sudden change, inquired the cause, and she, with a holy simplicity, related to them the vision that had been vouchsafed to her. The twenty-fifth day of a life thus modest and guarded came at length, and she was seized with a violent fever. On the thirtieth day the Blessed Virgin appeared to her anew, attended by the same band of holy maidens, and invited her to come to them. She, casting her eyes down in lowly reverence, said, "I come, Lady; behold, I come." And with these words she calmly expired.* Certain

* Die autem trigesimo, cum hora ejus exitûs propinquâsset, eamdem genitricem Dei cum puellis, quas per visionem viderat, ad se venire prospexit.

it is that if the slight defects of behaviour into which this innocent girl fell, had not been a hindrance and a blemish to her perfection, the Blessed Virgin would never have come down from heaven to caution her against them, nor would she have required her to correct them thoroughly before being received into the Heavenly Kingdom.

153. Third suggestion. The Director will insist, especially with Priests, Religious, and Nuns, as often as he chances to have the direction of such persons, on their attending to modesty in their looks, in their carriage, and in their every outward action; for in their case modesty affords great edification to seculars, while the want of it is to these latter an occasion of astonishment and scandal. Hence Jesus Christ in the Gospel gives them a very special command, that they let the light of their good example shine before the eyes of all. But to do this, as is plain, greatly depends on the order they maintain in their outward bearing.* St. Paul, speaking to Timothy of Bishops and Priests, says that it is necessary for such to *be of good report with them who are without;* which means none other than such as live in the world. Now this arises, above all, from modesty of the eyes, from circumspection in speech, accompanied by a seemly bearing of the person, and from becoming neatness in our dress.† The Apostle desires persons devoted to God's service to gain credit with seculars, not out of ambition or vain-glory, but solely that these may hold them in due esteem, may profit by their doctrine and instructions, and may take their rebukes in good part. It has been observed that a blemish on the face is more disfiguring than a wound or deep scar on any portion of our person that is covered. So, too, a trifling immodesty in Religious or in Priests—who are the noblest part, and, as it were, the face of the Church—is likely to give more scandal than a grievous sin committed by seculars, who are the less honourable members of

Quise etiam vocanti respondere cœpit, et depressis reverenter oculis, apertâ voce clamare: Ecce, Domina, venio: ecce, Domina, venio: in quâ etiam voce spiritum reddidit. Dial., lib. iv., cap. 17.

* Vos estis lux mundi . . . sic luceat lux vestra coram hominibus, ut videant opera vestra bona. Matth. v. 14, 16.

† Oportet autem illum testimonium habere bonum ab iis, qui foris sunt. I. ad Tim. iij. 7.

Christ's Mystic Body. Let us listen to St. Basil:—"An unbecoming action is of a different nature in one illustrious by his rank and in a person of low degree. If a mere plebeian play the buffoon or do anything unbecoming, this attracts no attention, as such things are common with that class of men; but if one who makes profession of perfection (as we may surely account Priests and Religious to do) is seen to fail in decorum, or to step a hair's breadth out of the path of duty, all take notice of the fault, and cry out against it as a grievous transgression.*

154. The Director should mark well how true this is. St. Gregory, in his Dialogues,† gives a narrative of the great virtue and extraordinary gifts which adorned Blessed Isaac, a monk in the neighbourhood of Spoleto. The holy Pope tells us that this monk was a man of the most sublime prayer and the deepest humility, while he was such a lover of holy poverty that he spurned, with generous disdain, the numerous possessions and revenues offered to him. Further, he had the gift of foreseeing the future, and the power to drive the devil out of the bodies of the possessed.‡ St. Gregory, however, does not conceal a certain defect which was found in the holy man, in company with all this virtue: and it was that he knew not how to repress the gladness of his heart, and could not refrain from showing it unduly by outward tokens. "But what fault is there in this?" you will say. "The expression of gladness, proceeding as it did from a holy cause, seems rather to have the appearance of a virtue than of a failing." Nevertheless, as the case was that of one making profession of a solitary and austere life, St. Gregory affirms that the Religious was blameworthy on account

* Neque enim, si quid indecorum geritur, id similiter in obscuris hominibus, et in iis qui illustres sunt, animadverti perinde solet. Nam de vulgo aliquis, si aut scurriles voces emittat, aut in ganeo crebrò versetur, aut alia hujusmodi flagitia agat, haud facile quisquam attendit; quippe cum quisque existimet facta illa universæ vitæ ejus instituto respondere. At qui vitæ genus perfectum profitetur, hunc, si latum unguem ab officio suo recedere visus sit, omnes confestim observant: ipsique probri loco illud objiciunt; et faciunt, quod in Evangelio scriptum est; *Conversi disrumpent vos.* In Reg. Fusius Explic., q. 22.

† Lib. iii., cap 14.

‡ Monachus, qui in terrâ possessiones quærit, monachus non est. Sic quippe metuebat paupertatis suæ severitatem perdere, sicut avari divites solent perituras divitias custodire.

of his extreme hilarity; and adds, that this alone would have sufficed to deprive him of a reputation for great virtue, had he not given proof of his holiness in other ways.* So true is it, that with those who are in a state of perfection, every outward act, not well regulated and modest, is sufficient to diminish, in the minds of seculars, that esteem and good opinion which persons consecrated to God are bound to preserve for His glory and honour. We may conclude then, with St. Jerome, that the modesty and outward composure of a Religious (and the same holds good of every ecclesiastic) should be such that his discourse, his gait, his countenance, and his whole exterior, may serve as a lesson in virtue.†

155. Fourth suggestion. Should the Director perceive that any of his penitents have become enamoured with this beautiful virtue of modesty, and are eager to attain it, the most effectual means he can prescribe will be the Particular Examination of which we spoke in the foregoing Treatise. But the penitent must be warned to take one failing at a time, and try to conquer it by this means. A general going to conquer a kingdom does not give battle on all points at once, nor strives wholly to subdue it at one blow; but he lays siege to each city in succession, and by capturing them thus, one after the other, he gradually extends his dominion in every direction. So too, if we wish by means of the virtue of modesty to subject all the movements of our senses and members to the rule of reason, we must first wage war against the eyes, the most wanton of our senses, and regulate them by the Particular Examen; then fight against the tongue, as being the most treacherous of our members, bridling this also; and so on successively with each one of our members, until we reduce them all to order by the same means. In this way we shall easily succeed in gradually rendering all our outward actions entirely subject to the will, and in keeping them in check; by doing which we shall

* Hic enim cum virtute abstinentiæ, contemptu rerum transeuntium, prophetiæ spiritu, orationis intensione esset incomparabiliter præditus, unum erat, quod in eo reprehensibile esse videbatur, quod nonnumquam ei tanta lætitia inerat, ut illis tot virtutibus nisi sciretur esse plenus, nullo modo crederetur.

† De ludo monasteriorum hujuscemodi volumus egredi milites, quorum habitus, sermo, vultus, incessus, doctrina virtutum sit. Epist. ad Rustic.

gain in the sight of others a certain lustre of modesty and decorous bearing.

156. Fifth suggestion. As regards the dress of women who wish to make profession of a spiritual life, the Director will strive to keep them aloof from vanity as far as in him lies. I do not say that they should be made to alter their style of dress, for this must not be done without mature deliberation, the consent of the members of their family, and a reasonable hope that the holiness of their lives will answer to the change in their dress; since it has sometimes happened that certain persons have come recklessly to cast aside the holy habit which they had put on, or have disgraced it by their evil ways. I advise only that all should be taught to dress as modestly as their condition will allow; for the great obstacles in the way of women giving themselves to the service of God are two in number: the beauty of their faces, of which they are so careful, and their vanity in dressing, on which they plume themselves so much. Experience shows, that when these two difficulties have been got rid of, persons of their sex easily withdraw from the world, cultivate modesty, retirement, prayer, and the practice of all the other virtues. St. Cyprian, speaking of virgins, says, "Women who clothe in silk and purple cannot clothe themselves perfectly in the virtues of Christ: adorned as they are with gold, jewels, and pearls, they lose every jewel of the soul, if peradventure they have made gain of any."* The holy Doctor had derived this lesson from the Prince of the Apostles, St Peter, who, addressing Christian women, forbids them to braid their hair after the fashion of idolaters, and to wear a profusion of gold ornaments or gaudy apparel.† St. Paul, on the other hand, allows some moderate adornment, saying, that the dress of women may be made beautiful with decency and modesty, still without broidered hair, or gold, or jewels, or costly array; all which have an appearance of luxury, and savour too much of love

* Serico et purpurâ indutæ, Christum sincere induere non possunt: auro et margaritis adornatæ, et monilibus, ornamenta mentis et corporis perdunt. De Habitu Virg., lib 4.

† Quarum non sit extrinsecus capillatura, aut circumdatio auri, aut indumenti vestimentorum cultus. 1 Pet. iij. 3.

of show.* If the Director have guided souls for some time, his own experience will have shown him that these Saints had good reason to speak in this tone, and therefore he will endeavour to keep women, particularly such as are devout, from these vanities. For my own part, I knew a lady who, after having turned her back on the world and entered upon a holy course of life, decked herself out gaudily on a certain occasion, and put on all her old vanities and past habits together with her dress. Such is the dominion exercised by vanity over the female heart.

157. Finally, if the Director would wish to attain an accurate idea of the style of dress and manner of life befitting a woman desirous of living devoutly in the world, he may find it in St. Gregory of Nazianzus. "The ornaments worn by a lady in the world ought to consist in the goodness and decorum of her behaviour; in keeping for the most part within doors; in frequent converse with God in prayer; in attending to her various work with the needle; in the overseeing of the doings of the female servants; in flying from gossip, and from familiarity with the men employed in the house; in guarding her eyes, her tongue, ay, and her face too, in embellishing which women commit so many faults; in seldom going abroad, but in conversing at home with estimable and esteemed companions of her own sex." † Let a woman do all this, and she may be sure that she is walking in the path of perfection.

* Similiter et mulieres in habitu ornato, cum verecundiâ et sobrietate ornantes se, et non in tortis crinibus, aut auro, aut margaritis, vel veste pretiosâ: sed quod decet mulieres promittentes pietatem per opera bona. I. ad Tim. ij. 9.

† Mulierum ornamentum est morum probitate, et elegantiâ florere: domi ut plurimum manere: colloquium cum divinis oraculis habere: fuso, et lanæ operam dare: ancillis opera mandare: servos vitare. oculis, labiis, genis vinculum injicere: pedem limine non frequenter efferre: pudicis quidem omnibus mulieribus delectari. Adv. Mulieres ambitiosius se Ornantes.

ARTICLE IV.

The hindrances to perfection arising from want of duly guarding the senses of Hearing and of Smell.

CHAPTER I.

EVILS ARISING FROM THE BAD USE OF THE HEARING. ADVANTAGES WHICH COME FROM THE GOOD USE OF THIS SENSE.

158. THE sense of hearing resides in the ears, within which sound, propagated by the air, produces special sensations. And as words are nothing but a certain sound formed by the tongue and lips of man, who by such means expresses his inner thoughts, it belongs to this sense to take in the words and discourse of our fellow-men. But as words, considered from a moral point of view, may be either good and praiseworthy or bad and reprehensible, we can make a good use of this sense of hearing by willingly listening to the former, or an evil use when we hearken to the latter with pleasure and satisfaction.

159 *Faith* in the divine mysteries, as the Apostle teaches, *comes by hearing* * For if we hearken not to the truth which we are bound to believe, and to the arguments which go to establish its credibility, we are perforce deprived of the knowledge which is a necessary preliminary to faith.† By means, too, of this sense, we receive from God those heavenly lights and inner motions which serve to arouse from the sleep of sin many Christians who have faith, it is true, but live not up to their belief. Daily experience, indeed, shows that there is not a more effectual means for reclaiming sinners to penance, than an atten tive hearing of God's Word. By means of the hearing, those mighty inspirations are received whereby God calls us to perfec-

* Fides ex auditu. Rom x. 17.
† Quomodo enim credent sine prædicante?

tion, as was the case with St. Antony, who while listening to the words of the holy Gospel, felt himself so powerfully moved, that he forsook the world and all that he had, and withdrew into the wilderness, to live alone with God. The like is also related of St. Nicholas of Tolentino who, on hearing a sermon on the vanity of earthly things, conceived such a disgust of them that he turned his back upon the world, and hastened to hide himself in a cloister

160. Nor is it only in public discourses that God makes use of our hearing to draw us on to perfection; but He also employs private conversations, as appears from ecclesiastical history, which tells of numbers who have been stirred up to strive after perfection by the private exhortations of their friends. The Blessed Raymond of Pisa, when one day playing the guitar, saw a great servant of God pass along the street. He felt a strong impulse to follow him, and, acting upon it, he threw aside his instrument, and proceeded to accompany the Priest. Hearing him soon after discourse of God with much sweetness and energy, he became all on fire with the holy words spoken and being seized with an extraordinary fervour gave himself wholly to God, and advanced to high sanctity. For my own part, however, I am much more moved by the great impression made on the heart of St. Augustine, and of his mother St. Monica, by the devout conversation they had together at the mouth of the Tiber: as he himself relates in the book of his Confessions. He says that they began to converse upon a pious subject, in the course of which they went on to admire the greatness of God as reflected in the objects which were before them; then their discourse soared higher, to the consideration (joined with pious affections) of other more noble works of God's almighty Hand, both in heaven and on earth. They next advanced to the consideration of their own souls; and then, soaring above all created things, their mind winged its flight, and plunged into the everlasting joys of the abode of the blessed, until at length they became silent, and all-absorbed in lofty contemplation.* By merely hearing the

* Erigentes nos ardentiore affectu in idipsum, perambulavimus gradatim cuncta corporalia, et cœlum ipsum . . . et adhuc ascendebamus interius cogitando, et loquendo te, et mirando opera tua, et venimus in mentes nostras,

conversation which these two holy souls were holding together on the things of God, their minds were gradually enlightened with those sublime illuminations,—there was enkindled in their hearts that rapturous ardour with which they were carried away, and in which they were happily lost in God. The same Saint further tells us of himself, that on hearing the psalms and devout chants of the Church, in the beginning of his conversion, God, by their means, instilled into his mind those lofty conceptions, and into his heart that unspeakable sweetness, which made him melt into tears of happiness.* So true is it that the sense of hearing is the ordinary channel by which God pours into our souls those supernatural lights and affections which stir us up either to conversion, to amendment, or to the highest perfection.

161. On the other hand, the devil makes use of this sense to draw souls on to their ruin, or at least to keep them far from the paths of perfection. I would ask, Whence comes it that, even among Christians, born in the bosom of Holy Church, and taught in the school of the Redeemer, so much store is set on honours, dignities and the pomps of the world? Why is so much importance attached to grandeur, luxury, and vanity? Why do men give themselves so readily to resentment, hate and revenge? How is it that they seek so greedily after money and worldly goods, and hanker so eagerly after riches? All this arises from the generality of the faithful talking of these passing things in terms of great esteem; from their extolling them and magnifying them, and pronouncing those happy who possess them. From which it follows that listeners conceive a high opinion of such objects, vain and empty though they be; and, by a natural association, our affections closely follow the guidance of the esteem we form, and

et transcendimus eas, ut attingeremus regionem ubertatis indeficientis, ubi pascis Israel in æternum, veritatis pabulo; et ubi vita sapientia est . . . et dum loquimur, et inhiamus illi, attigimus eam modice toto ictu cordis, et suspiravimus, et reliquimus ibi religatas primitias spiritus: et remeavimus ad strepitum oris nostri. Confess., lib. ix., cap. 10.

* In hymnis et canticis tuis suavesonantis ecclesiæ tuæ vocibus commotus acriter. Voces illae influebant auribus meis, et eliquabatur veritas tua in cor meum; et ex eâ æstuabat inde affectus pietatis, et currebant lacrymæ, et bene mihi erat cum illis Confess., lib ix., cap 6.

get entangled in such vanities. And that wide-spread corruption which is witnessed and deplored by those who have God's honour at heart, what is its source? Nothing else but the unguarded use of this same sense of hearing. On this there can be no question. And would you be convinced of this, ask the many shameless women, the many dissolute and abandoned youths, who now are living plunged in the filth of countless abominations—ask them, I say, what was the first link in that long chain of sin with which the devil at this very time holds them captives, and you will most surely find that, as a common rule, it was listening with pleasure to some immodest or imprudent conversation. By this it was that they conceived their first impure thoughts and lewd desires; by this did they drink of those first drops of wickedness, which have at length drowned them in an ocean of iniquity.

162. It is plain, then, that the salvation or ruin of man has its source in the good or evil use of this sense, and that according as the ear is carefully or heedlessly guarded, devout persons will find in it either their spiritual advantage or the ruin of their souls. For the ear is another of those openings whereby death and life find an entrance for the quickening or the ruin of our spirit. And what is most noteworthy, it is not a window like other windows, which may be opened or closed as we list, but one that stands ever open and cannot be closed; because, though we can succeed in keeping this sense far from evil discourse, we cannot shut our ears as we can shut our eyes or our lips, nor can we hinder words which present themselves from entering and soiling the whiteness of our soul. Let him, then, who makes profession of piety and devotion, frequent sermons, so that by the gate of the ears holy things may find an entrance into his heart; let him fly with the greatest horror from theatres, comedies and public shows, where all that is spoken,—love-sick discourse and amorous words,—infuses through the ears into the soul a deadly poison. Let him take heed not to listen to talk which is too free—that pest which destroys sound morals, according to the well-known adage, *Evil communications corrupt good manners.* Let him further guard against listening to that vain discourse which fills the head with worldly ideas, and dissipates the heart and mind. But let him

rather attend with pleasure to instructive, pious, and spiritual discourse, encouraging these with all his might, yet without affectation, among his friends and acquaintances; for such conversation fills the mind with godly thoughts, enkindles holy affections in the will, and is useful both to the hearers and the speaker—as was shown above in the case of St. Augustine. Nor will it lose its efficacy when held in simplicity between persons who stand on an equal footing. Indeed, this circumstance rather increases the benefit; for we frequently see that spiritual conversation is more effectual than even some sermons thundered from the pulpit by sacred orators.

163. We read in the Lives of the Fathers, that a saintly old man beheld Angels joyfully hovering over the monks who were holding pious discourse with each other; but when, on the contrary, their talk was worldly and to no purpose, he beheld the demons in their midst, grunting in the form of foul swine. Hence he went about through the monastery, crying aloud, "Brethren, forsake all your empty talk, which is the ruin of the soul!"* It may be noted that this great servant of God did not merely say that worldly conversation occasions some slight prejudice to devout persons, but that it is deadly in its effects on their souls; on account of the dissipation and other most baneful results it works within us. No wonder, then, that the foul fiends take delight in this vain conversation, and are glad to be present and give brutish tokens of their satisfaction.

164. On the other hand, godly discourse strengthens the soul, inflaming and encouraging it to virtuous endeavour; for while we listen to converse about holy things, Jesus Christ speaks at the same time to our hearts, since He is then present with us, according to the promise preserved to us in His holy Gospel.† Whence the same happens to us as befell the two disciples on the road to

* Cum autem aliud quivis loquerentur; statim angeli recedebant longius; indignantes contra eos. Veniebant autem porci sordidissimi, et morbo pleni, et volutabant se inter eos. Dæmones enim in specie porcorum delectabantur de superbiâ, et vanâ loquelâ eorum . . . Beatus autem senior hæc videns commonebat per monasteria fratres: Cohibete a multiloquio, et ab otiosis sermonibus linguam, per quam malum interius animæ generatur. Cap. 26, § 35

† Ubi sunt duo vel tres congregati in nomine meo, in medio illorum ego sum. Matth. xviii. 20.

Emmaus; hearing the words of Christ, they *felt their hearts burn within them.** God was pleased to grant ocular demonstration of this truth to St. Francis of Assisi and his children; for he, being one day in the company of some of his brethren, they began spiritual colloquy, during which they spoke of God with ideas so lofty and sweetness so great, as filled each of the company with deep admiration and spiritual comfort. Meanwhile, the Redeemer appeared in a ravishing and loving semblance in the midst of the devout gathering. At this sight, all being beside themselves with rapture, fell prostrate on the ground, and remained there absorbed for a time in most sweet ecstasy.† The devout man should then abhor the hearing of foolish and vain talk, but make it his delight to listen to wise, holy and profitable discourse; if he would have for his companions in conversation the Angels and their King, rather than devils out of hell.

165. I will add, that nothing is more suitable nor more befitting to a devout person, than willingness to lend an ear to godly discourse, and to keep it closed against profane conversation. For every one delights to be reminded of what he loves. The soldier is ever ready to talk of war; the student of science; the craftsman is never tired of listening to those that talk of his handicraft.‡ Just so, worldly men relish to hear the discourse of the world, and spiritual men are fond of hearing spiritual discourse. Each one may find in this a test by which he may discover to what class of persons he himself belongs.

CHAPTER II.

COMING TO PARTICULARS, THE HARM IS POINTED OUT WHICH THE SOUL MAY RECEIVE WHEN IT WILFULLY LISTENS TO MURMURING.

166. MURMURING, says St. Jerome, is a vice that so pervades Christendom, that scarcely one can be found who is free from

* Nonne cor nostrum ardens erat in nobis, dum loqueretur in viâ! Luc. xxiv. 32.

† In Chronic. Min. Galli, lib. i., cap 30. ‡ Tractant fabrilia fabri.

its infection. You will find persons consecrated to God, who live free from every stain of impurity; who keep their hearts far from all greed of gain and other guilty attachments; who never allow an improper word to escape their lips; who mortify their appetite by fasting; afflict their flesh with hair-shirts; in a word, are adorned with every virtue; but you will hardly find a spiritual person who does not murmur and criticise the actions of others; for this is the last snare the devil lays for them, and into this they are all continually falling.* The reader may hence infer the necessity we are under of speaking of a vice which is so foreign to Christian perfection, yet is so common among those who make profession of it. However, since listening to murmurs implies that there is some one who murmurs (as it is plainly impossible that there should be listeners unless there be a speaker), before proceeding to show the great evil of lending the ear to talk of this kind—which is the object of this Chapter—we must briefly show the heinousness of his sin whose tongue detracts from another's good name.

167. St. Bernard, treating of this subject, says that the tongue of the backbiter is a viper which poisons three persons with a single bite; a lance which pierces three men with one thrust; a three-pointed sword which makes three wounds with one blow.† Then, explaining what he means by the three wounds inflicted by the backbiter's tongue in every murmur it utters, he says that the first wound is received by him against whom the remark is directed, piercing him to the quick in his good name; the second is received in the ears of the listener, who is scandalised at the remark and brought into the occasion of sin; the third wound, more deadly than the others, is inflicted on the speaker,

* Pauci admodum sunt, qui huic vitio (scilicet detractionis) renuncient; raroque invenies, qui ita vitam suam irreprehensibilem exhibere velint, ut non libenter reprehendant alienam; tantaque hujusmodi libido mentes hominum invasit, ut etiam qui procul ab aliis vitiis recesserunt, in illud tamen, tamquam in extremum diaboli laqueum, incidant. Epist. ad Celant.

† Numquid non est vipera lingua detractoris? ferocissima sane, nimirum quæ læthaliter tres inficit morsu uno. Numquid non lancea est ista lingua? profecto, et acutissima, quæ tres penetrat ictu uno. *Lingua*, inquit, *eorum gladius acutus.* Gladius equidem anceps, immo triceps est lingua detractoris. De Triplici Custod. Manûs, Linguæ, et Cordis.

striking his own soul with so mortal a blow, that it makes it hateful and abominable in God's eyes: as the Apostle declares.*

168. "Nor," he adds, "will it avail to plead that there is no harm in a passing word which flies through the air, and is swept away by the wind. True, the backbiter's word does fly swiftly, but it wounds grievously; true, it passes quickly, but it burns cruelly."†

169. Yet would we understand more fully how deeply the enlightened mind of the mellifluous Doctor realised the infamy of the sin of detraction, and the horror in which he held it, we must read his Third Sermon on the Dedication of his Church, and we shall find that he goes so far as to give the name of traitors to the monks who dared to introduce into his monastery this hateful vice: he even calls them fellow-workers of the devil, since such, he says, are in league with these to spread scandal, to sow strife by the murmurings and whisperings of their tongues; and he charges them with the endeavour to change God's house into a den of demons.‡ What strong words! What burning zeal! What an abhorrence of detraction! How great must be the shamefulness of this vice!

170. Nor are we to believe that St. Bernard stands alone in this high estimate of the guilt of murmuring. Other saints and other Doctors have spoken of it in terms of the deepest detestation. St. Clement of Rome, in a letter of his recorded in Gratian,§ relates what was taught by the Prince of the Apostles: that there are three sorts of manslaughter; the first, that which destroys our neighbour's life; the second, the crime of those who hate him unto death; third, the sin whereby we rob him of his good name.

* Detractores Deo odibiles. Rom. i. 30.

† Dicimus: Levis res sermo: tenera, mollis, et exigua caro lingua hominis: quis sapiens magni pendat? Levis quidem res sermo, quia leviter volat; sed graviter vulnerat · leviter transit, sed graviter urit.

‡ Proditores sunt quicumque in hoc Domini castrum inimicos ejus introducere moliuntur: quales sunt utique detractores Deo odibiles, qui discordias seminant, nutriunt scandala inter fratres. Sicut enim in pace factus est locus Domini; sic in discordiâ locum fieri diabolo, manifestum est. Non miramini, fratres, si durius loqui videor, quia veritas neminem palpat. Omnino proditorem se noverit; si quis forte, quod absit, vitia quælibet in hanc domum conatur inducere, et domum Dei speluncam facere dæmoniorum. Serm. 3 in Dedic. Ecc.

§ De Poenit., Dist. 1.

And he tells us, to each of these three, as being of equal guilt, does God assign an equal penalty.* St. Jerome likewise calls every backbiter guilty of murder, on the authority of St. John and of Solomon; and he hesitates not to call it an enormous iniquity.† Nor should this mode of speaking appear strained or exaggerated; for granting that the backbiter does not shed the blood which flows in his neighbour's veins, yet he draws from him the blood of his good name, which is ever so much more precious. He robs him, not of the life of the body, which is less valuable, but of social existence, which is of greater importance; for the unfortunate person whom the tongue of malice has smitten, lives no more, as of old, in the good opinion or esteem of his fellow-men.

171. At least may we assert that detraction is far more heinous than robbery or theft, for, as the Wise Man says, *Better is a good name than great riches:* since it is of an order superior to that of all the wealth in the world, and thus is to be far more valued.‡ And certainly you will not find a single man of good sense who, to restore his good name, if lost, or to stave off injury impending over it, would not think that money, income, all his property and possessions, would be well expended. It follows, then, that a greater damage is done, and a more grievous fault is committed by him whose detraction deprives a neighbour of the good character which he before enjoyed among men, than by a thief who would rob him of his money, of his wealth, or of any other worldly possession. And here let us reflect, in passing, on the general blindness of Christians. If one of them were to discover that he had committed some twenty or thirty thefts in his lifetime, he would assuredly be ashamed of himself, and deem himself unworthy to live in the society of men. But if he be conscious of having twenty or thirty times injured his neighbour's fair fame—which is a more grievous sin—he feels no compunction,

* Homicidarum tria genera esse dicebat B. Petrus, et pœnam eorum parilem esse dicebat: sicut enim homicidas interfectores fratrum, ita detractores quoque eorum, eosque odientes homicidas esse manifestabat

† Grande scelus est cum detraho fratri meo: lingua mea fratrem interficio. *Qui* enim *odit fratrem suum, homicida est.* Videte quid dicat Salomon: *In manu linguæ, mors et vita.*

‡ Melius est bonum nomen, quam divitiæ multæ. Prov. xxij. 1.

no remorse, no regret: as if he had done no evil! What a delusion! What blindness! What a bewitching of our minds!

172. That I may not be suspected of a wish to enhance, more than truth allows, the grievousness of this sin or to exaggerate its deformity, let us use a measure which certainly cannot possibly deceive, and try if we can fathom the depths of its malice. The measure is, the punishments with which God visits this crime. We shall see how severe such chastisements are, and by a just and exact analogy, we may unfailingly infer the gravity of the offence. We read in the Book of Numbers,* that Mary, the sister of Moses, was covered from head to foot with a most foul leprosy for having murmured against her brother. And what is more astonishing (as St. Basil observes), though Moses interceded for her cure, he was not heard; and yet it was he himself who had been offended: so great was the anger of God against her. In the same book,† we read that Core, Dathan, and Abiron, in punishment of having murmured against the same Moses, were swallowed up alive by the earth, which closed over them, and over all that belonged to them; that two hundred and fifty of the leading personages, and afterwards fourteen thousand seven hundred of the multitude of the children of Israel, were burned alive by a fearful fire, which was rained down upon them from above in punishment of their murmurings against the Great Prophet; that, on another occasion, God sent fiery serpents to destroy this murmuring people; and finally, that they all but a few were condemned, in chastisement of their many repeated murmurings, to perish in the sands of the deserts of Arabia, through which they went wandering without being allowed to enjoy for a single day the delights of the promised land for which they yearned so longingly, and for which they had sought at the price of so much hardship. Most assuredly we nowhere read of God having visited other sins with such heavy scourges as are fire raining down from heaven, the opening of the bowels of the earth, and the sending forth of devouring serpents; leprosy, death, and the slaughter of whole nations. How heinous, then, must be that sin which God, Who is most just, most full of mercy even in His vengeance, punishes with such terrible severity!

* Num. xij. 10. † Ibid. xvj. 21, 24.

173. If from the pages of the inspired historian we turn to the annals of the Church, we shall still find instances of God's visiting detraction with the severest punishment. Out of many, I will choose but three, in which the wrath of God seems more plainly made manifest; and I will relate them shortly. The first is one reported by Thomas of Cantipré, who tells us that the circumstance happened under his own eyes to the person of an unhappy Priest, who was unworthy alike of the name and character. This man was in the habit of tearing to pieces with his treacherous tongue the good fame of his neighbours, and recklessly shedding the blood of their reputation. Being at the point of death, he fell into a paroxysm of such rage as to mangle his tongue with his teeth, and, what was stranger still, whenever he opened his mouth, an intolerable stench escaped from it; God wishing to manifest, in this case, the fulfilment of what the Royal Prophet says, that the tongue of the murmurer is the tongue of an asp, and that his mouth is a sepulchre of corruption: an observation made by the author just mentioned.*

174. The two other instances are related by Baronius,† one as having happened to a Priest called Donatus, the other to a Bishop of the name of Mauranus, whose fates were similar and equally deplorable. The one, while at table, cast reflections injurious to the happy and illustrious memory of St. Ambrose; the other, on a like occasion, having spoken evil of the glorious actions of St. Augustine in his brother's presence, they were both struck with mortal blows by an invisible hand, and covered the table with their own blood. Having been supported on the arms of others from the table to their bed, they miserably expired. Thus, concludes the author,—thus does God punish the backbiter's tongue.‡

175. But my murmurings, some one will perhaps say, are deserving neither of such rebukes, nor of such punishment, as they

* Quod quia lingua sua dolose egerat, et venenum aspidum sub labiis ejus; quasi sepulchrum patens guttur illius fœtorem teterrimum exhalavit, ut per quæ peccaverat, per eadem torqueretur. Apum, cap. 37.

† Tom. iij. An. 397, n. 34.

‡ Is finis virorum detrahentium fuit; quod videntes, qui tunc aderant, admirati sunt.

are but slight; and though they may tarnish, they cannot blacken. my neighbour's fair fame. To this I reply: If St. Bernard, that sworn enemy of detraction, were called on to answer to such a plea, he would say at once, that in detraction there is no slightness of fault. "Some one may perhaps fancy," he writes, "that in murmuring there may be a slight sin. Not so judged the Apostle, who warns us to take heed to ourselves against this sin more than against any other; not so judged Moses, who told the people that their murmurings did not smite him, but smote the heart of God; not so judged the same Apostle, who warned the Corinthians not to murmur, lest they too be destroyed; as was the fate of those who murmured and were excluded from the heavenly country, in distant exile from its happy portals."*

176. We cannot however deny, that in murmuring, as in other sins, there is levity of matter, and hence these words of St. Bernard are to be taken in the sense, that although it may, and indeed does, often happen, that in murmuring a venial fault only is committed, yet, for the following reasons, the evil is never small. First, That should never be accounted a slight evil which, in any manner, injures our neighbour in his fair fame. Honour is as dear to us as the apple of the eye. Now, even as the least touch on so sensitive a part as the eye is ever most painful, so too, every wound in our honour made by the tongue of another is always most intolerable, and ought not, in all justice, to be accounted a slight evil. Secondly, Murmuring, though it may chance to be slight in itself, has a certain deformity of its own, for which it deserves to be considered as a serious evil. I may make this clear by a comparison with theft, with which detraction has several points of resemblance. It is undoubted that to filch any trifling object is not a theft attaining to the grievousness

* Fortè aliqui leve peccatum æstimant murmurare: sed non hic, (nempe Apostolus ad Philip., ij. 14), qui ante omne monet cavendum. Puto autem, ne illum quidem leve putasse, qui murmurantibus aiebat: *Non contra nos est murmur vestrum, sed contra Dominum; nos enim quid sumus?* Sed ne illum quoque, qui dixit: *Non murmuraveritis, sicut quidam murmuraverunt, et perierunt ab exterminatione;* illo nimirum exterminatore, qui positus est in hoc ipsum, ut a terminis beatæ illius civitatis arceat murmuratores, et longe faciat a finibus ejus. In Sententiis.

of a deadly sin; yet, a nobleman, or any other person of honourable station, would be more ashamed to have it known that he had been guilty of a trifling theft than that he had fallen into some grievous sin or unchastity or revenge. Because theft is infamous, which, even in trifling actions retains its special deformity, rendering them disgraceful and, in every instance, imprinting a stain on the honour of all who commit it. Why can we not say the same of murmuring, which is a real theft and, what is worse, robs us of that which is most precious, even of that fair name which a person of good repute enjoys in the minds of his neighbours? Therefore, granting that the detraction be slight; granting that it be venial; still, it always is a great evil, as it robs our neighbour of what is most dear to him, always cuts him to the quick and puts him to torture. Though never so trifling, detraction is an infamous theft, an action unbecoming in a Christian, and above all in a Religious, who ought, more than all things else, to have at heart the virtue of charity.

177. But I have got so far on my journey that I have reached the end; for having shown the deformity of the vice of murmuring, I have also clearly shown how heinous is the fault of him that listens with pleasure to detractors. As the Holy Fathers say, it is one and the same sin to detract, or to encourage detraction by listening to the detractor; and this is still more true whenever any listener encourages the detractor's tongue, either by putting him questions, or by showing pleasure in his language, or, it may be, by not rebuking, or at least interrupting, his malicious talk, especially when then there is an obligation to do so. A well-known saying of St. Bernard is this: "I know not who does the greater harm, the detractor, or he that listens with pleasure to detraction."* For, as the same Saint elsewhere says, "One has the devil on his tongue, urging him to speak, the other in his ears, making him eager to listen." St. Basil inquires what punishment should be awarded to the Monk who utters detraction, and to his companion who listens to it; and he decides that both should be kept apart from the company and converse of the other Re-

* Detrahere, aut detrahentem audire, quid horum damnabilius sit, non facile dixerim. De Consid., lib. ii.

ligious, as being equally guilty: which he proves by quotations from Holy Writ.*

178. St. Jerome gives as the reason for this, that listeners to detraction are the cause of the very detraction which they feel satisfaction in hearing. Let us suppose the case that no one ever gave credit to detractors, nor listened to them. Such men would certainly never dare to set their malicious rumours afloat, and shame, at least, would make them hold their tongue. So that if any speak evil, the blame lies with those who readily give ear to them, and are the occasion of their wicked gossip.† Hence, in his letter to Demetrias, the Saint warns her not to murmur, nor to listen to those that do; so as not to take part by tacit consent in their sin, or to give encouragement to their vice, by willingly lending an ear to them, but rather to follow the advice of the Holy Ghost, to keep the ears fenced round with a hedge of thorns, so that words proceeding from an evil-speaking tongue may find no entrance.‡ He further says, that the first thought to be entertained by a person who is about to devote himself to the spiritual life, should be to arm himself against these slanderous tongues, for nothing can so disturb a devout soul as lending the ear to the talk of these mischievous murmurers. Such people stir up hate, anger, strife and discord, they dissipate the mind, rendering it unstable and inconstant. On the other hand, never to listen to words contrary to charity, begets steadiness of behaviour, and preserves a serene calm within the heart.§ And, in

* Exterminandi a reliquorum societate ambo. *Detrahentem enim proximo suo, hunc persequebar.* Et alibi dictum est. *Detrahentem noli libenter audire, ne sustollaris.* In Reg. Brevior., Reg 26.

† Quod si hæc in nobis esset diligentia, nec passim detractoribus crederemus, jam omnes detrahere timerent Sed hoc ideo malum celebre est, idcirco in multis fervet hoc vitium, quia pene ab omnibus audiuntur. Epist. ed Cel.

‡ Tu vero hoc malum ita fuge, ut non modo ipsa non detrahas, sed ne alii quidem detrahenti aliquando credas; nec detractoribus auctoritatem de consensu tribuas, nec eorum vitium nutrias annuendo. *Noli*, inquit Scriptura, *consentaneus esse cum derogantibus adversus proximum suum; et ne accipias super ipsum peccatum*, et alibi: *Sepi aures tuas spinis, et noli audire linguam nequam.*

§ Est sane tale hoc vitium, quod vel in primis extingui debeat, et ab eis, qui se sancte instituere volunt, prorsus excludi. Nihil enim tam inquietat ani-

conclusion, he makes use of these remarkable words, "Blessed is he who is so well armed against this vice that no ones dares backbite in his presence."* A blessedness of this kind was attained by St. Teresa. Either by cleverly diverting the conversation, or by mildly rebuking the murmuring which arose among her Nuns, she came at last to this, that none of her Religious durst start any topic of this kind in her presence. Thus it became a common saying in her convent, that where Teresa was, the backs of the nuns were safe from backbiters. This she herself tells us in her autobiography.

179. The above having been duly established, any devout person anxious not to go astray through the sense of hearing, and to become a partaker in the guilt of evil tongues, must subject himself to the rule which I am now about to lay down. Let him fly all converse with persons whose habit it is to censure their neighbours' conduct: let him obey the command of the Holy Ghost to this effect: *Have nothing to do with detractors;* and again, *Remove from thee a froward mouth, and detracting lips put far from thee.*† Should he happen to hear any detraction of importance, let him be on his guard to give no token of complaisance, in order, as St. Jerome says, not to take part himself in the detraction, nor have any share in the sin of another.

180. But this is not enough. He must further trample under foot all human respect, lay aside all unnecessary regards for the dignity of the speaker, and rebuke the detracting tongue (if so be that due and lawful respect for the person who detracts forbids it not), and remind the defamer of the damage which he is doing to his neighbour. Let him take for himself, in such a case, the

mum, nihil est, quod ita mobilem, et levem faciat, quam facile totum credere, et obtrectatorum verba temerario mentis assensu sequi. Hinc enim crebræ dissensiones; hinc odia injusta nascuntur. Hinc est quod sæpe de amicissimis etiam inimicos facit; cum concordes quidem, et credulas animas multiloquia lingua dissolvat. At contra, magna quies animi, magnaque morum gravitas, non temere de quoquam sinistre quid audire.

* Beatusque est, qui ita se contra hoc vitium armavit, ut apud eum detrahere nemo audeat.

† Cum detractoribus non commiscearis. Remove a te os pravum, detrahentia labia sint procul a te. Prov. xxiv. 21, et iv. 24.

advice given by St. John Chrysostom to the people of Antioch, on the manner of behaving in the like circumstances: "If any one desire to murmur, say to him with all freedom, 'If you wish to speak well of your neighbour, and to relate anything that redounds to his credit, my ears are open to listen. But if your intention be to speak evil of him, to reveal his faults and failings, or to blame his doings, I will close my ears against you. My ears are accustomed to receive the balm of good discourse, not the filth and ordure of backbiting.'"* But if the station of the slanderer is such that he is your superior in rank or authority, and hence does not allow you to address him in this style and to rebuke him with so much openness, try at least to divert the conversation and to start another subject more in keeping with Christian charity. But should you find that even this is not feasible, you may at all events cast down your eyes, put on a serious look, and show by your exterior what you are not allowed to express in words: that is, show him by the sedate behaviour which you assume, that such talk is unseemly in itself, and an annoyance to you. By this means you will administer a silent but effectual reproof, for, as the wise man says, *The north wind driveth away rain, as doth an angry countenance a backbiting tongue.*† Cassian relates, that a certain monk, called Machetes, had received this grace from God, that when in spiritual conferences holy things formed the subject of conversation, he was ever alive to what was going on, and was self-possessed, though the conference might last whole days and nights; but whenever any backbiting began to be introduced he immediately went off into a deep sleep.‡ You may not be able, by miraculous slumber, to show him who backbites in your presence the displeasure you feel at this talk, so repugnant to charity; but you may make him sensible thereof by your silence, and by the sadness of your countenance, whenever it will not be possible for you either to divert the conversation or to rebuke the backbiter.

* Dic proximo detrahenti: Habes aliquem quem laudes, et commendes: aures aperio, ut unguenta suscipiam. Si vero malum velis dicere, obturo aures: non enim stercus, et cœnum accipere sustinebo. Homil. 3.

† Ventus aquilo dissipat pluvias: et facies tristis linguam detrahentem. Prov. xxv. 23.

‡ Inst., lib. v., cap. 29.

I have hitherto spoken of the spiritual damage resulting to him who listens to backbiters, and as it is a fault into which we frequently fall, I have been somewhat diffuse on the point. Not but that a devout person should hedge the sense of hearing against other kinds of conversation which may be injurious to the soul, and even work its ruin. It is evident that we cannot be too careful not to listen to unchaste words or discourse, which not only are a token of the corruption of him that utters them, but result in the corruption of the hearer.* The same holds good of amorous words, especially when coming from one of the opposite sex; words which, gently making their entrance, corrupt the heart with the sweet poison of a carnal attachment, extinguish all sense of devotion, and at times bring us to cast off altogether the holy fear of God. Who does not see how important it is to close one's ears against false maxims, which pervert the mind; against evil counsels, which seduce the heart; against praise, which puffs up and engenders pride; against flattery, which deludes and hoodwinks such as are not on their guard; against worldly and empty talk, which distracts the mind from godly thoughts, and dissipates the heart by earthly affections. In a word, we must ever remember that the sense of hearing is not protected by any natural barrier, but remains open to every word falling from the lips of others, and cannot of itself avoid them. It belongs, then, to us to guard it against harmful discourse.

CHAPTER III.

THE HARM WHICH THE SPIRITUAL LIFE MAY RECEIVE FROM THE SENSE OF SMELL.

181. THE most innocent of all our senses, and that which least of all hinders our perfection, is the sense of smell, for it is the weakest of all our senses, and therefore, it has also less power to do us harm. Ravens, bees, and vultures are gifted with a much keener

* Corrumpunt bonos mores colloquia prava.

scent than man, whence they perceive from afar all kinds of odours, and the stench of carrion. The same applies to dogs, which can follow their masters or track their prey by the aid of the mere impressions which these have left in passing. Albertus Magnus says, that this arises from the fact that in man the sense of smell is close to the brain, which in our case is very large, and by its humidity and coldness impedes this sense from the perfect exercise of its office.* But, whatever the cause may be, certain it is that God has disposed this with the wisest foresight, for the beasts stand greatly in need of the sense in question, to distinguish the food suitable to them from that which would be hurtful, and, amongst so many objects, to discern what is in harmony with their nature, and what is not in harmony : for which reason it is fitting that in animals this sense should be particularly keen. On the other hand, man, being endowed with reason and understanding, distinguishes by their aid the various kinds of objects with far more accuracy.

182. Nevertheless, even the sense of smell may be prejudicial to spiritual life, if a devout person go in quest of delicious scents, search after them in flowers, essences and perfumes, and carry them about him, perfuming his rooms, and eagerly seeking the pleasures such fragrancy affords to this sense; it being unquestionable that to seek sensual pleasure for the sole purpose of gratification is unlawful and sinful. Such indulgences are unbecoming even in worldlings, and when such are sought after in excess, they are so displeasing to God that He has sometimes given tokens of His anger by inflicting signal chastisements. Judge, then, for yourself how displeasing to Him will be this indulgence in spiritual persons, who have devoted themselves to His service. The instance St. Peter Damian relates of the punishment wherewith God visited, for this very reason, a certain lady, the wife of a Doge of Venice, is known to every one.† Besides other extraordinary luxuries wherewith this lady pampered her body, she would have her chamber perfumed with so many sweet-smelling gums and other scents, that the Saint is ashamed to enumerate them, fearing lest his readers should tax him with

* Tract. De Odore. † Epist. ad Blanceam Comitiss., cap 11.

exaggeration.* But God was not long ere He showed His displeasure at the excessive indulgence of this lady; for He struck her from head to foot with a most loathsome ulcer, which consumed the flesh from her bones, and from her putrid limbs there came such an unbearable stench, that neither her relatives, nor even her slaves and domestics, could go near her room. Only one servant, who held a strong scent to her nostrils, could be found to enter there, and hurriedly to render the most necessary services, after which she hastened to make her escape. Being thus, before her decease, reduced to the condition of a mass of carrion, the lady miserably expired. Nobody mourned her death, nor was it a grief to any one, but a release; for she had become abominable to all by the intolerable bad smell of her sores. Thus would God, concludes the Saint, show to every one, by this living corpse, that our vile flesh does not deserve to be all scented with perfumes.†

183. But a devout person must not be content with merely refusing to regale his nostrils with a variety of scents; if he truly love the mortification of his senses—a virtue so sought after by the true servants of God,—he must further endeavour to afflict his sense of smell by unsavoury odours, or at least bear patiently with such, when necessity requires, whether on account of the nature of the locality where he lives, or the habits of those with whom he dwells, and more especially when Christian charity demands it, as in attending on the sick, either in hospitals or in their own homes; following in this the example of so many saints, who, animated by this spirit of mortification and charity, even enjoyed the unpleasant exhalations of the sick, as much as if they had been in the midst of a flower-garden, or in walks bordered with fragrant roses.

184. The way wherein the holy Abbot Arsenius tortured this sense may be truly called heroic. We read, in the Lives of the Fathers of the Desert,‡ that he kept in his narrow cell a vessel of

* Ejus vero cubiculum tot thymiamatum, aromatumque generibus redolebat, ut et vobis narrare dedecus fatear, et auditor forte non credat.

† Quid enim sit caro, docet ipsa caro: quodque perhibet mortua, testatur viva.

‡ In Vit. Pat., sec. 36.

water in which to soak the palm-leaves so as to soften them and make them fit to be manufactured into baskets, which was the usual occupation of these saintly monks. In the course of time the water became putrid, and gave forth an insupportable stench. Still he would never allow the water to be thrown away, nor his cell to be rid of the foul smell. The monks, when visiting him, often said: "Father, get this vessel of water emptied, for its excessive stench is fit to drive every one away from your cell." "No," would he reply; "as an offset to the gratifications I allowed my nostrils with scents and perfumes whilst I was in the world, I must now afflict them by this stench, and must thereby make satisfaction to God for my former indulgence, lest He punish it in the life to come with penalties incomparably more severe." The devout may learn hereby how to mortify this sense, especially if in their past lives they have indulged or gratified it to excess.

CHAPTER IV.

PRACTICAL SUGGESTIONS TO DIRECTORS ON THE PRESENT ARTICLE.

185. FIRST suggestion. The Director will have understood before this (and I should think his own experience will have long since taught him the lesson), that wickedness makes its first entrance into the hearts of youth of both sexes by the sense of hearing. As we cannot close them against words, sayings, jokes, and discourse, which may tarnish the brightness of their innocency, the only means to preserve them unsullied is to keep young men at a distance from evil-tongued and dissolute companions, and to warn young girls to abstain, as far as possible, from dealing and conversing with men, else their ruin is beyond repair. I will here content myself with reminding all of the teaching left on record by a great master of the spiritual life, from whom they cannot withhold credence. This is none other than the great Doctor of the Church, St. Jerome.

186. In his letter to Leta, the Saint sets forth after what manner she should religiously train her young daughter; and lays down as a fundamental rule never to allow her to hear a loose word, or any profane songs.* In his letter to Demetrias he insists on her guarding against listening to immodest words, these being the snares which dissolute youths set for the virtue of young women.† But, in order that such poisonous words may never reach the ears of tender maidens, with the imminent risk of defiling their hearts, he gives the following advice to Leta: "Keep thy daughter ever by thee: never allow her to leave the house but in thy company. Let no youth, no perfumed fop hover around her. In church, during the sacred watches of the night, do not allow her to stir from thee the length of a finger."‡ He then goes on to say, that, when going to her country-seat, she must not leave her daughter at home, for the reason given above, lest the venomous hiss of some treacherous asp reach her chaste ears. In a word, she must train her to such reserve that she may not be able to live apart from her mother, and that when separated from her she may fear and tremble.§ He lays down the same rule for Demetrias, telling her to avoid as a pestilence and a deadly poison all young men with crisped locks, and bodies and garments sweetly perfumed, for, as he observes, these scented people are not always sweet in soul.|| He expressly warns her against the friendship and familiar acquaintance of married ladies, on account of the danger of hearing from them talk which poisons the heart; as, indeed, often happens from their carelessness and

* Turpia verba non intelligat, cantica mundi ignoret.

† Numquam verbum inhonestum audias. Perditæ mentis homines uno frequenter levique sermone tentant claustra pudicitiæ.

‡ Numquam absque te prodeat in publicum: nec basilicas martyrum, et ecclesias sine matre adeat. Nullus et juvenis, nullus cincinnatus assideat vigiliarum dies, et solemnes pernoctationes sic virguncula nostra celebret, ut ne transversum quidem unguem a matre discedat.

§ Si quando ad suburbana pergis, domi filiam non relinquas: nesciat sine te, nec possit vivere, et si sola fuerit, pertimescat.

|| Cincinnatos pueros et calamistratos, et peregrini muris olentes pelliculas, de quibus illud arbitrii est. Non bene olet, qui bene semper olet: quasi quasdam pestes, et venena pudicitiæ, devita.

unconcern in speaking on subjects which it befits not a virgin to hear.*

187. To these most prudent counsels I will add another, that girls (and the same holds good of boys also) be carefully kept at a distance from ill-behaved young people, because one such in a neighbourhood suffices, as experience shows, to implant evil in the minds of all by vicious discourse, and to sully the innocence of all the rest. Such are the principles whereby the Director must guide youth. He must forewarn them against hearkening to words which, going in by their ears, would at length infallibly corrupt their hearts. Such are the maxims which he must strive to engrave on the hearts of parents, in order that they too may know how to guard their children's ears, by which, much more than by any other sense, death makes its entrance into guileless hearts. But he will perhaps object that it is impossible to keep young people nowadays under so tight a rein as to guard them from ever hearing what is unfit for them to hear. Then, will I reply, it is impossible to keep them guileless and pure, and much more to lead them in the path of Christian perfection; for, if it be not possible to keep the gates closed against those who would rob them of their chastity, it will be no less so to preserve this virtue in them unblemished.

188. Second suggestion. I said in the foregoing Chapter that it is not enough to keep aloof from backbiters, but that we should rebuke them when we hear them make use of words which could unjustly blacken another's fair fame. It must be observed, however, that this doctrine often breeds scruples and anxiety in timorous and delicate consciences; for, on the one hand, finding themselves placed amid backbiters, they would wish to fulfil their duty; yet, on the other, they are kept back by a certain shamefacedness which makes them shrink from breaking forth into such rebukes, and leaves them in fear, and troubled with the notion that they have been guilty of sin. In order, then, to free these timid souls from such perplexities, the Director must apply to their

* Matronarum, maritis et sæculo inservientium, tibi consortia declinentur, ne sollicitetur animus, et audiat quid vel maritus uxori, vel uxor locuta sit viro. Venenatæ sunt hujusmodi confabulationes.

case the counsel which masters of the spiritual life usually give to prevent us from going astray in these matters; and by the light of their advice explain and clearly set forth the doctrine I have laid down above. The backbiter is either our superior, our equal, or our inferior. If he be our superior, the penitent is not bound (nor would it, in many instances, be even lawful) to address to him a public rebuke, lest by so doing he should fail in due respect. Yet he must not show his approval of such talk by laughter or cheerfulness of look, nor by applauding the remarks made; and especially must he take heed not to induce the speaker, by putting questions, to continue his malicious discourse, or to aggravate its malignity, for fear that he co-operate in anywise in the sin and be guilty of it himself. But he must maintain an appearance of reserve and, as I have said above, must put on a certain serious air. St. Jerome makes a telling comparison in regard of this matter. An arrow, says he, that is strongly propelled, if it strike against a rock or some other hard body rebounds against him who shot it forth. Thus too, backbiting, when it meets with a grave countenance, which signifies disapproval and displeasure, rebounds against the backbiter, strikes him dumb, makes his heart sink and dries up the words upon his lips.* This course must always be adopted whenever there is no other means of hindering detraction. One may also begin to excuse and take up the defence of the person who is assailed by an evil tongue, as our Lord took on Himself the defence of Magdalen against the murmurings of Judas.† But this expedient is not always suitable, as at times the backbiter may endeavour to give proof of what he advances, and, instead of withdrawing, will go on detracting with more violence. Hence this means should be employed only when there is reason to await a good result from undertaking the defence of the absent party.

* Sicut enim sagitta, si mittatur contra duram materiam, nonnumquam in mittentem revertitur, et vulnerat, vulnerantem: ita detractor, cum tristem faciem viderit audientis, immo non audientis, sed obturantis aures suas, ne audiat judicium sanguinis, illico conticescit, pallet vultus, hærent labia, saliva siccatur. Epist. 4.

† Quid molesti estis huic mulieri? bonum opus operata est in me. Matth. xxvi. 10.

189. But if the backbiter be our equal, unless the penitent deem it profitable and opportune to administer to him a mild and charitable rebuke, he should at least divert the conversation, as I have already advised in a foregoing Chapter, and he should start some new topic of discussion. This was the custom of that illustrious Gentleman, renowned Chancellor, and far-famed Martyr of England, Sir Thomas More. His biographer tells us that whenever any discourse was started injurious to the character of any one, he immediately passed on to another subject. He would, for instance, without any exordium or preface, put in: "You may say what you like, but I maintain that this house is very well built, and that he who planned it was an able architect."* The backbiter, meanwhile considering that this sentence did not correspond to what he was talking about, became aware of his mistake, stopped short, and held his tongue. But if it be possible, without any too abrupt transition, to introduce another topic, it is always better. This abrupt method is seasonable only when other and more appropriate means of silencing a backbiter fail to occur to the mind.

190. Lastly, if the detractor be an inferior—as, for instance, a son, a servant, a wife, a scholar, a subject—the penitent must in nowise withhold reproof; since he is bound to correct the speaker, both by the obligation of his office and out of charity. He may address to him, in such case, these words of St. John Chrysostom to the people of Antioch :† "Let us flee, my children, let us flee detraction, that diabolical vice. It is the devil that tempts you to speak thus, in order that you may burden your conscience by speaking against others." These are the rules which the Director should give to his penitents, in order that the detraction they chance to hear may not have any power to tarnish their souls.

191. Third suggestion. The Director will also warn his peni-

* Dicat quisque quod volet ; ego dico domum illam pulcherrime extructam ; eumque qui fecit, excellentem esse in suâ arte magistrum, atque architectum. Th. Stapleton In Ejus Vitâ.

† Fugiamus, dilecti, fugiamus detractores, docti quod est totum satanicum barathrum insidiarum ejus hæc incessio. Ut enim nostra negligamus, et graviores nobis reatus constituamus, in hanc nos consuetudinem diabolus ducit. Hom. 3. ad Pop. Antioch.

tents against listening, or giving credence to certain backbitings which bear a semblance of zeal, but which in reality are the most malignant of all. I will brand them for him with the indignant words of St. Bernard: "Some there are who, unable to conceal the malice they bear within them, murmur against their neighbours' doings, but cloak their wickedness under the appearances of a false modesty, and under a masked humility. You may see them, before they vomit forth their detraction, begin with affected sighs, and then pour out their slanders with a sorrowful face, with eyes downcast and full of tears, with grave and hesitating speech. Such detraction as this does by far the most harm, as it wins readier credence, since the hearer thinks that all is spoken, not out of malice or passion, but with a feeling of commiseration, and with much reluctance."* The holy Doctor then proceeds to set forth the words these hypocritical backbiters are accustomed to make use of in order to conceal their venom. "It cuts me to the heart," will they say, "that he should have behaved in such a manner, for I wish him well, but I have not succeeded in correcting him as I desired." Another will say, "I was well aware that he had fallen into such and such a fault, and I should never have said a word about it, only, as it has been mentioned publicly, I cannot deny the fact, and must say, with tears in my eyes, that the thing really did happen thus;" and then they will add, "He is most certainly, in many things, worthy of praise, but, to tell the truth, in this matter he cannot be excused."

192. Others, as St. John Chrysostom says, make use of a different artifice in order to backbite without seeming to do so. They

* Alii autem quodam simulatæ verecundiæ fuco conceptam malitiam, quam retinere non possunt, adumbrare conantur Videas præmitti alta suspiria, sicque cum quâdam gravitate, et tarditate, mæsto vultu, demissis superciliis, et voce plangenti egredi maledictionem; et quidem tanto persuasibilem, quanto creditur, ab his qui audiunt, corde invito, et magis condolenti affectu, quam malitiose proferri. Doleo, inquit, vehementer pro eo, quod eum diligo satis, et numquam potui de hâc re corrigere eum Et alius: Mihi quidem, ait, bene compertus fuerat de illo istud: sed per me numquam innotuisset. Sed quoniam per alterum patefacta res est, veritatem negare non possum: dolens dico, revera ita est. Et addit grande damnum nam alias quidem in pluribus valet: ceterùm in hâc parte, ut verum fateamur, excusari minime potest. Serm 24 in Cantica.

disclose to certain persons their neighbours' secret faults, exacting from them the strictest silence, and recommending them not to tell any one what has been spoken to them in confidence, intending by this artifice to appear anxious for the character of others, at the very time that they are unjustly blackening it. "But do you not see," says the Saint, "that you yourself declare what you are doing to be vile, and worthy of blame? For if it be unlawful for your confidant to discover to others the fault of a neighbour, it was far more improper in you to be the first to reveal it."*

193. This being premised, as the Director should rebuke these hypocritical backbiters, if any such present themselves to him in the Confessional, and should give them to understand that the most venomous detraction, and that which does the greatest harm to our neighbour's character, is precisely that which is concealed under the cloak of pity, of commiseration and zeal (for, as St. Bernard says, such finds more ready credence from listeners); so must he warn simple-minded and timorous persons to guard their ears against the insinuations of these busy detractors, so full of zeal; and to place no trust in them, unless indeed—as may occasionally happen—they are led to speak on the matter through some real and just motive, to promote the advantage of their neighbour and the glory of God. For some there are who, in very deed, under the guise of harmless sheep, have the heart of a wolf for their neighbours. Christian charity teaches to hide, and not to speak of the faults which we may ourselves observe, or which may in any other manner come to our knowledge, to keep them secret, and never lay them bare before the eyes of others. We read in the Lives of the Fathers of the Desert, that a certain monk went to Abbot Pastor, and plainly told him that he intended to quit the desert, and to go elsewhere, because he had heard a very disedifying report of a brother monk. The servant of God replied that he should not credit such reports, which oftener than

* Hoc vere magis ridiculum est, quod cum aliquid arcanum dixerint, rogant audientem, et adjurant, ne cuiquam alteri amplius dicat; hinc declarantes, quod rem reprehensione dignam commiserunt. Si enim illum, ut nemini dicat, rogas; multo magis te priorem huic dicere non oportebat. Hom. 3 ad Pop. Antiochen.

not are false. The monk made answer, that his informant was an honest, trustworthy person. "But," rejoined the Saint, "if he were truly such as you describe him, he would not have told you these things." A most fitting observation, which should make us beware how we give ear to those who, under pretence of zeal, are ever blaming the doings of others.

194. Fourth suggestion. If the Director have charge of persons who attend seriously to their own progress, he should induce them to converse on spiritual things when they engage in social intercourse. First, because he will thereby cut off the occasion of much vain and empty talk, which is hurtful to spiritual life; and, secondly, such conversation enkindles fervour, even as hot coals placed together communicate their heat to each other, and help one another to burn. He must, however, forbid two things: one, retailing the instructions and directions they receive from their Confessors, as these confidences are (especially with women) a source of ill-feeling, jealousy, suspicion, and murmuring against their own Director; they are, in a word, the cause of countless evils: the second, communicating to others the favours or graces, if any, that they receive in prayer, or the acts of virtue they practise; for this is an occasion of vanity and self-complacency, especially in persons of the weaker sex.

ARTICLE V.

The hindrance to perfection resulting from the tongue, considered not as one of the five senses, but as the organ of speech.

CHAPTER I.

THE DIFFICULTY OF RESTRAINING THE TONGUE FROM TRANSGRESSING TO THE PREJUDICE OF SPIRITUAL LIFE.

195. In the second Article we spoke of the tongue, considered as the organ of taste; as one, that is, of those five senses which we

have in common with the brutes. We were not then studying it as the instrument of the noble function in which the brute creation can claim no share, and which, properly speaking, belongs not to sense but to reason; I mean speech, discourse, and conversation. The order of our plan did not allow of our previously treating this matter. But since the tongue is a great hindrance to Christian perfection, not only when it acts as an organ of bodily sense, but much more when it becomes the instrument by which the faculties of our soul disclose and make manifest the acts of the reason; it is fitting that, after having done our best to give rules for restraining the tongue in movements which belong to the viler portion of our nature, we should proceed to lay open some principles for its regulation when it is the organ of speech; acting as which it exercises a most noble power. To this subject then we shall devote the present Article.

196. It cannot possibly be doubted that of all the members of our body the most difficult to be kept in check is the tongue; for the Apostle St. James says as much in unmistakable language: *Every nature of beasts, and of birds, and of serpents is tamed, and has been tamed by the nature of man; but the tongue no man can tame.** "It is most strange," writes St. Augustine, commenting on these words of the Apostle; "man by his art can tame lions, and render tractable the fiercest wild beasts, yet he cannot tame his tongue. Man who tames all things else, cannot tame himself in the department of his tongue."† Hence the holy Doctor, knowing full well the unruliness of this member, and having in his own case experienced its violence, bitterly complains of it to God in his Confessions, and avows that he is unable to discover the ways and means of keeping it within due bounds. "The tongue," he says, "is an ever-raging furnace, at one moment casting forth words all heated with the fire of impatience, at another, inflamed by burning words of anger and indignation; now, words blackened

* Omnis natura bestiarum, et volucrum, et serpentium, et cæterorum domantur, et domita sunt a naturâ humanâ; linguam autem nullus hominum domare potest. Jac. iij. 7.

† Homo domat feram, et non domat linguam: domat leonem, et non frenat sermonem: domat ipse, et non domat seipsum. Serm. 4, De Verb. Dom. cap. I.

with the smoke of vanity; now, idle words spoken without any purpose; and now again, it suddenly bursts out in words which wound charity. Thou, my God, commandest me to restrain and keep it within due bounds. But though with my other passions and temptations I may rely somewhat on myself, with this only is it impossible."* In the same sentiment of profound humility does St. Gregory of Nazianzus complain of his tongue, and own that, despite his declining years and failing strength, he had not yet quite succeeded in bringing that member into perfect subjection.† Now if the very saints, who guarded their tongue so jealously in all that they said, could yet speak thus of themselves, what will become of us if we are not careful of our words? Into what numberless sins and faults must we needs fall! Unhappy creatures that we are!

197. St. John Chrysostom aptly remarks that, God knowing how dangerous and slippery is this organ of our body, has fenced it round with the double wall of the lips and teeth, so that it may not be wholly free to transgress by the words it utters.‡ The hands and feet are free in their several motions; there is no bar to the hearing of the ears, or to the smelling of the nostrils; the eyes are veiled by the single covering of the eyelids, interposed between the sight and the objects seen. Yet free and unfettered as are these senses, they are quite tractable compared with the tongue, which, although enclosed within a double fence of teeth, and within the strong rampart of the lips, cannot be tamed nor brought under effectual restraint.§

198. The saintly Abbot Pambo was well aware of this.||

* Quotidiana fornax nostra, est humana lingua. Imperas mihi et in hoc genere continentiam. Da quod jubes, et jube quod vis. Est qualiscumque in aliis generibus tentationum mihi facultas explorandi me, in hoc pene nulla est. Confes., lib. x., cap. 37.

† Morbo effœtum, et senectute fractum, et debilitatum, tamen non potuisse effugere linguæ indomitæ calamitatem. De Silentio in Quadrag. Jejun.

‡ Deus eam veluti muro duplici voluit circumdari. Nam dentium tegmine, et labiorum custodiâ lingua continetur, ne verba improvidâ garrulitate proferantur. Ad Baptizand.

§ Linguam autem nullus homo domare potest.

|| Hist. Tripart., lib. viij., cap. 3.

Hearing, on one occasion, from the lips of a holy monk these words of the Royal Prophet, *"I will take heed to my ways, so as not to offend by my tongue;** "Stop, Father," he said, "go no further. I will hear the rest when I shall have put this great lesson into practice." Being asked, after the lapse of many years, why he had not returned to the great servant of God, in order to have some further spiritual instruction, he replied, "Because I am not yet perfect in the first lesson which I received:" meaning by this, that, after years of strenuous endeavour, of watchfulness and mortification, he had not yet attained a perfect mastery over his tongue. Hence, too, for three whole years together, the Abbot Agatho kept a pebble in his mouth, in order, by sheer force, to restrain and, so to say, crush down this unruly member; very much as is done with snakes which, being able to slip through the hands with great ease, are fastened to the ground and then crushed with a stone.

199. And, indeed, no one can be so well aware of the truth of all this as Directors themselves, for whose behoof chiefly I am writing; since they continually experience it in the sacred tribunal where they exercise their sovereign authority. After long practice in hearing Confessions, they will have met with many individuals who have mended grave faults to which they were subject; generously forsaken the occasions which were to them a snare; uprooted from their hearts some cherished vice in which they were deeply immersed; even courageously renounced the pomps and vanities of the world, of which they had hitherto been slaves, deserving of the more pity as their slavery was voluntary. But the Confessor, depend upon it, has never met with persons who have gained perfect mastery over their tongue, even though he may have spent many years in the sacred ministry. For some are always sliding back into impatient or peevish words; others into idle and vain talk; this one cannot refrain from sarcasm, from those sharp sayings which are but little in unison with Christian charity; that other cannot keep his tongue from certain petty murmurings and criticisms in which he habitually indulges. Others, again, cannot keep themselves from always boasting. And as for those whose conscience is not

* Custodiam vias meas, ut non delinquam in linguâ meâ.

over-tender, the Confessor will find that they have ever the same blasphemies, the same curses, the same detraction, the same loose conversation on their lips. In a word, as the Son of Sirach has well said, *Who is there that has not offended with his tongue?** Such a one, if he can be found, is truly called "Blessed." *Blessed is the man that hath not slipped by a word out of his mouth.*† Such a one, the Apostle St. James goes on:—*If he offend not in word, . . . may be called a perfect man.*‡

200. But what follows from all this? Are we to allow our tongue to go on unchecked, uttering all sorts of words to the prejudice of God and our neighbour? Assuredly not. It follows rather that we must of necessity employ means for bridling it, of so much the greater efficacy as its unruliness is the greater. A fiery and spirited young horse that rears and plunges, neighs, snorts, and struggles, is not left to its own whims, but care is taken to break it in with a rougher bit and with sharper spurs, and, should these prove insufficient, no pains are spared to bring it under by severity, with thong and stick. In like manner, just because the tongue is so unruly and so difficult to manage, so liable to overstep the limits of what is lawful in its speech, we must, in its case too, employ the most effectual and the harshest means to keep it in check; so that it may not, as too often happens, hinder our progress towards Christian perfection. We shall now proceed to set forth in detail the nature of these means.

CHAPTER II.

MEANS OF BRIDLING THE TONGUE.

201. THE first means of bridling the tongue is to ask this grace of God, and to ask it unceasingly, repeating constantly with the Royal Prophet: *Set, O Lord, a watch before my mouth, a door of*

* Quis est qui non deliquerit in linguâ suâ? Ecclus. xix. 17.

† Beatus vir, qui non est lapsus verbo ex ore suo Ecclus xiv. 1.

‡ Si quis in verbo non offendit, hic perfectus est vir. Jac. iij 2.

*circumspection round about my lips, that they may not be thoughtlessly opened, and let out words displeasing to Thee.** St. Augustine sets forth, with that depth and subtlety which marks his genius, the necessity that exists of making use of this means in order to bring the tongue into subjection. "The tongue," says the holy Doctor, resting on the words of St. James, "no man can tame; hence thou canst not tame thine own, for thou art a man: so that thou must needs have continual recourse to God that He may do for thee what thou art not able to do for thyself." This the Saint makes clear by several well-chosen comparisons. "The horse," he says, "the camel, the elephant, the ass, the lion, do not tame themselves, neither can man tame himself. And as, to reclaim the horse and other animals from their savage state, the art and industry of man are required; so, to tame man and his unruly tongue, we also require the help and grace of God. Cease not, then, to have recourse to Him, to recommend thyself to Him, if thou wouldst tame thy tongue."† Nor could he have said anything more to the purpose. And thus it only remains for me to add that a spiritual person should especially beg of God the amendment of that fault of the tongue into which he has a habit of falling, and which, despite all the diligence he has used, he has not succeeded in amending. A patient is not content with asking the physician in a general way to heal his ailment, but points out the particular disease under which he is suffering; and for this he craves suitable remedies, for he feels that a special malady needs a special medicine. In this manner ought we also to deal with God.

202. Second means. After having recommended ourselves to

* Pone Domine custodiam ori meo et ostium circumstantiæ labiis meis. Ps. cxl. 3.

† Intelligamus carissimi: si *linguam nullus* hominum *domare potest*, ad Deum confugiendum est qui domet linguam nostram. Si enim eam domare volueris, non potes quia homo es: *linguam nullus* hominum *domare potest.* Attende similitudinem ab ipsis bestiis quas domamus. Equus non se domat: camelus non se domat: elephantus non se domat: aspis non se domat: leo non se domat: sic et homo non se domat. Sed ut equus dometur, bos, camelus, elephantus, leo, aspis, quæritur homo. Ergo Deus quæratur, ut dometur homo. Ergo, domine, *refugium tu factus es nobis.* Serm. 4, De Verb. Dom. cap. 2.

God, we must, on our part, make strong and firm resolutions, not once only, but repeatedly, to bridle our tongue. We should often ponder over the enormous evils to which an unrestrained and wanton tongue gives birth, so that being duly impressed and penetrated with some at least of these evils, we may urge our will to an energetic determination to keep it in check. *The tongue*, says St. James, *is a little member, and boasts great things. Behold how small a fire how great a wood it kindles.** The tongue is a fire; for from that little member proceeds the conflagration of anger, hate, revenge, slander, strife, and of numberless other evils. Well then might the Apostle say, *The tongue is a fire; a world of iniquity.*† Conformably with these words of St. James, St. Gregory of Nazianzus, when treating of the tongue, says: "Who will ever be able to recount the woes to which our tongues give rise? It alone, if it lists, is able to set house after house on fire, to enkindle strife between city and city, between subjects and their ruler; even as a spark falling amidst straw can grow into a vast and devouring conflagration."‡

203 *The tongue*, continues the same Apostle, *is among our members, so that it defiles the whole body.*§ St. Bernard aptly comments on this passage, saying: "Who can count the defilements which take their rise from this little member? There is the tongue which is ever given to vain and idle talk: and the lecherous tongue which breaks forth into unbecoming words, the proud tongue boasting of itself:—the former of these two being the slave of lust, the latter that of arrogance.¶ There is the deceitful tongue which

* Lingua quidem modicum membrum est, et magna exaltat. Jac. iij 5.

† Ecce quantus ignis quam magnam sylvam incendit. et lingua ignis est, universitas iniquitatis. Ibid. 5. 6.

‡ Quis autem, quot mala ex eâ oriantur, ratione consequi possit? Domum cum domo, si ita voluerit, urbem cum urbe, principem cum populo, populum rursus cum principe statim ac sine ullo negotio committit: non aliter atque igniculus stipulæ admotus in magnum incendium cito excrescens. De Silentio Quadrag. Jejun.

§ Lingua constituitur in membris nostris, quæ maculat totum corpus.

|| Quis sane numeret, quantas modicum linguæ membrum contrahat sordes? De Trip. Cust. Manûs, Linguæ, et Cordis.

¶ Est lingua dissoluta in sermonibus otiosis, est lingua impudica, est magniloqua; quarum prima lasciviæ, sequens arrogantiæ famulatur.

with its lies misleads, or with its flatteries betrays. There is the evil tongue which at one time stabs you in front by injurious and contumelious words; at another pierces you behind your back by calumnies and detractions."* The Saint concludes: "Since we have to give a strict account to God of every idle word, what will not be the rigour of the account required of us for so many lying words, words of anger, biting, insulting, vain, proud, impure, flattering words, and words to the prejudice of the fair fame of others?"† Is not this enough to make any Christian, especially one who is at all in earnest about his perfection, take a firm and generous resolution to keep in check this dissolute and unruly member, and to keep it within bounds even at the cost of his blood and of his very life? So much the more as our tongue is a treacherous and most daring member, which refuses to be subject to any one, be he sinner or saint, perfect or imperfect, secular or religious; but, so to speak, gets the upper hand of us all, and betrays us all into numberless faults.

204. St. Antoninus relates that the devil appeared one night to St. Dominic, who was in the church absorbed in devout prayer.‡ The Saint, nothing daunted at the vision, took occasion from it to inquire what were the snares which the fiend set for the Religious, in order to make them his prey. He, therefore, asked the demon what temptation was used against the Brethren while assembled in choir to sing the divine praises. The answer was, "I make them come late to church, and I make them hurry to leave it." The Saint next led the devil to the dormitory, and asked—"How do you tempt my religious in this place?" He replied, "I make them be long in getting to sleep, that they may be slow in rising, and come late to the Divine Office; and I strive, moreover, to disturb their minds with unclean thoughts."

* Est etiam lingua dolosa et lingua maledica, quarum altera in falsiloquam et adulatoriam dividitur: altera vero nunc in face contumelias irrogat, nunc detrahit in occulto.

† Quod si de omni vel otioso verbo, quodcumque locuti fuerint homines Deo reddituri sunt rationem in die judicii, quanto districtius de verbo mendaci, mordaci et injurioso, de elato, de lascivo, de adulatorio, de detractorio judicabuntur?

‡ Histor., Part. Tert. tit. 23. cap. 4, sec. 6.

St. Dominic then took the fiend to the refectory: "What are your temptations here?" was the question. "Some I urge," was the reply, "to intemperance by excessive eating, while I tempt others not to eat at all, so that they may become weak and unable to undergo the fatigues of their rule." At last they came to the public recreation-room, where the custom was that the friars should spend an hour in innocent conversation. "And here," said the Saint, "how do you tempt these servants of God?" At this question the demon began to roll his tongue about in his mouth, and instead of speaking, to make an inarticulate noise. The Saint becoming suspicious at this strange style of answer, compelled him to speak plainly. The demon then said, "This place belongs wholly to me;* it is here I make my profits:" meaning thereby that though they who conversed in that place were otherwise good and holy persons, they never left it without some failing or shortcoming. If, then, the tongue be the source of so many evils, from which none are wholly free, reason requires that everybody—those especially who really love their progress in virtue—should make a sincere and hearty resolution to keep it in check, whatever it may cost.

205. But, that such resolve may prove effectual, it is necessary for each person to watch over himself, and proceed carefully in his speech; to examine and weigh well his words; not doing like some, who open their mouths and let their words go forth without the least forethought. Such manner of conversing is full of sin and imperfection. Not so did King David, as he tells us of himself: *I have said, I will take heed to my ways, that I sin not with my tongue.*† St. Augustine, in his commentary on these words, says, that our tongue swims, so to speak, in a liquid medium, for which reason it easily slips." The Royal Prophet, knowing this, and seeing on the one hand the necessity which he was under to make use of this member, in order to manifest his thoughts, determined in his own heart to use it with such care, as not to utter words of which he would hereafter have to

* Hic locus totus meus est.

† Dixi: Custodiam vias meas ut non delinquam in linguâ meâ. Ps. xxxviij. 2.

repent. "Do thou likewise," adds the holy Doctor: "think well on what thou art about to say; reflect on thine inward thought, examine it carefully, and then manifest it to him who is listening to thee."*

206. St. Ambrose, commenting on the same verse, says, "There are ways which we must follow, and other ways against which we must guard: we must follow the ways of the Lord, and take heed to our own. Thou wilt take heed to thy ways (that is the path of thy perfection), when thou shalt be not over-ready and hasty, but slow and circumspect in thy speech." Because, as one who has to cross a deep river does not rush all at once into the water, but goes very carefully, and first tries the ford; so, when about to undertake discourse which abounds with so many occasions of fall, do not throw thyself into it, proceed slowly, speak with maturity and reflection.† An instruction which is wholly conformable with what is taught by St. James, whom we have so often quoted. *Let every man be quick to hear, but slow to speak* ‡

207. We read in the Lives of the Fathers of the Desert,§ that two monks embarked in a boat in order to reach the solitude where the Abbot St. Antony lived; for they were desirous of receiving from him some spiritual counsel. They found on board a venerable old man who was Abbot of the monastery in which he lived, and who, like them, was going to visit St. Antony. During the whole voyage the two monks never ceased talking together, while the old man did not once open his mouth, but maintained a rigorous silence. At length, they in talking, he in silence, arrived at the monastery where the great St. Antony dwelt. On their entrance, the Saint came at once to meet them,

* Non enim lingua frustra in udo est, nisi quia facile labitur. Videns ergo quam esset difficile, ut necessitatem loquendi haberet homo et in loquendo non aliquid diceret, quod se dixisse nollet . . . statuerat non loqui, ne aliquid diceret quod loquutum se esse pœniteret. . . . Custodi ergo vias tuas, et noli delinquere in linguâ tuâ: perpende quod dicturus es: examina, consule interiorem veritatem: et sic profer ad exteriorem auditorem. In Ps. xxxviij.

† Aliæ sunt viæ quas debemus sequi, aliæ, quas custodire: sequi vias Domini; custodire nostras. Potes autem custodire, si non cito loquaris.

‡ Sit autem omnis homo velox ad audiendum, tardus ad loquendum. Jac. i. 19.

§ De Mortif. Prop. Sens.

and courteously addressing the two monks, said, "I congratulate you upon the agreeable company which you have had during your journey in this saintly old man, and you, Father Abbot, on being escorted by these two good monks." "Yes, holy Father," replied the old man, "they are both good, and I take them to be so; but they always keep their door open:" meaning by this that they ever kept their mouths open, and cast forth, with little reflection and caution, whatever came into their minds or hearts.* And it was his opinion, that unless they looked to this failing, they would never be able to attain to much perfection. A spiritual man must then take heed not to leave his door open to every thought that wishes to go forth, but rather must keep watch and ward over it; and, as a diligent door-keeper, who takes care of the house of his soul, reflect what words it is meet to allow to go out, and what words it is proper to keep at home: lest his speech involve him in countless faults and sins. Even the pagans considered it blameworthy to speak without thought and without reflection. Thus we read of a certain Anasimo, a ready but random talker, that beginning one day to speak in the presence of a number of venerable people, Theocritus of Chios got up and said, "Listen attentively, for Anasimo is beginning to speak, with his usual flood of words, and his one drop of sense."† A severe rebuke this, and one calculated to make the man blush. In order not to deserve it, we should apply to ourselves the advice of the Wise Man, *Make a balance for thy words, and a just bridle for thy mouth,*‡ which comes to this, that we should proceed with reflection in our discourse, if we want to prevent our tongue leading us astray.

* Hoc autem dicebat, quia quodcumque ascendebat in corda ipsorum, hoc loquebantur

† Incipit flumen verborum, mentis gutta. Stobæus Serm 34.

‡ Verbis tuis facito stateram et frenos ori tuo rectos. Ecclus. xxviij. 29.

CHAPTER III.

SILENCE ANOTHER MEANS FOR CURBING THE TONGUE.

208. BY Silence, I am far from implying that a decent person is to make up his mind never to speak again. I would have him converse in all due moderation when speech is suitable, and hold his peace when it is time to keep silence. This is the lesson given by Ecclesiastes: *There is a time to keep silence, and a time to speak.** When it is time to speak, we should speak with due moderation; when it is time to be silent, we should keep silence rigorously. "The tongue," says St. Gregory, "must be held in with prudence; it must not be bound so fast as never to be loosened for a single word.† Account must be taken of times and seasons," continues the Saint. "At times it is the hour of silence; then we must tighten the reins over the tongue; but, when the time to speak has come, we must loosen the bridle: for, as inopportune speech is unseemly and so is undue loquacity, in like manner, to hold one's peace when it is time to speak, is unseasonable and a proof of negligence and disorder."‡ He then cites the words of the royal Psalmist: *Set a watch, O Lord, before my mouth, and a door round about my lips:* § and observes that David prayed God to set a door, not a wall, before his lips. Now, the difference between a wall and a door is this, as all know, that a wall keeps those in the house always shut in; while a door opens and shuts, and alternately admits visitors or debars them entrance. "Hence," he continues, "the Psalmist asks not for a wall to keep his lips ever closed, but for a door which he may open at fitting times to discreet speech, and which at

* Tempus tacendi et tempus loquendi. Eccles. iij. 7.

† Lingua directe frænanda est, non indissolubiliter obliganda. Pastoral., cap. 3. Admon. 15.

‡ Discrete quippe vicissitudinum pensanda sunt tempora, ne aut cum restringi lingua debet, per verba inutiliter diffluat, aut cum loqui utiliter potest semetipsam pigre restringat.

§ Pone, Domine, custodiam ori meo, et ostium circumstantiæ labiis meis. Ps. cxl. 3.

other times he may shut against all discourse, remaining absolutely silent."*

209. We are, then, to speak when it is proper to speak, when necessity or civility require it, whether for our own or our neighbour's advantage, or for the lawful solace which may be justly claimed by one whose mind is weary and needing repose. But we must shun excessive talk, in order to avoid dissipating our own soul, or annoying or being burdensome to those about us by superabundant discourse: never interrupting others, out of an eagerness to speak, when they are occupied in conversing. The Athenians had decreed the building of a sumptuous palace for a public purpose. Two of the most famous architects that could be found in their city were chosen. Having been introduced into the assembly in order to give their opinion, and to set forth their plans and ideas of the form that this magnificent building was to take, and of the means to give it majesty, beauty, and the fitting conveniences, one of them spoke in a copious and unbecoming style, which was irksome to all the venerable assembly. The other being called upon to give his opinion, summarily expressed it in these few words: "I am ready to carry out in act what the speaker has just proposed at such length."† This pithy and concise speech pleased the meeting as much as the unbounded and unseasonable discourse of the earlier speaker had disgusted them; so the commission for the work was given to the man of fewest words.‡ Hence our readers may learn that, in order not to make themselves troublesome to their hearers by their talk, they must follow the advice of Seneca, and not leave their tongues free to run loose in lengthy and superfluous speech, but restrain their impetuous desire of chattering: a kind of disease under which some labour.§

* Quod bene Psalmista considerans, dicit: *Pone, Domine, custodiam ori meo, et ostium circumstantiæ labiis meis.* Non enim poni ori suo parietem, sed ostium petit, quod videlicet aperitur et clauditur Unde et nobis caute discendum est, quatenus os discrete et congruo tempore vox aperiat et rursus congruo taciturnitas claudat.

† Ego opere adimplebo quod iste tot verbis amplificavit.

‡ Plut. apud Labat. tom. 3. De Operibus Bonis pro Popul.

§ Optimum est ad primum mali sensum mederi sibi, tum verbis suis minimum libertatis dare et inhibere impetum. De Irâ. Lib. iii.

210 Young people of either sex are especially called upon to observe this moderation of speech, according to the saying of Cleanthes; for as it belongs to them to learn rather than to teach, so it is more becoming to them to listen than to speak.* St. Basil, writing of virgins, states, that they should keep themselves much under control when speaking, and that when occasion offers of conversing with any person, they should listen a great deal and say very little.† Abbot Nesterotes, as Cassian relates, exhorting his monks in a spiritual conference to silence, turned to a certain John, at that time a mere youth, and said to him that it was particularly his duty to be silent, as to speak was not proper for one of his age, who ought to be wholly intent on hearing and putting into practice the lessons of his elders.‡ This is so true, that Abbot Pastor, on account of this very reserve in speaking, awarded to Agatho a praise which to some might seem excessive; for being engaged in a spiritual conference in an assembly of monks, he gave him the title of Abbot. The others marvelled greatly at so unusual a thing. "Why," they asked, "do you call Agatho an Abbot, seeing that he is only a youth of tender years?" "Because," replied Pastor, "his silence shows him to be such."§ By which saying he meant that nothing is so apt to win esteem and respect for a young man (and this is still more true of a young woman) as reserve in speech, especially when in company with their elders. For this is an unmistakable token of a modest and retiring disposition, and of a humble and well-regulated mind; virtues which have a peculiar suitableness in the young.

211. On the other hand, if a youth is eager to speak much, and, as we commonly say, to act the most important part, especially in

* Maxime juvenibus convenire silentium. Laertius, lib. vij., cap. 2.

† Castigatâ itaque locutione prudens virgo utetur, cumque tempestive quempiam oportuerit alloqui, multo audiet plura, quam dicet. De Verâ Virginitate.

‡ Observate in primis, et maxime tu, Joannes, cui magis ad custodiendum ea quæ dicturus sum ætas adhuc adolescentior suffragatur, ne studium lectionis et desiderii tui labor vanâ elatione cassetur, ut indicas ori tuo silentium: hic enim est primus disciplinæ actualis ingressus: omnis quippe labor hominis in ore ipsius: et ut omnium senior instituta, atque sententias intento corde et quasi muto ore suscipias, ac diligenter in pectore tuo condens ad perficienda ea potius, quam ad docenda. Collat. xiv.

§ Quia os suum facit eum nominari abbatem.

the company of grave and elderly people, such conduct is ever looked upon as an unsufferable impertinence and a mark of great forwardness. Laertius relates* of a certain youth, that being at a banquet, he began to chatter like a magpie, making more noise and uttering more words than all the others put together. Zeno, who was at the table, having borne with this for a long time, but being unable to put up any longer with such folly, raised his voice, saying, "Your ears seem to have been changed into a tongue:"† by which he meant that a young man should employ his ears to listen, rather than his tongue to speak; while on the contrary, this youth seemed to have no ears, and to be all tongue. The same philosopher said to a young man infected with the like disease of loquacity, "Remember that God has given thee a pair of ears, and only one tongue, that thou mayest listen much and speak little." He likewise rebuked another who was too fond of hearing himself talk, by observing, "See: with what a dangerous fluxion that poor youth is attacked, all his brains seem to be running away from his tongue!" A disgraceful reproof, which every young man who has been properly educated should be careful not to deserve.

212. Again, we must hold our tongue and keep entire silence when duty requires this conduct. A general rule meeting each individual case cannot, of course, be laid down upon this point; for Religious are bound to a kind of silence quite different from that which should be kept by people living in the world; and even among Religious the degree of the silence to be observed differs according to the different character of their particular Institute. This only can be said in general, that spiritual persons of all classes should endeavour to make for themselves a certain retirement which shall be in harmony with their condition, in which retirement they may keep a silence more or less rigid; for, as the Holy Ghost teaches, *In a multitude of words there wanteth not sin:*‡ whence we may infer that innocence and purity of conscience are usually the companions of solitude and silence, under the shadow of which we are able to enjoy a certain exemption from sin. The

* Lib. vij, cap. 1. † Aures tibi in linguam defluxerunt.
‡ In multiloquio non deerit peccatum. Prov. x. 19

Lacedemonians were much given to silence, and were very brief in their manner of speech. Hence a certain Spartan named Caryllus having been asked why Lycurgus had given so few laws to his fellow-citizens, replied, "They who keep silence and are sparing of their words do not need many laws:"* meaning that such are not liable to go astray. We conclude, then, that all who make profession of piety and devotion, should be careful to set aside certain intervals in every day when they may withdraw to their room, or to the church, in order to meditate or pray vocally, or to read some spiritual book; and, as far as may be, should labour in this privacy to gain recollection for the mind which has been dissipated and scattered by converse with their neighbours. We must remember that the Holy Spirit places our security wholly in the custody of the tongue: *He that keeps his mouth keeps his soul*,† giving us to know that he who guards his lips keeps his soul from all harm. In another place, again, the Holy Ghost declares, repeating this same truth, that he who keeps his tongue keeps his own soul from those sins which those commonly incur who are fond of talking much: *Whoso keeps his mouth and his tongue keeps his soul from trouble* ‡ And by the mouth of the Son of Sirach, God speaks yet more emphatically: *Who will set a watch before my mouth, and a seal of wisdom on my lips, that I fall not suddenly by them, and my tongue destroy me not.*§ Now, what is this watch, what is this seal, if not silence? To reflect upon our words and to ponder them is, no doubt, as we have before remarked, to place an efficient guard upon our lips; and yet it is not an altogether trusty guard; for much as meditation and reflection keep watch and ward over the lips, they leave them open. Silence alone is a most safe sentinel over the mouth, for this alone is the seal of which the Holy Ghost is speaking; and this alone, by keeping the mouth closed, secures us against every

* Pauca loquentibus paucis etiam legibus est opus.

† Qui custodit os suum, custodit animam suam. Prov. xiij. 3.

‡ Qui custodit os suum et linguam suam, custodit ab angustiis animam suam. Prov. xxi. 23.

§ Quis dabit ori meo custodiam et super labia mea signaculum certum, ut non cadam ab ipsis et lingua mea perdat me? Ecclus. xxij. 33.

transgression and every kind of fault. Hence silence is sure to save us from ruin, by giving us purity of conscience, never failing to fit us for a great increase of perfection. He then who is in earnest about his spiritual advancement, must practise silence, as far as is compatible with the state to which God has called him.

CHAPTER IV.

PRACTICAL SUGGESTIONS TO DIRECTORS ON THE PRESENT ARTICLE.

213. FIRST suggestion. As regards too great freedom of the tongue, the Director must take special care to keep an eye upon women, who are by nature given to much talking and who, by this fault, put a great obstacle in the way of their perfection. For as in the weaker sex reason is not strong, but the imagination very lively, it follows that speech in women is more under the rule of the fancy than of the intellect, and therefore the conversation of women is for the most part imperfect, not to say sinful. I really believe that the majority of them, if they had no tongue at all, would attain to greater perfection. An anecdote which may be seen in the life of St. Vincent Ferrer, is much to our present purpose. While preaching at Valencia,* a woman was brought to him who had been dumb from her birth. St. Vincent seeing the faith of those who had brought her, interrupted his sermon and, lifting up his eyes to Heaven, made a short prayer; then turning to the poor woman, he inquired of her before all the people what she wanted of him? The woman, who up to that time had never spoken a word, replied: "I want food and the use of my tongue." "Food," said the Saint, "shall not fail thee during the rest of thy days; but thou shalt not obtain of God the use of thy tongue, since of this He has deprived thee for thy greater good. Know that if thy tongue had been loose, and free to speak, it would have brought ruin on thy soul by the sharpness

* Apud Surium, lib. iij., cap. unico.

with which thou wouldst have misused it. Take heed then never to beg of God this favour, for if it were granted it would be to thee a great misfortune." "Holy Father," she replied, "I will follow your advice." At these words she became dumb again, and as unable to speak as she had been before. How many women are there in Christendom like this one, who would be saints if only they had no tongue! But the evil use they make of it from morning to night is a great hindrance in the way of their perfection, and for many it is even an occasion of everlasting ruin. Therefore in dealing with women, the Director must take especial care that they guard their tongues and do not make light of the faults which they commit by this member; and he must reprove them frequently for such faults, and must prescribe to them fitting means of procuring their amendment, such as I am going to point out immediately.

214. Second suggestion. The Director should take note of the peculiar faults into which his penitent falls in the use of the tongue. If the person be accustomed to meditate, the Confessor will prescribe that every morning some point of the meditation be applied to this subject, or at least that some reflection be made upon it, in order that, as I have said above, a strong purpose of amendment be formed. If, however, he be not accustomed to meditate, the Director will advise that this firm purpose be made in the prayers, which the penitent—being as I take for granted a devout person—will recite faithfully every morning. Thus he will be rendered more cautious throughout the day, and will be taught to keep strict watch over the tongue. The Confessor must earnestly inculcate upon all the necessity of continually recommending themselves to God in their prayers and Communions to obtain the grace necessary for the correction of these faults. We have already shown that the extirpation of faults of the tongue depends mainly on the grace of God.* *To man it belongs*, says Solomon, *to prepare his heart*, by good resolutions; *but to the Lord to direct the tongue*, by giving, in times of need, those effectual aids for its

* Hominis est animam præparare, et Domini gubernare linguam. Prov. xvj 1.

restraint which are, as a rule, not to be obtained without earnest prayer.

215. If the penitent relapse frequently into the same fault, the Confessor should impose some mortification, which may serve as a check to deter the person from repeating the like failing This was the custom of the saints in their anxious desire to make progress. Paul the Simple, a disciple of St. Antony, for a slip of his tongue, which in reality was not blameworthy, laid himself under the penance of not speaking for three whole years. Sulpitius Severus, as St. Jerome relates,* having, through his loquaciousness, been seduced into error by the Pelagians, imposed on his tongue the penance of never speaking again until his death, and he kept to his word.† St. Gregory of Nazianzus, conscious of having exceeded by too much speaking, put himself under the obligation of fasting and silence for the space of forty days. His purpose in so doing was twofold—first, to punish his guilty tongue, and next, to bring it by this long silence to due moderation. This he himself confesses.‡ I know that the Director neither can, nor should, lay his penitents under such severe penances for the slips which they make with their tongue, but yet he may assign to them mortifications according to their strength, condition, and degree of virtue. He may tell them, for instance, to withdraw to their room, and to spend an hour in silence, on the days upon which they shall have allowed their tongue an undue freedom; or else he can counsel them to abstain some one day from wine; to mortify their tongue with the taste of wormwood, or of some other bitter drug; or to humble this proud member by forcing it to make a certain number of crosses on the floor, or by

* In Catalog. Illust. Virorum.

† A Pelagianis deceptus, agnoscens loquacitatis culpam, silentium usque ad mortem tenuit, ut peccatum, quod loquendo contraxerat, tacendo penitus emendaret.

‡ Ego cum præcipitis sermonis impetu mediocritatis regulam excessisse perciperem, nullum melius remedium inveni, quam ut eam excelso pectore premerem; ut lingua mea, quæ dicenda, et quæ tacenda sunt, addisceret. Cujus facti mei (hoc est quadragenarii jejunii, et silentii) si causam quæris, idcirco a sermone prorsus abstinui, ut sermones meos moderari discam. De Silent. Quad. Jejun.

condemning it to ask pardon of the person whom it has wounded. Should the fault committed have been one against charity, he may give other penances of a similar nature.

216. Third suggestion. As regards silence, the Director will rigorously insist, with religious and nuns, on such observance of it as their rule requires. He will therefore exhort them to keep as much as possible, and in so far as their occupations permit, retired within their cells, and there to occupy themselves in handiwork or in useful studies, in prayer or in spiritual reading; for it is beyond belief how much silence contributes to the spiritual life, and how it ripens and gives it increase. St. James says, *If any man think himself religious, bridling not his tongue, but deceiving his own heart, this man's religion is vain.** And the Prophet Jeremiah assigns the reason, saying, that in solitude God imparts Himself to the soul, and *raises it above itself* with the gift of prayer.† On the contrary, continual talk fills the mind with countless empty phantasms, dissipates the spirit, spoils recollection, indisposes for prayer, takes away the opportunity for practising virtue, and occasions a multitude of sins, as I have already shown. In a word, it robs us, little by little, of every spiritual gift, and makes us wholly unable to recover our loss.

217. This is why the saints held silence in such esteem, and practised it so rigorously that in many their practice might be deemed somewhat excessive. St. Romuald, leading a most austere life in the wilderness, spent seven whole years without speaking to a single person.‡ St. John, called the Silent, maintained, during the space of forty-seven years, a continual and rigorous silence.§ Palladius relates|| that the Abbot Ammon, who ruled over three thousand monks, lived among them in such strict silence, that the monastery, despite the number of the religious, seemed a real solitude. Thomas of Cantipré¶ relates that, in a Benedictine monastery in Brabant, a certain monk was so given to silence,

* Si quis putat se religiosum esse, non refrænans linguam suam, sed seducens cor suum, hujus vana est religio Jac. i. 26.

† Sedebit solitarius, et tacebit, quia levavit se super se. Thren., iij 28.

‡ S. Pet. Damian. in Vitâ.

§ Cyrill. apud Sur. 13 Maii.

|| In Hist. Lausiac., cap. 48.

¶ De Apib., cap. 13.

that for sixteen whole years he had never uttered one single word; and that God was pleased to make manifest, by a wondrous miracle, His approval of this devout silence. The monastery being on fire, the first words the monk uttered after so long a time were the following: "Stop, fire! advance no farther." At these few words, coming from those usually silent lips, the conflagration was at once extinguished. I do not relate these things as proposing them for an exact imitation. I am quite aware that it is proper for religious of either sex to speak when their office requires it, when charity to their neighbour suggests it, or when the rule or custom of their house allows or commands it for the purpose of innocent recreation. I only say, that beyond these cases, if they are in earnest about the perfection which so befits their state, they must love retirement, their cell, silence and solitude. Above all, the Director should take care not to encourage loquaciousness in nuns under the pretext of keeping them contented, as is the practice of some Confessors, who say that so long as nuns speak as much as they like to each other only, no harm is done. True, there is not the same amount of harm in nuns chattering together from morning to night without stopping, that there would be if this were done with seculars at the *grille*. But even this would be a great evil; as it would cause much dissipation of mind, would be an incentive of petty passions, and would occasion numberless faults. It is a piece of folly to pretend to keep a woman who is shut up within four walls happy by mere chattering. God alone can render nuns cheerful, and alone can content their hearts with that inner peace and calm which He sheds upon them by His grace. The Lord is not to be found in the midst of gossips, but in silence and in solitude, as I have observed above.

218. As regards seculars, I have already remarked that we must adapt ourselves to their condition and occupations, so as to obviate the inconveniences and trouble to which an indiscreet silence might easily give rise. And this the more, since it is the will of God that each one should practise virtue in accordance with the requirements of his state and calling. Certain it is, however, that women, being commonly much detained at home, have greater convenience for practising some sort of silence and

retirement than men, who are usually occupied in more distracting employments. Hence, Directors of women may warn them not to go from house to house calling upon their neighbours, nor, except when some requirement of duty or courtesy exact it, to admit within their own house the useless visits of female acquaintances; but to content themselves with the company of their own family. This will be for them an excellent means of practising silence, and will cut off the occasions of countless sins of the tongue. And if their domestic duties, and the charity which they owe to those of their household, allow them to withdraw for some hours of the day to work within their own chambers, the Director may counsel them this kind of retirement as a useful means of keeping themselves recollected in the presence of God while at their work. But to speak in general terms, we should urge all seculars (as I laid down in the foregoing Chapter) to make it a duty to secure, during a certain portion of the day, the retirement and silence necessary for attentive prayer, for meditation, or for spiritual reading; in the measure of the spiritual gifts and the capacity and condition of each one. For besides being needful for the salvation of their soul—an object which should be to them of primary importance, since if the soul be lost all is lost—these spiritual exercises contribute much to the success of our temporal interests, according to the blessed promise of our Redeemer:—*Seek first the kingdom of God and His justice, and all other things shall be given to you over and above.**

* Quærite primùm regnum Dei, et justitiam ejus: et hæc omnia adjicientur vobis. Matth. vj. 33.

ARTICLE VI.

The hindrance to Christian perfection caused by our ill-regulated and unmortified passions.

CHAPTER I.

THE ENUMERATION OF OUR PASSIONS, AND HOW THEY ARE A HINDRANCE TO PERFECTION.

219. WE have already said, at the beginning of the present Treatise, that amongst those hindrances to the attainment of perfection which have their seat within us, some belong to the outer senses; others, again, to the inner senses, that is, to the passions which reside in the sensitive appetite Of the hindrances opposed by the five outer senses we have sufficiently treated in the foregoing Articles. We have now to speak of those hindrances which the inner senses put in the way of our perfection. I mean the impediments arising from the passions of our appetites corrupted by the sin of our first Parent; which, in theological language, are termed the *fomes peccati*, the incentive to sin.

220. St. Thomas numbers eleven passions, six of which belong to what he calls the *concupiscible*, and five to the *irascible* appetite.* Under the former heading are classed love, hate, desire, abhorrence, joy, and sadness; to the latter belong hope, despair, fear, boldness, and anger. Now all these passions take their rise in the passion of love, as in their well-spring and fountain-head; it is love that sets them all in motion, that excites them all, it alone, so to speak, gives them life For from love proceeds hate, a turbid affection of the soul which is nothing but the displeasure we feel at what is adverse to the object of our love. From love and hate flow all those other affections or passions which band together against reason, and make war upon it. So that if we reduce the matter to its first principles, to love we must

* 1, 2, q. 23, art. 4.

refer the origin of the several emotions which disturb our heart's peace; as we may easily discover by examining singly the exact nature of each taken separately. Thus, desire is nothing but the tendency or movement towards a beloved object in its absence. Abhorrence is the shrinking of the soul from what is not present, but is an object of hate. Joy is a calm and delightful repose in the possession of a beloved object. Sadness, the pain and affliction felt at the presence of what we hate. Hope, an extension of our desire, tending to some good end difficult of attainment, but which we love and deem it possible to reach. Despair is but a failing of hope, and a sinking of the mind, with reference to the same loved object, when it is thought to be impossible of attainment. Fear is a paralyzing emotion with regard to some great evil which, though absent, threatens us and from which we shrink. Boldness is a bracing of the soul to overcome the obstacles which stand between it and the possession of the object of love, or the destruction of the object held in hate. Anger is a burning feeling against what is contrary to self-respect and self-esteem (which is naturally an object of our love), tending to seek the compensation of revenge. Thus do all our passions when duly examined recognise the passion of love as the parent from which they all derive existence.

221. Now, to understand thoroughly how the above-mentioned passions place hindrances in the way of Christian perfection, we must notice an error into which some servants of God fell in the early ages of the Church, and which St. Jerome attributes to Origen. Some writers were then of opinion that a spiritual man might and ought to annihilate all his passions by the practice of virtue, so thoroughly as to be wholly undisturbed by any, even the slightest emotion, and attain so perfect a calm as to be able to live without any trouble of soul in the tranquil exercise of all the virtues.* St. Jerome mentions with special

* Doctrina tua, Origenis ramusculus est. In eo enim psalmo, in quo scriptum est (ut de ceteris taceam), *Insuper et usque ad noctem erudierunt me renes mei;* asserit, virum sanctum, de quorum videlicet et numero es, cum ad virtutis venerit summitatem, ne in nocte quidem ea pati, quæ hominum sunt, nec cogitatione vitiorum aliquâ titillari. Ad Ctesiphon adv. Pelagianos, Epist. 133.

disapproval the view of Origen, who, as the Saint believed, held that one who had reached to the summit of perfection would be exempt, even in time of sleep, from any effects of human frailty, and that his mind would always be free from every impure fancy. According to St. Jerome, the propagators of this error were Evagrius of Pontus, with his disciples Palladius and Ruffinus, to whom were joined, from among the monks, Ammonius, Eusebius, and Euthymius. Orus and Isidore were afterwards of the number of the Bishops of those times who were condemned as Origenists. Later on, this imperturbability, or, as it was frequently termed, impassibility of the soul, became yet more dangerous and detestable, when the heretics Pelagius, Jovinian, and Priscillian published it as a portion of their teaching.

222. Besides St. Jerome, another of the early Fathers, St. Augustine, waged fierce war against this error, and maintained that when our passions are regulated by reason in the proper manner, it is a manifest heresy to say that such passions are sinful, and should be accounted as ailments or weaknesses of the soul.* St. Augustine proves his point triumphantly, by the example of Christ Who, dwelling amongst us free from all sin, would yet be liable to the passions of the body and experience its emotions whenever He deemed advisable.† This the Saint proves from the particular instances related in the holy Gospels, such as when our Blessed Lord in holy indignation grieved over the hard-heartedness which He perceived in the Jews;‡ when He mourned at the grave of Lazarus, showing signs of most real grief; and, again, when He rejoiced at the thought that the raising of Lazarus from the dead would bring numbers to the true faith.§ Another proof adduced is the ardent desire of Jesus to eat the Passover with His disciples;|| and the sorrow, the sadness, the bloody sweat which overwhelmed Him as the hour of

* Cum rectam rationem sequantur istæ affectiones, quando, ubi oportet, adhibentur: quis eas tunc morbos, seu vitiosas passiones audeat dicere? De Civit. Dei, lib. xiv. cap. 9.

† Quamobrem etiam ipse Dominus in formâ servi vitam agere dignatus humanam, sed nullum habens omnino peccatum, adhibuit eas, ubi adhibendas esse judicavit Ibid.

‡ Marc. iij. 5. § Joan. xj 15, 33, 35, 38. || Luc xxij. 15.

His Passion drew nigh.* Now, if Christ Who had His passions in subjection and in obedience to His will, consented to feel their emotions in so many divers manners, who may hope to attain to a state in which he will be wholly free from the slightest involuntary disturbance?† To the example of Christ St. Augustine joins that of the Apostle St. Paul, who *rejoiced with those that rejoiced* and *wept with those that wept;* who complained of conflict and wrestlings without, of fears within; who *desired to be dissolved, and to be with Christ,* who yearned to see the Romans and Corinthians face to face; whose sadness and heartache for the obstinacy of the Jews were unceasing, who mourned bitterly for the ruin of certain sinners.‡ The holy Bishop of Hippo concludes by saying that, if all these emotions passions and affections, which had their source in the love of virtue and in perfect charity, be sinful, vice itself must be called virtue.§ In a word, St. Jerome was perfectly justified in saying that these spiritual Stoics wished to have man without human nature, and to make him, though existing in the body, as if he were without a body.||

223. From all this we may gather: first, that a spiritual man, do what he will, can by no means attain to a state in which he will never feel any uprising of passion, since he always bears about with him that nature which has been spoiled and defiled by the sin of Adam; a nature which he has taken in his mother's womb, and which is always tending to throw out fresh shoots of disordered affections.

* Matth. xxvj. 38.

† Cum ergo ejus in Evangelio ista referantur, quod super duritiâ cordis judæorum cum irâ contristatus sit: quod dixit: *Gaudeo propter vos, ut credatis:* quod Lazarum resuscitaturus etiam lacrymas fuderit: quod concupierit cum discipulis suis manducare pascha. quod propinquante passione, tristis fuerit anima ejus usque ad mortem; non falso utique referuntur. De Civit. Dei. Ut supra.

‡ Gaudentem cum gaudentibus, flentem cum flentibus, foris habentem pugnas, intus timores; cupientem dissolvi, et esse cum Christo; desiderantem videre Romanos; Corinthios æmulantem; magnam tristitiam, et continuum dolorem cordis de Israelitis habentem; luctum suum denunciantem de quibusdam peccatoribus. Ibid.

§ Hi motus, hi affectus de amore boni, et de sanctâ caritate venientes, si vitia vocanda sunt, sinamus, ut ea, quæ vere vitia sunt, virtutes vocentur. Ibid.

|| Hoc est hominem ex homine tollere, et in corpore constitutum esse sine corpore.

Our passions may and should be mortified, and kept within due bounds; we may weaken them so as to lessen their movements, and thus succeed in overcoming them more easily, and in being attacked by them less frequently; but they cannot be utterly extinguished, so as to be no longer felt. It was a singular privilege of the ever-blessed Virgin to be preserved from every irregular motion of passion, as it was her singular gift to be preserved untainted by original sin. But whoever has sinned in Adam, with Adam must suffer some rebellion of the passions, so long as life lasts within him.

224. Secondly: the passions, when regulated by right reason, by the light of faith, by the theological and moral virtues (as were the passions of Christ, of the Blessed Virgin, of St. Paul, and the other saints), far from being sinful, or an obstacle to perfection, are a help to its attainment, and by their activity facilitate the practice of virtue.

225. Thirdly: The passions which are opposed to perfection, and which precipitate countless souls into everlasting ruin, are those only which are unmortified and inordinate; regulated neither by reason nor by the light of faith, but opposed to the righteous dictates of them both, following the inclination of corrupt nature, and helped by our frail will in complying with the demands of that nature.

226. From these disorderly passions arise all the sins and vicious habits which are the ruin of our souls. I have said above, that love holds the first place among the passions, that it communicates motion to them all, and draws them after it, working out its inclinations. Now, it is precisely from inordinate love that all the vices which war so furiously against the soul take their rise. If the reader will but reflect attentively, he will see clearly that this is the explanation how all the above comes to pass. He will see that pride originates in an inordinate love of our own excellence, which makes us scorn subjection and desire to be raised over the heads of all our fellow-creatures; that covetousness arises from an excessive love of property, money, and gold which it worships as its god, that lust is the result of an inordinate love of our bodies, which makes us crave for pleasures forbidden

by the law of God, and by our right reason; that anger takes its rise in an excessive love of our own honour, which we would defend by unreasonable means; that gluttony results from a too great love of our bodies, which we wish to gratify by an excess in food; that envy springs from an over great self-love, which is afflicted at the good of others, as if this were a hindrance to our own; finally, that sloth itself comes from an inordinate self-love, which shrinks from holy things under the apprehension that they will surely become a burden to us. Thus the reader may perceive that every vice, and consequently every hindrance placed in the way of perfecting or saving our souls, arises from inordinate passions, and especially from the passion of love when not regulated either by the light of reason or by that of faith, but excited, and as it were inflamed, by the brutish impulses of sensuality To what height the obstacles may grow which our unmortified passions place in the way of our spiritual progress and of our advance in Christian perfection, will appear in the following Chapter. To show this is the object of the present Volume.

CHAPTER II.

A MOST SERIOUS HINDRANCE TO CHRISTIAN PERFECTION ARISES FROM OUR ILL REGULATED AND UNMORTIFIED PASSIONS

227. If that be true which, with St. Thomas of Aquin, we have laid down as the very foundation of the whole spiritual edifice which we are now engaged in building up; if Christian perfection mainly consists, in the first place, in the love of God, and, secondly, in the love of our neighbour; further, if perfection is so much the more sublime as this love is more ardent and more pure, it follows in strict consequence, that what is most opposed to charity is also most contrary to Christian perfection. But what is there that wages a fiercer war against the love of God than our unmortified and unsubdued passions, rebellious alike to the laws of reason and of faith? since with their disorderly movements they

are in open revolt against all that God requires of us, and they tend directly to shake off the yoke of His law, in the perfect keeping of which law the very essence of the love of God consists. And further, I ask, what is there that stands in the way of the practice of the moral virtues (the ultimate and most requisite disposition for the attainment of the same love of God) so much as unruly passions not kept in check by the dictates of reason, and the vices springing from these unbridled passions as from an evil root, spreading their growth over our souls? Surely, no greater impediment to perfection can be found. For it is impossible that any of us should be able to exercise humility if we have not yet trampled pride underfoot; or to enjoy the sweet fruits of meekness, if we have not yet stifled the outbursts of anger; or to possess our souls in patience, when we have not silenced the murmurings and chafing of our frail nature amid labours and adversities; or to practise obedience, when we know not how to bend our self-will and to subject it to the will of another. The same holds good of all the long catalogue of virtues. So that if it be impossible to attain to the perfect love of God without the moral virtues, to which it belongs to open the door and give entrance to that love within our souls; and if, too, it be impossible to acquire these virtues without mortifying and subduing our passions; that man may well despair of attaining to even a low degree of perfection, who is not fully resolved to go against his evil inclinations, to overcome them, to wage war with them and to withstand them, by bringing them into subjection both to reason and to faith. So true is this, that St. Augustine, whom we have quoted on this same matter elsewhere, hesitates not to say that the diminution of our passions is the increase of charity; and where passions no longer exist (understanding this in accordance with what is possible in our present life, as we explained above), charity becomes perfect.* Hence, concludes the Saint, he who would grow in charity, must take care to moderate his passions and to bring down their strength by unceasing mortification.†

* Nutrimentum caritatis est imminutio cupiditatis; perfectio, nulla cupiditas.

† Quisquis igitur eam nutrire vult, instet minuendis cupiditatibus. Lib. lxxxiij. Quæst 9, 36.

228. We find in the Holy Scriptures a lively and expressive figure of this most important truth in the two altars, one of whole burnt offerings, the other of incense.* The former was made of brass, and stood outside the Holy Place, in the Court of the Tabernacle, and on it was burnt the flesh of the victims which had been offered to God. The latter was made of gold, and was placed within the Tabernacle, and on it were burnt savoury perfumes before the Ark of the Lord. It was a rite of Jewish worship, that the fire for burning the incense in the presence of God should be taken from the altar of whole burnt offerings. St. Gregory the Great, aptly commenting on these rites of the Old Law, remarks, that the altar of whole burnt offerings, upon which were consumed the victims immolated in honour of the Most High, is an emblem of the compunction and mortification with which we should consume our carnal vices, and destroy the corrupt inclinations of our flesh, to the honour and service of the Almighty, to whom such sacrifices are ever most acceptable. He further says that the altar of incense signifies the love of God, figured by the gold which covered this altar, and that in this love of God our soul loses itself, being consumed in sweet affections before its Lord. But it is to be noted that the altar of holocausts stood without the Tabernacle, while that of incense stood within; to show that, before being enkindled with divine love, the old man and his vices and lusts must be consumed as a perfect whole burnt offering in the fire of mortification; and that by no other flame can the sweet perfumes of the love of God be enkindled.†

229. Whoever, therefore, would burn in the flames of this love

* Exod. xxvij.

† In tabernaculo duo altaria fieri jubentur, unum exterius, aliud interius: unum in atrio, aliud ante arcam: unum quod ex ære coopertum est, aliud quod auro vestitur: in æreo consummantur carnes, in aureo accenduntur aromata. . . . Multi plangunt mala, quæ fecerunt, et incendunt vitia igne compunctionis, quorum adhuc suggestiones in corde patiuntur. Quid isti nisi altare sunt æneum, et in quo carnes ardent? quia adhuc ab eis carnalia opera planguntur. Alii vero a carnalibus vitiis liberi, amoris flammâ in compunctionis lacrymis inardescunt, supernis inesse civibus concupiscunt, Regem in decore suo videre desiderant, et flere quotidie ex ejus amore non cessant. Quid isti nisi altare sunt aureum, in quorum corde aromata incensa sunt, quia virtutes ardent. Homil. 22 in Ezech.

of God, which sweetly consumes the soul, making it perfect, must first be tried for a long time in the fire of mortification, and must be purged therein of the dross of his vices; he must dry up the peccant humours of his disorderly passions, and burn, reduce to ashes and wholly destroy, as far as in him lies, all his perverse inclinations. And this is precisely what our Blessed Lord teaches us with His own lips, saying, *Whosoever will come after Me*, that is, be My follower, friend, lover, spouse, *let him deny himself*, that is, go counter to his own desires, *and follow after Me*, namely, by bearing the cross of continual mortification.* Again, *If any one take not up his cross and follow Me*, by means of an unceasing self-denial, *the same is not worthy of Me*, nor of My love: says our Lord in another place.†

230 St. Paul, in his Apostolic letters, insists upon the same teaching. He writes: *They that are Christ's*, in other words, the faithful followers of Christ, *have crucified their vices and the disordered appetites of their concupiscence*, with the nails of holy mortification.‡ And again: *Mortify therefore your members which are upon the earth;* and which have been formed of earth.§ And not to leave undetermined the manner of practising such mortification, the Apostle adds: *Put off the old man with his deeds*, by withstanding his evil inclinations, and striking them down with all the energy of the spirit; *and put on the new man, who is renewed in knowledge after the image of Him that created us;* being made conformable, that is, to Christ and His holy Gospel.|| He further reminds his disciples that between the flesh and the spirit an intestine war ever rages, and that there can be no truce between these two deadly foes. Again he writes: *The flesh lusts against the spirit;* namely, by the uprising of its appetites, rebel-

* Qui vult venire post me, abneget semetipsum, et tollat crucem suam, et sequatur me. Matth. xvj 24.

† Qui non accipit crucem suam, et sequitur me, non est me dignus. Matth. x. 38.

‡ Qui autem sunt Christi, carnem suam crucifixerunt cum vitiis, et concupiscentiis. Gal. v. 24.

§ Mortificate membra vestra, quæ sunt super terram. Coloss. iij. 5.

|| Exspoliantes vos veterem hominem cum actibus suis, et induentes novum. Ibid. iij. 9.

ling against it, and exciting within it great tumult and disorder; but *the spirit lusts against the flesh*, striving, with the aid of divine grace, to subject it to God's holy laws.* Do you, then, he continues, if you would be spiritual and perfect, ever *walk in the spirit*, siding with it against the inordinate lusts and inclinations of the flesh, and be ever ready to keep them under, and to mortify them.† Lastly, he encourages us to the practice of this mortification by his own example: *I so fight, not as one that beats the air: but I keep under my body, and bring it into subjection;* severely chastising it, so that it may be subjected to the spirit whether it will or not.‡

231. And it should be noticed, that the Apostle is not content that such mortification be mild or intermittent; but he will have it to be so severe and unceasing as to resemble that very mortification which our Divine Redeemer practised in His own Person.§ For, as a soldier who is face to face with the foe, has only to cease from the conflict in order to be conquered, so, with far greater reason we, who have as many enemies within us as we have concupiscences and vices, must never suffer the sword of mortification to drop from our hands, that thus we may be able to strike down every inordinate craving as soon as it begins to stir; sometimes withstanding the irregular motion of some passion that begins to waken, and sometimes cutting off the head of some vicious or imperfect affection which we feel is arising within our breast. Hence St. Augustine, commenting on these words of the same Apostle: *if by the Spirit ye mortify the deeds of the flesh*:‖ says, that the real task, the ceaseless struggle of every devout person, truly in earnest about his perfection, should be the fervent mortification of the evil inclinations of his rebellious flesh; which he should mortify from morning till night, bridling them, weakening their

* Caro concupiscit adversus spiritum, spiritus adversus carnem: hæc enim sibi invicem adversantur. Gal. v. 17.

† Spiritu ambulate, et desideria carnis non perficiatis.

‡ Ego sic pugno, non quasi aerem verberans; sed castigo corpus meum, et in servitutem redigo. I. Cor ix. 26

§ Semper mortificationem Jesu in corpore nostro circumferentes. II. Cor. iv. 10

‖ Si spiritu facta carnis mortificaveritis, vivetis.

power, and, as far as he can, depriving them of their very existence.*

232. But, if this be the case, it must needs be said that certain spiritual persons, who give themselves up to devout exercises, but care not to do violence to themselves in subduing some of their unruly petty passions, who strive not to crush the risings of these passions by a continuous and vigorous resistance, but allowing them, on the contrary, to range unchecked amid the objects of their cravings, it must needs be said, I repeat (unless St. Paul be wrong, and Christ Himself have deceived us), that such persons are straying from the path of perfection; since, whatever trouble they may be taking, they are omitting the very thing which is most necessary to attain perfection. They are assiduous in prayer, they fast often, they visit churches, they frequent the sacraments. So far so good. But they shrink from doing violence to themselves in order to overcome certain appetites, certain affections and certain emotions of their soul. Such persons are pressing forward, I admit, but not in the right path.† People of this class will undoubtedly never reach any notable degree of perfection.

233. In confirmation of the doctrine of both the present and the preceding Chapters, I will give an illustration taken from the Lives of the Fathers of the Desert.‡ A saintly monk, who for fifty years had led a most austere life, and had tasted nothing but bread and water, and who had always been on the watch to mortify his passions, allowed himself one day to utter the following words: "God be praised, I have already utterly extinguished within me, lust, covetousness, vanity, anger; I have at length slain every one of my evil inclinations." Abbot Abraham happened to hear of this, and, taking pity on the simplicity of this servant of God, went to him, in order to warn him of the error. On entering into his cell, the Abbot said, "Tell me, my good old man, if, on returning to your cell, you should find seated on your bed a beautiful woman, gaily dressed and handsomely decked out,

* Hoc est opus vestrum in hâc vitâ, actiones carnis spiritu mortificare, quotidie affligere, minuere, frænare, interimere. Serm. 13, cap. 9.

† Bene currunt, sed extra viam.

‡ De Discret., n. 6.

who were courteously to greet you, would it not occasion some evil thought in your mind?" "Yes, Father," replied the monk; "but I would drive her out at once, nor should I venture to touch her with one of my fingers." "You see then," replied the Abbot, "that lust is not yet dead within you, as you thought; it is only deadened." He continued, "But if, when walking along the road, you should discover some gold coins lying among the heaps of stones by the wayside, would you not feel the desire of picking them up?" "I should, Father," replied the aged monk; "but then I should despise the thought, and would not take the trouble to stoop for the money." "So you see, Brother," chimed in the Abbot, "that covetousness is only mortified in you, not dead." And, pressing further his questionings, "If," he went on, "two monks were to call upon you, one of whom was fond of you, and in the habit of speaking in your praise to everybody and of extolling you to the skies; while his companion hated you, hardly bearing to look at you, and blackening your character by evil insinuations, would you receive them both with the like good grace and affection?" "Naturally, no," replied the old man; "but still I would do violence to myself, and I would entertain them both with the same charity." "You see again," replied the Abbot, "that pride and anger are not yet dead within you, but only deadened." He ended by observing "that the passions are alive in every one, but that holy men keep them bound up and confined by the fetters of mortification."*

234. We may hence infer how undeniable are the two principles which have been inculcated throughout the present Article. First, that we can mortify, but not slay, our passions; we can diminish their violence, but not wholly rid ourselves of them, so as to prevent their disturbing us by their rebellion with greater or less frequency. Secondly, that the way to mortify our passions is that which the good old monk put into practice; we must, that is, resist them; we must oppose them as soon as ever they make themselves felt, using contrary acts, put forth with all vigour and generosity. Thus, for instance, an unclean thought presents itself

* Vivunt ergo passiones, sed tantummodo a sanctis viris quodammodo religantur.

to your mind—drive it away at once, with a firm protestation, that you choose to die rather than consent to such abominations. A movement of anger or impatience arises within your heart—stamp it out without delay, by an act of patience and meekness. Or, it may be, a thought of pride or self-complacency puffs you up—lower yourself straightway by an act of profound humility. You notice welling up in your bosom a certain bitterness or feeling of aversion against your neighbour—stifle it by an act of charity and of love. And so in like manner with all the other inordinate affections of the soul. On this greater or less mortification of our appetites depends our greater or less spiritual progress; for that is but too true which the author of the "Imitation of Christ" says, "Our progress is ever in proportion to the violence we do to ourselves."* If then, Directors would have their penitents to advance speedily, let them hammer repeatedly at this nail; for if the spirit of interior mortification once effect an entry into men's hearts, we shall soon see them flying rather than walking along the path of perfection.

CHAPTER III.

CERTAIN RULES TO BE OBSERVED IN MORTIFYING THE PASSIONS IN ORDER TO ATTAIN MORE EASILY TO THE DUE QUIET OF THE SOUL.

235. THE first rule I shall prescribe for the mortification of our passions, and for speedily bringing down their pride, shall be borrowed from Cassian, that great master of the spiritual life. He tells us that the spiritual man should seek to discover what vice or passion is the most lively in his soul; what rules him most by its inner motions, and what causes him to fall most frequently. Against this, a truceless war is to be declared, until it be wholly subdued. In other words, we must make up our mind ever to thwart our predominant passion, and constantly to

* Tantum proficies, quantum tibi ipsi vim intuleris. Imit., lib. i., cap. 25.

withstand its inordinate motions with all our might and main. It is thus that generals act when engaging the army of the foe; they attack that battalion which is the strongest, and which offers the most stubborn resistance; for when they have disposed of this, it becomes easy to put the rest of the army to rout. So too, if we but conquer our predominant passion, we shall have no longer any difficulty in mastering the rank and file of our lesser evil propensities.*

236. The very means of which the devil makes use, namely, employing our passions to work our ruin, is precisely that which we should adopt in order to put him to flight and to mount to a higher degree of perfection. St. Gregory says that the devil, always lying in wait for our souls, takes notice of the passion or vice to which each one of us is most given, and directs all his temptations to that particular point. Thus, one of an open and sanguine temperament the demon strives to allure by sensual gratification and by vanity. In those of a melancholy, harsh, and rugged character, he stirs up motions of anger, of pride, and great sternness; for he perceives that such persons are inclined to passions of this nature. It is by artifices and industries such as these that the great deceiver traps countless souls, and with them peoples hell.† Now the very same stratagems of which the common foe of mankind makes use for our ruin we should employ for our salvation. Let us then examine what is the passion that has acquired the greatest dominion over our souls, what vice has struck the deepest root in them; and against this passion particularly let us arm without delay, with the determination to overcome it by dint of resistance, and to cast it to the ground by repeated blows of contrary acts.

* Ita adversus vitia arripienda sunt prælia, ut unusquisque vitium, quo maxime infestatur, explorans, adversus illud arripiat principale certamen; omnem curam mentis, ac sollicitudinem erga illius impugnationem, observationemque defigens. Collat. v., cap. 14

† Intuetur inimicus generis humani uniuscujusque mores, cui vitio sint propinqui, et illa opponit ante faciem, ad quæ cognoscit facilius inclinari mentem: ut blandis ac lætis sæpe luxuriam, nonnunquam vanam gloriam, asperis vero mentibus iram, superbiam, vel crudelitatem proponat. Ibi ergo decipulam ponit, ubi esse semitam mentis conspicit; quia illic periculum deceptionis inserit, ubi viam esse invenerit propinquæ cogitationis. Moral., lib. xiv., cap 7.

Nor should we lose heart on account of the violence wherewith it assails us, in seeking to cause us to follow after its evil propensities: rather should we put our trust in God, and fight manfully in the hope that He will finally give us the victory, by the help of His mighty arm.

237. As soon, continues Cassian, as we shall find that we have sufficiently mortified one passion—from its having no longer the strength to force our will, and from the ease by which we overcome its assaults—we must dive anew into the recesses of our hearts to find out what passion comes next in order, as being most troublesome to us; and against this we must take up the arms of mortification in order to overcome it, relying meantime on God's gracious help.* In this wise we shall succeed in gradually extirpating the various evil propensities that have taken root in our hearts, and which stifle the growth of the seeds of virtue and hinder perfection from flowering within us. St. Augustine prescribes this very method for subduing our passions. Commenting on the words of the Apostle, *If by the spirit ye mortify the deeds of the flesh, ye shall live*, he says: 'When you shall have overthrown one passion by mortification, pass on to another that is yet vigorous. Trample underfoot that which you have laid low, and gird yourself to the struggle with that which resists you. True, the former enemy is dead, but this one continues to live; refuse to consent to it, and you are putting it to death. When you have gone so far as to cease to receive any pleasure from it, you will have put it to death."† He then concludes with these remarkable words: "This should be our continual occupation, this the daily task of our Christian warfare, to mortify our passions."‡ This method of subduing our passions—prescribed as it is by saints

* Cum se ab eâ (scilicet passione) senserit absolutum, rursus latebras sui cordis simili intentione perlustret et exploret, quam inter reliquas perspexerit diriorem atque adversus eam specialius spiritûs arma commoveat. Moral., lib. xiv., cap 7.

† *Si spiritu facta carnis mortificaveritis, vivetis.* Rom. viij 13. Calca mortuum, transi ad vivum · calca jacentem, confligc cum resistente. Mortua est una delectatio, sed vivit altera: et illam, dum non consentis, mortificas. Cum cœperit omnino non delectare, mortificasti. Serm. 13, cap. 9.

‡ Hæc est actio nostra, hæc est militia nostra.

and masters of the spiritual life—must doubtless be the most fitting and the best suited to every one; for as a spiritual man would strive in vain to uproot from his soul, at one effort, all his evil inclinations, he must perforce endeavour to extirpate them one by one, beginning with that which is most hurtful; like the gardener who wishes to clear his ground of noxious weeds.

238. It was precisely this very method that St. Dorotheus employed to bring his disciple St. Dositheus in a short space of time to the summit of perfection; as he himself informs us in the life which he has written of his disciple. The saintly master examined what was the ruling passion to which his young pupil was most subject, and straightway he began to mortify this one in the youth. When he had sufficiently brought one passion within bounds, he applied himself to discover some other inordinate affection, and strove to bring about a detachment from that one also. For instance, if he saw him too much attached to a book, to a knife, or any other implement which the novices were allowed to use, he immediately took it from him. If he noted in him the least vain self-complacency in any handiwork which the youth had faithfully completed, he would not deign to cast a single glance upon it. If any sagacious question were propounded, which might have furnished a motive of vanity, no answer was given. Meanwhile, the Brethren marvelled greatly at seeing Dositheus (who, on account of his weak health, was unable to fast, to watch, or to take part in the other austerities of common life) attain within a brief space a remarkable degree of perfection. Hence, moved by a holy curiosity, they asked him, from time to time, what was his special exercise of virtue? His candid reply was: "To mortify all my inclinations, and to submit my will." And in very deed, by means of this interior mortification alone, he attained, within the limit of five short years, to such high sanctity, that he was soon after his death raised to an eminent degree of glory and placed on a level with the greatest saints of his Order. So true is it that the royal road to perfection is the mortification of our inordinate lusts and passions. If, then the reader feel not the courage to cut down at a single blow these domestic enemies of his perfection, he may make use of the method which St. Doro-

theus employed with his young disciple, and resolve to meet them singly, and one after the other, always making that one bear the brunt of the battle which is known to be the strongest and the most unruly.

239. Second rule. In order thus to conquer our passions by means of mortification, we should crush them at their earliest rising, and stamp out the first sparks which they light up within our soul. For otherwise, if we suffer them to grow, they will gain so much strength that it would soon become morally impossible for us to conquer them. St. Augustine, on the words of the Psalmist, *Happy shall he be that shall lay hold of thy little ones, and dash them against the rock*,* asks what is meant by these *little ones*, who, at their birth, are to be dashed against the rock? He replies that they are passions new-born within our soul.† Dash, then, against the rock these little ones, while they are yet little and make their first appearance, lest growing, they increase in strength and dash thee against it.‡ "But peradventure," he continues, "ye are in fear lest, though kept under, such passions will not die. Dash them then against the Rock, which is Christ; keep them under for the love of Jesus: thus shall you be in safety, and they shall be wholly destroyed."§ These concluding words of the quotation well deserve our attention, as setting forth the most effectual and most godly way of mortifying our irregular affections. At their very first upheavings, we should raise our thoughts to Jesus Christ, and make strenuous endeavour to overcome them for love of Him. "Lord," we should each one of us exclaim, "I will not give way to this angry feeling, nor utter this offensive word, nor take this revenge, nor will I allow mine eyes to glance at this object, nor will I dally with this thought, for love of Thee." It cannot be told what vigour such loving affec-

* Beatus, qui tenebit et allidet parvulos suos ad petram. Ps cxxxvj 9.

† Quid sunt parvuli Babyloniæ? Nascentes malæ cupiditates. In Ps. cxxxvj.

‡ Ne enim cupiditas nequam pravæ consuetudinis robur accipiat cum parvula est, allide illam.

§ Sed times, ne elisa non moriatur. Ad petram allide. *Petra autem erat Christus.* . . . In petrâ ædificamini, si non vultis tolli aut a fluvio, aut a ventis, aut a pluviâ.

tions impart to the soul, and what courage they inspire to repel the onslaught of any passion, however violent; and the victories thus won, St. Augustine observes, are far more assured, far more stable, and of far greater merit.

240. I have always been greatly pleased with a comparison which St. Ephrem employs to show the vigour wherewith every one should check the first risings, the first motions of passion. If, he says, when a slight swelling appears on our bodies, we neglect to have it looked to in the beginning, little by little it grows into a disgusting ulcer; and if the first drops of matter which it throws out are not carefully wiped off, the ulcer becomes putrid and mortifies, so as to infect the whole body. In the same way, if we take not heed of the first motions of our unruly passions and if we withstand them not by a prompt resistance, they extend, and spread through the vitals of the soul, so as to bring darkness upon it, to unnerve its strength, and wholly infect it with the all but incurable ulcer of sin.*

241. A certain monk, an able Director of souls, as St. Dorotheus relates, made his disciples see this truth with their eyes and touch it with their hands†—if I may use this expression. The venerable old man was holding spiritual converse with them in a cypress wood, when he ordered one of their number to pull up a plant which he pointed out, that just appeared above ground. The youth did as he was required with the utmost ease, using one only of his hands. Then he was told to pull up one that had already begun to strike root. He pulled it up with the same hand, but not without an effort. He was then told to do the same to another plant which had already attained to the size of a sapling. In this case he had to use both hands, and to pull with all his strength, in order to get it out of the ground; for it was deeply rooted in the earth. The Abbot at length commanded the novice to pull up a tree that had already grown into a thick trunk; but here all his efforts were unequal to the task. The

* Nisi citius passiones, quæ in te cernuntur sustuleris, ulcus efficiunt: nisique parvam putredinem curaveris, in infinitum excrescent, omnemque substantiam tuam corrumpent. Serm. de Perf. Monach.

† Serm. 11.

holy old man then observed: "Thus is it with our passions: when they are yet, so to speak, tender, and begin to make their first appearance within us, a little vigilance and mortification is all that is needed to uproot them. But if we suffer them to grow, far greater toil and trouble are required in order to overcome them. But should we, without taking any heed to check them, suffer them to strike deep root in our hearts, no human power can extirpate them; to do that the all-powerful hand of God will be required. Hence, my children, do you watch over the first inordinate motions of your souls; trample them down without delay, as soon as ever they are born,* by contrary acts, if you really desire to make considerable progress in the way of the Lord."

242. We have all often proved the truth of this story by our own sad experience. An unholy thought presents itself to the mind: if it be at once cast off, no harm is done; but if the mind allow it to remain a little while, the thought excites a certain feeling of delectation, which, in its turn, kindles desire, and the desire passes on to carry itself out in shameful deeds deserving of everlasting death. Of this, too, we are warned by St. James.† Or again, a certain tender feeling of attachment to a person of the opposite sex may arise in our hearts. If we withstand it and keep away from the person who is the object of the attraction, the feeling will soon pass away, and we shall be saved from the enormous ills which may result from encouraging it. But if we foster the inclination, however apparently innocent in its beginnings, it will soon degenerate into an impure affection, and will turn out to be a hook baited in hell, having power eventually to draw both persons into irreparable ruin. A strong movement of anger arises in our hearts at some insult received. If we make a sacrifice of the feeling to God, we shall at once put out the spark that would be enough to cause a mighty conflagration. But if we consent to the feeling of our frail nature, and begin to ponder over

* Allide parvulos ad petram.

† Unusquisque tentatur a concupiscentiâ suâ abstractus et illectus. Deinde concupiscentia cum conceperit, parit peccatum. peccatum vero cum consummatum fuerit, generat mortem. Jac. i. 14.

the words, the motives, and other circumstances which aggravate the insult, anger degenerates into hate; this, in its turn, is kindled into revenge, and the end of all will be that an irreconcilable enmity will spring up. Again; the devil may suggest to a devout person a thought of want of trust in God. If the tempted at once lift up his heart to God, and make an act of hope in the boundless goodness of the Almighty, the enemy departs in confusion. But if he who has been moved to distrust give admittance to this pusillanimous thought, diffidence grows into discouragement, and discouragement degenerates into profound melancholy, with the evident risk of falling into the slough of despair. Thus do our passions grow greater and greater, in this manner do they become more and more inflamed; in this wise do they gather ever increasing strength, so as wholly to rob us of our virtue: unless at their first uprising we check them without delay, by instant mortification.*

243. This vigilance over the first motion of our passions was admirably put into practice by St. Monica, the mother of the great St. Augustine, and hereby she succeeded in subduing them so completely as to master them thoroughly. Her holy son relates of her that she was married to a man of a very hot temper who, though much attached to her, being at times beside himself through his passionate disposition, not unfrequently flew into a rage with her, and then would insult her with cutting reproaches, and at times too outrage her feelings with insufferable taunts. The holy woman, who assuredly was not herself made of stone, must naturally have felt the inward risings of resentment at being thus treated by her own husband. Nevertheless, when so sorely tried, she *lifted herself above herself*, not to allow the least vent to her passion; being wholly intent on checking its very first movement. Hence, St. Augustine bears witness, that on such occasions she always held her peace, and never allowed a single syllable to escape her lips.† As soon as the storm of her husband's

* Principiis obsta · sero medicina paratur,
Cum mala per longas convaluere moras.

† Noverat non resistere irato viro, non tantum facto, sed ne verbo quidem. Confess., Lib. ix., cap. 9.

passion had calmed down, and all the inner disturbance of his soul was quieted, she gently put him in mind of his fault. The result was, observes St. Augustine, that while the quarrels of other matrons with husbands of a far meeker temper were the talk of the town, and while the faces of some of these women bore marks of the blows which they had received, his mother never had to tell, nor could she have told, of any, the slightest, quarrel with her husband. Now, let us suppose that St. Monica had failed to check the first impulses of resentment that her husband's passion must surely have stirred up within her; that she had allowed them some escape, in some angry gesture or in some tart reply; it is plain that a furious war would have raged between the two. And she also would have borne, like her neighbours, the shameful traces of domestic strife. On the contrary, by withstanding the first motions of passion, and by denying it the outlet of a single word, she attained to a height of heroic virtue (rarely to be met with among married women), which enabled her to live in complete agreement, in undisturbed peace, and in perfect love, with her irritable partner. They who would master their bad passions and obtain over them a glorious victory, have but to *go and do likewise.*

CHAPTER IV.

FURTHER RULES FOR MODERATING OUR PASSIONS.

244. *The life of man is a continual warfare,* says holy Job.* The battle-field is within us, and we may count foes as numerous as the passions which we nurture in our bosoms. But what renders this conflict still more formidable, is the fact that our adversaries are not subject to death, though struck, wounded, and laid prostrate after countless blows, they always spring to their feet again, renew the attack, and strive to work our ruin. In order, then, not to become faint-hearted, remiss, and careless in so stern a conflict,

* Militia est vita hominis super terram. Job vij. 1.

we must set before our eyes, as a fundamental principle of the spiritual life, that so long as we are in this world we shall have to struggle with our unruly passions. I do not deny that after a long practice of self-denial our corrupt inclinations will be at length subdued and conquered. But I must not be understood to mean that these passions of ours will lose all power of movement, and be unable to give any more annoyance after their defeat. I have just now laid down the very contrary, and St. Bernard states the same in very significant language, when he says: "Believe me, brethren, our passions, though pruned down, will put forth fresh shoots; though driven out, will return; though extinguished, will be kindled anew; though put to sleep, will wake again."* When we say that our passions are mortified, we mean that they are rendered less active, that they have lost their nerve, and have been weakened to such an extent that their motions are less active, less violent, less troublesome and less dangerous; for which reason they can be overcome by spiritual men with greater ease and quicker speed. Still the battle is ever raging, because the foe never dies. We must then always grasp tight the sword, and be prepared to strike down now this, now that, brutal appetite, as soon as it uplifts its head, and rises in daring rebellion against the spirit.

245. St. Gregory, in his commentary on these words of holy Job, *And the beasts of the land shall be tame*, observes: "By these beasts are signified our passions, which by their motions rise up against reason, and may truly be said to urge us from within ourselves to what befits the brutes, to things that suit more the nature of brutes than that of man.† Who is there," he continues, "that living in the flesh, may fairly believe himself to have quite tamed these wild beasts, when even the Apostle of the Gentiles, though rapt to the third heaven in lofty ecstasy, heard within himself the roarings of those fierce and untamable brutes, our

* Credite mihi, et putata repullulant, et effugata redeunt, et reaccenduntur extincta, et sopita denuo excitantur. In Cant. Serm. 58.

† *Bestiæ terræ pacificæ erunt.* . . . Possunt per terræ bestias motus carnis intelligi, qui dum mentem nostram irrationabilia suadendo lacessunt, contra nos bestialiter insurgunt. Moral. lib vj, cap. 16.

passions?"* Next, he adds, for the encouragement of men of good will, this holy and wholesome doctrine: "Far other is it to hear the roaring of these savage beasts (namely our passions) than to feel their bite. They who deny themselves in nothing, and refuse to mortify their inclinations, not only hear the roar of these beasts but are wounded by them, and mangled with the gashes of the many sins committed in obedience to their dictates. But such as practise mortification, keep them straitly confined behind the bars of continence, and suffer them not to come near enough to be able to bite."† Therefore we may conclude that so long as we live in this mortal body we must ever remain on the watch against ourselves, even as one who lives in the company of savage beasts; that we must ever keep a tight hand on the reins of continence and on the bridle of mortification, to bind the jaws of these implacable brutes, which are always, one after another, seeking to tear us to pieces.

246. We read in the Lives of the Fathers of the Desert that a monk, who was living the life of a solitary in a forest, went to visit Abbot Theodore in order to complain to him of the inward disturbance which he experienced on account of the activity of his passions. At his first visit, the Abbot replied as follows: "Since you cannot enjoy peace in the calm of solitude, go and dwell with others in a monastery, and live under the obedience of the Abbot who governs it." The hermit went his way, and lived for a time with some monks; but soon returned to renew his complaints to the Abbot, saying that even in the monastery he was troubled by the turmoil of passion, nor could he, though dwelling in that holy place, find the peace after which he sighed. The Abbot then asked him: "Tell me, Brother, how long a time has passed since you first became a Religious?" "Eight years," was

* Quis enim adhuc in hâc corruptibili carne subsistens, has terræ bestias plene edomat, cum ille ad tertium cœlum raptus egregius prædicator dicat: *Video aliam legem in membris meis repugnantem legi mentis meæ, et captivum me ducentem in lege peccati, quæ est in membris meis?*

† Sed aliud est has bestias in cavo operis sævientes aspicere, aliud intra cordis caveam frequentes tenere. Redactæ namque intra claustra continentiæ, etsi adhuc tentando rugiunt, usque ad morsum tamen, ut diximus, actionis illicitæ, non excedunt.

the answer. "Know then," rejoined the Abbot, "that it is now sixty years since I began to profess the monastic life, and all this time I have never passed one single day without being disturbed by some passion or other." Thus the solitary was given to understand that, so long as this miserable life lasts, a servant of God must ever be in readiness to fight against the rebellion of his lusts; that although, by generous mortification, the war may wax less fierce, and victory become more easy, yet for all that we can never be at perfect peace with enemies such as ours, that know no pity.

247. Now, in order that this mortification of our passions may not be considered more difficult than it is, and in order that we may have confidence in being able to rid ourselves of them, another rule is to be observed. We should change the matter and the objects of our passions; we should supply them with a different aliment, and whereas they have hitherto been bound down to the vile and worthless things of earth, we should force them to be occupied with the holy and precious goods of Heaven. In such wise, though we may not hope to uproot our passions from our hearts, we shall sanctify them and change them from the hindrance they were, into an instrument and means of perfection. To reduce this suggestion to practice, we should act as follows: The passion of love—let us suppose—is grovelling in an attachment to some worldly object, let it turn to God, and from the sinful imperfect affection that it was, it will be transformed into His holy love. In like manner, the desire, nay, the hankering that we feel for the transient things of earth may be directed to the things of Heaven; and thus our fear of temporal losses may be changed into a wholesome dread of such as are eternal: thus can our hopes at once become heavenly, and our harmful terrors be changed into a saving fear. The gratifications we were always seeking from the miserable delights of earth, we shall now seek in converse with God in the practice of virtue and spiritual exercises, and thus our pleasures, from being either sinful or dangerous, will become safe and holy. This, beyond question, is the easiest, the most agreeable, and the most effectual way of subduing the unruly passions of our souls; giving them, that is to say, a new

sphere of action, a different food, and occupying them with good, profitable, and holy objects. In a word, to pretend to conquer our concupiscences by mere resistance, without supplying them with other objects, is too violent a strain to be lasting; for, as St. Augustine says, the heart of man cannot live long without some affection and some pleasure, which it must seek either in the creature or the Creator, in things of time or in things of eternity.* All this teaching I have borrowed from Cassian.†

248. But in order to withdraw our inclinations from the things of earth, and to give them a relish for supernatural and divine objects—which lie beyond the ken of our senses—we must, of necessity, exercise ourselves much in meditation upon heavenly things and in the reading of devout books. We must hold familiar intercourse with God in prayer; we must frequently, during the day, keep ourselves in His presence, and often speak of spiritual matters. For, although holy things are far above our senses, if they be assiduously pondered, they take shape and reality in our imagination, and make an agreeable impression on our hearts. Thus the sensual appetite easily directs its affections to them, and finds in them a far sweeter gratification than it had hitherto derived from the filthy objects of this world. And, further, if it should please God to vouchsafe a very special grace, our passions will, by this means, not indeed be wholly extirpated (as we have already shown, more than once, that this is impossible), but so calmed down, as only slightly and rarely to be an occasion of disturbance. Instances of this may be seen in the case of certain saints who seem to have become wholly insensible to all earthly objects.

249. Cæsarius relates‡ that a monk of the Cistercian order had

* Aut infimis delectatur aut summis.

† Non possunt desideria præsentium rerum reprimi vel avelli nisi pro istis affectibus noxiis quos cupimus amputare, alii salutares fuerint intromissi. Nullatenus enim valet vivacitas mentis absque alicujus desiderii, vel timoris, vel gaudii, vel mæroris affectione subsistere, nisi hæc eadem in bonam partem fuerint immutata. Et idcirco si carnales concupiscentias de cordibus nostris desideramus extrudere, spirituales earum locis plantemus protinus voluptates, ut his noster animus semper innexus, et habeat quibus jugiter immoretur, et illecebras præsentium, et temporalium respuat gaudiorum. Collat. lib. xii., cap. 5.

‡ Miracul., Lib. x. cap. 6.

attained to so high a pitch of sanctity that by the very touch of his garments he wrought great and frequent miracles. His Abbot, reflecting that the manner of life of this religious differed in no one point from that of the rest of the brethren, wondered exceedingly at the many prodigies which God wrought by his means. Calling him aside one day, "Tell me, my son," he said, "Tell me in all simplicity, what is the cause of the many miracles you work?" "Father," replied the monk, "I do not myself know; for I never fast more than the others, nor do I ever prolong my prayers and vigils beyond what the custom of our monastery requires. I can only guess at one cause, and this I mention to you in confidence, as you are my Superior. I am neither elated by any prosperity, nor cast down by adversity; when praised, I am not puffed up; if despised, I do not trouble myself; when I have plenty, I thank God; if not enough, again I thank Him; when sick, I am not sad; if in health, I do not rejoice." On hearing thus far, the Abbot rejoined: "But tell me, when, some months hence, the soldiers ravaged with fire and sword all the estates belonging to our province, did you not feel disturbed?" "No, Father," was the reply, "I at once left all to God's holy will." The Abbot then saw that the holiness of this monk consisted not in outward things—in these he was like his brethren, and therefore his sanctity made no show in the eyes of others—but was nourished by a perfect mortification of all his passions, obtained by means of the great love of God which had struck most deep root in his heart. Such, then, is the easiest as well as the most effectual way of moderating, or rather I should say, of giving order to, the disordered affections of our souls, called passions. By such means we change our passions into holy affections, applying them to spiritual things, but especially directing to God Himself the passion of love, which, as the mainspring and regulator of all the others, will, when sanctified itself, sanctify all the others, since the rest of the passions are dependent upon love for their every movement. Now this is the very course pursued by the holy monk of whom we have just been speaking.

CHAPTER V.

PRACTICAL SUGGESTIONS TO DIRECTORS ON THE SUBJECT OF THE PRESENT ARTICLE.

250. FIRST suggestion. A long practice in the sacred ministry will have convinced directors of consciences that there are many indeed who make profession of piety and aspire to Christian perfection, but there are very few who attain it in even a middling degree. The reason for which is no other but this: that few are at all in earnest about mortifying their inclinations and subduing their passions. No Confessor but has met with some who make all their perfection to consist in fasting, or else in long vocal prayers, or in lengthened visits to the church, or in frequent Communions, or at least in afflicting their bodies by the use of instruments of penance. But few, very few, are they who strive in real earnest to overcome every motion of resentment; to subdue every rising of anger within their souls; to get the better of every slight feeling of rancour or aversion against a neighbour from whom they have received some offence; to bear meekly and peaceably every gainsaying and detraction which touches them to the quick; to wean their affections from possessions or persons whenever they feel that the attachment is too great; to subject their own will and their own views to the will and views of another; to conform themselves wholly to God's designs in all the mischances which may befall them; and so on of other things. This is why many there are who occupy themselves with aiming at the spiritual life, but few are they who make any notable progress in the way of perfection.

251. It must not be supposed that I am blaming prayers, meditations, frequentation of the sacraments, fasts, and bodily austerities. Directors cannot but have noticed how earnestly and frequently I have recommended these devout practices. But I am urging that if these practices are to be profitable, and are to lead to the end proposed—that is to perfection—they should be made to bear on the mortification of the passions. For fasting

and the rest are the remote means of perfection, while the inward mortification of our appetites and inclinations is the proximate means; seeing that by this we acquire all the moral virtues which pave the way to the perfect love of God. If, then, a devout person be accustomed to meditate, the Director will see that the meditations be directed to the uprooting of all imperfect inclinations, and that a portion of the mental prayer be employed in making firm resolutions to mortify these and keep them under. If the penitent have the habit of praying vocally, he must be instructed always to beg in his prayer for grace to conquer his predominant passion. If he frequent the sacraments, let him be told to offer them up to obtain a plentiful grace by which he may subdue some prevailing bad inclination. If he be addicted to fasting, or to the use of any other bodily austerity, let him aim at subjugating the flesh and all his unruly passions to the spirit. In a word, Directors must take pains to convince those whom they guide that all the devout practices which we have mentioned are only means to interior mortification; just as interior mortification is itself the means for acquiring those virtues which are the proximate and the ultimate disposition for obtaining the love of God in its perfection. Let them, therefore, not weary of inculcating upon all the pregnant sentence of the author of the Imitation: *Progress in virtue is in proportion to the violence done to ourselves.** All who travel by any other road will tire themselves greatly, and advance but little. Should, then, Confessors find penitents prone to excess in prayer, or to indiscreet penances, a limited allowance should be appointed; and such persons must be told to make up for what they would like to do in the way of great penance by interior mortification, and by overcoming themselves in some special point on which they appear inclined to yield to themselves; with the assurance that to do this will be more acceptable to God than anything else. They will thus omit a favourite practice of virtue, only to supply its place by one that is much more profitable.

252. Second suggestion. If the Director find his penitent fervent in the practice of the virtues, and desirous of advancing, he

* Tantum proficies, quantum tibi ipsi vim intuleris. Imit., lib. i, cap. 25.

should try to help him in the exercise of this interior mortification. He should examine what is the predominant passion, and must apply his skill to mortify this defect. If, for instance, he find the person much given to pride, let him take occasion to rebuke him, let him keep from showing the esteem he may have conceived of him, and command him to exercise himself in humble and lowly employments; for the humiliation of the body is commonly followed by that of the heart. If the penitent be seen to be over-fond of liberty, society, and amusement, the Director must put what restraint he can on his mixing too freely with the world. Above all, he should break the will in those matters on which it is most set, however spiritual and holy such matters may be: for there can be nothing holier than to give up our own opinion and to go against our own will.

253. Such were the means employed by the great St. Antony to lead Paul the Simple in a short time to a sublime degree of perfection.* This man having detected his wife in adultery, had fled, without saying a word, from his house and family, and had wandered a homeless outcast through the wilderness. While thus a fugitive in the desert, he chanced to come across the holy Abbot Antony. Inspired from above, he threw himself at once at his feet, and gave himself up to him as his disciple. Under the training of this great saint, he attained, within a few years, to such a height of holiness, that he wrought wonders even more stupendous than those of his master. Hence, St. Antony feared lest the multitude of those who came to his pupil for succour might interfere with the progress of his contemplation; and sent him to the farthest parts of the desert, where few would be found to overcome the difficulty of access. But by what means, think you, did this great Patriarch of monks so speedily raise his disciple to such sublime holiness? By none other than the unceasing mortification wherewith he continually exercised him. At times he would say to him, "Stay here kneeling in prayer at the door of my cell, until I come out," and he would keep him in this posture a whole day and night together, secretly observing meanwhile, through the lattice of his window, the behaviour of his dis-

* In Vitis Patrum, In Vitâ S. Pauli Simpl.

ciple, whom he ever found immovable in prayer. At other times, he would order him to draw water from the well and then spill it on the ground, and would keep him whole days employed in this useless labour. At others, he would set him to make baskets, and when the work was done to perfection, would scold him for not having done it aright, and tell him to undo the whole and to begin anew: and would frequently lay upon him countless other tasks very trying to nature, and even repugnant to reason itself. By this continual mortification, by breaking his will in a thousand different ways, he soon formed him into one of the greatest saints of the Desert. Of so great avail is an expert Director, who knows how to mortify in fitting seasons the natural inclinations of his penitent. It should, however, be borne in mind, that such mortifications are to be proportioned to the spiritual strength of the penitent, lest they be more than his actual state will allow him to bear: else, far from being an exercise of his virtue, they would become a danger of its being overladen and failing.

254. Third suggestion. The Director must not rest content with his penitent's checking his vicious appetites only, but must endeavour to induce him to mortify those appetites which tend to things lawful indeed in themselves, but yet not necessary; for, as St. Gregory says, "It belongs to the servants of God always to keep from what is unlawful, and frequently even from what is lawful." * By denying ourselves lawful gratifications we become more sure of not taking such as are either sinful, imperfect, or dangerous: for self-love being kept under and weakened by these supererogatory mortifications, will not venture to require what we are forbidden to grant. Besides, God deals more generously with souls which He sees to be liberal and generous in denying themselves, for His sake, in those matters in which they might lawfully find pleasure; and He fills such with a superabundance of graces and favours, of divine and supernatural gifts.

255. St. Ambrose, in the funeral oration pronounced by him over the Emperor Valentinian, relates many such acts of self-denial which had been practised by the deceased. The Emperor

* Habent quippe sancti viri hoc proprium, ut semper ab illicitis longe sint, a se plerumque etiam licita abscindant. Dial., lib. iv., cap. 11.

was very fond of the Games in the Circus; yet he abstained from them so entirely that he would not have them celebrated even on his birthday.* He was passionately addicted to the chase, and to the sport afforded by the wild beasts which were exhibited in those days at the public shows. But he deprived himself of this pleasure by causing all the animals to be slaughtered on one day.† His enemies, not knowing what to say against so blameless a life, objected against him his over-eagerness to take his meals before the usual time. He not only corrected himself in this particular, but began to fast frequently; so that many a time, in order not to be wanting in the politeness so befitting his imperial dignity, he was present at grand banquets, but would, with heroic self-denial, remain without eating during the whole of a sumptuous repast.‡ Word was brought to him that the young nobility of Rome was being fascinated by the charms of a certain actress. He summoned her to the palace; and then would not vouchsafe to her a single glance, both to mortify his own curiosity, and to teach thoughtless young men how they should guard their hearts against the love of women. And, what is still more to be admired, we may add, that he acted thus while yet unmarried, and before he had become attached to the lady who afterwards was the partner of his throne.§

256. The like acts of self-denial in abstaining from lawful pleasures are related of other personages, illustrious both by their birth and by their virtues. St. Francis Borgia, for example, when

* Ferebatur ludis Circensibus delectari. Sic illud abstersit ut ne solemnibus quidem principum natalibus, vel imperialis honoris gratiâ, Circenses putaret esse celebrandos. In Obitu Valent.

† Aiebant aliqui ferarum eum venationibus occupari, atque ab actibus publicis intentionem ejus abduci. Omnes feras uno momento jussit interfici. Ibid.

‡ Jactabant invidi, quod præmature prandium peteret. Coepit ita frequentare jejunium, ut plerumque ipse impransus convivium solemne suis comitibus exhiberet, et quo religioni sacræ satisfaceret, et principis humanitati. Ibid.

§ Scenicæ cujusdam formâ, ac decore deperire Romæ adolescentes nobiles nuntiabatur. Jussit eam ad comitatum venire: deductam tamen numquam aut spectavit, aut vidit. Postea redire præcepit ut et omnes cognoscerent irritum ejus non esse mandatum, et adolescentes doceret ab amore mulieris temperare, quam ipse, qui potuit habere in potestate, despexerat. Et hæc fecit cum adhuc non haberet uxorem. Ibid.

Duke of Gandia, would often while out hawking and when the falcon was hovering over its quarry, about to seize it in its claws, keep his eyes downcast, and thus forego the greatest, perhaps the only, pleasure of the sport. St. Aloysius Gonzaga also, compelled, while Marquis of Castiglione, to be present at public shows, never would lift up his eyes to glance at any object of interest, and thus changed his very diversions into a means of great mortification. But far more noticeable was the self-denial of King David when all-parched with a most burning thirst. Fevered as he was, he could not refrain from uttering an expression of his yearning for the crystal stream that came forth from the well at Bethlehem.* On hearing this, three valiant chiefs went to the camp of the Philistines, and, hewing their way through the hosts of the foe, reached the mouth of the well, and filling a helmet with the water, took it to the king. The sight of this clear, cold spring-water must have greatly enhanced the thirst that was burning the body of the saintly king; but yet he made a sacrifice of it to the Almighty, and refused to taste a single drop.† Directors should accustom their penitents to forego, by similar acts of self-denial, even lawful gratifications. For instance, one of them would like to look at something very curious, instead of looking at it, let him make a sacrifice to God.‡ A person often feels a desire to utter some clever saying, or some witty word; instead of saying it, he should make an offering of it to God, and hold his peace. Again, if the thought occurs of taking some favourite amusement, he should offer the pleasure to God, and renounce the gratification. The same principle will apply to numberless gratifications which present themselves in the course of the day. If the Confessor succeed in bringing his penitents to the exercise of this kind of mortification, he will soon behold them wing a rapid flight to the very summit of perfection: for, in the same measure as self-love is diminished by mortification, in that does the love of God increase.§

* Oh si quis mihi daret potum aquæ de cisternâ, quæ est in Bethlehem juxta portam! II. Reg. xxiij. 15

† At ille noluit bibere, sed libavit eam Domino. Ibid. 16.

‡ Libet eum Domino

§ Diminutio cupiditatis augmentum caritatis: perfecta caritas nulla cupiditas.

ARTICLE VII.

Hindrances to Christian Perfection from the love of Worldly Goods and Riches.

CHAPTER I.

REASONS WHY THE LOVE OF GAIN AND OF WEALTH IS INCOMPATIBLE WITH CHRISTIAN PERFECTION.

257. THE lofty summit of Christian perfection rises within us in the inmost region of our souls. Now, many obstacles thwart us when we would scale the heights which bring us near unto God, placing us in close union with Him. Of these, some are in the immediate vicinity of our souls, as they arise from the inner and outer senses, and may be termed interior obstacles; while other hindrances have their place outside our souls, arising from riches, honours, and other attractive objects, and these may be termed exterior obstacles. But, in contrast to the course usually adopted by the general of an army, who, wishing to carry a high and strong position, begins by first surmounting the obstacles which the outworks oppose to his progress, and only then proceeds to master the greater obstacles presented by the inner fortifications; in direct contrast, I say, with such, we have first striven to overcome the internal hindrance, whereby the senses clog our onward ascent to the summit of perfection; and we now proceed to overturn those external hindrances which impede our advance. I trust that by following this order we shall succeed in our purpose. In the present Article I mean to treat of the impediment which the love of gain and the desire of riches are able to put in the way of our perfection; and then I shall pass on to that which arises from the love of honours and of other objects that charm us, to which I shall devote the following Articles.

258. St. Augustine settles this point in a few brief words. "The desire of gaining or preserving the goods of fortune is the bane of charity, and consequently the ruin of perfection; for

charity being once undermined by this deadly poison, the whole spiritual edifice must needs totter to its fall."* This alone might suffice to show how incompatible with perfection is an inordinate attachment to riches. But that the reader may be more deeply impressed with this truth, I will show him how it happens that the love of wealth wages so fierce a war on charity and on improvement in all other virtues, which, like trusty handmaids, follow in the train of charity, and accompany her as their queen.

259. St. Bernard gives three reasons for this. First, the love of wealth entails great labour and anxiety in its acquirement. Secondly, it begets a great fear of losing what we have gained. Thirdly, it causes us great sorrow when the loss of our property actually occurs: troublesome passions, destroying all peace, and occasioning poignant grief: all incompatible with the practice of virtue and the struggle after perfection.† And this is what our Lord hints at when He says, that "riches are thorns which choke every good impulse that arises within us."‡ "Just so," says St. Gregory; "because riches are the thorns which prick our hearts with anxious cares, inflicting upon them mortal wounds."§ The same holy Doctor, commenting elsewhere on the self-same words of Jesus Christ, distinguishes the three kinds of thorns whereby, according to St. Bernard, riches tear our hearts and keep us far from God and virtue. "Riches," he says, "like sharp thorns torture our souls, and make them bleed with the cares which we have to bear in amassing them; with the fears we feel of losing them; with the pain and bitter grief which follow on their loss."‖

* Venenum caritatis est spes adipiscendorum, aut retinendorum temporalium. Lib lxxxiij, Q., Quæst. 36

† Divitiarum amor insatiabilis longe amplius desiderio torquet animam, quam refrigerat usu; utpote quarum acquisitio quidem laboris, possessio vero timoris, amissio plena doloris invenitur. Serm. De Convers. Ad Clericos, cap. 12.

‡ Et exortæ spinæ suffocaverunt eum.

§ Spinæ sunt quæ cogitationum suarum punctionibus mentem lacerant, et quasi inflicto vulnere cruentant. Hom 15, in Evang.

‖ Divitiæ veluti spinæ animum hominis timoribus, sollicitudinibus, angoribus pungunt, vexant, cruentant. Moral., lib. ij, cap. 27.

260. And he is right. What cares do not worldlings feel, what toils do they not undergo, in heaping up money and treasure! What labours do not their shops and warehouses witness! What fatigues accompany their journeyings by land and sea! How much strength is worn out on books, in the case of literary men! What ruin of health! How many anxious forebodings of loss of profits, of sudden falls in the market, of rivals balking us in our plans! How many sleepless nights, how many anxious days, how many meals eaten without relish, before the gain we longed for is made our own! But supposing that we succeed in our efforts, and fill our coffers with gold, increase our estates, enlarge our houses, and double our incomes, shall we at length be satisfied, and rest content with our riches? By no means; but, on the contrary, then it is that toil and anxiety will be followed by the second pricking, so aptly described by the saints whom we have quoted: then it is, exactly, that there begins to arise in our soul the fear of losing what has been gathered at the cost of such wearing toil. If the sky, in stormy weather, re-echo with thunder and be illumined with lightning, immediately there comes a fear lest a violent shower of hail lay waste our fields. If the heavens be too sparing or too prodigal of their rain, should the weather be too dry or too wet, too cold or too warm, there arises the alarming prospect of a bad harvest. This man dreads lest a jealous competitor should oust him from a lucrative situation, lest an unfavourable judgment should deprive him of a rich inheritance Another man suffers fears arising from robbers, from servants, from persons employed on his property, from members of his own family, nay, even from his very children, thinking that they may some day waste in a moment what it took him long years and extraordinary efforts to amass. And, to adopt the words of St. Basil, I may further add that, if a dog bark, we are frightened lest the alarm be caused by some one attempting to rob us of our money or our goods.* Even Juvenal, the satirist, ridicules the poignant fears which agitate the hearts of persons

* Canis latrat, avarus putat furem esse. Mus forte perstrepit, in avari cor salit, quemlibet vel puerum suspectum habens. Filios jam grandes ut insidiatores aspicit. Hom. 21, In Aliq Script. Loca.

attached to wealth; writing, that when one of such travels with a full purse, he is not only afraid at the sight of a sword, but trembles from head to foot at the shadow of a reed stirred by the wind.*

261. But by far the most painful thorn is the grief that the lover of wealth must needs feel when it comes to be lost. If one of his ships laden with merchandise founders at sea, how his heart aches! If he is non-suited in a court of law, what bitterness he feels! If his money is purloined, if his debtors fail, if his house is burnt, he straightway goes through a real martyrdom. If he finds that one of his clerks has broken his trust, or that one of his family has incurred a debt, or that one of his friends has betrayed him, what sorrows, cares, and untold anguish will be his portion! Now, how is it possible, may I ask, for a heart distracted by such anxious thoughts, by such sordid passions, by such gnawing cares, to converse with God; to bear any love to virtue; to feel any earnestness in its practice? All this necessarily supposes peace, great calm of heart, complete serenity of mind.

262. And here I will tell an interesting story, which will serve very well to illustrate this gospel truth. Father John Edeus† relates, that a very wealthy person lived in a mansion adjoining the cottage of a poor day labourer, and that his bed-chamber was so close to the hut of this poor working-man as to enable him to hear all that was said, and to take notice of all that was done, within it. He observed that his needy neighbour was always cheerful and merry, and never showed the smallest sign of being heavy at heart. When the man came home at night, fatigued with his day's work, he would light his poor fire, and then would either sing a cheerful ditty, or joke pleasantly with his wife, or play quite happily with his little family. He would then lay him down on his hard bed, and give no further sign of consciousness until his wife aroused him at dawn of day to his accustomed labour.

* Pauca licet portes argenti vascula puri,
Nocte iter ingressus, gladium contumque timebis;
Et motæ ad lunam trepidabis arundinis umbram.

Juven., Sat. 10.

† In Fascic. Virt. et Vit

Turning to his own case, the rich man wondered that he could never succeed in gaining for himself a single moment of unmixed cheerfulness, forasmuch as his days were full of sorrow, his nights disturbed, and his dreams troubled. While brooding over this disparity, it occurred to him that his very wealth and his large estates were the cause why his quiet was disturbed; and that, on the other hand, the poverty of his humble neighbour was itself the real source to which the poor man owed his great contentment and his great happiness. To make sure of this surmise, he adopted a plan which would be sure to test the truth of his conclusion. He took a purse full of money, and in the middle of the night, gently pushing open the ill-secured door of his neighbour's cottage—for it never was very carefully fastened—he hung the money upon the latch inside, and thenceforward took pains to attend particularly to everything that went on. Next morning, the poor labourer got up as usual, and, discovering the purse, was quite beside himself for joy at the sight of so much gold and silver. But very shortly he was plunged into countless anxious thoughts as to how he was to hide his treasure, and how he was to spend it. That day he did not go to his work, but stayed at home in silence and deep thought. Then it occurred to him that should his wife or children get to know of his good fortune, they would not be able to keep the secret, but would bruit it about, with the risk of his losing the treasure. Next he began to fear lest his neighbours, and even members of his household, might rob him of what thus happily and beyond all his expectation he had acquired; and not finding any safe hiding-place for his little store in his wretched hut, he adopted the following plan. He hid it in the pallet of his bed, and, feigning illness, laid him down on it, as if to keep guard over it with his whole person. From this time forward he no longer sang as of yore, nor was he heard to laugh, neither did he romp with his little ones. At night-time he tossed uneasily on his bed, and could not control deep sighs, which were mistaken by his wife for an effect of his illness; they being, all the while, the result of the covetousness which had already made its way into his heart, and was fast poisoning its peace. The gentleman being now convinced that his wealth was the sole cause of all the anxiety and trouble which he suffered, called at the cottage, and asked the wife what had become of her husband, since for some days past he had not heard him talk, or sing or laugh, as up to that time had been his habit. She replied that he was confined to bed with a pain in his side. "No," answered the gentleman, "that is not his ailment. I know what it is; but, doubt me not, he will soon be cured." He then went to the bed of the pretended patient, and said, "My good man, the purse you found hanging at your door is mine. Give it back forthwith, or I will at once go and denounce you to the judge and have you hanged as an infamous thief." Alarmed at such a threat, the poor labourer hastened to restore the purse, and went back to his work; found his peace of heart once more, and recovered his sleep. This anecdote requires but little comment, as the story shows of itself that the attachment to wealth and worldly store is the growth of thorns of which Jesus Christ speaks; which, by countless prickings, pierce the heart of men with anxieties, alarms, and sorrows, rendering it wholly unfit for any practice of virtue and pursuit of perfection; both of which essentially require calm and tranquillity of soul.

263. So true is this, that many—even among pagans, deprived as these were of the light of Faith—have deemed it impossible to acquire the moral virtues which they were striving most earnestly to acquire, unless they first knew how to despise riches. St. Jerome instances the notable example of Crates the Theban, who, taking ship for Athens, that he might there study moral philosophy, cast overboard all the money which he possessed, saying, while stripping himself so generously of his wealth, "Go to, lust of riches! I drown thee in a sea of water, lest thou overwhelm me in an ocean of cares."* In his letter to Paulinus, the holy Doctor plainly says that Crates acted thus, because he did not think it possible to possess together the double treasure of riches and virtue.†

* Crates ille Thebanus, rejecto in mare non parvo auri pondere: Abite, inquit, pessum malæ cupiditates. Ego vos mergam, ne mergar a vobis. Contra Jovin., lib. ii.

† Non putavit se simul posse virtutes et divitias possidere.

264. St. Augustine alleges the examples of some illustrious personages—all of them idolaters—who despised riches, and held poverty in high esteem as being the mother and guardian of the moral virtues to which they were aspiring. He sets up for our admiration a certain Lucius Valerius, who kept himself so poor amid all his greatness, that, though he was Consul when he died, they did not find money enough wherewith to discharge the cost of his funeral, so that the people had to bury him at their own expense: also Cincinnatus, the Dictator and head of the whole Republic, whose only property was a small farm which he ploughed and tilled with his own hands, and who after having most gloriously triumphed over the enemies of his country, returned to his small patch of ground and his plough, to earn his bread by his labours and sweat: Fabricius, too, who spurned the costly presents of King Pyrrhus, and even refused the fourth part of his kingdom rather than part with the priceless treasure of his poverty. The holy Doctor infers from these instances that a Christian should make no great account of renouncing earthly goods and of living in voluntary poverty to gain a blissful country and a never-ending happiness, when these men, pagans as they were and having no such hope, despoiled themselves of the goods of fortune out of the desire they had for the virtues which, even without grace, are the natural ornament of the human soul.* We will conclude, then, in our turn, that if in the eyes of the pagans themselves the love of money, of riches, and of earthly goods, was such a hindrance to the attainment of natural and human virtues (for with all their strength they could

* Quomodo audebit se extollere de voluntariâ paupertate Christianus, ut in hujus vitæ peregrinatione expeditior ambulet viam, quæ perducit ad patriam, ubi veræ divitiæ Deus est. cum audiat vel legat, L. Valerium, qui in suo defunctus est consulatu, usque adeo fuisse pauperem, ut nummis a populo collatis ejus sepultura curaretur? Audiat, vel legat Q. Cincinnatum, cum quatuor jugera possideret, ut ea suis manibus coleret ab aratio esse abductum ut Dictator fieret; victisque hostibus, ingentem gloriam consequutum, in eâdem paupertate mansisse? Aut quid se magnum fecisse prædicabit, qui nullo præmio mundi hujus fuerit ab æternâ illius patriæ societate seductus: cum Fabricium dicit tantis muneribus Pyrrhi Regis Epirotarum, promissâ etiam quartâ parte regni a Romanâ civitate non potuisse divelli, ibique in suâ paupertate privatim manere voluisse? De Civ. Dei, lib. vj., cap. 18.

not strive for anything higher than this), virtues which of themselves rank the lowest of all, how much more powerfully will not such attachments hinder us from acquiring the supernatural and heaven-born virtues which belong to a more elevated sphere; since they make us like unto God, unite us to Him in this life, and fit us for the everlasting possession of Him in that which is to come? How can we hope, with our hearts entangled in such affections, to mount to any high degree of Christian perfection?

265. No wonder then, I may remark with Cassian, that, instead of the prophetic spirit which Giezi might have obtained, descending upon him as by hereditary right from his great master Eliseus, he should have received instead the chastisement of a foul leprosy, covering him from head to foot; because his heart was defiled by greed of gain. Nor are we to be astonished if the unhappy Judas, whom the preaching of our Divine Master had converted, who had been trained in His school, instructed and enlightened by heavenly doctrine, should have fallen from the lofty pitch of holiness whereunto he had been called, and should have plunged himself headlong into the bottomless pit of perdition; seeing that this wretched man was possessed by love of money. No wonder, too, that Ananias and Sapphira were, by an unseen hand, struck dead at the feet of the Prince of the Apostles; for they cherished within their hearts the love of gold, in the very act of despoiling themselves of their possessions.* We may conclude, then, with the Wise Man, that *He that loves gold shall not be justified*,† since the greed of gain and the love of perfection are too much opposed to each other ever to be united in one and the same person.

* Giezi, ea quæ nec antea quidem possederat, volens acquirere, non modo gratiam prophetiæ non meruit possidere, quam per successionem veluti hæreditariam a suo habuit magistro suscipere: verum etiam e contrario æternâ leprâ Sancti Elisei maledictione, perfunditur. Judas autem volens resumere pecunias quas antea Christum secutus abjecerat, non solum ad proditionem Domini lapsus, apostolatûs perdidit gradum, sed etiam vitam ipsam communi exitu finire non meruit, eamque violentâ morte conclusit. Ananias vero et Sapphira reservantes partem quamdam ex his, quæ possederant, apostolico ore morte mulctantur. Instit., lib. vij., cap. 14.

† Qui aurum diligit non justificabitur. Eeclus. xxxj 5.

CHAPTER II.

THAT EXCESSIVE LOVE OF WEALTH IS OPPOSED NOT ONLY TO PERFECTION BUT TO SALVATION.

266. THEY *that will be rich*, says the Apostle, *fall into temptation and the snare of the devil.** And he goes on to explain what this snare is, *And into many foolish hurtful lusts which drown men in distraction and perdition.*† A poisonous serpent lurks amid these thorns; if, then, fearing to be pricked by them, you keep far from them, the serpent will be unable to do you harm; but if you love these thorns as though they were roses, and go near them, and try to pluck them, the reptile will dart out upon you and pierce you with its venomous fangs. "Thus," says St. John Chrysostom, "does the hellish serpent lie hid amongst thorns of riches, and lurking in this covert await his prey."‡ If, through covetousness and lust of gain, you linger in their neighbourhood, with an inordinate desire of acquiring wealth, the infernal serpent will entangle you in his temptations, will sting you in countless ways, and will infect you with the poison of mortal sin: for of a truth, as the Apostle says, there is no evil under the sun which is not caused by love of gold.§

267. Most certainly it is so: for what sin can we point out in this wretched world, what vice is there, but proceeds from this poisoned source? You may inquire whether the desire of wealth can be the cause of infidelity and heresy? But why put the question? Does not St. Paul tell us that this very thing is the cause of sins against Faith? He had just previously laid down that *covetousness is the root of all evil.* Then he proceeds to tell us, that *some having coveted after gold, have erred from the faith*, turning their

* Qui volunt divites fieri, incidunt in tentationem et in laqueum diaboli. I. Tim. vj. 9.

† Et in multa desideria inutilia et nociva, quæ mergunt homines in interitum et perditionem. Ibid.

‡ Diabolus veluti serpens spinis occultatur inter divitiarum imposturam assidue latitans Hom. in Epist. ad Rom.

§ Radix omnium malorum est cupiditas. I. Tim. vj. 10.

backs upon God and upon His truth.* St. Ambrose accounts for this fact as follows: "The love of money," he says, "involves the mind of him that covets it in such darkness that it bewilders and even blinds him, leaving him without light wherewith to discern God and the truth of God's holy faith."† And St. Augustine agrees with St. Ambrose, for he discovers in the covetous heart a certain kind of idolatry. "Since," he remarks, "these wicked persons make money their main end, and use God as a means: inasmuch as they do not spend their money with a view to God, but honour God for the sake of gain; and hence they make money their last end."‡

268. You may ask, perhaps, how can greed of gold be the cause of injuries and injustice done to our neighbour's prejudice? But whence, I answer, come so many unlawful and usurious bargains, so many lawsuits unjustly begun and carried through, so many thefts and robberies, so much unfair dealing in commerce, so much oppression of labourers and of the poor? What, may I ask in turn, is the wellspring from whence streams forth the poison of so many deeds of injustice, if it be not the lust of gold which prevails in the human breast? But inordinate attachment to wealth, you may rejoin, has no part or lot in the abominable vice of impurity. Good God! how many maidens trample underfoot the flower of their virginity, how many wives defile the marriage-bed, how many widows sully their fair fame, for some vile profit! How many are they who spend their money in purchasing the chastity of others, their riches being the origin of their impure life! But love of riches, you may still insist, is not chargeable with part or share in perjury, hatred, and murders. On the contrary, I reply, what numbers are there who, for the sake of gaining

* Quam quidam appetentes erraverunt a fide. Ibid.

† *Radix omnium malorum est cupiditas, quam quidam appetentes erraverunt a fide* Vides ergo quia qui pecuniam habet, fidem perdit: qui aurum redigit, gratiam prodigit. Avaritia autem cæcitas est; errorem religionis inducit. Cæca, inquam, est avaritia, sed diversis fraudum occulata ingeniis: non videt, quæ divinitatis sunt; sed cogitat, quæ cupiditatis sunt. Serm 59, De Avaritia.

‡ Non sicut perversi, qui frui volunt nummo, uti autem Deo, quoniam non nummum propter Deum impendunt, sed Deum propter nummum colunt. De Civ. Dei, lib. xj., cap. 25.

an unjust suit, or of selling their goods at a little higher price, boldly swallow the pill, bitter though it be, of perjury! What hate, what rancour, ever raged in the heart of any man, unless the first fuel had been supplied by interest? How many assassins, rendered more cruel than the very tigers, imbrue their hands in human blood for the sake of a scanty gain! At least, you will add, this sordid vice has nothing in common with sacrilege. But, O God! what numbers take upon themselves the dignity of the Priesthood, called, not by Divine inspirations, but by motives of interest; lured on by the prospect of gain! How many, many such, end by making a hideous medley of masses, sacraments, and sacrileges, and become so much the more execrable in God's sight as they more frequently administer holy things!

269. Let the reader attend to what happened to St. Launomar, and he will see whether what I advance be true or not.* A nobleman of the name of Hermoald, being laid low by a grievous illness, sent the Saint a present of forty crowns, begging of him to intercede on his behalf, and to obtain from God his recovery. The Saint refused to accept the money, and repeatedly sent it back; but yielding at length to the prayers and earnest entreaties of the messenger, he took the sum, and going into his oratory, laid it upon the altar, beseeching God to be pleased to accept of it for the cure of the sick person. Then taking up the purse, he drew forth, one by one, each coin that it contained, and began to examine each in turn with an attentive eye, or rather, I should say, with the eye of a prophet enlightened from above. Having thus gone through every one of the pieces of money, he singled out one, and calling the messenger, said to him, "This is the only piece that I mean to accept: the only one that I can take with any pleasure. This one only coin have I found undefiled and free from fault; all the others are tarnished by robbery and injustice. Return the coins to thy master, and tell him that such money cannot avail to appease God's wrath, *for the sacrifices of the wicked are an abomination to the Lord.*"† Of forty pieces

* Apud Vinc. Bellovac., lib. xxj., cap 84.

† Victimæ impiorum abominabiles sunt Domino. Prov. xv. 8.

of money, one only was found pure, unstained, and free from sin: all the others were soiled, tarnished, and encrusted with the filth of guilt. Now, if this same holy man could go into the dwellings of certain rich persons, who are always hankering after money, and if he were able to direct the clear view of his mind into those purses crammed with silver and gold which are so carefully locked up in desks, chests, and safes, how many meannesses, what abominations, would he not discover in the midst of all this abundance of money? How he would make such people blush at their crimes, and how would he cause them, compelled by the evidence of the truth, to confess with St. Paul that the love of riches is the root of all evil!*

270. This being the case, the awful threats so frequently recorded in Holy Writ against those who covet riches are not without foundation, on account of the great difficulty, even, I may say, the moral impossibility, such are in of saving their souls. *Where are they that hoarded up silver and gold, wherein men trust, and made no end of their getting? They are banished and gone down to hell.*† And with His own mouth Christ says, *Woe to you, ye rich, for ye have your comfort here.*‡ It must be borne in mind that on the lips of Christ, "Woe," according as the interpreters of the Scriptures explain, implies damnation; and this view is borne out by the very words of our Saviour Himself, Who on another occasion, says, *How difficult it is for those that are rich to enter the Kingdom of God!*§ *It is easier for a camel to pass through the eye of a needle, than for a rich man to enter the Kingdom of Heaven:*|| if he be covetous. St. Gregory, in his comment on these words, concludes, that very rarely does a wealthy man, whose heart is set on his riches, attain to the eternal bliss of Paradise; since, according to our Saviour's words, it is morally impossible, as far as it

* Radix omnium malorum est cupiditas. I. Tim. vj. 10.

† Ubi sunt, qui argentum thesaurizant, et aurum, in quo confidunt homines? Exterminati sunt, et ad inferos descenderunt. Baruch. iij. 18.

‡ Væ vobis divitibus, quia habetis hic consolationem vestram. Luc. vj. 24.

§ Quam difficile, qui pecunias habent, intrabunt in regnum cœlorum. Luc. xviij. 24.

|| Facilius est camelum per foramen acûs transire, quam divitem intrare in regnum cœlorum. Matth. xix. 24.

depends upon himself; and hence a miracle of divine grace is required for such a man to be saved.*

271. We read in the Chronicles of the Order of St. Francis of Assisi,† that while Brother Leo was one day attending St. Francis in his sickness, after having fulfilled this charitable office, he withdrew to a corner of the cell to pray. When thus engaged, he was rapt in ecstasy, and transported in spirit to the banks of a wide and rapid river. There he beheld certain Friars, laden with bundles, who entered the bed of the river with the object of reaching the opposite bank. Some were swallowed up in whirlpools and drawn under the current; others, having gone over a third part of the distance, were swept away by the impetuous waves and carried off to perish miserably in the middle of the stream. Some were drowned at a quarter or a fifth of the distance from the opposite bank; others, when they had all but reached the dry land. The servant of God, at the sight of so many fatal accidents, was moved with compassion for the poor wretches, but was unable to give them any assistance. All of a sudden, he beheld other Friars, without bundle, or package, or burden of any kind: these he saw enter the bed of the river with activity and courage, ford it without accident, and safely reach the other side. St. Francis having known meanwhile the vision of Brother Leo, summoned him, and commanded him to give an exact account of all that God had made known to him during his prayer. When he had complied, the Saint exclaimed, "Now, Brother, that which you have seen is no dream, no vain fancy or illusion of the devil: it is the very truth. The mighty river you beheld is the world, the passage through which is so fraught with dangers. Those who, weighted with burdens, perished miserably in the waters, signify the Religious who do not live detached from goods of this earth, but covet them, seek after them,

* Rarum valde est, ut qui aurum possident, ad requiem tendant, cum per semetipsam Veritas dicat: *Difficile, qui, pecunias habent, intrabunt in regnum cœlorum* Nam qui hic multiplicandis divitiis inhiant, quæ alterius vitæ gaudia sperant? quod tamen, ut Redemptor noster valde rarum, et ex solo divino miraculo evenire posse, monstraret: *Apud homines*, inquit, *hoc impossibile est: apud Deum autem omnia possibilia sunt.* Moral., lib. iv., cap. 3.

† Lib. ii, cap. 11.

and strive to procure them with great endeavours. The others who, without incumbrance, crossed with ease to the opposite shore, are the religious who live detached from all temporal goods, in perfecty poverty of spirit. They it is who reach in safety the shore of eternal bliss." Now, applying this mysterious vision to our present subject, I will observe, that if some petty trifles (for, at all events, the property of these hapless religious could not have been more than trifles) proved so great an obstacle to the attaining eternal salvation, as even to occasion everlasting ruin; what will be the case of seculars who hanker with such ardent longings after riches, whose thoughts are all about making profit, about hoarding, enlarging their establishment, increasing their incomes and extending their possessions, with the accompaniment of those burdens on their conscience which are ever joined with this insatiable appetite of possessing? What, I ask, will be their lot? Will they be saved in the end? It may be so, I know: but I cannot persuade myself that it will so be. For the words of our Lord are too plain to be mistaken: *They that love money shall with difficulty enter the Kingdom of Heaven.*

CHAPTER III.

THE REMEDY AGAINST THE HINDRANCES PLACED BY RICHES IN THE WAY OF CHRISTIAN PERFECTION.

272. THE great means of not falling into the snares which the devil has concealed among the thorns of riches in order to drag us down to hell, and if he succeed not in that, to withdraw us at least from the perfection of Christian life, is a total detachment of our affections from wealth and money; whether we have acquired these already or are in search of them, whether we retain them or renounce their possession. This is that true poverty of spirit, so highly extolled by Jesus Christ, and so greatly recommended by the saints; securing us against all the injuries which our spiritual life might receive from temporal possessions. This,

moreover, is the essential perfection of Christian poverty, whereby those who live in the world may, if they will, in the very midst of their riches, vie in perfection with Religious themselves; without which it will avail even religious but little to have outwardly stripped themselves of worldly goods by their voluntary renouncement.

273. St. Ignatius Loyola has explained this poverty of spirit and inner detachment by an apt and most expressive comparison.* "He that is poor in spirit," says this Saint, "must behave as a statue amid the temporal goods which he possesses, or which are allowed him for his necessities. A statue is neither joyous nor sad at whatever may happen: it allows its owner to strip it or to clothe it as he sees fit. If you put a tattered robe on a statue, or throw around it a garment of embroidered silk, all overlaid with pearls, the figure is indifferent whether it bears on its shoulders either one or the other vesture. If you place in the hand of a statue a purse full of gold, or another filled with earth, it is as ready to hold the one as the other. In the same manner, then, should each one of us—whether he be the absolute master of money or of landed property (as are people of the world), or whether we have merely the use of these (as is the case with religious)—comport himself with the like indifference and the like detachment. We should live without affection or esteem for such objects; in readiness either to part with or possess them, to forego or to enjoy them, as God wills and as His most wise Providence may dispose." Such as do this are in God's sight truly *poor in spirit;* and if, being seculars, they abound in wealth, this will in nowise hinder them from reaching the loftiest heights of Christian perfection.

274. All this fits in most admirably with the teachings of the Holy Fathers. St. Gregory the Great, speaking of St. Peter and St. Andrew, asks, what was it that these two great Apostles forsook when they left all to follow our Redeemer, seeing that they possessed scarcely anything that they could leave behind them in the service of so great a Master? He goes on to answer his own objection and says, that in cases such as those just chosen from

* P. Ribaden. et P. Maffei. In Vitâ S. Ign.

the Scripture, we must take note, not so much of the amount or quantity given up, as of the inner disposition of the heart. And as these two Apostles kept for their own use not one even of the trifling objects which they had hitherto possessed under their lowly roofs, and as they had put away all desire of possessing the least thing,—living in perfect detachment of the heart from all earthly goods,—we must own that they forsook much, and might truly say, *Behold, Lord, we have left all things*, and are become poor for Thy sake.* The holy Pontiff continues: "We however act not in this wise; for not being poor of spirit we remain attached to what little we have, and even covet that which we have not."† St Augustine, in like manner, pursuing the same line of thought says that Peter left much, since he left all that he had or desired to have. And, adds the Saint, was there ever a poor man known whose heart teemed not with hopes and expectations of acquiring the fragile and passing goods of this world? or who, amid his penury, did not wish to improve his position in life? St. Peter, therefore, left much when he cut away from his heart all covetous desires.‡ St. Jerome, writing to Paulinus, says, "That man has given up all to God who has given himself—that is, who has given up all the affections of his heart, by detaching it from all the goods of fortune." And he confirms this teaching by the example of the Apostles, "who gave up merely some few fishing-nets and a crazy old boat; yet was their sacrifice most acceptable to Christ, and rewarded by Him with the highest gifts" Again, the Saint points to the example of the widow, who dropped her mite into the treasury, of which mite our Blessed

* Ecce nos reliquimus omnia.

† Ad vocem dominicam uterque iste piscator quid, aut quantum dimisit, qui plane nihil habuit? Sed in hâc re affectum potius debemus pensare, quam censum. Multum reliquit, qui nihil retinuit: multum reliquit, qui quantumlibet parum, totum deseruit. Certe nos habita cum amore possidemus, et ea, quæ minime habemus, ex desiderio quærimus. Multum ergo Petrus, et Andreas dimisit, quando uterque etiam desideria habendi dereliquit Hom 5 in Evang.

‡ Multum dimisit, fratres mei, multum dimisit. Quid? non solum dimisit quidquid habebat, sed etiam quidquid habere cupiebat. Quis enim pauper non turgescit in spe hujus sæculi? quis non quotidie cupit augere quod habet? ista cupiditas præcisa est. In Psalm. ciij., Conc 3.

Lord made as great account as if she had deposited in it all the riches of Crœsus. For Jesus Christ looked not so much to the low value of the boats which the Apostles had left, or to the smallness of the coin given by the widow, as He did to the inward disposition of their hearts.* So true is it that the very pith and marrow of Evangelical poverty consists in the unseen detachment of our heart.

275. From this well-grounded doctrine flows a consequence which cannot but be very consoling to such seculars as seriously strive after perfection, and which must also be very alarming for such religious as are less in earnest about the matter than suits their state. The consequence to which I allude is the following. A secular can be more poor in spirit amid his wealth than a religious in his voluntary poverty, if the former be not attached to his possessions, if he be ready to part with them when required by God, or by duty, and if, moreover, he covet nothing of what does not belong to him. The contrary however is the case if a religious desire any of those things which he has renounced for God's sake, or if he be attached to the trifles allowed him for his own use; for—as it has been truly said by St. Gregory, Pope—in these matters God has more regard to the disposition of the heart than to the object to which it may choose to attach itself.†

276. The story related by John the Deacon, in his Life of St. Gregory the Great, is well known.‡ As it illustrates the truth of the doctrine with which we are now concerned, it will be useful to recall it once more to memory. A hermit of great virtue had stripped himself for God's sake of all his worldly goods, and had retired into a forest to serve the Almighty in continual prayer, fasting, and other bodily austerities. He had kept nothing for himself except a cat, which he had taken with him as a companion in his solitude, and he was in the habit of caressing it and allowing it to lie in his bosom. One day being in prayer,

* Totum dedit Deo, qui seipsum obtulit. Apostoli tantùm navem, et retia reliquerunt. Vidua duo æra misit in gazophylacium, et Crœsi divitiis præfertur.

† Affectum potius debemus pensare, quam censum.

‡ Lib. x., cap. 14.

he besought the Lord to be pleased to show him what reward was in store for one who, renouncing the world and all its wealth, had wholly devoted himself to the divine service. The following night, while he was asleep, God made known to him that such a one might expect in heaven a place as high as that of Gregory, the Bishop of Rome. The hermit was grieved at this answer, and mourning as one who could not be comforted, went about the whole day repeating the following sorrowful complaints: "Poor creature that I am! After having renounced all my worldly means, I am not to expect a greater reward than that reserved to Gregory, who is rolling in riches! What will it avail me to have left home, parents, possessions, revenues, splendour, and luxuries of all kinds, if my recompense is to be only equal to that of one who possesses all these things in greater plenty than was mine?" After having thus spent some days in weeping and lamentation, the Lord God spoke to him again, saying, "It is not for his wealth that a man is rich in My sight, but for his detachment from the lust and affection for riches. Know, then, that your heart is more attached to that cat of yours, which you are all day long stroking and patting, than Gregory is to all his wealth, which in his heart he makes of none account and spends in deeds of charity." At these words the good hermit awoke, and understanding what had hitherto escaped his notice, namely, what was the essence of true poverty of spirit, he began to serve God with greater detachment and in lowlier humility. Seculars, especially such as are married and who cannot lawfully leave their possessions, may be encouraged by this anecdote, since by detachment of heart and the good use of their wealth, they may equal, nay, even may surpass, the poverty of the most austere religious. Let religious then, in their turn, tremble lest, after having despoiled themselves of their temporal goods, they remain, on account of trivial and petty attachments, more rich in God's sight than if they had never renounced what they once possessed, and had kept all but without such attachment. And if any one of them perceive that he has become a slave of the trifles whereon he has set his heart, let him blush for himself who, having done so much, loses all for the sake of so little.

277. But we must observe carefully, before going any further, that it is no easy matter to discover whether our hearts are set upon the goods of which we are the owners, or of which, as poor men, we are allowed the use; and thus it is difficult to determine whether there exists within us that poverty of spirit which is an earnest of the Heavenly Kingdom.* For, the love of worldly possessions is not like personal attachments in the world, which, as a rule, are so warm, fervid and lively, that we cannot hide them from ourselves, and are constantly betraying them to others by outward signs and tokens. The former class of attachments—love of property and love of money—lie hidden deep in the heart, and as they burst not forth into emotions they may be secretly lurking there without our being aware of their presence. In one case only does the attachment discover itself and make itself known; and this is when we fear that we shall be robbed of our possessions, or when we actually have to part with them, whether through violence or of our own free will. If such privation be calmly accepted, with resignation to God's will, it is a sure sign that the heart was free from such attachment. But if, on the contrary, grief and heart-burning be the result, it is clear that an attachment did exist, since the loss or privation is so bitterly felt. To discover whether or not a bandage adheres to a wound, all we have to do is to take it off. If in lifting it up no pain be felt, it is a clear token that the linen was not sticking to the wounded part; if pain be the result, it shows that an adhesion had been formed; and the greater the pain, the more strong the adhesion. The same applies to the subject which we are now treating.

278. I will make what I have just said clearer by the story of Ptolemy, King of Cyprus. Valerius Maximus relates, that this prince had gathered together such heaps of gold, and amassed such vast hoards in his treasury, as to make him a probable subject of apprehension and suspicion on the part of Rome itself. The Romans, taking umbrage at his immense wealth, determined, out of regard for their own security, to make themselves masters

* Beati pauperes spiritu, quoniam ipsorum est regnum cœlorum. Matth. v. 3.

of the island, and to subject it and render it tributary to their Republic. This project came to Ptolemy's ears, who, foreseeing that his treasures would be his undoing, had them stowed away in ships which were pierced with holes in order to sink them in the main sea, and thus deprive the Romans of all hope of so rich a prey. Let us pause here to make a brief observation. Who would not have believed that the heart of this king was in no way set upon his great riches, which he was so ready to throw into the water? At any rate, it would seem plain that he preferred his life and freedom to his treasures, because, in order to preserve the former, he was determined to give up the latter. But this would be a false inference; for when he came to the point of having to part with his treasures, he showed how deeply the attachment to riches had sunk in his heart, since, having reached the open sea with the above-mentioned vessels, as soon as he came to the spot where his gold and silver and jewels were to be swallowed up and lost to him for ever, he suddenly felt such a pang in his heart at the idea of this privation, that he had not the courage to give the word of command, and returned with his precious cargo to the shore; showing by this conduct that not only had riches the mastery over him, but that he was their abject slave.*

279. And so it is. As we said above, when a bandage is taken off, the wound smarts and by smarting proves how fast it was sticking. Just so, if a spiritual man would find out whether or not there exists in his heart the like attachment to worldly pelf, let him watch himself when God deprives him of a portion or of the whole of his riches, by some sudden disaster which visits the family, or by rivals hindering his gains, or doing some other injury to his interests, and let him examine whether, in such cases, he resigns himself to God's will in the total or partial loss of his wealth, without losing peace of heart. If so, he may rest assured that he is not enslaved to his goods and money, but is free from all attachment and in possession of true poverty of spirit. But if

* Procul dubio hic non possedit divitias, sed a divitiis possessus est: titulo, rex insulæ; animo autem, pecuniæ miserabile mancipium. Lib. ix. De Avarit., cap. 4.

on these occasions, he feels much grief, great affliction, and can find no means of restoring peace to his heart, he may rest convinced that he is attached to his wealth, and bound thereto by the chain of a most imperfect and most dangerous affection. Of this there can be no doubt, for it is impossible that the human heart should feel the pain of separation from an object to which it is not attached.

CHAPTER IV.

THE MOST EFFECTUAL MEANS FOR FREEING OURSELVES FROM ATTACHMENT TO RICHES, AND FOR ATTAINING TRUE POVERTY OF SPIRIT.

280. I HAVE just stated that loss of goods, money, and property in general, is the touchstone for testing whether or not the heart of man be set upon them, and, as a consequence, whether he possess poverty of spirit, or be devoid of this virtue. I now add, that this privation is not only a sign whereby to know, but a remedy, and perhaps the most effectual one, to remove the like attachments; to sunder the chains that bind us in slavery to silver and gold; and to obtain true freedom of spirit. For which reason every spiritual person should deprive himself wholly, or in part, of his possessions, in the manner set forth by the rules of Christian perfection, as will now be explained.

281. St. Barnabas the Apostle, so Baronius relates,* having heard from the lips of Jesus Christ these words, *Sell all that thou hast, and give it to the poor,*† sold forthwith all his valuables and distributed the proceeds to the poor, reserving to himself only a small piece of ground for his own sustenance. But after Christ's Ascension into Heaven, being further enlightened, he sold even this, and laid the price thereof at the feet of the Apostles. The

* Tom. I., A.D. 34.

† Vendite quæ possidetis, et date eleemosynam. Facite vobis sacculos qui non veterascunt, thesaurum non deficientem in cœlis. Luc. xij. 31.

early Christians, who were truly earnest in their desire of Christian perfection, being aware of the counsel given by our Lord, *If thou wouldst be perfect, go and sell all that thou hast, and give it to the poor*,* frequently sold their possessions, and carried the proceeds to the Apostles.† Whoever will do likewise, in imitation of these most saintly Christians, may have full assurance of attaining that poverty of spirit to which Christ has promised happiness upon this earth, and far greater bliss in Heaven above. Because, so generous an abandonment of all the goods of fortune, of necessity presupposes, that our attachment to wealth is entirely extinguished.

282. But if we go one step further and, not content with stripping ourselves of all that we have, bind ourselves before God by vow never to possess any earthly thing, we shall succeed far more thoroughly in sundering all attachment, and in bursting those meshes with which the devil covers wealth and with which he entangles the frivolous; since by this vow a man uproots from his heart not only the actual love of riches, but all hope of ever possessing any for the future. Now, this is precisely what Religious do by their solemn vow of poverty. The first example of this vow was set by the Apostles, whom St. Augustine believes to have bound themselves under oath to poverty. He forms this conclusion from the words of St. Peter, *Behold, we have left all things*.‡ The Apostles found imitators in their disciples, concerning whom St. Augustine,§ St. Jerome,‖ St. Gregory, Pope,¶ St. John Chrysostom** affirm, that by this same vow they put away from themselves all manner of interest and property in earthly goods. From the Apostles and their followers, in the course of ages, religious poverty took its rise. Hence religious are more prepared than any others for the attainment of poverty of spirit, if they will but manage to act up to

* Si vis perfectus esse, vade, et vende quæ habes, et da pauperibus. Matth. xix 21.

† Nemo quidquam suum esse dicebat: sed erant illis omnia communia Act. iv 32.

‡ Lib. xvij. De Civit. Dei, cap. 4.

§ Serm. 17. De Verb. Apost.

‖ Ad Demetriad.

¶ Lib. i., Ep 35.

** Auctor., cap. 5.

what they have promised to God with such generous self-renouncement, and under such heroic strictness of obligation; never taking back, even in affection, any part of what they have so solemnly renounced: else, under the guise of poverty, they will (as I have said above), be richer than many seculars who are detached from their possessions; and will be less disposed than many who remain in the world to pursue after perfection.

283. But, as all cannot attain to this heroic self-despoilment of their goods, on account of wife, children, and other relations, whom they are bound to support; or for other reasonable considerations, which may have place in each and every walk of life; every Christian who would be a disciple of the Saviour, and who desires to make progress in spirit, must strip himself, at least in part, of riches and wealth. Having taken what is requisite for the suitable maintenance of himself and others dependent upon him, he must distribute the remainder with open hand to the poor, and employ it in works of religion or piety. Whoever refuses to do this, cannot pretend to be exempt from an inordinate attachment to his property; seeing that he cannot make up his mind to forego what is not needed for his own sustenance: thus plainly convicting himself of an excessive attachment to earthly possessions. He may, indeed, afflict his body with disciplines and fastings; he may reduce it by long prayers and watchings; but notwithstanding all this, he will never be able to make much progress in perfection, since his attachment to wealth will always be a great impediment in the way of his advancement. St. John Chrysostom, speaking of interested motives, sets forth this truth with great clearness by the following comparison:—"A ship laden with a valuable cargo, but beyond the power of her tonnage to carry, is liable to founder through the weight of the very riches which she bears within her bosom; but if her freight be moderate she will make the port in safety."* "In like manner," says the Saint, "if a Christian, by keeping everything for himself, becomes overladen with money and possessions, his riches may lead him to sink in an ocean of grievous

* Si quando in navigiis est onus justo gravius, demergit cymba: cum vero est moderatum, prospero fertur cursu. Serm. De Avar.

faults, and even of unquenchable fire." But if, retaining only a moderate portion of his revenues, so much as is required for a fitting maintenance, he spend the rest on pious works, his very wealth will help him to sail prosperously to the haven of perfection. It would be needless to allege, in proof of this, the examples of charitable persons who have been generous in spending their means upon the relief of the poor; such stories abound, and every town can record many such. It will suffice to call our reader's attention to one of the most heroic acts of renunciation of riches that can be found in the pages of history, namely, that of St. Mechtildis and her brothers. It is related by Thomas of Cantipré, who was her contemporary.

284. This holy virgin was born of the royal race of Scotland. An illustrious offshoot of that kingly stem, she was brought up amid the pleasures, the luxuries and the splendour of court life. She had four brothers, the eldest of whom, after having distinguished himself in the army, turned his back on warfare the palace and his wife, going as an exile and wanderer through the world, begging his bread, and obtaining as an alms the poor pittance necessary to sustain life. The second brother, who was an Earl, trampling under foot the plenty of the royal palace, withdrew into a vast wilderness, there to lead a poor and solitary life. The third was an Archbishop who, laying aside his mitre and crosier, became a poor Cistercian monk. The fourth, Alexander by name, remained at home, as the King wished him to succeed to the throne. One day Maud, who was then not more than twenty years old, calling the last named of her brothers, began to speak to him in the following terms, addressing him in a compassionate tone of voice—"What will become of us two, my dearest brother? Our other brothers, in order to win a heavenly crown, have renounced an earthly kingdom, and have left you their kingdom of this earth, with the danger of your losing the throne prepared for you on high. A sorry exchange indeed! What do you mean to do? what course are you going to adopt?" Alexander, bursting into tears, turned to his sister and said—"What would you advise me to do? Speak! since I am determined, for the sake of my soul's welfare, to put into execution whatever you think best." Seeing

him so well disposed Maud replied—"My wish is, that we also should both renounce the riches of earth in order to win the never-failing treasures of heaven. I propose that we should fly together from our father's palace." Without more ado, they each put on a disguise, and, thus concealed, made their way to a far-distant country, where Maud taught her brother to milk the cows and to make cheese of their milk. As soon as she saw him expert in this lowly occupation, they passed over to France. On their arrival there she placed him in a Cistercian monastery, called Fanium, to take charge of the dairy, and stayed with him until the monks, being satisfied with the ability of which he gave proof in this humble occupation, admitted him as a lay-brother into their community. Seeing him thus permanently settled in God's service, Maud said to him—"Brother, we have earned a great reward by leaving the palace, but it will be still greater if we now separate from each other never to meet again." These words went like arrows straight through the heart of Alexander. He wept bitterly, feeling greater sorrow in parting with his saintly sister than he had felt in giving up the crown; yet making an effort to control himself, he became resigned. Maud then withdrew to a village, hid herself in a poor cottage, where she earned a scanty pittance by the work of her hands; sleeping on the bare ground, and exercising herself in continual prayer; during which God ofttimes raised her to Himself in ecstasy, and, overwhelming her with heavenly delights, repaid her even here below for the great sacrifice that she had made for His sake.

285. I am aware that one must be of royal blood to make the like acts of self-renouncement. Still we may imitate this holy virgin to a certain extent, and may in some sort follow the example even of her brothers. If we cannot forsake sceptres, crowns and kingdoms, and have not the courage to deprive ourselves of our possessions, we can at least retrench what is not necessary for our condition; not indeed for the purpose of heaping up new hoards by these economies, but in order to give the value to God in the person of His poor. We can at least deny ourselves some comfort, pleasure or pomp, forego some greater gain, with a view to spend the price on the worship of God, on churches, or altars,

or on other works of Christian piety. But if we refuse to do even this little for God's sake; if, cleaving to our treasures and possessions, like some sea-creature to a rock, we seek vain pretences for greedily keeping all to ourselves; we shall ever be far from Christian perfection, and further still from poverty of spirit. But, what is worse than all, we cannot expect God to act generously with us, when we show ourselves so sparing and so miserly in our dealings with Him.

CHAPTER V.

PRACTICAL SUGGESTIONS TO DIRECTORS CONCERNING THE PRESENT ARTICLE.

286. FIRST suggestion. The Director will meet with persons who seem to be spiritual, because their conversation is most blameless, because they abhor the pomps and vanities of the world, and are assiduous in long vocal prayer. Yet if he search into their interior he will discover much that is wrong, on account of their inordinate attachment to their money and worldly goods; an attachment betraying itself by the stinginess of their dealings with those of their household, by the hard bargains they drive with their servants, workmen, tradesmen, and tillers of their lands; by their little love of and compassion for the needy, and by their neglect in relieving them in their distress: above all, by an excessive striving to hoard, which absorbs their every thought. The Director must make no account of the apparently good spiritual state of such persons as these, since true devotion and true spirituality are incompatible with so sordid a passion as covetousness. He should strive rather to make them become spiritual by dinning into their ears the warning given to the rich man of the Gospel parable—*Thou fool, this night thy soul shall be required of thee; and the things thou hast provided, whose shall they be?** Thy children

* Stulte hâc nocte animam tuam repetent a te: quæ autem parasti, cujus erunt? Luc. xij. 20.

or grandchildren will enjoy them, but what shall it avail thee that they be well off on this earth, if it be thy lot to burn in fire for a time, or for everlasting? Let the Confessor impress these truths upon penitents of such a character, and get them often to meditate on the great end of all, which is death; a consideration of much effect for uprooting such attachments from our hearts. Because, since death strips us of our temporal possessions, the assiduous meditation upon our coming end strips our hearts of their affection for these goods.

287. Another most effectual means for healing this class of spiritual maladies will be, to reflect frequently on the poverty of Christ, Who, dwelling amongst us in mortal flesh, had not a roof to shelter Him, though King of Heaven and Monarch of the Universe. From His own lips do we hear, *The foxes have their holes, and the birds of the air their nests, but the Son of Man has not whereon to lay His head.** A most powerful remedy against the fever of covetousness is frequently to bring before the mind that hankers after worldly goods, the poverty in which Christ was born, lived, and died; to represent it to ourselves—thus St. Cyprian represented it to his people—as the inseparable companion of our blessed Lord, ever abiding with Him, and appearing in His clothing, in His dwelling, in His kinsfolk and companions. Christ at His birth preferred to sumptuous palaces the shelter of a stable. His Mother laid Him there upon the straw, and placed Him in a lowly manger. Instead of royal purple, Jesus chose to be clad in miserable rags; instead of being clothed in fine linen, He willed to be wrapped in a handful of tatters. Such was the dwelling selected for Himself by the Maker of the World. such the delights which marked His birthday. As He grew up, He dispensed with servants and handmaids, who would have been out of keeping with the scanty furniture of His abode, with the smallness of His means and the frugality of His diet. When preaching His Gospel He would have no rich or wealthy disciples, but preferred to choose poor fishermen as His companions. The Mother was poor; poor was the Son; the cottage He lived in was poor; the

* Vulpes foveas habent, et volucres cœli nidos: filius autem hominis non habet ubi caput suum reclinet. Matth. viij. 20.

shelter it afforded was poor. Such are the examples which Christ has left to His true followers in the Church militant.* Such, too, are the maxims which the Director should inculcate upon certain falsely devout and covetous persons, in order that they may make them a subject of their repeated consideration at the foot of the Crucifix; for if these be leisurely and repeatedly pondered, they will avail to uproot by degrees from their hearts the attachment therein engendered by a mistaken esteem of riches.

288. Second suggestion. The Director must be aware that those who strive to join piety and avarice have countless excuses wherewith to palliate their greed of gain. They imagine a thousand necessities of their children, their grandchildren and other kinsfolk; they forecast countless dangers and disasters; extending their anxious cares to a distant future, being wholly absorbed in the idea of leaving their family after their death well provided for, in wealth, in comfort and in security. What is worse, blinded as they are by covetousness, they deem this a justification for being sparing of their alms to the poor, unfair in dealing with their neighbours, and penurious with themselves. The Director must not listen to these excuses, as such motives are not suggested by reason but by the passion which rules within them. He must rather urge these penitents to behave with befitting generosity, both to those of their household and to strangers; he must urge them to give abundant alms, not only on account of the merit attaching to this practice, but also because, by frequently parting with their money, they will gradually learn to become detached from it. For this purpose he will frequently put them in mind of what has been already observed, that they should take heed not to rob Christ in the person of His poor, lest in the dreadful judgment-day they too come to hear from His lips the

* Nulla domûs ambitio, nisi declinatorium in stabulo, mater in fœno, filius in præsepio. Tale elegit fabricator mundi hospitium. hujusmodi habuit delicias sacræ Virginis puerperium. Panniculi pro purpurâ, pro bysso in ornatu regio laciniæ congeruntur. . . . . Pedissequas substantia familiaris non patitur, mancipiorum obsequia sumptus tenuis, et inops mensa excludit. . . . Christus pauper discipulos divites aspernatur Pauper mater, pauper filius, inops hospitium, his, qui in formâ hujus scholæ in ecclesiâ militant, præbens efficax documentum. Serm. de Nativit.

awful reproach.* He should not be too ready to allow them to aim at increasing their income, enlarging their establishment, and hoarding up for their children and relatives; since, were these motives sufficient to dispense us from alms-giving, no one would be bound to this virtue however rich he might be, even were he Crœsus himself. Who is there, indeed, in the world but might add to his store, and by constantly doing this become able to leave his heirs rolling in riches? But this pretext for not giving alms is a vain one, and has been condemned by Innocent XI., who condemned those who taught that scarce any one can be bound to give alms out of what is superfluous to his position in life, since even kings need all that they have.†

289. Third suggestion. If the penitent be a religious, the Director must make a distinction in what concerns the use of money and other property, between the substance of the poverty which the penitent has vowed and the perfection of the virtue; in order to be sure of guiding this soul aright. The substance of religious poverty consists in this, that the religious man or woman is deprived of the dominion over any kind of property or money, being allowed only the use of things; and this use, moreover, is permitted only with the knowledge of, and in dependence upon, lawful superiors. The religious must bear in mind, that by the act of consecration which was made to God when the vows were taken, we renounced by the vow of holy poverty all right and claim to our own possessions, and undertook a strict obligation to God never more to have dominion over any earthly good whatever, and never to possess them as if our own. So that, after our Profession, we are no longer, nor can we ever hope to be, master of anything, not even of the habit which we wear, everything belonging to our Monastery or to our Order. And by the same vow we further undertook the obligation of not making use of any of these things of which we cannot be proprietors, except with the special or general leave of our Superiors.

* Esurivi, et non dedistis mihi manducare: sitivi, et non dedistis mihi bibere. Matth. xxv. 42.

† Vix in sæcularibus invenies, etiam regibus, superfluum statui, et ita vix aliquis tenetur ad eleemosynam, quando tenetur tantùm ex superfluo statui.

And though it may suffice, as far as regards the substance of the vow, that this leave be merely implied, it is always safer to obtain an express permission.

290. Whence it follows that if a religious of either sex give, receive, sell, buy, or in a word dispose of any temporal thing without the necessary permission, that person commits a twofold grievous sin; or, to speak more exactly, incurs by one mortal sin the guilt of two grievous faults. For there is theft in disposing of what is not, and cannot be, the property of a religious; and there is sacrilege in violating a promise made to God by a solemn vow. St. Jerome relates, on this point, an awful instance, of recent occurrence in his day, which happened in a monastery of Nitria. I will quote his own words: "A monk, who was sparing rather than covetous, left at his death a small sum of money, which he had earned by making baskets. All the monks of the neighbourhood met in solemn conclave, to the number of five thousand, in order to determine what was to be done with the money which the deceased had secretly amassed. Some would have it given to the poor; others thought that it should be spent on divine worship, and applied to the Church; while not a few were of opinion that it would be the best plan to hand it over to the relatives of the deceased. But the Abbots Macarius, Pambo, and Isidore, with all the most revered of the Fathers of the Desert, by a special inspiration of the Holy Ghost, decreed that this money should be buried with the monk who had retained it as his own, and that, when it was placed at his side, the assembled brethren should say, 'Be thy money with thee unto perdition.'" * This event struck such terror into all the monks of Egypt, that not one of them would have dared to dispose of a penny without leave.

* Quidam ex fratribus parcior magis, quam avarior, et nesciens triginta argenteis Dominum venditum, centum solidos, quos lina texendo acquisierat, moriens dereliquit. Initum est inter monachos consilium (nam in eodem loco circiter quinque millia diversis cellulis habitabant) quid facto opus esset. Alii pauperibus distribuendos esse dicebant: alii dandos ecclesiæ: nonnulli parentibus remittendos: Macarius vero, Pambo, et Isidorus, et cæteri, quos patres vocant, Sancto in eis loquente Spiritu, decreverunt, infodiendos cum eodem, dicentes: Pecunia tua tecum sit in perditionem. Nec hoc crudeliter quisquam putet factum. Epist. ad Eustochium.

291. St. Gregory relates a similar instance as having happened when he himself was in Rome, and Abbot of his monastery.* A deceased monk was discovered to have been in possession of three crowns. The Saint having heard this, commanded that the wretched man should be buried in a dung-heap, and that while this ignominious burial was being performed, the Community, in imitation of the ancient monks, should say those awful words "Thy money be with thee unto perdition." The Director may now see what an enormous sin it is for a religious to keep or to dispose in anywise of money or any other thing as though it belonged to him; without obtaining due leave. Should he happen to meet with any person consecrated to God in holy seclusion who has fallen in this way, he will impress upon the person the grievousness of his sin, warning him, and telling him to be very cautious for the future to keep in strict dependence upon his lawful Superiors in the use of goods and money. Should the Director wish to learn from me what quantity is required to render the religious who disposes of anything without leave, guilty of grievous sin, I will answer, that the same sum which is required for a mortal sin of theft suffices for a mortal sin against the vow of poverty; but as authors do not agree as to the precise quantity required in the former case, neither are they unanimous in fixing what quantity would constitute a grievous breach of the vow of poverty.

292. Thus far, then, for what touches the mere substance of religious poverty. But the Director should beware of resting satisfied with so little in the case of religious, who are under grave obligation to tend to perfection. While treating of seculars in this Article, we were not content with their merely avoiding mortal guilt in the use which they make of their property, but we required of them the pursuit of perfection proportioned to their state of life. Much less should we remain content with this in religious, who have vowed poverty hoping not only to keep from sin but to attain perfection. To reach then the perfection of this virtue which, despoiling our outer man of the goods of earth, enriches the soul with everlasting treasures, three

* S. Greg. Dial., lib. iv., cap. 55.

things are, as it appears to me, requisite. First, to retrench whatever is vain or superfluous; secondly, to bear with patience, if we cannot feel joy in, the privation of what is necessary; thirdly, to keep up an entire detachment from the necessary or suitable objects which are allowed us for our use.

293. As to the first requisite, it is plain on the very surface that nothing is so contrary to the state of poverty as to possess things which are superfluous, and much more things that are useless, since even they who pass for rich in the world do not usually abound in what is superfluous for their position in life. The world says, "Blessed is he that has;" while Christ, on the contrary, says, "Blessed is he that has not, but makes himself poor."* The religious should then ask himself with whom does he intend to be happy, with the world or with Christ? If he replies that he seeks the happiness which Christ bestows, both in this and the next life, on His followers and all faithful imitators of His poverty, then let him be told that he must strip himself of all superfluous comforts, even as His Saviour chose to forego them. Such was the practice of St. Teresa, who frequently during the year searched every part of her cell with a spiritual eye, and on discovering anything superfluous, made an offering thereof to the Lord, renouncing it for His sake. Moreover, she tells us of herself, that when she found anything useless, she was unable to recollect herself in prayer until she had parted with it, God giving her thereby to know how jealous a lover He is of holy poverty, since a trifling superfluity was such an obstacle to the reception of His favours. But as religious poverty is not kept with the same rigour in every Order and Institute, I would lay down this rule for knowing what each religious should look upon as a superfluity. I would attend to the practice of those who are the most observant, the most exact, whose conscience is the most delicate, in each Order or Community; and all that is not conformable with the simplicity of these exemplary religious in their dress, their cells, and the common things allowed for daily use, I would set down as a superfluity deserving retrenchment.

294. As regards the second point, I will remark that, as never

* Vade, et vende ea quæ habes, et da pauperibus.

to suffer any privation of what our state demands is to be rich indeed, so nothing is more appropriate to religious poverty than to have to bear with the want of some things which are really necessary. For if religious were never to stand in need of anything connected with food, clothing, habitation, or their daily employ, what would be the merit of the virtue of poverty? In what would their vow produce an imitation of our Saviour's poverty? In what respect would they be like to Christ? Let them look for a while into the life of Christ, as did St. Cyprian who was quoted above, and see how many necessaries were ever wanting to Our Lord. Let them but cast a glance on the cave at Bethlehem where He was born; they will find neither cradle wherein to lay Him nor fire to warm Him. Let them consider the lowly cottage of Nazareth where He dwelt; they will find it unfurnished, comfortless, and not much superior to the poor dwelling of His infant days. And if they look at Him during the time of His preaching, they will find Him without house or home, or shelter that He can call His own. Beholding Him on the Cross, they will see Him stripped of His very garments, dying naked in the sight of all the people of ungrateful Jerusalem. A religious should rejoice, therefore, when necessaries fail him, seeing that this little taste of poverty likens him to his Lord, and wins for him a treasure of unfading glory in Paradise. Never should he, like an imperfect religious, allow himself to be constantly complaining of those in charge because they do not provide everything in sufficient abundance: murmuring at the Superiors because they are wanting in vigilance: grumbling at the underlings because they are neglectful in the care that they should take of him.

295. With regard to the third point, I have already shown in the third Chapter, that the poverty of spirit which is the quintessence of the virtue of poverty consists in the detachment of the heart from every temporal thing. Nor is it to the purpose to say that the attachment is to some trifle only, and hence is of slight moment; because every attachment, whether great or small, clogs the soul in its progress towards perfection. Whether you hold a bird by a thin thread, by a piece of twine, or by a thick rope, it cannot escape, nor poise itself on its wings in the air, nor soar

aloft. And so in like manner, it matters not whether the devil keep our hearts captive by an attachment to great or small things; we are equally unable to rise to God freely and without check, and to soar to perfection; much less of course can we attain poverty of spirit, which requires a heart disengaged from every kind of attachment. If, then, the Director have charge of nuns or other religious, who have devoted themselves to God by the vow of holy poverty, he will take care that they keep to more than the mere essentials of this virtue, and he will strive to secure its perfect observance, by inculcating on them what I have set forth above.

296. Fourth suggestion. I have many a time and oft met with Confessors of religious persons who freely allowed their penitents to give and to receive presents and money. Where these Confessors got their power to do this is, I must own, more than I can tell. If they acted thus in virtue of an express and special license of the Superior, it was all right; if otherwise, their permissions were illicit and invalid. Because, religious having made their vows in the hands of the Superior, and not of the Confessor, they depend on the former, not on the latter, in the use of temporals. To their Superiors, then, they must have recourse, not to their Confessors, for the permission that they may seek to obtain.

ARTICLE VIII.

Hindrances to Christian perfection arising from the inordinate craving for Worldly Honour and Glory.

CHAPTER I.

THE DISTINCTION BETWEEN AMBITION AND VAINGLORY, AND IN WHAT THE MALICE OF THESE TWO VICES CONSISTS.

297. Among the objects which, by their allurements, make war upon the soul from without, Worldly Honour and Glory rank next

to Riches. Wealth bewitches us and keeps us far from God by the glitter of gold and silver, while honour and glory separate us from God by a certain empty show which is peculiar to them. And if, as we have seen in the foregoing Article, riches are a great hindrance to our spiritual progress, worldly honours and glory are its ruin. This truth we shall now proceed to demonstrate.

298. I must begin by explaining what is meant by the words honour and glory, lest they be mistaken for one and the same thing, while in reality they are quite distinct. It will be necessary to explain what are those passions of ours which rush headlong in pursuit of these two bright phantoms, worldly honour and glory, and in what consists the disorder of our loving them. Honour, says St. Thomas, implies a certain respect or homage paid by us to another in acknowledgment of his excellence.* Thus by bending the knee, or by bowing down, or performing other acts indicative of respect, before kings, emperors, and other high personages of this world, we are said to do them homage in acknowledgment of their eminent dignity; and from such acts honour results. "Glory," says the same Saint, "is to set forth some quality or action which, becoming known, brings honour to the person and secures him esteem and praise, whether that which is published be a bodily gift or some quality of the soul."† Thus by making public a victory won by some brave commander, or an heroic act by which some Christian forgives his sworn foe, glory is gained; for such deeds, becoming public, secure for the one a reputation for courage, and for the other the character of a virtuous and holy man.

299. This being presupposed, the passion or vice of Ambition, according to the Angelic Doctor, is an inordinate desire of honour, whereby we seek for marks of homage which may witness to some endowment or excellence possessed by us.‡ The vice of vainglory is an inordinate craving for glory, whereby the vain per-

* Honor importat quamdam reverentiam alicui exhibitam, in protestationem excellentiæ ejus. 2, 2, q 191, art. 1.

† Nomen gloriæ proprie importat manifestationem alicujus de hoc, quod apud homines decorum videtur; sive illud sit bonum corporale aliquod, sive spirituale. 2, 2, q. 132, art. 1.

‡ Ambitio importat appetitum inordinatum honoris. 2, 2, q. 131, art. 2.

son desires that some quality or praiseworthy action of his be made manifest for the sake of the esteem and praise which he hopes to gain; so that vainglory has for its object the glory of the world, while ambition covets the honours of the world. But as both honour and glory may be wished for and sought after virtuously and without any stain of vice, St. Thomas proceeds to show wherein consists the disorder of these two vicious passions.

300. Treating of ambition, the Angelic Doctor shows that its inordinateness or disorder consists in these three things:—First, we may seek a homage far beyond our deserts, which we always do when we are destitute of that quality, to the true existence of which this homage should bear witness. Secondly, we may seek honour for ourselves without referring it to God, to Whom alone it is due, since whatever is excellent in us we have from His gift, from Whom *every good and perfect gift descends.* Thirdly, we may rest in the honour received as in our last end, without directing it to the profit and advantage of our neighbours.* Consequently, if we seek after such honour only as is really due to us, and if we refer it wholly to God in sincerity of heart, and make it available to the spiritual or temporal weal of others, we shall not incur the blame of ambition. When we act thus, we act with that uprightness of heart which entirely excludes the three above-mentioned disorders. Thus wise and conscientious princes are accustomed to act, when claiming due honour from their subjects, knowing that this is needed for the good government of their people, and feeling that they are the vicegerents of God, to Whom the homage paid to their persons is finally referred. It must, however, be borne in mind that, ordinarily speaking, it is not lawful for one not placed in such exalted positions and dignities to desire, and much less to strive to obtain, them; because they are an occasion of honour to the person who holds them on account of the exalted rank to which they raise

* Tripliciter autem appetitum honoris contingit esse inordinatum. Uno modo per hoc, quod aliquis appetit testimonium de excellentiâ, quam non habet, quod est appetere honorem supra suam proportionem. Alio modo per hoc, quod honorem sibi cupit, non referendo in Deum. Tertio, per hoc, quod appetitus ejus in ipso honore quiescit, non referens honorem ad utilitatem aliorum. 2, 2, q. 191, art. 1.

him, and it is most difficult to desire such dazzling objects without some inordinate affection, and most difficult, consequently, to keep clear of the sin of ambition or even of presumption, should the person in question be unfitted for the post which he covets.

301. Then proceeding to vainglory, the same holy Doctor discovers three disorders in the desire of glory akin to those of ambition in its striving after honour.* The first disorder has place when the vain person desires glory on account of some gift which he does not possess; or of some noble act which he has not performed; or seeks for it on account of something base and trivial which he has done, but which is in nowise worthy of praise. The second disorder consists in seeking glory of men, whose judgments about us are so mistaken and false, and who oftentimes praise what is not praiseworthy, but, on the contrary, deserving of blame. The third disorder has its rise in not giving the glory of our good deeds to God, to Whom alone all glory is due, as the Apostle teaches;† or else in failing to direct it to our neighbour's welfare, but rather in drinking up the whole of it ourselves and becoming, so to speak, intoxicated with it as if it were wholly ours. Whence it follows, that whoever desires a glory free from these three blemishes—in other words, who desires glory for deeds truly deserving of honour and praise; whoever wishes it not for himself, but to give it to God; whoever covets it as a means of doing good to others, does not incur the guilt of vainglory.

302. Trusting that our readers will now perceive both the distinction existing between ambition and vainglory, and also the deformity of these two vices, we will next proceed to show how opposed both are to Christian perfection. In the succeeding Chapter, which we shall immediately commence, we shall

* Uno modo ex parte rei, de quâ quis gloriam quærit: puta, cum quis quærit gloriam de eo, quod non est, vel de eo, quod non est gloriâ dignum, sicut de re fragili et caducâ. Alio modo ex parte ejus, a quo gloriam quærit: puta hominis, cujus judicium non est certum. Tertio modo ex parte ipsius qui gloriam appetit; qui videlicet appetitum gloriæ suæ non refert in debitum finem, puta ad honorem Dei, et proximi salutem. 2, 2, q. 192, art. 1.

† Soli Deo honor, et gloria. I. Tim. i. 17.

briefly describe the war waged against perfection by ambition, while the following will show how much more dangerous a foe it has in vainglory.

CHAPTER II.

THE FIERCE WAR WHICH THE PASSION OF AMBITION WAGES AGAINST SPIRITUALITY.

303. THE ill-regulated desire of honour, called by us Ambition, wars so fiercely against spiritual persons, and obstructs so mightily their progress that, as the Holy Fathers say, many who had overcome all other wickedness, have been in their turn overcome and undone by this vice of the spirit. Let us listen to St. Ambrose speaking on this point:—"Ambition is the most dangerous of our sins, because it gently invites and pleasantly allures us to dignities. Whence it often happens that they whom lust has been unable to defile, and avarice could not overthrow, nor any other vice vanquish, have at last fallen into the slavery of ambition and have come to lose the favour of the Lord their God."* St. John Chrysostom says the same, but much more plainly and emphatically:—"Ambition blinds our minds. To despise riches is easy in one who chooses not to care for them; but it is far more arduous and difficult to despise honour when it is paid to us by the multitude. To do this, belongs only to persons of an angelic mind and of high wisdom, whose thoughts are already raised from earth to heaven. There is," he continues, "no vice which tyrannises over us as this one which, triumphing over every heart, reigns supreme everywhere."†

* Hoc ipso periculosior ambitio est, quod blanda quædam est consiliatricula dignitatum; et sæpe quos vitia nulla delectant, quos nulla potuit movere luxuria, nulla avaritia subvertere, facit criminosos. Lib. iv. in Luc., cap. 4.

† Adcæcat mentis intuitum præsentis gloriæ furor: nam pecunias quidem contemnere, volenti satis est facile; honorem autem a multis collatum despicere, multi laboris indiget, magnæ sapientiæ, angelicæ cujusdam animæ ipsum cœlestis celsitudinis verticem tangentis. Non est enim, non est, inquam, vitium ita tyrannicum, et ubique dominans. Hom. 43 ad Popul. Antiochen.

304. St. Cyprian, going into particulars, and treating of persons consecrated to God, who for this reason are, more than others, bound to lead a devout life, says, that ambition takes root even in the hearts of Priests and secretly takes up its dwelling within their bosoms.* But no one of the Fathers has gone so deeply into this subject, in order to fathom the deformity of the vice, as St. Bernard who, setting himself to describe it as it is in itself and to paint it in its true colours, speaks of it with the utmost possible severity. "Ambition is a subtle poison, which easily insinuates itself everywhere; a secret venom, a hidden pestilence of the soul. It is the artificer of deceit, the mother of hypocrisy, the source of envy, the parent of vice, the incentive to all manner of villainy, the rust which eats into virtue, the moth that devours sanctity, bewitching our hearts, changing even remedies into disease, and from the very medicines themselves breeding sickness and death."† Let the reader consider attentively this portrait of ambition drawn by the practical hand of St. Bernard, and then let him say whether a more hideous monster than this vice has ever appeared in the world.

305. It was not without reason, then, that saints (who, to use the words of St. John Chrysostom, by their heroic virtues were lifted up above the earth) shrank with such abhorrence from station, dignities and honours. They were full of alarm lest they should fall a prey to the hideous monster of ambition, and be irretrievably enslaved in its embrace. St. Gregory, as is related in his life, having been elected Supreme Pontiff and Chief Bishop of the Catholic Church, went and hid himself in an obscure cave in order to flee the splendours of this eminent dignity. But being betrayed by a gleaming pillar of fire, and seated, as it were, by force on the papal throne, he wrote to the Emperor Maurice, entreating him in the most urgent terms not to consent to his election; that thus, if the choice had been disapproved of, he might have escaped the honours to which he had so rooted an

* Etiam in sinu sacerdotum ambitio dormit: ibi sub umbrâ recubat, in secrete thalami se fraudulenter occultat. Serm. de Jejun. et Tentat

† Ambitio subtile malum, secretum virus, pestis occulta, doli artifex, virtutum ærugo, tinea sanctitatis, excæcatrix cordium, ex remediis morbos creans, generans ex medicinâ languores. In Ps. xc.

aversion.* St. John Chrysostom, in order to flee from ecclesiastical dignities, hid himself in the desert and buried himself in solitude. Being, however, discovered by Flavian, through a revelation of God, he was consecrated and afterwards compelled to ascend the archiepiscopal throne of Constantinople.† St. Ambrose, chosen by the unanimous acclamation of the people and of the reigning Emperor to the See of Milan, secretly left the city by night and fled away. But God so directed his steps by an extraordinary providence that, after having travelled all night long he found himself at daybreak at the city gate from which he had started on his journey.‡ St. Jerome was so adverse to honours that, though in priest's orders, he abstained from exercising the functions of his sacred ministry in the monastery in which he dwelt for many years § The holy hermit Ammonius, fearing to be made Bishop, cut off one of his ears in order to render himself by this mutilation, ineligible for the episcopal office.|| St. Malachy, on his election to the episcopate, so steadily refused this dignity that it became necessary to threaten him with excommunication in order to force him to accept it.¶ But I should never make an end were I to tell of all the great souls who have shrunk from honours with more abhorrence than others would fly from dishonour and disgrace. The reason was, that they knew how difficult it is to find ourselves surrounded with homage and not to leave some opening to ambition; not to allow this vehement passion to force us out of the path of perfection. Hence they looked upon lofty dignities as so many points of danger, thinking that the greater was the height to which they were raised, the more easy and the more disastrous would be a fall into the abyss below.

306. Meanwhile, with the evidence of this truth before them, what have so many worldlings to say in their excuse, who, blinded by the glare of empty honours, run headlong after them, and place

* Joan Diac. In Vitâ S. Gregor.
† Metaphrast. In Vitâ S Joan. Chrysost.
‡ Paulin. In Vitâ S Ambr.
§ Epiph. Epist ad Joannem.
|| Pallad , Hist. Lausiac, cap. 12.
¶ S. Bernard. In Vitâ S. Malachiæ.

all their happiness in being the object of the homages of their fellow-men in this miserable world? What can those many ecclesiastics say for themselves, whose only desire is to attain to some post of honour in the Church, and who direct all their endeavours to this object, sparing neither toil nor fatigue; who make use of the credit of their friends, of the patronage of the great; and who if, after endless intrigues, they succeed in obtaining their wish, give themselves up to a life of repose and contentment, as though they had reached the very centre of all possible bliss? The same, too, must be said of those Religious who, after having turned their backs upon the honours of the world, eagerly search for these very same honours in religious life; covet posts of responsibility, dignities, benefices, preferments, within the narrow limits of the cloister; and when balked of their desires, lose their peace of mind, filled with numberless regrets, countless rancorous feelings, complaints without end. How can they attempt to reconcile this spirit of ambition with the spirit of that perfection after which religious are bound to strive?

CHAPTER III.

THAT VAINGLORY IS ONE OF THE MOST DEADLY FOES TO CHRISTIAN PERFECTION, SINCE IT INFECTS ALL OUR ACTIONS, AND TAINTS THEM WITH A MORTAL POISON.

307. To kill a man is nothing more nor less than to separate his soul from his body by some violent action, the result of which is that what was a man becomes a corpse, retaining the semblance of a human being, though it be a man no longer. Now this is just what Vainglory does to every virtuous action to which it attaches itself; it robs each of our good deeds of whatever is good, supernatural, meritorious and holy in it; and changes each into a corpse, which bears the semblance of virtue to the eyes of man, but in the sight of God is made hideous and a mere deformity, by this vainglory; it, in one word, kills all our good actions by

the alluring poison of self-complacency. One man gives an alms, and while he is in the very act of bestowing it, vainglory steps in and mars the virtuous deed. The beholders of the charitable act esteem it to be holy, but God looks upon it as an abomination, because vanity has sucked out of it whatever was virtuous, holy and meritorious, its very soul in fact; changing it into a corpse which retains the appearance of a living virtue, but is in reality nothing but a dead and vicious act. The same holds good of every other act of Christian perfection. And the reason of all this is plain; for our good works being animated by the godly purpose which moves us to bring them forth to the light of day, derive from this motive, joined with interior assisting grace, all their supernatural character, all their lustre and merit. But by vainglory insinuating itself, the good motive is set aside and is supplanted by a sinful one, which wholly destroys it.

308. Hence our Blessed Saviour solemnly warned those who, when they gave alms, published the fact with the sound of a trumpet, in order to attract the esteem and praise of men;* or who, in their fasts, affected a certain austerity of countenance for the purpose of letting men know that they were fasting.† He said that for such there would be no reward in the world to come; ‡ because vainglory had robbed their actions of whatever merit they might have had, transforming them into loathsome carcases, which, far from pleasing God and moving Him to bestow a recompense, only provoked His wrath and chastisement. These ill-starred persons are in like case with King Ezechias, who, having boastfully shown the rich treasures of his palace to the ambassadors of the King of Babylon, heard from God, by the mouth of His prophet Isaias, that in punishment of this vanity he was to lose all the treasures in which he had taken so much pride.§ In like manner do we, by mingling vainglory with our actions, rob ourselves of all the spiritual riches we might otherwise have amassed by their

* Tubâ canunt ante se, ut honorificentur ab hominibus. Matth. vj. 2.

† Exterminant facies suas, ut appareant hominibus jejunantes.

‡ Receperunt mercedem suam

§ Auferentur omnia, quæ sunt in domo tuâ, et quæ condiderunt patres tui usque in diem hanc, in Babylonem non remanebit quidquam, ait Dominus. IV Reg. xxx. 17.

means; so that they add neither to our merit here nor to our reward hereafter.

309. In the Chronicles of the Cistercian Order, we read of a monk who was gifted with a most excellent voice, and was, moreover, a most accomplished singer. The poor man, however, misusing these gifts, when he joined with the other monks in choir, together with his wish to praise God, harboured also a longing desire to hear himself commended; and took more pleasure in the honour which he received from his fine voice, than in the praise which God received from the Divine Office. It pleased the Lord to make known to all the monastery what little account He made of the praise which this monk gave Him with so much vanity, and how destitute of merit was that manner of singing the Office. It happened then one morning, that after he had finished intoning a responsory, there appeared in the midst of the choir, visibly to all present, a loathsome blackamoor who, dancing about, and clapping his hands, and applauding, by other uncouth gestures, the chant of the unhappy monk, cried aloud, "What a splendid voice! how well he has been singing!"* The reader will bear in mind that nothing is more pleasing to God's ears than the chant of His praises, especially in the company of many of His servants: but if vanity glides in to taint this service, nothing can be more grating to God's ears, or more pleasing to those of the devil. So fatal is the poison wherewith this vice infects our every good deed. With St. Basil then may we conclude, "Let us fly from vainglory, the moth-worm of virtue, the enemy of our soul; for however agreeable and attractive it may be, it gently robs us of all our good works, and sweetly pillages all our spiritual store; disguising its fatal venom in a honeyed draught, and with its sweetness poisoning alike the mind and heart."†

* O bene cantavit: optime cantatum est.

† Fugiamus inanem gloriam, dulcem spiritualium operum spoliatricem: jucundum animarum nostrarum hostem; tineam virtutum, blandissimam bonorum nostrorum deprædatricem, eamdemque mellis illitu fraudis sui veneni coloratricem, et mortiferi hominum mentibus poculi porrectricem. Constit. Monast., cap. 11.

CHAPTER IV.

VAINGLORY A DEADLY FOE TO PERFECTION, WHICH IT ATTACKS AT THE HEAD OF A COMPANY OF SEVEN VICES.

310. St. Thomas, following the view taken by St. Gregory the Great, does not number Pride among the Capital Sins, but sets it apart by itself as the Queen of these vices, which follow in its train and form a hideous court around it. Hence, instead of pride, he places at the head of the capital sins, its first-born daughter, namely, Vainglory.* The holy Doctor next proceeds to represent this vice under the figure of a hydra, from whose empoisoned womb spring forth seven other vices for the destruction of Christian perfection. Those vices, says the Saint, which are subordinate to the end and object of some one capital sin are the children of that sin, and may also be termed the branches or offshoots of that evil trunk.† Now, there are seven vices which tend, either directly or indirectly, to the vain putting forward of our own excellence, the sole end and darling object of vainglory; so that it may be said that the offspring of this frightful monster, the offshoots of this poisonous root, are seven in number. Boasting makes our merits known in a direct manner by the use of words; Presumption parades them by deeds; Hypocrisy shows by deceit, making a pretence of spiritual gifts which are not possessed. We also make a show of our excellence in an indirect manner, when we refuse to admit our inferiority to others. Now this may take place, as regards the mind, by Obstinacy in our opinion, which we pertinaciously refuse to abandon for that of another, though it be more solidly grounded.

* Gregorius autem in libro trigesimo primo Moralium, superbiam ponit reginam omnium vitiorum, et inanem gloriam, quæ immediate ab ipsâ oritur, ponit vitium capitale: et hoc rationabiliter. 2, 2, q. 132, art. 4, et q. 162, art. 8.

† Dicendum, quod ut supra dictum est, illa vitia quæ de se nata sunt ordinari ad finem alicujus vitii capitalis dicuntur filiæ ejus. Finis autem inanis gloriæ est manifestatio propriæ excellentiæ. Ad quod potest homo tendere dupliciter: uno modo directe, sive per verba, et hæc est jactantia: sive per facta, etc. 2, 2, qu. 132, art 1.

As regards the will, this is done by Discord, when we are unwilling to give up our own engagements or occupation for the sake of compliance with another's request. As regards our words, vainglory is shown by noisy Disputes, by loud and quarrelsome outbursts, when maintaining our own opinion. As regards our deeds, it is manifested by Disobedience whenever we refuse to be subject to the commands of those who are set over us. Thus, according to the Angelic Doctor, from this evil root of vainglory spring forth these seven detestable offshoots,—Boasting, Presumption, Hypocrisy, Obstinacy, Discord, Quarrels, Disobedience. The reader may now see for himself what an enemy vainglory is to perfection, which it invests on all sides, banded together with these seven vices, combining its efforts with theirs, and sparing no pains for its destruction. He may now determine whether a spiritual person is capable of making any progress, unless he uproot from his heart the last fibre of this poisoned root, which is so fertile a parent of evil.

311. For this cause, our Divine Lord, seeing His disciples full of complacency and vain rejoicing because the demons showed themselves subject and obedient to their commands, rebuked them at once, and warned them of their evil disposition; for He knew very well the fatal effects which would result if it once grew up and spread itself within their hearts.* He trampled these first motions of vanity under foot by recalling to their memory the awful fall of Lucifer, hurled headlong from heaven on account of the complacency which he took in his sublime prerogatives: † as St. Cyprian most aptly observes in his commentary upon this passage.‡ And we may here take notice how much every feeling of vainglory is to be shunned since, despite the meekness, gentleness and kindly bearing of Jesus, especially

* Verumtamen in hoc nolite gaudere, quia spiritus subjiciuntur vobis. Luc. x. 20.

† Videbam satanam, sicut fulgur de cœlo cadentem.

‡ Gloriabantur aliquando discipuli, et complacebant sibi in miraculis congratulabundi, quod eis etiam dæmones obedient; sed repressa est, incipante Domino, simplicitatis eorum præsumptio. *Videbam*, inquit, *satanam descendentem de cœlo.* His verbis eorum animis intimans. . . . quia ante hominis conditionem superbientis diaboli ruinam vidit. Serm. de Jejun. et Tentat.

in dealing with His disciples, He no sooner saw them yielding to this vice than He resolved to terrify them by bringing to their mind the fall of Lucifer from the heights of heaven into the bottomless depths. In doing this, He implied a threat of a like fall for them, from the high station to which He had raised them if, in the future, they did not rid themselves of all such vanity.

312. This truth was fully realised by that saintly monk whom Abbot Pastor pointed out to his religious as a model of humility, since he always shrank from the praise and esteem of men, and even went in fear of the vainglory which so often springs from this cause.* The holy man dwelt in a poor cell in the neighbourhood of Constantinople, in great poverty and seclusion, and in very remarkable austerity of life. The Emperor Theodosius, having heard of his sanctity, wished to see him and to converse with him face to face. Leaving behind him his escort of guards and his whole attendance of courtiers, he entered, without making himself known, into the cell of the solitary, and, after a short conversation, seeing nothing in this poverty-stricken place but a few pieces of dry bread, the emperor asked to be allowed to partake of some refreshment. The good hermit at once laid the table, putting thereon water and salt, his own usual fare; and they took their meal together. When the meal was ended, the emperor made himself known. The solitary, in confusion, prostrated himself with his face to the ground out of veneration and reverence, and began to apologise for the frugal way in which he had entertained his august guest. Theodosius raised him up with his own hands, and declared that he was fully satisfied with this poor and simple reception, and saying that he envied much the happy lot of the monk, he took his leave. After his departure, the holy man bethought himself that the emperor's visit would pave the way for people of all classes, both high and low, to come to his hermitage, and that the courtiers, in imitation of their master, would make a point of coming to visit him. He began to fear lest, amid these crowds anxious to pay him respect, the devil should glide in and tempt him to vainglory; lest he should

* In Lib. Sent. Patrum, § 18.

grow fond of praise, and take pleasure in the esteem and good opinion which others would testify of him; whence a great decrease of fervour, and perhaps the total ruin of his spiritual life, would follow. He therefore, without any hesitation or delay, left his hermitage that very night, and fled into Egypt, in order to live alone and unknown amid the holy Fathers of the Desert. Here we have the case of a man who was deeply aware of the many vices and evils to which vainglory gives rise, since he fled so anxiously from every temptation which might be occasioned by the homage and esteem of the world. He did not act as some imperfect spiritual persons who, far from hiding their gifts, display them and flaunt them and who, instead of fleeing praise, go forth to seek and to meet it. No wonder that these people feel gratified thereby, become filled with vanity, are puffed up, end at length by indulging in vainglory, and in losing every sentiment of true spirituality.*

CHAPTER V.

VAINGLORY IS SHOWN TO BE SO GREAT AN ENEMY OF CHRISTIAN PERFECTION THAT NO OTHER IS AS DIFFICULT TO OVERCOME.

313. HAVING shown how formidable an enemy to Christian perfection vainglory is, and with what a number of vices it is leagued in the war it carries on, I may now add, that it is an all but unconquerable foe, because it is so treacherous that not only is it impossible completely to crush it by the acts of a perfect life, but it finds its nourishment in our good actions themselves, and from these strengthens itself for the fight. There is no evil, as St. John Chrysostom aptly observes, which has not some opposite virtue by which it may be overcome and which may not be finally destroyed by repeated acts of resistance. Thus fornication has chastity for its foe, pride is opposed by humility, anger by meekness, covetousness by an open-handed disposition, envy by

* Evanescunt in cogitationibus suis.

charity, sloth by fervour. Vainglory alone has no opposite virtue by which it may be surely overcome, for it takes occasion to raise its head from whatever good a man may do in order to keep it in check; and even in the humiliations which would seem most fitted for its destruction finds matter for vain self-complacency. The holy Doctor alleges an excellent reason for this, saying: "All evil springs from some vice; vainglory alone has its origin from what is good; so that, far from being extirpated by good deeds, these are its food."* Whence we infer that vainglory is a vice peculiar not to sinners, but to spiritual persons: since a fornicator, or a robber, or a murderer has nothing to be vain about, but, on the contrary, has much to make him ashamed of and to cover him with confusion.†

314. Although Cassian uses different words, yet he gives expression to the same views as to the power of this vice to undermine every work of perfection without being itself vanquished. He says: "Every other propensity is weakened by practising acts of a contrary tendency; vainglory is the only vice which constantly rises with renewed strength after it has been thrown to the ground. The other vices have dominion over those who allow themselves to be overcome by them, but this one makes head even against those who gain the victory over it and, from its very defeats, takes occasion to assail its conquerors." Which after all, comes to saying that vainglory often takes its rise from the very acts of self-humiliation which are performed with a view to its overthrow.‡ Then going into details, he illustrates this

* Omnia mala quæ sunt in mundo, habent contraria bona, per quæ superentur; ut puta fornicatio castitatem, superbia humilitatem, iracundia mansuetudinem; et nullum est malum, quod non habeat contrarium bonum, per quod superetur, exceptâ vanâ gloriâ. Ideo, quantavis bona feceris, volens compescere vanam gloriam, tanto magis excitas eam. et causa est ista: quia omne malum a malo nascitur, sola autem vana gloria de bono procedit · et ideo non extinguitur per bonum. sed magis nutritur.

† Denique inter homines peccatores tentatio vanæ gloriæ non habet locum. Fornicator enim, aut raptor quomodo tentatur in gloriâ vanâ, qui non habet unde glorietur? Hom. 15 in Matth.

‡ Omnia vitia superata marcescunt, et devicta per singulos dies infirmiora redduntur. . . . Hoc verò dejectum acrius resurgit ad luctam. . . . Cetera genera vitiorum eos tantum impugnare solent, quos in certamine superaverint.

doctrine by several examples taken from ordinary occurrences. "If, for instance, to get rid of vainglory, you put aside your splendid apparel, vanity will assail you under your humble garb. If, to parry the strokes of vainglory, you cease to speak eloquently and learnedly and impose on yourself a rigorous silence, even this reticence and reserve will supply your vanity with the food by which it may be made strong to smite you. If you make no secret of your fasts, vanity lays hold of you. If you fast in secret to avoid the praises of others, vainglory will creep into this your contempt of glory."*

315. Hence St. Jerome, in his letter to Eustochium,† compares vainglory to our shadow, which ever follows the body, just as vainglory itself always follows close upon the foot-prints of virtue, and as our shadow still keeps up with us, however fast we may run, so the more a virtuous man flies from vainglory, the more conscious does he become of being held tight in its embrace. "It avails not," says the same holy Doctor, writing to Rusticus, "to withdraw into the remotest deserts, to retire into the gloomiest caverns, into the darkest caves, to avoid the assaults of this vice; for it follows us wherever we may go.‡ Thus," adds the Saint, "vainglory has penetrated into the deepest solitudes in order to assail men of a most austere life; for when they give themselves to prayer and fasting, when they withdraw themselves from the conversation of men, they at once begin to look upon themselves as persons of some merit, and take a vain complacency in their good actions."

316. The reader may now judge how true it is that this vice has a something about it that renders it invulnerable; since even

Hoc vero suos victores acrius insectatur: quantoque fuerit validius elisum, tanto vehementius victoriæ ipsius elatione congreditur. Instit., lib. xj., cap. 7.

* Cui sub specie splendidæ vestis cenodoxiam non potuit diabolus generare, pro squallidâ, et incultâ conatur inserere. Quem scientiæ, et elocutionis ornatu nequivit extollere, gravitate taciturnitatis elidit. Si jejunet palam, gloriâ vanitatis pulsatur. Si illud contemnendæ gloriæ causâ contexerit, eodem vitio elationis obtunditur.

† S. Hier. ad Eustoch., Epist 22.

‡ In solitudine cito subrepit superbia: et si paulisper jejunaverit, hominemque non viderit, putat se alicujus esse momenti.

the practices of perfection, far from destroying it, cause it on many occasions to spring up again with fresh complacency and vigour. He may hence infer how much it is to be dreaded by spiritual persons, and how cautious they ought to be not to allow it any approach to their minds and hearts. It is beyond question that the greatest servants of God have ever stood in more immediate dread of this vice than of any other; and that, to avoid its assaults, they have frequently made use of extraordinary means, which might at first sight be deemed indiscreet. The reason is, that they judged no remedy to be unfitting, no precaution unsuitable, if it could but guard them against the surprise of this vice. Thus, in the Lives of the Fathers of the Desert,* we read that Abbot Simon, a venerable man, having heard that the Governor of the province was coming with all his retinue, to pay him a visit and beg a blessing at his hands, when urged to prepare himself for duly receiving a person of so high a rank, gave answer: "Leave me alone for a short time while I go and prepare myself." At these words he went forth from his cell, and at a short distance from it began to eat bread and cheese. The Governor, with his noble escort, finding him on their arrival thus engaged, made no account of him, saying: "Is this the holy hermit of whom we have heard such wondrous reports? to me he does not seem different from other people." After which the Governor turned his back upon the Solitary with little if any show of respect. But the monk was overjoyed at this behaviour, as he had thus shielded himself against the assaults of vanity, to which so honourable a visit might naturally have exposed him. A similar instance is related of Abbot Moses.† Having, like the other, heard that the Governor was about to call upon him and to consult him, he feared lest some emotions of vanity might be occasioned by an event which was so much to his credit. He therefore made up his mind to fly from the monastery, which in fact he did, betaking himself in the direction of Egypt. It chanced that on his road, he fell in with the very person whom he was seeking to avoid. On the latter inquiring of him where Abbot Moses lived, he replied: "Do not trouble yourself to make his acquaintance, as he is a mere fool, and a

* Cont. Inan. Glor., n. 8.

† Ibid., n. 2.

heretic to boot." The Governor, however, discovering that he was not far from the monastery, continued his journey, and on arriving, entered the church to say some prayers. On being received by those who were in charge, he told them that he had come to see the Abbot Moses, but that on his way he had heard some very strange reports concerning him; for an aged and venerable monk had told him that he was not the saint the world took him for, but a fool and, worse than that, a heretic. "But what sort of a looking man was this monk?" they rejoined. The Governor replied that he was a tall man, of withered aspect, bronzed complexion, and dressed in a habit that was very much worn. "But," said the monks, "that is the very Abbot whose acquaintance you wish to make." On hearing this the Governor wondered very greatly, and was much edified at the humility shown by the holy Abbot, who, on the other hand, was secured against any temptation to vanity.

317. As we are on this subject, I will not pass over a stratagem which one of these Solitaries cleverly employed in order to get rid of the vainglory which was on its way to surprise him amid the pomp and circumstance of an exceeding great honour.* This good man went to visit a sick youth, in accordance with the desire of the boy's father, repeatedly expressed. On approaching the dwelling of the invalid, he beheld his parents and friends coming forth with lighted torches in their hands, as is customary in processions of holy relics. Fearing to be taken unawares by vainglory, what did he do? He turned off to a neighbouring stream, stripped himself of his clothes, and commenced washing them. Seeing him in this condition, the company began to conceive a bad opinion of him, and deeming him undeserving of the honour they had destined for him, put out their torches and returned to their own homes. Meanwhile the father of the sick youth, who had accompanied the Solitary, said to him: "Father Abbot, why have you committed so gross an impropriety? Are you not aware that the people take you for a saint, but after seeing you naked in this stream, they have changed their minds and think you are possessed by the devil?" "Just what I wanted,

* Ex Lib. Sentent. PP., § 3

replied the monk;* "I wished to do away with the esteem and good opinion which they had formed of me, and to put to flight the vanity of which I was beginning to feel the temptation."

318. The reader may see from this how much the saints have always feared vainglory: how many and various were the artifices of which they made use to shield themselves from its attacks. not hesitating to destroy their good reputation in countless ways in order to escape being entangled in the snares of vain self-complacency. Hence, too, we may learn with what vigilance a spiritual person should keep guard over his heart, lest he yield to this vice, which insinuates itself into all good deeds, and the more in proportion as these are the more holy. For this reason we have called vainglory an all but unconquerable enemy of Christian perfection. I do not pretend that we are to put in practice conduct like that which we have just recorded Such extraordinary actions are to be justified only by supposing that those great servants of God were inspired to perform them by a special movement of divine grace. But we must, at all events, not seek for, and on the contrary, avoid praise, which is the aliment of this vain and frivolous passion; and we must, by contrary acts, repress without delay the first upheavings of vanity within our hearts: further, we must make use of the other remedies which will be briefly described in the following Chapter.

CHAPTER VI.

CERTAIN METHODS BY WHICH WE MAY STRIVE TO OVERCOME AMBITION AND VANITY.

319. THE first means of all is to be fervent and persevering in begging from God the grace to root out these vices from our soul. Although this is a remedy for all the diseases, without exception, to which we are subject, it may be called a specific for the cure of ambition and vainglory. And this is so true, that St. John Chry-

* Et ego volebam hoc audire.

sostom goes so far as to say that prayer is the only remedy against these two vices. "There can be no other remedy," he remarks, "against vainglory but prayer; and prayer itself, unless you take heed, will become the parent of vainglory."* The reason of this may be found in the ease wherewith this insinuating vice mingles with our every action, as we have already shown. So that no other than the Almighty Hand of God has power to uproot it, when once it has established its dwelling in our hearts. But this effectual help is vouchsafed only to long, earnest, and fervent prayer. Hence, if any one feel prone to this vice, he must resolve to beg of God the amendment of it in all his prayers; to entreat this favour in all humility, acknowledging before God how insufficient is man of himself: he must ask earnestly for it with hope, awaiting with absolute trust the help of the Divine Goodness, which is ever most ready to shed favours upon us, especially when we make petitions for graces which are in perfect conformity with the Divine Will. By constant prayer of this nature we shall at length find that this vice has been uprooted from our hearts; the work having been done gradually, if not all at once.

320. In order to conceive a firm and vivid desire of the extirpation of the said passions, that thus our prayer may be fervent and availing with God, it will be of great use to consider, in addition to the motives alleged in the foregoing Chapters, how contrary to the spirit of Christ is the spirit of ambition and vainglory. When our Blessed Lord was in the wilderness and was tempted by the devil to the sin of ambition, He spurned the tempting fiend with indignation, saying, *Get thee hence, Satan.*† Again, when the people were about to make Him their King, Jesus took to flight, and withdrew to a mountainous country to escape the honour.‡ He made repeated declarations of His abhorrence of praise,§ and showed this abhorrence in deeds: as when He imposed silence on the demons who were proclaiming

* Nullum remedium potest esse contra vanam gloriam, nisi oratio sola. Et hæc ipsa vanitatem generat, nisi caute prospexeris, si forte bene oraveris. Hom. 15 in Matth.

† Vade Satana. Matth. iv. 10. ‡ Joan. vj. 10.

§ Si glorifico me ipsum, gloria mea nihil est.

Him the Son of God:* as also when He commanded the leper whom He had healed not to make public the miraculous cure which had been wrought by His Divine Hands.† Intending by such acts, as St. John Chrysostom observes, to set us a powerful example of the abhorrence with which we ought to shrink from worldly honour.‡ In place of such honour and such glory, Christ chose dishonour, humiliation, contempt and confusion: His choice was to be filled with reproach, contumely, and outrage. By considerations such as these, a devout person will certainly succeed in awakening within himself a lively confusion at being so unlike his Divine Master, and an ardent desire of uprooting from his heart vices so unbecoming in a follower of Christ. And thus prayers will become more fervent, glowing, and more availing.

321. The second means is, that the person be fully persuaded, first; that whatever good he may possess in the order of nature or the order of grace, is a pure gift of God; and next, that of himself he is only sin and nothingness. He should allow the grand maxim of St. Paul to sink deep into his heart, *What hast thou that thou hast not received?* that is, gratuitously, from God. *But if thou hast received* all things as a gift from God's beneficent hands, *why dost thou glory as if thou hadst not received?* Why vaunt it? Why take complacency in it? Why seek for praise on its account, as if it came from thyself and not from Him, as though it were not His but thine own?§ The same Apostle further adds that we are unable, of ourselves, to conceive a good thought unless God bestow on us the power, and that by our own strength we are incapable of forming it.|| How much less capable are we of forming devout affections, and carrying out

* Exibant autem dæmonia a multis clamantia, et dicentia, quia tu es Filius Dei; et increpans non sinebat ea loqui: quia sciebant ipsum esse Christum. Luc. iv. 41.

† Vide nemini dixeris. Matth. viij. 4.

‡ Ideo enim nulli dicere jubet; ut doceat non diligendam ostentationem, et gloriam. Hom. 26 in Matth.

§ Quid habes, quod non accepisti? si autem accepisti, quid gloriaris, quasi non acceperis? II. Cor. iv 7.

|| Non quod simus sufficientes cogitare aliquid a nobis, quasi ex nobis; sed sufficientia nostra ex Deo est. II. Cor. iij. 5.

virtuous designs, doing holy actions, and whatever else wins the esteem and praise of people in the world!

322. "Wouldst thou know," says the Prophet Osee, "what thou hast of thine own? I answer: thy sins and thy everlasting ruin."* The many sins we have committed in times gone by; the countless imperfections of the present; the grievous crimes into which we should surely fall at every moment if God upheld us not by His Almighty Arm; the everlasting damnation which had been our lot long since had not the mercy of the Almighty interposed in our behalf; all this is our own; in this no one else can claim a share. But if there be in any one of us some good quality, or if we do any action that is praiseworthy, this belongs to God, Who of His mere goodness bestows it upon us.†

323. Wherefore St. Bernard, so penetrated with this truth of faith, upbraids with great vehemence those vainglorious persons who rob God of His honour and appropriate it to themselves. "Whence thy glory," he says, "vile and loathsome dust? Is it from thy holy living? But this is not the work of thy spirit, but of the Spirit of God, by which thou art hallowed. Or is it thy power of working miracles that invests thee with brightness? But thy hands are only the instruments of such miracles; God alone, by His supreme power, is the worker in all these wonders. Thou art puffed up peradventure by the applause of the people, whom thine eloquence delights. But tell me, who has given thee a tongue, and knowledge and fluency? Are not these the pure gifts of God? Is not thy tongue, while thou preachest, in the power of God Who uses it even as a writer uses his pen when he writes? All these things, properly considered, are talents intrusted to thee by the Lord in order that thou mayest traffic with them; and thou hast a charge of giving, when called upon, a strict account of the increase thou shalt have earned."‡ Such are the

* Perditio tua ex te, Israel: tantummodo in me auxilium tuum. Oseæ xiii 9.

† In me tantummodo auxilium tuum.

‡ Tibi unde gloria, o putride pulvis, unde tibi? De vitæ sanctitate? sed *Spiritus est, qui sanctificat;* spiritus, dico, non tuus, sed Dei. Si prodigiis, aut signis effulgeas; in manu tuâ sunt, sed virtute Dei. An blanditur popularis favor, quod verbum bonum, et bene, forte deprompseris? Sed Christus

maxims with which the heart and mind of every Christian should be deeply impressed, so that when the first motions of vanity and complacency are felt he may reject them with disgust, and render to God in its entirety whatever glory and honour may accrue from each one of the gifts of the Almighty. But, what is more, by a deep and repeated consideration of this truth, we may come at length to be enabled to regard our own excellence with as much detachment as if it belonged not to ourselves but to some one else, and to feel no uprising of vanity when the thought of it comes to our mind, or when we hear it extolled by the lips of another.

324. St. Jerome records that St. Hilarion had attained this degree of perfection; for at the age of seventy, although he had before his eyes the great monastery which he had founded, the immense multitude of monks who dwelt there in the most perfect austerity and regularity of life; although he saw the people who thronged to him from every part of the world, either to be healed of their diseases, or to be freed from the demons, or at least to receive his blessing; not only did he never rejoice in his heart at this extraordinary popularity, and at the great account which the whole world made of him, but on the contrary he sobbed most bitterly. And when they asked him why he wept so abundantly, and why he broke forth into such piteous lamentations, he replied: "Because the world imagines there is something good in me; because I fear that God will recompense me in this life for any service which I may have done Him; because, on account of the throngs that press around me, I can no longer enjoy the quiet of the solitude which I have sought for in the desert." Unmistakable tokens these that he was in nowise attached to this applause, to these marks of reverence, and to the high esteem in which he was held by men, but that he referred all to God, and was in his own heart as detached from them as though he was not the object of these honours.* But what the holy Doctor adds

donavit os, et sapientiam. Nam lingua tua quid, *Calamus scribæ?* et hoc ipsum mutuo accepisti. Talentum creditum est, repetendum cum usurâ. Serm. 13 in Cant.

* Sexagesimo vitæ suæ anno, cernens grande monasterium, et multitudinem

further, is worthy of special notice: "Others may wonder at the great miracles of this Saint, at his prodigious abstinence, his profound humility, his deep insight into divine things; for my own part, what astounds me is that he could, with such magnitude of soul, have trampled under foot the great glory and high honour which so many obsequious crowds flocked to pay him. And this my wonder is increased when I remember that not only persons of low degree pressed around him, but that ecclesiastics, priests, bishops, and entire communities of monks gathered together at the door of his cell; that high-born ladies, nobles, governors of provinces, and persons of rank and influence, flocked to see him, merely to receive a drop of oil or a morsel of bread blessed by his holy hands. Yet so many and such honours availed not to arouse within this saintly old man a single movement of vanity; but left him in trouble and affliction, because he was not allowed to remain in his beloved solitude, forgotten, abandoned and unknown." *

325. To the astonishment expressed by St. Jerome we may add that of St. Bernard, who, when speaking of those noble souls that made no account of the glory of the world, says, that it is a great and extraordinary virtue to be unconscious of your own greatness at the very time that you are doing great things: to be in ignorance of your holiness while it is apparent to all the world, yourself alone excepted: to be admirable in the sight of others, but contemptible only in your own eyes. "This is a virtue," writes the Saint, "which I deem more stupendous than all other virtues

fratrum secum habitantium, turbasque eorum, qui diversis languoribus, et immundis spiritibus occupatos ad se deducebant, ita ut omni genere hominum solitudo per circuitum repleretur, flebat quotidie, incredibili desiderio conversationis antiquæ recordabatur. Interrogatus a fratribus quid haberet? Cur se conficeret? ait: Rursus ad sæculum redii, et recepi mercedem in vitâ mea. Homines Palestinæ, et vicinæ Provinciæ æstimant me alicujus esse momenti, etc. In Vitâ Ejusd.

* Mirentur alii signa, quæ fecit: mirentur incredibilem abstinentiam, scientiam, humilitatem. Ego nihil ita stupeo, quam gloriam illum, et honorem calcare potuisse. Concurrebant episcopi, presbyteri, clericorum, et monachorum greges, matronæ quoque, Christianorum grandis tentatio: sed et potentes viri, et judices, ut benedictum ab eo panem, vel oleum acciperent. At ille nihil aliud, quam solitudinem meditabatur. Ibid.

put together."* To attain this virtue, however, there is no other method than the one which we have marked out above, which is to meditate without ceasing, and to distinguish between what we have of ourselves and what comes to us from God. If to these considerations there be added a ray of light from above which, as was observed at the beginning of this Chapter, God will never withhold from him who asks it in humility faith and perseverance, we shall be enabled to make so fair a distribution, that the soul will never ascribe to itself any gift or excellence by which it may see itself to be adorned, nor any honour which it may receive on that account; but being fully despoiled and entirely detached from everything, will refer all to God, and even amid applause and homage will ever remain in deep self-abasement, knowing full well that of itself it can lay claim to nothing except to its many miseries.

CHAPTER VII.

OTHER MEANS OF COMPLETELY SUBDUING THESE TWO VICES.

326. ANOTHER effectual means of not being surprised, or at least overcome, by vanity, is to direct all that we do purely to the glory of God, as St. Paul exhorts us to do: *Whether ye eat or drink, or whatsoever else ye do, do all for the glory of God.*† Cassian, too, inculcates this practice as most effectual in keeping our hearts safe from this hurtful monster of vanity. "A champion of Christ," he says, "who wishes to fight bravely in the arena of perfection, can put to flight this monster of vainglory, this many-headed hydra, if he never undertakes any action out of motives of vanity, but always proposes to himself a good and upright end,

* Magna, et rara virtus profecto est, ut magna licet operantem, magnum te nescias et manifestum omnibus, tuam te solum latere sanctitatem: mirabilem te apparere, et contemptibilem te reputare. Hoc ego ipsis virtutibus mirabilius judico. Serm 13 in Cant.

† Sive ergo manducatis, sive bibitis, sive aliquid facitis, omnia in gloriam Dei facite. I. Cor. x. 31.

endeavouring to keep it in view while actually engaged in the work." The reason hereof is plain; since, if in the beginning of our works our aim be the good pleasure and the glory of God, we must at once check any desire of honour or of our own good repute, which may redound to us from that on which we are employed. And if in the progress of the work vanity begin to stir, it is easy to avoid it by renewing our original intent of acting for God's glory alone, and by again referring our work to the sole end which in the beginning we proposed to ourselves.* This was the practice of St. Bernard; for when he was tempted by the devil with thoughts of vanity while in the act of delivering a learned and eloquent sermon, he would turn to the tempter with these memorable words, "I did not begin my discourse for thee, neither will I leave it off for thee.† From the very beginning I fixed the eye of mine intention on the glory of God: it is for His honour alone that I mean to finish what I am now doing."

327. Battaglini, in his history of the illustrious king of Poland, John Sobieski, records an action which is not only most edifying, but is eminently worthy of our admiration.‡ This great hero having routed the Turkish squadrons, and raised the siege of Vienna in Austria, entered the city in triumph, surrounded by his victorious soldiers, and hailed by the cheers of all the inhabitants; but before going to any other place, he went to the Court Church of the Discalced Carmelites, where he ordered a *Te Deum* to be sung in thanksgiving for his victory. But as no musician was at hand to intone the festive chant, not brooking any delay in giving to God the praise which the world was attributing to himself, he gave out the opening words of the Canticle in person, with a loud voice, and continued to sing alternately with the people. Then asking the priest what prayer was to be said in conclusion,

* Athleta Christi, qui verum, ac spiritualem agonem legitime certare desiderat, hanc multiformem variamque bestiam superare festinet. . . . Primitus, nihil proposito vanitatis, et inanis gloriæ capessendæ gratiâ nos facere permittamus. deinde ea, quæ bono initio fecerimus, observatione simili custodire nitamur, ne omnes nostrorum laborum fructus, post irrepens cenodoxiæ morbus evacuet. Inst., lib. xj., cap. 18.

† Nec propter te cœpi, nec propter te desinam.

‡ Anno 1685, num. 23.

the king, who had begun the hymn of thanksgiving, determined to end it also, which he did with the following words: *Not to us, O Lord, not to us, but to Thy name alone be the glory* of the illustrious victory.* In the campaign, then, which this prince, who was no less pious than heroic, had undertaken against the Ottoman forces, he proposed to himself no other end than the glory of God; hence he found no difficulty, at the end of his undertaking, in referring to God, by a public and solemn attestation, the glory which accrued from it, instead of appropriating the honour to himself. It would have been far otherwise if, in taking the field against the enemies of the Christian name, he had proposed to himself, instead of the glory which would accrue to God from the defeat of the foe, to render his own name famous by this great military achievement and to immortalise it with posterity. Certain is it that after the prosperous issue of the battle, he would not have given the glory to God, but would have taken for himself all the praise, honour, applause and popular acclamations that greeted his entrance into the city. Now, from his behaviour on the occurrence of so great an event, we may take a lesson as to what our own conduct should be in trivial matters; so that when approval or praise follows upon what we have done we may not be puffed up by vain self-complacency. In putting our hand to any work, let us set God before us as our main end; directing our actions to Him, and protesting, in all sincerity, that we desire nothing but His glory alone, His good pleasure, the fulfilment of His most holy will. This we should do habitually in our every action, in order that by the frequent practice of renewing our purity of intention, a certain zeal for God's glory may take root within us, and that we may be rid of the natural inclination which we all have to seek our own honour.

328. Another means of avoiding temptations to vainglory is to conceal our gifts and talents, and the praiseworthy and virtuous actions which we are in the habit of performing. St. Gregory suggests this course by a most apt and appropriate comparison. "Whoever," he says, "has found a rich treasure, does not expose it to view in the public places, nor does he carry it openly about

* Non nobis, Domine, non nobis, sed nomini tuo da gloriam.

with him through the crowded streets; for to do this would be to invite robbers to come and deprive him of it: but, on the contrary, he conceals his treasure from every eye, knowing well that the less the treasure is seen the safer it is. In the same manner, whoever amasses by godly deeds a store of virtues and merits, must keep them from the eyes of others, lest the devils, like so many thieves, assail us with feelings of vanity and plunder all the spiritual wealth we have earned by the toils of a virtuous life.*

329 St. John Chrysostom urges on us the same advice; he would have us carefully conceal the gifts which we have received from God, if we do not want to lose them by disclosing their existence; and he enforces his counsel by the use of a comparison much like that of St. Gregory so lately quoted by us. "A costly garment," he says, "embroidered with gold and silver, if hung up in a public place, attracts the covetous gaze of those who pass by, tempting them to plans of theft and rapine; but if shut up in a chest, it remains quite safe. Thus too do the riches of virtue, when displayed and set forth to the public eye, invite our hellish foes to filch them away clandestinely by the uprisings of vanity; but if kept concealed in the heart, they will remain there without any risk of being lost."† Hence also our Blessed Saviour warns us how, in time of prayer, we must enter into our chamber, close the door and pray to our Father in secret, so that others may not be witnesses of our prayer. And again He tells us to wash our faces when we fast lest, by the sad and pallid look of our countenances, we give outward sign that we are fasting; and, in the same way when we give alms, to give them in such privacy, that our *right hand may not know what is done by the left hand.* Full

* Inventus thesaurus absconditur, ut servetur. quia studium cœlestis desiderii a malignis spiritibus custodiue non sufficit, qui hoc ab humanis laudibus non abscondit. In præsenti etenim vitâ, quasi in viâ sumus, quâ ad patriam pergimus. Maligni autem spiritus iter nostrum, quasi quidam latrunculi, obsident Deprædari ergo desiderat, qui thesaurum publice portat in viâ. Hom. 11 in Evang

† Sicut aurum, et vestem pretiosam, cum in publico ponimus, multos ad insidias provocamus; si vero domi recondamus, in tuto cuncta servabimus; sic si opes virtutum palam, quasi venales assidue portemus in mente, inimicum irritabimus ad furtum: si vero nemo id alter sciérit, nisi quem nulla occulta latent, tutissimo in loco consistent. Homil. 3 in Matth.

well did our Divine Teacher know that, from the display of our good deeds, the moth of vainglory and vain self-satisfaction is generated, which gnaws at, mars and destroys all the virtues with which we seek to clothe ourselves. And therefore Jesus Christ employs these expressions in order that we may most carefully hide our good deeds, lest any of them come to meet the eyes of our fellow-men.

330. Let me now illustrate this doctrine by an instance of heroic concealment, whereby a nun was enabled not only to hide her virtue but even to impart to it the lustre of an eminent sanctity. The story is narrated in the Lives of the Fathers on the authority of St. Basil.* It seems, then, that there lived in a convent of four hundred nuns, one sister of most rare virtue; for she sustained herself only on the fragments of bread which were left on the table by her sisters in Religion, and on such miserable scraps of meat as were found in the dishes when these were being cleaned, and yet enjoyed both in and out of prayer a continual union with God, was glad when she met with ill-treatment; exulted in affronts; and though not seldom provoked beyond measure, never allowed any words to escape her lips that could in the least offend against charity. This nun, seeing that in a community of so many religious women, whose eyes were most quick to observe the conduct of their companions, it was hopeless to hide the many gifts which God had heaped upon her, bethought herself of a plan, extraordinary indeed, but the best suited to her mind for the purpose of hiding the whole body of her virtues from public notice. She began by feigning insanity and, not long afterwards, managed by strange cries and contortions to persuade the nuns that she was possessed by the devil. Her imitation was so true to the life, that it gained full credit in the community. Hence it came to pass that she was the sport and butt of every one as insane, and was abhorred by all as one possessed; she was forbidden the society of her companions and kept in the kitchen to do the work of a scullion. The veil, worn by the others in honourable token of the perpetual virginity which they professed, was taken from her, and in place of it her head was covered with vile rags.

* De Prævid. num. 2.

Some would rail at her with bitter mockery, others would pursue her with biting words, or heap blows upon her, while some found a diversion in drenching her with dirty water, filling her nostrils with mustard, and making her, in a word, the victim of their cruel pastime. Meanwhile, St. Pitherius, who was living in a certain desert and solitary place called Porphyricum, was visited by an Angel of the Lord, and commanded to go to such a convent, where he would meet with a nun who surpassed him in holiness; and the token by which he was to single her out from her numerous companions was the crown that she wore on her head. He hastened to the convent, and all the community crowded round him to do homage to his sanctity, of which they had conceived a very high opinion. He scanned each one with an attentive eye, but perceiving in none the token given to him by the Angel, he inquired whether there was any other nun in their convent. "There is," was the answer, "one other. But do not take the trouble to see her; she is mad. More than that," some rejoined, "the poor thing is possessed by a devil." "Bring her hither," said the Saint. The nun at first refused to come, fearing, most likely, some discovery which would be no less dangerous than honourable to her. However, she came at length. On her appearing, the holy solitary understood that her strange head-dress was the crown mentioned by the Angel, and without hesitation, he knelt at her feet and begged her blessing. The nuns, all astounded at this sight, exclaimed, "Stay, holy Abbot; she is a mad woman, undeserving of such honours." "You are mad yourselves," he replied, "not to have discovered the holiness of your companion. God grant I may stand at His judgment-seat adorned with as many merits as she will then possess." On hearing this, the nuns were all confounded, and blushed for very shame at the thought of the evil treatment with which they had shown their contempt of the sister for so long a time, and each strove to be first in falling at her feet and begging her pardon, some for their insults, others for their blows, others for their mockeries, all for the outrages of which each one felt herself to be more or less guilty. But she, fearing to lose, through this honourable discovery, the gifts which she had hitherto so securely preserved and increased by this long and artful concealment, fled from the convent, as in those times there were no rules of enclosure and stability, nor could it ever be found out to what corner of the world she had gone in which to hide her great virtues and secure them from being filched from her by so incorrigible a thief as vanity.

331. We must, however, add two observations of our own to this story: First, although we should all imitate this holy woman by our care to keep concealed the good with which God has gifted us, lest by displaying it the strong wind of vanity carry it away and beggar us of it; still, we are not allowed to imitate her in the means which she adopted to hide this virtue; because such extraordinary courses require, as will be shown in our next Chapter, a very special inspiration from on High—such as we may reasonably suppose to have been vouchsafed to this holy nun—without which, expedients of this nature are not lawful, and must never be employed. Secondly, I observe, that although we should ever incline, as far as it depends upon ourselves, to practise virtue in secret; yet, at times, edification, our neighbour's spiritual advantage and, as a consequence, the glory of God, require us to make public what good we can do · according to the teaching of our Blessed Lord Himself.* This is especially the case with those who, having care of souls, are bound to forward the salvation of all under their charge by setting a good example. In such circumstances however, as St. Gregory observes, though the good be made public, we must take care, in the secret depths of our heart, to form an upright intention of contributing solely to God's glory by means of the edification which our neighbour may receive from our virtuous deeds.†

* Videant opera vestra bona, et glorificent patrem vestrum, qui in cœlis est. Matth. v. 16.

† Sic autem sic opus in publico, quatenus intentio maneat in occulto, ut et de bono opere proximis præbeamus exemplum; et tamen per intentionem quâ Deo soli placere quærimus, semper optemus secretum. Hom. 11 in Evang.

P. 262 is over 2 pages error of type.

Director will give them to meditate upon these truths, recommending some book where these considerations are set forth in a plain and distinct manner: as progress in spirit is out of the question until the fumes of vainglory have been banished from the mind.

334. Second suggestion. In women vanity usually shows itself in appearing abroad in rich dresses, in being decked out in costly jewels, in being clothed with rare and magnificent apparel. The reason of this weakness is, that, on the one hand, women are excluded from all interest in literature, military affairs, politics; and are incapable of being chosen for posts of honour, charges, dignities and other honourable employments. On the other hand women, no less than men, have vanity rooted within their nature. Being precluded from occupying the passion of vainglory in things of greater moment, they spend it wholly in attention to their personal charms. But if they would make profession of devotion and piety, they must be careful to moderate this excess of adornment; for such vanity is incompatible with true devotion and solid perfection. Cæsarius relates,* that at Mayence, a lady, splendidly dressed, came one morning to the church to hear Mass. A Priest, zealous for God's service, beheld in the train which, like a proud peacock, she dragged after her, a number of demons under the shape of deformed and hideous blackamoors, who, clapping their hands, and grinning at each other, were having great sport, swarming up and down the borders of her dress, like so many fish inside a net. The servant of God ordered the demons not to depart, and turning to the people who were present at the divine service, invited them to contemplate the loathsome sight. The lady, finding that she was made sport of by the demons, and moreover an object of disgust to the beholders, returned home in confusion, and stripping off her costly garb, would never wear it any more. Now, if the demons took so much pleasure in her vain ornaments, it is a clear sign that these were injurious to the soul of her that wore them; and, what is worse, were doing still more harm to those who were led away from God by such fascinations. The Director must

* Mirac., lib. v, cap. 6.

be really humbled by a true knowledge of his own miseries. To drive away, then, the fumes of vainglory which have arisen in the soul of a penitent on account of the number or quality of the natural gifts possessed, the Director may employ the maxim which St. Basil used to set before his flock, in the following words:—"You are puffed up by your wealth, by the illustrious race of your forefathers, by the glory of the country of your birth, by the beauty of your exterior form, by the honours you receive from persons of all ranks. Turn your thoughts, I pray, upon yourself. Consider that you are only a mortal man, that you are nothing but dust and ashes, and that all your grandeurs will at the end dwindle into a handful of filthy earth. Tell me where are they who once filled the highest posts of power in the city in which you dwell? where are now those mighty lords, those governors of provinces, those brave warriors who headed powerful armies? where those kings, those tyrants? Have they not melted away into vile dust? What memorial is now left of their life save in a fragment of bone? Does not their once glorious career resemble the passing glory of a fiction acted upon the stage? Cast, I beseech you, cast a glance into their tombs. Can you distinguish amid this dust, amidst these particles of bone, the master from the slave, the poor man from the rich, the galley-slave from the prince who loaded him with chains?"* And assuredly there is no such effectual means of emptying out the wind with which vanity fills the soul, and which so puffs up men of this world, as the frequent consideration of what they will all soon come to, and what those are at present who once were far superior to them in every worldly advantage. If any such persons show an inclination for a devout life, the

* Tibi uni mire places ob avitæ gentis claritudinem? immo dico gaudio subsilis ob patriæ celebritatem; ob elegantiam corporis, denique ob honores ab omni gradu hominum tibi delatos? Attende tibi: mortalis enim tu. Quippe terra es, et in terram abibis. . . . Ubi, jam dic qui civitatum amplissimos magistratus capessebant? ubinam invicti rectores? ubi exercituum duces? ubi tyranni? Nonne omnia pulvis? nonne sunt in fabulam conversa omnia? Memoria vitæ eorum in quam paucis ossibus retinetur! In horum sepulchra deflecte parumper oculos. Posse tene speras discernere inter famulum, et dominum? inter pauperem, et divitem? inter vinctum, et eum, a quo vinctus erat, regem? Hom. 3 in Verba Moysis: *Attende tibi ipsi.*

CHAPTER VIII.

PRACTICAL SUGGESTIONS TO DIRECTORS ON THE SUBJECT OF THE PRESENT ARTICLE.

332. First suggestion. The Director need not be further warned of the incompatibility of the spirit of vanity and ambition with any serious progress in perfection. In meeting then, with persons who living habitually in the grace of God wish to apply themselves with fervour to His service, and who aspire to a devout and spiritual life, the Confessor must from the outset ground them on the sure and solid foundation of self-knowledge, by inducing them to meditate frequently upon what they have of themselves, and what they have received from God, so that they may learn to form a low and mean estimate of themselves, such as may keep them habitually in confusion at the sight of their miseries, and may enable them to refer with ease all the good they possess to that God Who is the true author of all good. This self-knowledge is one of the main ground-works of spiritual life, since it strikes down the two chief enemies of that life, namely, vanity and ambition. Give me a person who is well-grounded in this humble self-knowledge, and you will soon see that person, I will not say go forward only, but fly rapidly up towards the summit of perfection. If, on the contrary, the penitent fail of this, he will ever go limping along the spiritual path; halting and stumbling, without making any remarkable progress. Hence, a Director cannot insist too much upon this point.

333. Nor is this advice to be understood as though it concerned only supernatural gifts, or such as belong to the order of grace, in cases where we have little difficulty in acknowledging the liberal hand of the Almighty Giver; but we must apply the counsel to all natural endowments and advantages of riches, birth, talent, knowledge, prudence, pleasing address, outward beauty and other such blessings. Because to whatever object vanity may attach itself, it becomes an obstacle to spiritual progress. The fact is, that God does not commonly impart Himself to any one, unless the person

therefore strive to free his penitents from such hindrances, especially if they be spiritually inclined and accustomed to virtuous practices. If, without risking any inconvenience, he can rid them of all ostentation of dress and every vain ornament, let him do so, for he will thus go to the very root of this evil. But, as we have before observed, if prudence do not allow of his doing this, he must at least enjoin moderation in the use of such ornaments. He must engage women to dress as modestly and in as unpretending a style as their state of life allows; he should make them cover themselves sufficiently, and explain to them that when they put on any dress, they should take care not to desire only to be admired (which could not be excused of vanity and fault), but merely to comply with the requirements of decorum, or with other reasonable motives which may oblige them to the use of a moderate degree of adornment of their persons. For example, their motive in dressing well may be to avoid being singular and making themselves too much unlike other ladies of the same rank in society, so as to give outward show of their being spiritual persons: or to escape the error of certain women, who purposely seek to publish to the world by their dress, demeanour and even sometimes by affected forms of speech, the devotion which they fancy themselves to possess.

335. The Director may learn from St. Bernard himself—that great master of the spiritual life—the course to be followed with these vain females. One of the sisters of this Saint came to see him in his retirement at Clairvaux; she was arrayed in a splendid dress, which was covered with jewels and adorned with costly lace. St. Bernard, on hearing of the pomp with which his sister was visiting his sacred cloister, refused to go to the door, but sent her word that she was a net of the devil, who made use of her finery to ensnare others and to drag them along with her to hell. Neither would the brothers of the Saint, with the single exception of one, by name Andrew, go to meet her; and all that he said to her was, that she looked to him like a lump of filth wrapped up in silk and brocade. All in confusion at receiving such treatment and hearing such rebukes, the poor lady burst into tears, and promised to do all that her saintly brother might require.

St. Bernard then consented to come down to her, and his first word was to forbid her that pomp, parade and costliness of dress, of which she was so fond.* He then proceeded to give her some lessons in the spiritual life. She kept the promise which she had made to him, and putting away all her jewels and finery, began a devout and secluded life; and at the end of two years withdrew into a convent, with the consent of her husband, to lead a holy life. The Director may learn from this great Saint the way to make women holy. He must destroy, or at least moderate, in them their love of show, and must convince himself that a woman who has got so far as to make little account of her personal charms and of vanity in dress, and who is not anxious to appear attractive in the sight of others is, by this very fact alone, most disposed to devote herself entirely to the spiritual life and to the service of God Almighty.

336. Third suggestion. The Director must never allow his penitents to omit any suitable good work out of fear of vainglory. I will explain my meaning. Some there are who neglect to confer with their Directors on the inspirations and favours which they receive from God in prayer: they never discover to their Confessor the penances, mortifications, and other holy works which they are in the habit of performing, because, in speaking of these matters, they experience certain motions of vanity; so that they omit all mention of them, lest such feelings might arise within their breasts. Others leave off their visits to churches, their frequentation of the sacraments, their attendance on the sick in hospitals, and such like pious works; because, in doing these acts of virtue, they feel tempted to vanity. It must be strictly forbidden to such persons to omit any good deed in the hope of avoiding vanity; or else the devil, becoming aware of this fear may, by suggesting some vain thought or other, succeed in driving them, one by one, from all the good habits they have formed. They must direct their intention to God, making interior protests that they are acting purely for His glory; and without taking any notice of movements of self-complacency which may

* Primo verbo omnem ei mundi gloriam in cultu vestium, et in omnibus sæculi pompis, et curiositatibus interdixit. In Vitâ S. Bern., lib. 1., c. 6.

arise, they must persevere to the end in their course of conduct. A Solitary called on Abbot Pastor, and told him that he abstained from acts of charity, since all he did was tainted with vainglory.* The Abbot rebuked the Hermit, and to make him sensible of his error, set before him the following parable:—There were two farmers living in one village, one of whom was slothful, while the other was industrious. The one neglected to sow his seed, the other sowed his field in due season. The first had no crop at all, the second reaped a little wheat mixed with darnel. "Which of the two," asked the Abbot, "appears to have acted best?" "The second," replied the solitary, "for it is better to reap a little, of course, than nothing." "Just so," was the answer, "and if you cease from well-doing out of fear of vainglory, you will reap no merit; but if you persevere in doing good, although in the course of your actions there may be some slight admixture of the tares of vanity, yet you will gather some harvest of merits for Paradise." To this we may add that if, when vanity arises, we delay not to check it by exercising our right intention, no darnel will be found growing with our wheat, but our harvest will be full, entire, and abundant, when we go to enjoy it in Paradise. Hence, there is no need to leave off our good works on account of these groundless fears, but we should despise them and go forward with a holy liberty.

337. Fourth suggestion. The Director must not allow his penitents to win for themselves a reputation of folly, imprudence and want of good sense, with a view to shield themselves from temptations to vanity; for it is the will of God that we should proceed in our actions in all wisdom and uprightness. We ought all to be quite content if we bear with the lessening of our good repute in humility and peace when others form a bad opinion of us without our furnishing them with any occasion. I know full well that St. Simon Salo, and St. Philip Neri, and other saints, have made use of such means in order to be taken for fools. But, as we said just now, they were moved to behave as they did by an extraordinary inspiration of the Holy Ghost, apart from which it is not right to do such things. Nor should the

* Ex Lib. Doct. PP., Lib. De Orat., n. 7.

Director approve those of his penitents who, for the purpose of avoiding vanity, speak evil of themselves at every second word they utter, and call themselves "miserable sinners," "imperfect," "wretched creatures," and the like:—First, because under these affected forms there often lurks a secret vanity of appearing humble and lowly in the estimation we have formed of ourselves, though it no less frequently happens that the person in question does not advert to this subtle form of delusion. Secondly, granting that these self-accusations are sincere, listeners usually give no credit to them, but compensate by redoubled expressions of esteem for our depreciation of ourselves, so that, in the upshot, the person is exposed to the peril of vainglory by the very means which he has employed to escape from the danger. It is far better, then, that each one should have deeply rooted within him an exact knowledge of himself and his miseries; a knowledge leading him to self-contempt and to a sincere ascription of all that is good in him to Almighty God: and he must be ever ready to hear mention made of his defects and foibles, when they are commented upon by others.

338. Abbot Serapion was one day visited by a Monk, who at every breath called himself a sinner, unworthy of the religious habit which he was wearing.* The holy Abbot wanted to wash the stranger's feet, as was his custom whenever monks came to see him, but the other would not allow of it, declaring that he was only fit to be trodden underfoot by every one. The Abbot made him sit down to dinner, and gave him a frugal meal. During the repast he took occasion to remark to him, in a gentle and charitable spirit: "My son, if you would advance in religious perfection, remain retired in your cell, attend to yourself and to manual labour. Such perpetual passing from one desert to the other, such constant wandering amongst the Solitaries, cannot be of spiritual advantage to you. In no place is God found so easily as in our cell and in solitude." On hearing this remark, the vexation of the monk rose to such a pitch, that he could not abstain from showing outwardly some very clear marks of his irritation. Serapion perceiving this said: "How now, brother, what is this I see? Just now

* Ex Lib. Doct. PP., Contra Inanem Gloriam., n. 11.

you were calling yourself a vile sinner, unworthy of the ground you tread upon and of the air you breathe, yet, because I have charitably admonished you of your failings, you are full of confusion and altogether disturbed. You delude yourself, brother; if you wish to be truly humble, there is no need for you to publish your faults; wait for others to tell you of them, and when that happens bear with it in peace, ay, and rejoice thereat in your inmost heart." This second rebuke opened the monk's eyes, and showed him the difference between counterfeit humility and that genuine self-abasement to which alone it belongs to triumph over vanity. He ended by begging the Abbot's pardon, and returned to live a solitary life in his own cell. The Director must strive to make his penitents understand the same truth, and must lay down for them the rule of never speaking of themselves either in praise or blame: not in praise, because this would be an incitement to vanity; not in blame, because to do this is very seldom an effectual remedy against this ruinous vice.

ARTICLE IX.

Obstacles to perfection likely to arise from other outward agreeable objects.

CHAPTER I.

THE HINDRANCE TO PERFECTION ARISING FROM THE INORDINATE LOVE OF OUR PARENTS.

339. BUT it is not wealth, nor worldly glory, nor honour that is the only dangerous object which, by its agreeable fascination, withdraws devout persons from perfection. There are other objects no less fascinating which bar our spiritual progress, and form a serious obstacle to our further advance. Among these are to be ranked,

in the first place, parents and relatives who, from the ties of natural relationship, from the natural affection which results from it, from long and familiar intercourse, have the power to enkindle within us a love little in conformity with, and at times even wholly contrary to, the dictates of Christian charity, and so avail to keep us far from that perfection which is mainly grounded on the law of charity.

340. Were this not the truth, Christ would never have said these words: *If any one come to Me, and hate not his father and mother, his wife and children, his brothers and sisters, and even his own life, he cannot be my disciple.** Nor would our Divine Redeemer, on the other hand, have held out this splendid promise. *Whoso shall forsake his house, his brothers and sisters, his father and mother, his wife and children, his lands, for My name's sake, shall receive a hundredfold, and gain everlasting life.*† If then we may not hope to be disciples and followers of Christ unless, with a holy hate, we forsake or at least cease inordinately to love, those bound to us by ties of blood, it must needs be certain that any inordinate affection for our relatives is a great hindrance to the following and imitation of Christ, and consequently to Christian perfection. If Our Saviour promises a reward of a hundredfold here below, and in the world to come eternal and unfading glory, to such as tear themselves from those nearest and dearest to them, renouncing hope of living with them in this life, it necessarily follows that great perfection is found in this generous detachment: and that, on the other hand, over-attachment to our relations may easily become a matter of great imperfection.

341. But even if our Blessed Lord had not spoken on this subject at all, our daily experience would speak to us plainly enough; for it shows us numbers who, through an ill-regulated attachment to their kindred, are estranged from God and are absorbed, far more than they should be, in commerce, trade and worldly inter-

* Si quis venit ad me, et non odit patrem suum, et matrem, et uxorem, et filios, et fratres, et sorores, adhuc autem et animam suam, non potest meus esse discipulus. Luc xiv. 26.

† Et omnis, qui reliquerit domum, vel fratres, aut sorores, aut patrem, aut matrem, aut uxorem, aut filios, aut agros propter nomen meum, centuplum accipiet, et vitam æternam possidebit. Matth. xix. 29.

ests; so as to lose all spirit of devotion, and every feeling of piety; and, what is more deplorable, our own experience furnishes instances of some who, for the sake of their children and descendants, fear not to lose their own souls, by charging their conscience with the burden of money made by unjust dealings and exorbitant profits. It is idle, therefore, to expect any progress in Christian perfection, unless we uproot from our hearts so harmful and dangerous an affection which, if it lead us not to eternal ruin—as we know to have been the case with some—will ever keep us immersed in a very ocean of failings and imperfections.

342. But to proceed with perfect clearness in so important a matter, we must distinguish two distinct kinds of affection that we may bear towards our kinsfolk. The one is the love which nature itself enkindles in our hearts towards those who are of the same blood; a love not very different from that which brute beasts entertain for their offspring; for nature does not make even a tigress a mother without instilling into her a tender love for her cubs, and inspiring these with a reciprocal affection for their dam. This natural affection, if regulated by the rules of right reason, is lawful and virtuous; but if it pass these bounds, it is faulty and, with persons of too easy a conscience, may become the source of many grievous sins, which will often drag them to eternal perdition.

343. The second kind of love is that which Christian charity dictates and regulates by her holy laws. As we are commanded by this charity to love our neighbour for the sake of God, our first beginning, last end and eternal bliss; so, too, does it lay us under the obligation of loving our parents for the same motive and, as St. Thomas teaches, loving them with even greater affection than what mere nature inspires.* Now, this love for our kindred, when in accordance with the rule of charity, is wholesome and meritorious, and can be of no prejudice to perfection. On the contrary it is a help, inasmuch as it is regulated by charity the queen of all the virtues, and as it is directed to God, from Whom, as from its native well-spring, all our perfection is derived.

* 2, 2, q 26, art 8.

344. Hence St. Gregory the Great says that if we would be united to God, we must so detach ourselves from our parents, as not to care for, or to ignore, the carnal love which springs from the ties of blood, and yet we must love them all the more truly and all the more holily in God. He observes, moreover, that we are bound always to acknowledge their relationship to us, and to give them help when in need in preference to all others: adding, that just as a flame which bursts forth into a conflagration first seizes upon the fuel that is closest to it, so our affection should first attach itself to those who are most near to us by their birth and origin. But this must be so ordered, that love for our kindred hinder not our progress in spirit; and we shall succeed in attaining this excellence, if we ennoble our affection by the love of things heavenly and divine, ordering and directing it unto God.* And further on, the same Saint remarks in still plainer terms: "That godly men cease not to cherish and to aid their kindred in their need, but that they so moderate and rectify this affection by the holy and spiritual love which they bear to God, as not, on account of their relations, to deviate from the path which leads to Heaven."†

345. It must, however, be borne in mind, that love for God can hardly extinguish the carnal, low and imperfect love which nature enkindles within our breasts for our kinsfolk, so as to change it into a spiritual and godly affection, if we remain constantly in their society. For the presence of objects so naturally

* Extra cognatos quisque, ac proximos debet fieri, si vult parenti omnium verius jungi, quatenus eosdem, quos propter Deum viriliter negligit, tanto solidius diligat, quanto in eis affectum solubilem copulæ carnalis ignorat. Debemus quidem et temporaliter his, quibus vicinius jungimur, plus ceteris prodesse, quia et flamma admotis rebus incendium porrigit, sed hoc ipsum prius, unde nascitur, incendit Debemus copulam terrenæ cognationis agnoscere, sed tamen hanc cum cursum mentis impedit, ignorare; quatenus fidelis animus divino studio accensus, nec ea, quæ sibi sunt in infimis conjuncta, despiciat, et hæc apud semetipsum recte ordinans, summorum amore transcendat. Moral., lib. vii, cap. 6.

† Neque enim sancti viri ad impendenda necessaria propinquos carnis non diligunt; sed amore spiritualium ipsam in se dilectionem vincunt quatenus sic eam discretionis moderamine temperent, ut per hanc in parvo saltem, ac minimo, a recto itinere non declinent.

pleasing; familiarity of intercourse, both continuous and confidential; the several tokens of affection and the many kind services that we daily receive from them; the love which we perceive that they bear towards us :—all serve as fuel which feeds our carnal affection for them and keeps it constantly alive. Hence, the above-quoted holy Doctor has aptly said, that whoever would be joined to God in the bonds of perfect charity must separate himself from the company of his kindred.*

346. We shall see this more clearly from divers facts narrated in the Lives of the Ancient Fathers, which show how much these great servants of God dreaded not only the conversation and familiar intercourse, but the very sight, of their relatives. We may first cite the instance of Abbot John. This holy man, in order to avoid receiving his sister who, after a separation of twenty-four years, wished to go to his monastery to pay him a visit, resolved to visit her himself, but so as not to be recognised.† He set out with two other monks, all three dressed in the habit of pilgrims, and on arriving at her convent, asked her for a little water to quench his thirst. Having drunk it, he went his way, without uttering a syllable or making himself known. On his return home, he wrote to his sister to tell her she had gained her object and had seen him again, as he was one of the pilgrims whom she had refreshed with water; that she must be content with that, and not give him any further trouble. We may also mention the example of the Blessed Theodore, disciple of St. Pacomius,‡ who arranged not to see his mother on her coming to visit him in the desert, despite the letters of recommendation she had obtained to his spiritual father, Pacomius, to make him use his authority and compel the young man to meet and converse with her. The holy youth contrived so fully to convince his master that such an interview could not result in his spiritual profit, that Pacomius did not venture to lay a command upon him, and thus he managed to baffle the artifices and expectations of his mother. And the monk Prior § was ordered by St. Antony to pay his sister a

* Extra cognatos quisque, et proximos debet fieri, si vult parenti omnium verius jungi.

† Ex Lib. Sentent. PP., s. 31.

‡ Ibid, s. 33.

§ Ex Eodem Lib., s. 30.

visit, and to hold conversation with her; he complied, not to be wanting in obedience, but kept his eyes closed during the whole interview. And the monk Mark, in like manner, when obliged by his Abbot to go and speak to his mother who was waiting for him at the monastery gate, presented himself before her in a tattered garment, his face begrimed with soot, and without once lifting up his eyes to her countenance addressed to her and her companion no more than the words, "May ye fare well." then turned his back upon them and went his way.* I could mention many more instances of a similar detachment from relatives, which occur in these ancient and edifying narratives of the Fathers of the Desert.

347. We may hence draw the two following conclusions:—First, how prejudicial to spiritual life is the love of flesh and blood; since the holy men of whom we have been speaking, whose great desire of perfection is well known, had so much dread of love of kindred that they took precautions against it by using means most extraordinary and which appear, at first sight, indiscreet. Secondly, in order to detach our hearts from our kindred it is necessary, or at least highly expedient, to keep at a distance from them; and it was because these servants of God understood this so completely, that they shrank from all conversation with them, from every occasion of intercourse, from all meetings, even from seeing them. Whoever then is thoroughly in earnest about his spiritual advancement, must if possible forsake all his kindred, in conformity with the counsel of our Blessed Lord and the practice of religious men, and burst in sunder at one blow the agreeable fetters of that imperfect and natural love which binds him to them. And, moreover, he must bear in mind that after having torn himself from his relatives, he must not hang about them; since it is a peculiarity of this deceitful affection that it breaks out anew with greater intensity after having been once extinguished. At least, if he cannot wholly leave them, he must keep apart from them as much as he is able· for, as to extinguish a fire nothing avails so much as depriving it of fuel, so, to maintain the heart in detachment, the surest means is to keep at a distance

* Ex Lib. Doct. PP.,—Lib. de Obed., n. 2.

from the agreeable objects which are the material with which its affections are occupied. But even if this be not feasible, he should learn, while dwelling amid his kindred, to moderate natural affection by the rules of charity, and to manage so as to subject carnal love to that of God. This, I own, is more difficult, but still it is attainable if, without paying attention to the inclinations of nature, we frequently protest before God that we love our kindred solely because it is His will—that we love them to promote their temporal and spiritual advantage, because it is the Almighty pleasure that we should promote it—that we will never do them any service which we know to be in any degree displeasing to the Divine Majesty. Such acts, frequently made from the heart, will avail to weaken carnal love and to render it subject to that of God; and thus it will no longer be a mere animal affection, but reasonable, well-regulated and holy; nor will it set any hindrance to our advance in Christian perfection. These maxims may shock such worldlings as are accustomed to be guided in their affections by natural instinct, after the fashion of the brute creation. Yet they are Gospel truths, taught by Christ, confirmed by the teaching of the Holy Fathers, and sanctioned by the practice of eminent servants of God, as we have already shown. By the neglect of these maxims we may account in part for the fact that we fail generally to discover in persons living in the world—even when they are devoted to piety—that spiritual growth which may be seen in Religious; at least when these are in earnest about their progress in perfection.

CHAPTER II.

ON THE HINDRANCES TO PERFECTION WHICH ARISE FROM ATTACHMENTS GROUNDED ON CARNAL AND SENSIBLE LOVE FOR AGREEABLE OBJECTS.

348. If carnal love for our kindred be so great a hindrance in the way of perfection, far greater is that which arises from a certain carnal and sensible love for other outward objects, and which

is grounded on a certain congeniality of temper rather than on ties of blood. When this love becomes too ardent, it often occasions great evils and even eternal ruin. But, in order not to be misunderstood, I must first make some preliminary remarks. Friendship, as defined by St. Augustine, is a mutual love between two persons founded on the reciprocal communication of goods.* Hence, there can be no real friendship between any two individuals unless they share and have in common such goods as either may possess.

349. It follows from this, that as there are manifold kinds of love, and various goods which may be enjoyed in common, so too there are divers descriptions of friendship. There is an evil friendship which joins two persons together in a vicious love, in the common enjoyment of brutal gratifications: such as are the pleasures of the senses. In reality, this in nowise deserves the name of friendship, since the objects shared in common are not really good, but supremely evil; and also because they are to be found among the brute beasts, which are incapable of entertaining friendship. There is another kind of friendship, which is holy, by which two persons love each other with the supernatural love of charity, and partake together of God Himself and of the everlasting bliss which they hope to enjoy in company. Such, for instance, was that which existed between St. Teresa and St. Peter of Alcantara, who loved each other intensely, with a holy love, having in view the glory of God, which they were banded together to forward; and who shared one with another those gifts which their spirits enjoyed in God, even so much as to remain at times in the midst of their intercourse rapt in God in sublimest ecstasy. Thus, too, we read that St. Gregory of Nazianzus and St. Basil were knitted together in the closest friendship, founded on their great virtues and their deep familiarity with sacred science; whence they lived in company for the space of thirteen years in the greatest harmony, in the desert of Pontus. Thus, too, an inviolable and virtuous friendship existed between St. Augustine and Alypius, in consequence of which they were converted and

* Amicitia est humanarum divinarumque rerum, cum benevolentiâ et caritate consensio. Ep. 155 ad Mart.

baptized together, and returned in each other's society to their own country where, one having been chosen Bishop of Hippo, the other Bishop of Tagaste, they remained till their death most closely united in the bonds of a holy affection. Again, between the celebrated Cassian and St. Germanus there existed a holy intimacy, based on the desire they both felt to promote perfection in the cloisters of Europe; which made them travel together over the several provinces of Scythia, Palestine, Mesopotamia, Cappadocia, Egypt, the Thebais, and other regions of the earth, everywhere searching for examples of religious perfection. There is another kind of friendship, which is not blameworthy, and yet is not holy or virtuous,—at least, if we consider that virtue which belongs to the order of grace. This kind of friendship is indifferent, that is, neither good nor bad, and implies a mutual attachment arising from a common enjoyment of earthly and temporal advantages. Such is the friendship that exists among soldiers and among men of letters; it is grounded, in the one case, on community of profession, and in the other, of pursuits of learning. Lastly, there is another description of friendship, which cannot be called either vicious like the first, or godly like the second, or even indifferent like the third, since it is very prejudicial to the spiritual life. This consists in a tender, sensible affection, founded on outward comeliness and grace in dress, voice, or deportment; on gaiety of disposition, and on a certain sympathy of temper and character. To distinguish this from the other kinds of friendship, we may term it imperfect friendship. This is the kind of attachment of which we intend to treat in this place, and which we maintain to be a most great impediment to the spiritual life, and the very ruin of perfection. Friendship of this kind may exist betwen persons of different sexes or of the same sex; and although it is more dangerous and pernicious in the former case, it is by no means free from peril in the second.

350. We have said that friendships of this kind are positively imperfect because, granting—as we all along suppose—that they have no evil and unlawful object, they are founded upon a sensible affection which is wholly carnal; their sole aliment being outer charms and exterior attractiveness. When attachments of this

nature become at all intense, they give rise to numberless jealousies, quarrels, suspicions, embittered feelings, and countless other forms of disquiet, full of trouble and anguish. From this we can easily understand how imperfect must be that root of which so many turbulent passions are the multifarious growth.

351. We further assert that these friendships are highly injurious, since it is enough for a devout person to be entangled in one in order to lose all the spiritual good that he may have acquired. The magnet may be called the queen of stones, for though less prized than many that are called precious on account of the beauty of their colour and on account of their brilliancy and rarity, it possesses a virtue by which it surpasses all the others put together. With a wondrous power of sympathy, it draws iron to itself, and thus can boast of subjugating to its force of attraction that substance which masters all the firmest rocks and all the hardest metals. It ever turns to the Pole, and thus guides the mariner amid the storm when all the stars of heaven are darkened, leading him across the foaming billows to the haven of his desire. But to deprive the magnet of its rare virtue, it suffices to put it into the fire, when it will soon become as useless as any of the pebbles upon which we tread when walking along a high road. The like happens in the case which we are considering.

352. To illustrate this, let us take the instance of some man who is devout, given to prayer, eager for the sacraments, charitable to those of the household, obedient to those placed in authority, and humble withal; one, in a word, who, like the loadstone, attracts the regard and admiration of all the world by the lustre of many virtues. We will suppose that such a one contracts a tender and impassioned attachment for a certain companion (it will, of course, be far worse if the person be of the opposite sex), that he gets entangled in this friendship, that his affections grow warmer and warmer, and eventually burst into a flame. You will soon see—although there may be no evil purpose in his friendship—that he, like the magnet, will lose all his virtue. He will speedily lose the spirit of prayer; for his interior being in turmoil, the divine light can no longer pierce through to illumine his mind or enkindle his heart: he will attend at church by a mere

bodily presence, but his thoughts, and possibly his eyes also, will go rambling after the object of his affections. He loses, too, his relish for the sacraments, which are become insipid to him; the poisoned draught of sensible attachment having destroyed the fine sense of his soul's palate. He loses all confidence in his Confessor, to whom he no longer lays himself bare, nor frankly declares the infirmity of his miserable soul and the weakness to which he has been reduced; either because he is ashamed to appear so miserable, or because he fears lest his Confessor, when he comes to understand what is the matter, will prescribe an energetic remedy. He loses charity, because, agitated by jealousy, suspicion, and fancies of all kinds, he no longer looks upon his fellows with the same eyes. He begins to nourish antipathies, to cherish innumerable petty spites, to break forth into acts of rudeness, into sharp and biting words. He loses obedience and submissiveness to those set over him because, being rebuked for his weaknesses, he turns angrily against his corrector, like a wounded snake, is insincere in his excuses and obstinate in his disobedience. Thus does the loadstone become a useless object, fit only to be trampled underfoot.

353. The same holds good of a girl just ready to enter life, who is pious, modest, obedient to her mother, respectful to those of her household, attentive to her duties, fond of retirement, who shrinks from the eyes of the public, and delights in going to church, whither she is drawn by her love for holy functions and her eagerness for the sacraments. If such a one become violently attached to a young man of her own station in life, being won by the charms and attractions which she discovers in him, you will presently see her wholly changed, although in the ardour of her feelings no evil thought as yet presents itself to her mind. She will become indevout, neglectful of the sacraments, and caring nothing to visit churches except when hoping to meet with the object of her affections. She will always be anxious to go out of doors in order to see her beloved one, and to be seen of him. She will be careless of domestic duties, and will very frequently be met with at the door and seen at the windows, from both of which she hitherto kept aloof. When rebuked by her mother for

her unwonted irregularities, you will hear her reply with insolence, and declare to her parent's face that she will not obey her, but will pursue her own course, despite all orders and prohibitions. Was I not, then, right? Are not these tender attachments most prejudicial to the soul, even granting them to be free from the taint and malice of grievous sin, seeing that they strip the soul of all virtue, perfection, and good, and reduce it to so wretched a plight?

354. But what is still worse, such friendships founded on imperfect affection make the love of God rapidly grow lukewarm and, if they are very ardent, finally deprive it of all warmth. Because God alone is the lawful Master of our hearts, which He desires to possess with His holy love; nor can He endure any other affection in them, unless it be subordinate to the love of Him, and by this love regulated in all its motions. And this is surely not the case with the soft affections of that friendship which is now under consideration. But when God is excluded from the full possession of our hearts, He withdraws from them and leaves them in a state of utter tepidity. The Philistines having utterly routed the forces of the Israelites by repeated defeats, took possession of the Ark of the Covenant, the richest and most highly-prized booty that could have fallen into their hands. In their joy at having so noble a prize, they bore it in triumph to their own city and set it in their Temple side by side with their idol Dagon, thinking thus to do honour to the God of the Hebrews by placing Him on an equality on the same altar with their god. They were mistaken; for the next morning, on opening the gates of the Temple, they found that their idol was fallen from its altar and was lying prostrate before the Ark of the true God.* They afterwards placed the image which, unmoved by human hands, had thus fallen, very near to the Ark; but the following day a far more lamentable sight awaited them, for not only was their idol cast down, as on the previous occasion, but its arms and head were broken off.† By this prodigy God has given us to know that He

* Cum surrexissent Azotii alterâ die, ecce Dagon jacebat pronus in terrâ ante arcam Domini. I. Reg. v.

† Rursus mane die alterâ consurgentes, invenerunt Dagon jacentem super faciem in terrâ ante arcam Domini; caput autem Dagon, et duæ palmæ manuum ejus abscissæ erant super limen. I. Reg. v.

will reign alone in the temple of our hearts, that if there be any idol which our affections have set upon a pedestal within our hearts, it must be cast down, hewn in pieces, shivered into fragments and utterly destroyed. In a word, the gilded ark of divine love must be allowed to rest and shine alone on the altar of our hearts, without any other love to share its dominion. The sole companions it allows of are such affections as are subordinate in their movements to itself, and regulated by its holy dictates. We must needs, then, infer, that these impassioned friends either have not God's love abiding within them, or that this love is very cold, so long as they cherish an affection which, being sensible and tender, is the more vile and carnal, and the more opposed to the holy love of God in the soul. Such as indulge in these ardent friendships have not God within them ; for instead of enkindling in their breasts a love for His unspeakable charms, they cherish rather an affection for earthly attractions, for a vile beauty which is wholly opposed to the divine love. How, then, can we wonder if every trace of virtue and perfection is slowly yet surely effaced from the hearts of these unhappy persons, who show the slight account they make of God and of that love of Him which is the source of all our spiritual good ? Should not these most disastrous results suffice to make us abhor such attachments as are tender and full of passion ? Should they not lead us to free ourselves of them at whatever cost, if perchance we are already entangled therein ? Is it enough, in order to ward off such evils, to say that friendships of this kind are lawful merely because they are not openly vicious ?

CHAPTER III.

FRIENDSHIP, FOUNDED ON A TENDER AND SENSIBLE LOVE, BESIDES BEING MOST IMPERFECT AND INJURIOUS, IS FURTHER MOST DANGEROUS.

355. Great as is the injury occasioned by such friendships or mutual attachments as are founded upon certain bodily endow-

ments that we discover in the person beloved, the damage done to our soul by these friendships is equally great, because the love which at the outset was merely tender, and remained unmixed with any vicious element, little by little degenerates into a merely sensual attachment, results at length in the ruin of souls, and proves to be the beginning of everlasting damnation. Nor is this peril confined to cases where an attachment is formed between persons of a different sex: the danger in tender friendships exists between persons of the same sex. This opinion will, I am aware, be deemed over-rigorous by some who are ensnared in these attachments. Let, then, St. Basil speak in my place. "Young men," he writes, "should flee from too intimate a friendship for others of their own age, and should keep aloof from such attachments, as they would from a raging furnace; for the devil, corrupting the affections by snares of this kind has often enkindled in many the flames of impure lust, and caused them to burn in everlasting fire."* And lest the reader might doubt whether the Saint is not alluding to the criminal friendships mentioned by me, in passing, in a former Chapter, he may remark, how the Saint forthwith adds, that "in the beginning, the devil lured on these miserable persons by an affection which to them seemed spiritual and charitable, but that corrupting them, little by little, through his artifices, he has ended by precipitating them into an abyss of great evils." And the Saint further continues: "Some even of those who had escaped safe and sound from the stormy sea of this world, have made shipwreck in the haven of Religious Life, where they seemed to be in security."† Let not the reader be scandalised at this language, which is not mine but that of the holy Doctor.

356. But should the weighty warning of a saint of such great

* Juvenis sive ætate, sive animo fueris, æqualium tuorum consuetudinem defugito, ab illisque te non secus atque ab ardentissimâ flammâ procul abducito. quandoque illorum operâ usus adversarius, plerosque olim incendio dedit, et sempiterno igni cremandos addixit. Serm. de Abdicat. Rerum.

† Spirituales primo caritatis vanâ quâdam specie illectos, in teterrimam postea voraginem præcipites deturbavit: et qui ex medio pelago sævientibus undique procellis, tempestateque incolumes evaserant, eos jam intra portum securos unâ cum ipsâ navi, vectoribusque submersit.

authority not suffice to show the danger lurking in these tender attachments, the personal experience of a great saint may succeed in convincing us. St. Teresa, in the thirty-second Chapter of her Life, relates, that being one day in prayer, she felt herself on a sudden transported to hell, and confined there in so narrow a niche or hole, as to be quite incapable of stirring hand or foot. She could distinguish nothing in this narrow prison, for a thick darkness overhung it; yet, she adds that in spite of the darkness she was forced to behold whatever could be a torment to the sense of sight. She felt the burning of the fire, but could find no words capable of conveying the severity of the torture that it inflicted. As regards the other bodily torments she observes, that in the opinion of her physicians, she had undergone such excruciating agonies in her illnesses that they were enough to cause her death; yet these agonies appeared to her a mere trifle in comparison with what she had to suffer in that infernal dungeon. As to the sufferings of the soul, she speaks as follows.—"All this was nothing in comparison with the torture, anguish, oppression and affliction of my soul: my despair and bitterness of heart were so great, that I am at a loss to describe them." Now, while the Saint was enduring the full force of these torments, God made her understand that she was in the place which the devils had in store for her, should she have continued her former mode of life.

357. We must here observe, that her only failings in the past consisted in certain personal attachments which had long retarded her spiritual progress. The reader must not for a moment indulge the thought that these attachments of St. Teresa were tainted with the least savour of vice or impurity; for, as the Saint bears witness in the same book, she had a natural abhorrence for all manner of unchastity. Moreover, Father Ribera, who had been her Confessor, states, in the memoir he has written of her, that these attachments, which he had narrowly watched, were free from all grievous fault, and were but a series of slight shortcomings, by reason of the ardour of her personal attachments, and some remote danger to which she exposed herself by their indulgence. In a word, her friendships in nowise differed from those soft and

impassioned friendships of which we are now treating. Still, had St. Teresa persevered in these attachments, notwithstanding they were free from vice, they would, by slow degrees, have landed her in that pit of fire, of which God gave her some experience after she had long since escaped these toils. Who then, after considering this example, will be ready to say that such friendships are lawful, innocent, and free from danger?

358. We may further add an observation, which will confirm the truth that we are inculcating. When St. Teresa was engaged in these affectionate intercourses with friends, her life was by no means lax or indevout: she spent several hours daily in prayer, and exercised herself in all manner of virtue, so much so, that re calling to mind the many virtues which then adorned her, she wondered that they should have been insufficient to ward off damnation.* "When I considered that, however sinful I was, I always had some intention of serving God, and forebore from certain things which I saw people of the world were doing without the slightest scruple; that when suffering grievous bodily ailments, I bore them through God's grace with much patience; that I was not given to murmurings or detraction; that I felt aversion for no one; that covetousness and envy had no such hold upon me as to occasion any action that might grievously offend our Lord; that, sinner as I was, I kept the fear of God, as I may say, constantly before my eyes: yet, with all this, I was shown the place the devil held in store for me," &c. Such being the case I will reason as follows:—If the soft and tender attachments, from which St. Teresa could not preserve herself for a certain time, would have dragged her, in the end, into the bottomless pit of ruin, despite the virtuous devout and spiritual life she strove to lead amid these shortcomings, what will become of so many young men and women, and even of some nuns, who are devoid of religion, careless about prayer, and without any virtuous practices; who get entangled in such attachments, foster them, and add fuel to the flame which is burning in their hearts, by their looks, words, presents and studied kindnesses; and, instead of breaking the chains by which the devil expects to drag them

* In Eod. Cap.

down to hell, they hug them every day more closely than before? Wherefore let those, whom this concerns, think of it.

359. Nor does it avail to urge that such friendships are devoid of danger, because the object of the attachment is a spiritual person. This excuse is worthless; for St. Bonaventure expressly and pointedly affirms, that when the object of an undue affection is a spiritual person, not only is such friendship not secure against grave dangers, but it is for this very cause more likely to be dangerous. And the reason is, that its very spirituality causes us to be less guarded and more ardent in our affection; and, moreover, spiritual gifts, enhancing bodily advantages, render the object more attractive, and hence more dangerous * The Director then must not admit any excuse, when there is a question of these tender and affectionate friendships, even between persons of the same sex; for love being the most vehement of all the passions, it is naturally the most fraught with peril. We may rest assured that love is a passion which becomes intense in proportion to the encouragement which it receives; and the more impassioned it is, the more readily does it degenerate from its holy beginnings. We must consequently be on our guard, and be quick to stamp out the first sparks of a fire which, if neglected, may burst out into a very conflagration of impurity.

CHAPTER IV.

PRACTICAL SUGGESTIONS TO DIRECTORS ON THE PRESENT ARTICLE.

360. First suggestion. Certain Confessors, seeing close attachments full of tenderness and disquieting passion arise between women (sometimes even between women of a pious disposition), take no heed of the matter. Indeed, there are cases known

* Noverint spirituales, quod licet carnalis affectio sit omnibus periculosa, et damnosa, ipsis tamen est magis periculosa, maxime quando conversantur cum personâ quæ spiritualis videtur. Nam quamvis horum principium videatur esse purum, frequens tamen spiritualitas domesticum est periculum, et malum occultum bono colore depictum. Opusc. de Purit. Conscient., cap. 4.

of some Confessors who have gone so far as to say, that there can be no harm in such persons loving one another. In truth, not only is there no harm, but it is a great point of perfection when they are mutually attached by the love of charity or, at least, by a love which is virtuous, void of danger and not out of keeping with the dictates of reason and of charity. But if they love each other with an impassioned love, which is founded upon nothing but gracefulness of person, manners and character, such attachment is most certainly not a mere evil, but a total ruin of the spiritual life, and not seldom an occasion of the soul's perdition, as the Director will have seen in the foregoing Chapters.

361. The Director must be aware that love is the predominant passion in women, because they are usually gifted with a tender heart, which easily opens to this affectionate softness and finds great difficulty in resisting it; as indeed is the case with everything that is conformable to our natural tastes. Moreover, women have a very vivid imagination, so that when it has once taken the impress of a beloved object, they are much affected, and find very much difficulty in forgetting it. Now, if it be their lot to be kept within doors, and if they have no occasion of finding in a person of the opposite sex an object for the love which predominates within them, they conceive attachments for one another; and if they should happen to meet with some companion or friend who is recommended to them by any remarkable external advantage, they conceive an affection for her and, as it were, lose all self-control in their love. From this there results a great turmoil of passion, a countless number of faults, and an entire cooling down of fervour. And, moreover, if this affection is suffered to grow immoderately, very grievous failings may follow from it: for this passion is one that blinds us, and against which no one can feel secure. Any Director of experience will bear me out in what I here assert. We may take it as an established principle, that a Confessor should not only make much account of these tender friendships, but that he must spare no pains in uprooting them, for while these are left undisturbed, all his efforts to lead his penitents to perfection are wholly useless.

362. Second suggestion. But that the Director may be able to

open the eyes of his penitents to the true nature of the injurious and dangerous friendships of which I am speaking, he must learn to recognise them; and hence it will not be useless to lay down for his instruction some signs by which he may discover them in his penitents. Some clear signs are frequently to think of the person when distant, and often to imagine that we are conversing in his company as if he were present, and that too in time of prayer when we should be thinking only of God—for our thoughts follow the lead of our affections; to address him, when present, in terms of affection, to show constant little marks of tenderness, to go on talking for ever without feeling wearied, not to be able to tear ourselves from the person, and to feel that we are doing violence to ourselves when obliged to part. Other signs will be, to make him many presents in order to provoke a turn of affection, to discover to him our own character, to render him all sorts of trifling attention and services, to praise immoderately all that belongs to him, to get angry at the slightest remark made to his disfavour, as if every straw that touches our beloved one were an arrow that pierces us to the heart's core. Further tokens are, to feel affliction at the want of correspondence on the part of the person beloved, to complain of his being negligent, to tell him that he is ungrateful, to give certain childish tokens of displeasure, to break off the friendship for mere trifles, but to be ready to take it up again more warmly than before. Again, to feel a great affliction if others share the favour of our friend, and to fear that we are going down in his esteem, to experience great jealousy, to be much agitated and disquieted, to conceive aversion for a rival, to break out into words of resentment, to come to an open rupture. Should the Director discover in a penitent all of these signs, or even some of them, he must not hesitate, but be assured that this pernicious affection is enkindled in the penitent's heart; even as he would conclude that a house was on fire if he saw smoke escaping from the roof. In such cases his whole care must be to effect a cure of so great an evil.

363. Third suggestion. The first remedy is to make the penitent aware how grave an evil he has incurred, so that he may conceive the desire of cure and make use of the remedies

prescribed for that end ; for, as a patient cannot be restored to health who does not wish to be cured, so, a person seized with this passion will never get rid of it unless he earnestly desire to be set free. Nor will it be very difficult to persuade these poor blinded souls of the grievousness of their ailment, if an experienced Director, without giving heed to the pretexts and excuses wherewith they palliate their attachment, be earnest in setting before their eyes the faults which they commit, the lukewarmness into which they have fallen, and the greater evils impending over them; of all which we have already spoken. Another remedy is a hearty recourse to God. These affections are, at times, so deeply rooted, especially in the hearts of women, that it needs the hand of God to pluck them forth. Now, there is no other means of obtaining this mighty aid but to earnestly ask for it. St. Teresa consulted a Jesuit Father concerning a certain friendship which had obtained great hold upon her. The Father, seeing how needful detachment was for her spiritual advancement, but finding her weak and vacillating, ordered her in the first instance to have recourse to the Holy Ghost, to beseech his help by reciting daily, for a week, the hymn *Veni Creator*. While the Saint was one day making this prayer, God gave her to hear in her inmost soul a few of those all-powerful words which spiritual writers call *living*, by which He uprooted from her heart all affection, not only for the person to whom she was attached, but to every one else in the world; so that it became henceforth impossible for her to attach herself to any one by like affections. Let each and every one who may find himself entangled in these toils, recommend his soul to God, and he too will receive help from on high, if not in the extraordinary manner in which it was vouchsafed to this Saint, at least help of great power, and then he will succeed in fulfilling his purpose.

364. The third remedy is to keep away from the beloved person. This remedy is the most arduous for very impassioned lovers; but then it is the most effectual and the most important. In vain do we look to extinguish a flame which blazes up and spreads about on every side, widening its circle in every direction, if we do not remove the fuel on which it feeds. In exactly the

same way is it sheer folly to pretend to stifle an affection which has taken possession of the heart, unless we keep away from the person who, being its object, adds fuel to it and fans it by his presence. Such penance in separation is most painful, I acknowledge; but then for our own soul, our own salvation, our own perfection, it is worth while to endure even a death agony.*

365. A fourth remedy is to remove whatever stimulates the passion; not to allow our eyes to wander in search of the person beloved; not to look at him full in the face; to cease from studied civilities and kindnesses; and when we are compelled to meet him whom we love, at the call of duty or civility, to do so with a serious mien, gravely and without needless lingering: above all, to cut off all sorts of presents, whether of great or small value: for, as St. Jerome writes, godly love does not run after feasts and tender and affectionately-worded letters.† Further, if the affection have not been already manifested, it should be kept concealed; for love, like fire, when kept covered up dies out by degrees, but bursts into a flame if uncovered.

366. Fourth suggestion. The foregoing prescriptions apply in cases where such tender friendships have already been contracted. But in any case, the whole care of a Director should be to guard his penitents from contracting these pernicious friendships, for it is much easier to prevent so great an evil than to cure it. He must therefore make use, in his guidance of penitents of either sex, of the advice which St. Basil lays down for his monks.‡ The Saint does not approve that in monasteries the monks should be allowed to form small gatherings apart from the community, nor to indulge in particular attachments; but will have each to show equal charity towards all the brethren. And he most aptly observes, that charity regards all indiscriminately with an equal eye, while carnal love takes the point of view the most in accord with its own whims. Still more strictly does the Saint forbid a monk to converse with women without a just cause, or to keep up a

* Agonizare pro animâ tuâ.

† Crebra munuscula, et sudariola, et fasciolas, et vestes ori applicatas, et oblatas, et degustatos cibos, blandasque et dulces litterulas, sanctus amor non habet. Ad Nepotian.

long discourse with them. The reason why is plain, for although every sensible affection may be dangerous, when there is a difference of sex it may be most dangerous, and may soon become vicious. We must be careful to keep fire from any combustible matter, especially from such things as tow or straw, which most easily catch flame. Now, men and women are to each other as straw and fire; by familiar intercourse they soon enkindle in one another affections which lead to perdition. Let men therefore avoid conversing with women, and never permit themselves to hold such intercourse except for a reasonable motive. Another warning the Director would do well to keep in mind is, that when his penitents, either male or female, are beginning to attach themselves to any one with sensible affection or friendship, he must apply the remedy at the outset. It is easy to cure diseases, if only we take them in hand at the beginning, but if they be allowed to grow and to get a hold on the susceptible frame of the patient, they become incurable. The same may be said of these affections. Hence, *Principiis obsta.*

ARTICLE X.

Hindrances to Perfection from the outward attacks of the Devil.

CHAPTER I.

THAT PERSONS WHO STRIVE AFTER PERFECTION ARE EXPOSED TO THE ASSAULTS OF OUR INFERNAL ENEMIES.

367. THE hindrances of which we have so far been treating, whether proceeding from within or without the soul, keep us far from God, and make us stray from the paths of Christian perfection, not by direct assault, but by luring us with the appearance of some earthly good. Thus, the senses and passions draw us after them by the bait of the pleasures which they offer; honours, glory, and riches bewitch the mind by their false glitter;

friends and kinsfolk win our hearts by the attractiveness of affection. And though all these objects be grievously prejudicial to our souls, they have no direct intention of harming us; they profess to minister to our gratification; they aim at our satisfaction, not at our perdition. Not so the devils, who by their artifices and temptations set great hindrances in the way of our perfection, and that with the purpose of debarring us from so great a good, and in case of success, of dragging us into terrible disasters. Hence we should stand in greater dread of them, as the implacable enemies and unwearying opponents of all spiritual progress, and should guard ourselves with greater caution against their snares and deceits. In order, then, that we may avoid the fate of so many unhappy persons who, overcome by their attacks or hoodwinked by their deceit, are daily suffering all loss of spiritual good, and even eternal salvation, we will treat in the present Article of the temptations of these enemies of ours, and set forth the methods in which they may be overcome. And as the principal purpose of the present work is the direction of those souls that aspire to perfection, we will, in this first Chapter, prepare them for the fray by showing them what that is which the devils mainly aim at in their temptations.

368. We learn from St. Peter, that *the devil goes about like a roaring lion seeking whom he may devour.** He is never still, always active, always hoping to swallow us up when he has caught us in his snares. He is urged to this restless energy by the hate which he bears to God, and by the envy which he entertains towards us. And because he is well aware that such as strive after perfection are the most acceptable to God, and the most sure to mount those bright thrones from which he and his companions were cast down on account of their pride, the Wicked One bears them a more implacable hatred, and wages against them a fiercer war by his temptations. Hence St Jerome might well say, that the devil is not most busy in pursuing infidels, and such as live out of the bosom of Holy Church; because he looks upon them as already won. But he strives for the undoing of Christian souls,

* Adversarius vester diabolus, tamquam leo rugiens, circuit quærens quem devoret. I. Pet. v. 8.

and among these, to use the expression of the prophet Habacuc, chosen souls are his most agreeable prey.* Thus did he fix his eager eye on holy Job, whom he made the butt of countless formidable assaults, in order to devour him. He aimed at Judas, an Apostle of Christ, one of the pillars and foundation-stones of Holy Church; and when he had torn him to pieces by the assaults of a sordid greed of money, he extended his designs to all the other Apostles in a body, desiring to sift them all by his evil suggestions, and to grind them to powder as flour is ground by a mill. Of this our blessed Lord gave them warning †

369. St. Gregory is of the same mind as St. Jerome, since he says, that the devil cares not to disturb those unhappy souls of whom he has gained full and unquestioned possession. ‡ But we who drive him forth from our hearts, who refuse to be his subjects, and by the practice of virtue wage war against him, are assailed by his temptations. And in very truth, what king, what tyrant ever waged war with his loyal and obedient subjects? War is for those who resist, who are refractory, for rebels who would shake off the yoke of subjection, who chafe when feeling the bit and bridle of obedience. Now, such are virtuous souls who withstand the devil; not sinners who obey and own subjection to his tyrannous sway. Hence it is against the former that our infernal enemies set all their snares, employ all their machinations, and wage the most truceless war in the endeavour to obtain the victory. And so true is this, that St. John Chrysostom goes so far as to say, that you will find no one who was very dear to God who has not been tried by most grievous temptations. § And he

* Non quærit diabolus homines infideles, non eos qui foris sunt, et quorum carnes rex Assyrius in ollâ succendit. De ecclesiâ Christi rapere festinat. Escæ ejus, secundum Habacuc, electæ sunt. Job subvertere cupit, et devorato Judâ, ad cribrandos Apostolos expetit potestatem. Ad Eustoch. de Custod. Virgin.

† Expetivit vos satanas ut cribraret tamquam triticum.

‡ Eos pulsare negligit quos quieto jure possidere se sentit. Circa nos vero eo vehementius incitatur, quo ex corde nostro, quasi ex jure propriæ habitationis expellitur. Moral., lib. xxiv., cap. 7.

§ Prorsus si quis omnia enumerare velit, plurima tentationum emolumenta reperiet: nullusque umquam ex his, qui Deo maxime cari, atque acceptabiles fuerunt, sine pressuris vixit, etiamsi non ita nobis videatur. De Provid., lib. i.

proves this assertion by the example of St. Paul who, though a most ardent lover of our Lord, and most tenderly beloved by Him, far from being exempt from these disturbances, was more than any one made the butt of the most violent temptations. Spiritual persons may take comfort from this when their minds are clouded and darkened by evil thoughts and their hearts filled with impious and filthy temptations; for these diabolical disturbances are plain tokens that they are dear to God and hence are the enemies of His enemies. Let this encourage them for the struggle, as they may be assured that the greatest heroes of the Church were not exempt from the like suggestions.

370. In the Lives of the Fathers of the Desert, it is narrated, that a solitary, a great servant of God, was led by his Guardian Angel into a monastery which was inhabited by a saintly community, all being entirely devoted to the service of God. On first setting foot on this holy spot, he was astonished to see it surrounded by such swarms of devils, that they surpassed in number the flies which settle on carrion, or the bees that buzz round a hive. He saw devils in the church, in the choir, in the cloister, in the dormitory, in the refectory, in the cells, devils everywhere. But far greater was his astonishment when, being led by his Angel outside the monastery, he could see no demons on his way through the city, save that in passing the town gate he discovered a solitary one, who was lounging idle and unemployed. "But wherefore," he inquired of his angelic guide, "so many devils for a handful of monks, while there is but one for this vast city?" "Because," replied the latter, "the townspeople do the devil's will already, so that they have no need of the devil to tempt them; not so, however, the monks; they withstand him and refuse to be his subjects. Hence these wicked ones gather together in great numbers around the Religious, and spare no pains to force their will." In a word, then, it is but too true that Lucifer deals with us after the fashion pursued by princes with revolted cities, which are invested on every side by numerous armies, are battered by artillery, and at length forcibly brought into subjection by all the might of their arms. But when the city has surrendered

and the citizens have been brought back to their allegiance, the king sets a single governor over them, who rules them in peace.

371. Hence it is not without reason that the Spirit of God warns us, *Son, when thou comest to the service of God, prepare thy soul for temptation.** Figure to yourself that you are entering upon a field of battle, where you will be hemmed in on all sides by the fiercest temptations of the fiends of darkness; for as you rebel against them, they will spare no artifices to win you over to their side. St. Gregory, commenting on the above words, speaks in the following admirable style:—"When thou comest to the service of God, the spirit does not invite thee to an agreeable undisturbed repose, but summons thee to wars, struggles, conflict, combats. The devils, leagued together for thy ruin, will allow thee no peace. And the more thou shalt show thyself determined not to yield and shalt withstand their behests, the more violently will they pursue thee with countless evil suggestions in order to break down thy constancy."†

372. We may judge hereby of the delusion of some who, wishing to serve God, whether in Religion or in the world, think to enjoy a calm, uninterrupted peace of soul and changeless serenity of mind, a very paradise of content. I do not deny that it is for a spiritual person a source of great comfort to feel himself free from the defects to which he was formerly subject; a great relief to be untroubled by certain stings of remorse which used once to gnaw his heart, and certain well-grounded fears of damnation. I do not deny that it is a great encouragement for him to feel a well-founded hope of being in grace with God, and in looking forward to entering one day upon the possession of an everlasting inheritance. Neither do I deny that God, from time to time, refreshes these faithful souls with the dew of His heavenly con-

* Fili, accedens ad servitutem Dei, sta in justitiâ, et præpara animam tuam ad tentationem. Ecclus. ii. 1.

† *Fili, accedens ad servitutem Dei, sta in justitiâ, et timore, et præpara animam tuam ad tentationem* non enim ait, ad requiem, sed ad tentationem: quia hostis noster adhuc in hâc vitâ nos positos, quanto magis nos sibi rebellare conspicit, tanto magis nos expugnare contendit. Moral., lib. xxiv., cap. 7.

solation. But still we must remain ever convinced that such consolations are often chequered with temptations, whereof some are loathsome, some blasphemous, some tumultuous, some disquieting; so that this peace is often clouded by fears, scruples and anxiety. In a word, we must ever bear in mind this great truth, that the devil is an implacable enemy who never leaves us in peace, and never ceases from troubling all who are faithful to God; for, as it has been excellently observed by St. Jerome, it is impossible that a man be not tempted in this life. Hence, in the Lord's Prayer, we put up our petition to God, not indeed as seeking to avoid temptations (for we must needs be tempted), but begging strength and vigour to overcome them.* We say this much, not to dishearten devout persons by the prospect of truceless conflict, but rather that by being forewarned, they may be forearmed for the struggles awaiting them, and that, relying on the divine aid, they may take courage, so that when attacked by the foe they may fight bravely and win the wished-for victory.

373. Abbot Theodosius, whilst bowed down by the weight of years, was fond of relating that, being in the flower of his age, he was planning a generous flight from the world, in order to devote himself wholly to God in solitude, when he was, of a sudden, rapt in ecstasy and made to behold with the eyes of the mind objects far other than those which present themselves to our bodily vision. He saw a man standing by him, bright and shining like the sun who, taking him by the hand, said, "Come along with me, for thou wilt have to fight like a valiant warrior." He then was led to a large amphitheatre filled with men some of whom were of most beauteous mien and clad in garments white as snow; while others were of sinister aspect and clothed in black like gloomy shadows. Whilst the youth was gazing fixedly on these divers objects, there appeared suddenly in the midst of the theatre a blackamoor of such immense stature that his head seemed to reach the clouds, and he heard from his guide that this was the

* Impossibile est humanam mentem non tentari. Unde et in oratione dominicâ dicimus *Ne nos inducas in tentationem;* non tentationem penitus refutantes, sed vires sustinendi in tentationibus deprecantes. In Matt., lib. iv., cap 26.

terrible foe with whom he must wrestle. At this news the poor youth grew pale, his blood froze in his veins, he shuddered with horror and trembled from head to foot. Turning to his guide he began to beseech him, with scalding tears, not to let him be exposed to so great a danger, for the adversary was so mighty that even if the strength of all mankind was united in his single arm, he would yet be unable to overcome him. "There is no help for it," replied the guide; "fight with this man you must, so enter boldly and with confidence into the lists. I will be there close at hand; and I will aid you in the great struggle, and as a prize of victory, will encircle your brow with a shining crown." The young man took heart, went to encounter the formidable giant, and by the help of his trusty guide overcame and mastered him; soon he laid him low in the dust, and was to be seen wearing on his head the bright crown which had been promised. Immediately on the fall of the giant, the crowd of black men took to flight, yelling hideously, while the troop of bright and comely youths burst out into thunders of applause for the noble guardian who had so opportunely assisted the inexperienced youth in this fierce battle, and had set so glorious a crown on his brows.*

374. The meaning of this symbolic vision is obvious. God wished in this manner to show the young Theodosius, when he was on the point of abandoning the world and of devoting himself to the monastic life, that to dedicate ourselves to His service, is nothing else but to expose ourselves to a furious battle with the giant powers of hell. But the Almighty, wishing to encourage him, showed at the same time, that, on the one hand, the devils stand by to make sport of his defeat, while, on the other, the Angels stand by while we are fighting, to applaud our victories; and that, though the foe be formidable, we must not on that account lose heart, since we ought to bear in mind that Jesus Christ, figured by the man in shining vesture, stands ever by us to assist us here and to reward our victories in Paradise with a crown of unfading glory. We have but to rely on Him and to fight bravely, and the victory and its prize are certain. Let us, then, be convinced that this present life is a ceaseless warfare with the

* Sophron., Prat. Spir., cap. 66.

unseen spirits,* who hem us in on all sides, and as brave champions of the Crucified One, let us always remain sword in hand, ever ready, ever equipped for the fight.

CHAPTER II.

SOME OF THE HOLY PURPOSES FOR WHICH GOD ALLOWS HIS GREAT SERVANTS TO BE MUCH TEMPTED BY THE DEVIL.

375. We read in the Catholic Epistle of St. James, that *God tempts no man.*† In Deuteronomy we find it written that God tempts His servants.‡ These expressions may seem not a little strange, for it would appear impossible to reconcile the statement that God tempts some persons, and that He tempts no one. But, as St. Augustine observes, the contradiction is only apparent, for one may tempt another in two ways—with a purpose of seducing him and leading him astray, or with that of trying his fidelity and of giving him the due reward. The former is the temptation of seduction, the latter that of trial; the former belongs to the devil, by the second God Himself tempts us, or permits His enemies to ply their temptations.§

376. Now one of God's main purposes in allowing His servants to be tempted is precisely this: to try those that love Him, those that are loyal to Him, and dearest to Him. Diabolic suggestions are put into our mind for the purpose of seducing us, as is clear from the fact that they aim at making us fall into an abyss

* Militia est vita hominis super terram. Job vij. 1.

† Ipse autem neminem tentat. Jac. iij.

‡ Tentat vos Dominus Deus vester. Deut. xiij. 3

§ *Ne forte tentaverit vos, qui tentat, et inanis sit labor vester* (I. ad Thessalon. iij.): atque hic intelligitur diabolus, tamquam Deus omnino non tentet: de quo alio in loco Scriptura dicit: *Ipse autem neminem tentat.* Nec contraria est ista sententia ei, quâ dicitur: *Tentat vos Dominus Deus vester.* Sed solvitur quæstio, cum vocabulum tentationis diversas intelligentias habeat, eo quod alia sit tentatio deceptionis, alia tentatio probationis. Secundum illam non intelligitur qui tentat, nisi diabolus: secundum hanc vero tentat Deus. Ep. 146 ad Consen.

of sin first and then of punishment; but on God's side, they are trials, which He allows in order that by their means our faithfulness may be put to the proof, whether it can bear the test of being tried in the furnace of these hellish molestations; and that we may show how steadfast is our constancy, how pure and unalloyed our love. Any pilot of the slightest experience, says St. Basil, can steer a ship when the weather is fine and the sea calm; but the able pilot is proved in the storm, amid the raging of the winds and the beating of the waves. Every soldier, however cowardly he may be, can pretend to bravery in his own camp, but the truly brave soldier is known by his bearing on the battlefield, surrounded by the swords of the foe. The athlete is tried on the race-course, the wrestler in the lists, the high-minded in calamity, and the Christian, who is a faithful lover of his Redeemer, in those temptations of the devil to which he is exposed by his Divine Captain.*

377. What did God aim at in that arduous and heart-rending command which He gave to Abraham, requiring him to sacrifice his favourite son on the top of Mount Horeb? Did He wish merely that the Patriarch should mercilessly put to death his only son? By no means. He wanted only to try his faithfulness. And wherefore did God deprive the innocent Tobias of his eyesight, and condemn him to drag on his life amid gloom and darkness? Was it to deprive him of all earthly comfort, and to make him mourn unceasingly?† Surely not; for Raphael, in unfolding to Tobias the divine counsels, told him that, because he was acceptable to God, it was necessary that temptation should try him.‡ And why was holy Job given up to the devil, who made such sad havoc of his goods, his children, of his very body? Was it to make him the most unhappy of mortals? To say so would be to utter a blasphemy. God had no other end in view than to give an illustrious proof of the patience of His servant.

* Ut gubernatorem navis tempestas, athletam stadium, militem acies, magnanimum calamitas; sic Christianum hominem tentatio probat. Orat. II, de Patient.

† Quale gaudium erit mihi, qui in tenebris sedeo, et lumen cœli non video?

‡ Quia acceptus eras Deo, necesse fuit ut tentatio probaret te. Tob. xij. 13

And this is what He aims at when He allows those who are devoted to His service to be the object of the most violent temptations, whether the devil assail them with the stings of incontinence, with thoughts of unbelief, with blasphemous suggestions, with want of trust, with despair or gloom; or whether the fiend torture them with scruples and anxiety. The Lord's purpose in allowing this is to try the fidelity of His servants and put their love to a rigorous proof. This was what He did to His most faithful servant St. Paul, whom He made the sport of the most distressing temptations.* When, therefore, any one finds himself assaulted on all sides by the most abominable suggestions of the demon, far from losing heart, he should rejoice, since these diabolical assaults are sure tokens of the love which God bears him; he must not lose courage, but animate himself to the strife, in order that he may prove how faithful he is when God Almighty exposes him to trial.

378. Another end which God has in thus allowing His servants to be tempted is to ground them in virtue. Virtue is not to be won except by conflict; and, as those trees which grow on mountain-tops strike deepest root, just because they are more exposed than others to the violence of the winds and storms; so, the virtues most deeply rooted in the soul are those which have had to withstand the shock of temptation, and the strivings of the devils with their wicked suggestions. It is most easy to account for this. Virtue is nothing else but a facility for doing virtuous acts, engendered by the frequent repetition of these same acts. But how shall virtuous actions be frequently repeated, if attacks of temptation be altogether wanting? How shall he who is never crossed make acts of patience? Or one who is never provoked perform acts of meekness and gentleness, or exercise chastity if never tempted to the opposite vice, or make acts of humility in the absence of humiliations? The same holds good of every other virtue. But if it be true to say that we cannot exercise virtue, at least cannot often exercise it, without the onslaught of temptation, it must needs follow that virtue is not to be acquired without temptation. Every one has heard of the counsel given by Scipio

* Datus est mihi stimulus carnis meæ, angelus satanæ, qui me colaphizet.

Africanus in the Roman Senate, when the question of destroying Carthage, the rival of Rome, was debated. Against the almost unanimous sentiment of his colleagues, he would have that city preserved, though it was an implacable foe of the Roman Commonwealth, for, as he wisely suggested, its arms would serve as a whetstone to Roman valour. In like manner, too, I say that the devils and their temptations are the whetstone of the virtues, since they afford them exercise, and render them more robust by their assaults.

379. We may now understand the meaning of the reply which God gave to the repeated prayer of the Apostle of the Gentiles, that he might be delivered from the temptations with which he was so cruelly harassed: "*My grace is sufficient for thee, for virtue is made perfect in infirmity.** It is not expedient for thee to be freed from this trouble and temptation, because in the midst of these contests virtue is refined. My grace is sufficient for thee, since aided by it thou art able to withstand the assaults of thine enemies, and to come out of the combat a glorious conqueror." Cassian concludes from this, that our most loving Saviour has done us a greater favour in exposing us to the conflict with temptations than if He had wholly freed us from them, because if amid these combats we but remain steadfast in well-doing, we shall attain to an eminent and sublime degree of virtue, according to those words which God spoke to St. Paul: *Virtue is made perfect in infirmity.*†

380. In the Lives of the Fathers of the Desert, it is recorded,‡ that a youth, who had been placed under the care of a saintly old man, being fiercely assailed with temptations to sensuality, generously resisted the onset of the enemy, and was ever on the watch to chase away every unholy thought, and constantly care-

* Sufficit tibi gratia mea: nam virtus in infirmitate perficitur.

† Majora nobis per colluctationem tentationum laudis contulit præmia benigna erga nos gratia Salvatoris, quam si omnem a nobis necessitatem certaminis abstulisset. Etenim sublimioris, præstantiorisque virtutis est, persecutionibus ærumnisque vallatum manere semper immobilem. . . . et acquirere quodammodo de infirmitate virtutem: quia virtus in infirmitate perficitur. Coll. XXIV, cap. 25.

‡ § 7.

ful to check every bad feeling. And as the poor young man continually felt this struggle of the flesh against the spirit, he strove to keep the body in subjection by unwearying prayer, rigorous fasts, long watchings, and extraordinary bodily labours. One day, his Ghostly Father, seeing him so hard pressed and harassed, said, 'My Son, would you have me pray to God to deliver you from these grievous temptations which do not leave you a moment's peace?" "No, Father," he replied, "for though I feel acutely the misery of these diabolical persecutions, yet I know by experience how useful they are; for, by God's grace, I combat, resist to the last, and practise continual acts of virtue. Now, Father, I pray more than of old, I fast more often, watch longer, and strive in a thousand ways to keep my rebellious flesh in subjection. Better were it, then, that you beseech God to help me effectually by His grace, so that I may fight vigorously, bear with patience this grievous molestation, and by means of these very temptations, make much progress in perfection,* that with the Apostle I may at length be enabled to exclaim, *I have fought the good fight, I have finished my course; henceforth there is laid up for me a crown of justice.*"† This young man did indeed fully understand how much temptations contribute to our acquiring Christian virtue; for, out of his eagerness to make progress, he cared not to be freed from temptation, preferring his spiritual advancement to his repose. Let some faint-hearted devout persons cast an eye on this saintly youth—they who, when overtaken by temptation, are troubled, disquieted, mourn and lose heart, saying that all is lost because they are tempted; like those delicate and dainty patients who, finding the medicine bitter, refuse to take the draught which is to restore their health. Let the example of this good monk encourage such persons to fight manfully against the demons who attack their virtue, resting assured that, amid all these temptations, they will not only retain the virtues which they seem to have hitherto acquired, but, more than this, will perfect and strengthen them.‡

* Et faciam etiam cum tentatione proventum.

† II. ad Tim. iv. 7, 8

‡ Nam virtus in infirmitate perficitur.

CHAPTER III.

OTHER REASONS WHY GOD ALLOWS TEMPTATIONS.

381. I HAVE said that God aims at grounding us well in virtue in slackening the chain which binds the tempter, and in allowing him to approach us with his suggestions. I now further add, that among all other virtues, the Almighty specially intends to establish us in a profound humility, which is the foundation of the whole spiritual life. We read in the Book of Ecclesiasticus, that whoever has not been tempted knows nothing about himself, understands nothing: *The man that has not been tempted, what does he know?** for it is only in time of temptation that man realises his weakness, and becomes conscious of his own misery. We shall do well to reflect how little the Prince of the Apostles knew himself before he was put to the test of temptation. In hearing Christ warn him of that great want of faithfulness whereby he was so soon to deny his Master, he showed that he in nowise feared for himself, but, confident of his own strength, he all but gave the lie to Our Saviour saying: *Even though I die with Thee, I will not deny Thee*† And going still further in his boldness, he adds, *Even though all should be scandalised in Thee, I will not be scandalised.*‡ Overweening presumption! But in what did it all end? When tempted, not by a crew of devils, but by a poor serving-girl, he found out his weakness, confessed it, and wept over it bitterly. As St. Augustine observes, before he was tempted St. Peter presumed upon himself; in temptation he came to know what he was and he learned humility.§

382. The same happens to us, says St. Gregory, when, undisturbed by temptation, we feel not the frailty of our flesh and the infirmity of our spirit;—and hence conceive a great opinion of our

* Qui non est tentatus, quid scit? Ecclus. xxxiv. 9.

† Etiamsi oportuerit me mori tecum, non te negabo.

‡ Etiamsi omnes scandalizati fuerint in te, sed non ego.

§ Petrus, qui ante tentationem præsumpsit de se, in tentatione didicit se. In Psal. xxxvj.

merits, esteeming that we have advanced in virtue, have acquired great strength, and need be afraid of no one. But when temptations gather around us, and bear us down by their weight, then, indeed, are we able to lay our fingers on our misery; we take up humble and lowly thoughts, we see plainly the danger we are in of falling headlong, and by godly fear we secure ourselves against such a disaster.* This was a second reason why God allowed St. Paul to be tormented by those unceasing temptations of the flesh. He would keep His servant humble amid the multitude of the revelations and extraordinary favours which He was pleased to lavish upon him: and this the same holy Apostle well knew, and to this he himself witnesses: *And lest the greatness of the revelations should exalt me, there was given me a sting of my flesh, an angel of Satan, to buffet me.*† In short, God acts with us as a pilot deals with his ship, which he fills with ballast in order to make it sink the deeper in the water; for if it were too light, it would become the sport of the winds and waves, and would probably end by being wrecked. So too does God, the true Guide and Pilot of our souls, keep us, by the weight of grievous temptations, plunged in the knowledge of our miseries; lest we be driven to and fro by the blasts of vanity, and cast on the rocks of many faults, with the risk of being lost eternally.

383. Sarah, a virgin and anchoret, was for thirteen years together grievously harassed by a foul spirit of uncleanness. She did not, however, pray to be delivered from this trouble, but humbling herself before God, asked merely for strength. The devil, furious at such constancy, redoubled his assaults, and made a last effort to overcome her. But she, humbling herself still more deeply, begged with all the more earnestness for help from on high. The enemy, seeing at length that there was no means of making

* Mirâ hoc nobiscum dispensatione agitur, ut mens nostra culpæ nonnunquam pulsatione feriatur: nam esse se magnarum virium homo crederet, si nullum unquam earumdem virium defectum intra mentis arcana sentiret. Sed cum tentatione irruente quatitur, et quasi ultra quam sufficit, fatigatur, et contra hostis sui insidias munimen humilitatis ostenditur: et unde pertimescit se enerviter cadere, inde incipit fortiter stare. Moral., lib. ij., cap. 27.

† Ne multitudo revelationum extollat me, datus est mihi stimulus carnis meæ, angelus satanæ, qui me colaphizet. II. ad. Cor. xij. 7.

her fall into sin, appeared to her in visible shape, exclaiming, "Thou hast conquered, Sarah! thou hast conquered!" hoping that, falling into some act of vanity or presumption, she might lose that profound humility which was the principal fruit that she had gained in her past struggles. On hearing this, the abashed but prudent woman replied, "No, not I, foul fiend, but Christ has worsted thee in me."* The devil frequently employs this artifice with certain heedless spiritual persons. Seeing he cannot prevail over them by his temptations, nor strip them of God's grace, he strives to rob them at least of the humility which they have been taught in their struggles, and which is the main end that God has in view in permitting them. He endeavours either to make them vain of their triumphs, or, if wearied by their continual conflicts, to draw them into want of trust, into discouragement, disquiet, trouble, and complaints; all of which are contrary to holy humility; so that while they on the one hand overcome temptations, they may on the other be overcome thereby. Let, then, each one who knows himself to be wanting in this particular, open his eyes, and whenever temptation shall assail him, let him acknowledge his misery in calm and peace; let him fathom the precipice into which he would fall headlong were God's holy Hand to be withdrawn, humbling himself in the Lord's sight, in sincerity of heart; let him cry for help, which he will surely receive, for God forsakes not unless He be forsaken.† He will thus come forth from temptation adorned with one of the most lovely of virtues, holy humility; which is just what God intended in exposing him to these contests.

384. There is another end, of very great advantage to us, which God has in view in allowing us to be exercised by temptation: it is to give large increase to the store of our merits in the present life, and so to enhance the splendour of our crown in the life to come. As St. James says: *Blessed is the man that endureth temptation* with patience, and overcomes them with fortitude, *for when he is tried, he shall receive the crown* which God has promised to

* Non ego te vici, sed Deus meus Christus. Eriber. Rosveid., In Vitis Patrum., lib. iij.

† Deus non deserit, nisi deseratur.

them that love Him; of merits on earth, and of glory in heaven.*

385. For the better understanding of this truth, every one who is in the state of grace should know, that as often as he rejects any diabolical suggestion, in order not to offend God, he gains by the holy act which he thus performs, at least one additional degree of grace, to which corresponds a higher degree of glory above and thus, by repelling temptation, he is preparing for himself an unfading crown in paradise. For, even supposing that he could lay claim in his heavenly country to that degree of glory alone, which he has earned by one single act, this would be sufficient to render him everlastingly happy, and to entitle him to reign for endless ages on a starry throne How many crowns, then, will he not win if he be frequently tempted, and if the temptations which assail him be violent, troublesome, wearying; since it is plain, that our victories are rendered more complete and glorious by the number and fierceness of the battles by which they have been won!

386. We read in the Chronicle of the Cistercian Order, that a certain monk was one night furiously assailed by impure temptations, which he manfully struggled with and overcame. That very night, a lay-brother of the monastery, who was in the country looking after a farm, had the following vision. He beheld a lofty column whereon hung a golden crown of most cunning workmanship, and which was everywhere studded with precious gems. While he was gazing upon it, full of admiration of its beauty and value, he saw a young man of charming aspect who, taking down this splendid diadem, gave it into his hands, saying: "Go to such a monk" (naming him) "and give him this crown, which he has won in the course of this very night." On coming to himself, the Brother was quite puzzled to know whether his dream was a diabolical delusion or a heavenly

* *Beatus vir. qui suffert tentationem: quoniam cum probatus fuerit, accipiet coronam vitæ, quam repromisit Deus diligentibus se* . . . Jac. i 12. Non timeamus tentationes; sed magis gloriemur in tentationibus, dicentes: *Quando infirmamur, tunc potentes sumus*. tunc enim nectitur corona justitiæ. S. Ambros. in Luc., lib. iv., cap 4.

vision. The next morning, therefore, he went to the Abbey, and as a precaution against all deceit, he communicated to his Superior all that he had seen and heard on the foregoing night. The Abbot summoned the monk in question, inquired what had happened to him the preceding night; and on hearing the violence of the temptation wherewith he had been assailed, and the brave stand he had made against it, understood that the crown seen by the lay-brother in his dream, was a figure of the immortal crown of glory which God had in store for him as the prize of the victory which he had gained over his infernal foes during the preceding night.

387. Such then is God's purpose in allowing us to be tempted; to prepare for us palms and crowns of immortal glory: a remark of St. Ambrose.* Hence, when we feel the assaults of our enemies, let us at once lift up our eyes to those bright crowns which our heavenly Captain holds out to us if only we be faithful to Him: and let the hope of so great a reward animate us to the conflict, as the same holy Doctor exhorts.† And if, according to the Apostle, those who strove in the race-course consented to forego every gratification that could diminish their strength,‡ and this to obtain a crown that perishes and *is corruptible*,§ how much more should we abstain from the pleasures with which the devil lures us, and check the passions by which he inwardly disturbs us, that we may win the heavenly and incorruptible crown prepared for us in glory everlasting? *But we an incorruptible crown.*||

388. If then it should happen to any one that he is assailed by continual, violent, and horrible temptations, let him not think himself forsaken of God, nor envy those who lead a life free from such turmoil; for this is not a token of being forsaken, but rather of God's care and protection, in that He makes these troubles serve for our present advantage, and for the

* Qui vult coronare, tentationes suggerit. Ut supra.
† Et si quando tentaris, cognosce quia paratur corona.
‡ Qui in agone contendunt, ab omnibus se abstinent.
§ Et illi quidem ut corruptibilem coronam accipiant.
|| Nos autem incorruptam.

increase of our future reward, as I have before shown, and as St. John Chrysostom most emphatically assures. "No one," says the Saint, "should consider that he is overlooked or forsaken by God, on beholding himself exposed to the onslaught of violent temptations; for this is the surest token he can have that God takes special care of him." * For just as a father who loves his son, spares not the rod and makes him feel its strokes, refusing to be moved to pity by tears because he seeks the present amendment and future advantage of his child; so, St. Paul tells us, God causes those whom He tenderly loves to pass under the rod of such trials,† since He desires their perfection in this life and their glory in the life to come.

389 I will conclude with a narrative left on record by Sophronius, concerning a certain Monk and Priest, Conon by name, who lived in a certain Monastery called Pentucola.‡ It was his duty to anoint with the sacred chrism, and to cleanse in the waters of regeneration such Catechumens as were presented for baptism. Now, in fulfilling this ministery for women, he felt grievous temptations, and on this account, he had more than once determined to leave his monastery and to withdraw from these disquiets. He was on the point of carrying out his purpose, when St. John the Baptist, the Patron of the place, appeared to him, saying, *Bear and persevere.* It chanced soon after that a young Persian girl, of singular beauty, came for baptism, and the servant of God, fearing some grievous assault of the devil on this occasion, actually left the monastery in order not to be in the way of the danger. While he was on his way, St. John the Baptist again appeared, and stopping him, bade him retrace his steps. But first he made him sit down, and forming on his body three signs of the Cross, freed him for ever from these temptations, addressing to him at the same time the words: "Conon, I had intended that for these struggles thou shouldst receive

* Ne existimemus esse signum, quod nos dereliquerit, vel despiciat Dominus, si tentationes nobis inferantur, sed hoc maximum sit nobis indicium, quod Deus nostri curam gerit Homil 33 in Gen.

† Quem enim diligit Dominus, castigat. Hebr., xij. 6.

‡ In Prat. Spir., cap 3.

great rewards, and shining crowns in the Heavenly Kingdom; however, since thou carest not for them, I now deliver thee from thy contest with the flesh, but thou in consequence must forego so splendid a guerdon."* And so it fell out, for the good Priest, returning to his monastery, resumed his sacred office without ever afterwards feeling the least rebellion of the senses. I would not infer from hence that these temptations should be desired. St. Thomas teaches the contrary,† because we may not lawfully make them an object of desire since they impel us to evil. But I will say that we should accept such temptations in resignation and peace, when God permits them, and pass through the trial with a profound humility; above all, resisting them with great courage, knowing how much they contribute to our acquiring virtue here and an increase of glory hereafter.

CHAPTER IV.

CERTAIN MEANS FOR OVERCOMING THE TEMPTATIONS OF THE DEVIL.

390. THE first means of overcoming the suggestions of the devil is to lose no time in rejecting them. If we are slow, or delay resisting the temptations of the enemy, we shall expose ourselves to the danger of consenting to them. Such is the advice which St. Jerome gives to the virgin Eustochium: "Suffer not evil thoughts to grow within your mind. Crush the enemy while he is yet weak, for if you allow him to gain strength, he will inflict upon you a mortal wound. Pluck out the tares of temptation as soon as they shoot up in your heart; let them not strike their destructive roots therein, and at length render it wholly vicious:‡

* Crede mihi, presbyter Conon, volebam te pro hâc pugnâ mercede donari: sed quia non vis, ecce abstuli a te hoc bellum; mercede autem hujus operis carebis.

† 3. p., qu. 41, art. 2.

‡ Nolo sinas, cogitationem (libidinis) crescere. Nihil in te Babylonium, nihil confusionis adolescat Dum parvus est hostis, interfice. Nequitia, ne zizania crescat, elidatur in semine.

for it is plainly impossible that temptations should not find place in our frail body, and he, therefore, is happy who drives forth the viperous brood of evil thoughts at their first appearance, and dashes them against the Rock which is Christ, by at once raising his mind to Him."*

391. St. Cyprian maintains the same view: "We must needs withstand the first stirrings of diabolical temptations, and we must be careful not to foster the serpent of evil suggestion as soon as it makes its appearance in the mind and heart; else it will grow into a poisonous monster that will shed its venom on the soul and cause our death."† And St. Gregory supplies us with the reason: "The suggestion of the infernal serpent," he says, "is, at its origin, soft and tender and can be easily crushed under the heel of virtue; but if allowed to grow and to make an entrance into the heart, it gains an irresistible strength and, by its violence, subdues the wretched soul which it makes the slave of sin and of the devil."‡ So that it is of equal importance to lose no time in driving away temptations, and to resist them should they insist on staying in the mind.

392. A person under temptation should therefore act as is done when a spark flies out and falls upon some one who in winter-time is warming himself at the fire. We all of us know that he does not wait to stare at it with a curious eye, but he shakes it off at once, otherwise the smallest delay would cause it to burn his garment. In the same way, and with the same promptitude, should we get rid of certain thoughts that the devil slips into our minds; of certain feelings which he stirs up in our breasts, which set on fire and, after the slightest delay, burn the

* Filia Babylonis misera : beatus qui retribuet tibi retributionem. *Beatus, qui tenebit, et allidet parvulos suos ad petram.* Quia enim impossible est in sensum hominis non irruere innatum medullarum calorem, ille laudatur, ille beatus prædicatur, qui cum cœperit cogitare sordida, statim interficit cogitatus, et allidit ad petram : *Petra autem erat Christus.*

† Primis diaboli titillationibus obviandum est ; nec coluber foveri debet, donec in draconem formetur. Serm. de Jejun. et Tent.

‡ Prima serpentis suggestio mollis et tenera est, et facile virtutis pede conterenda; sed si hæc invalescere negligenter permittitur, eique ad cor oditus libenter præbetur, tantâ se virtute exaggerat, ut captam mentem deprimens, usque ad intolerabile robur excrescat. Moral., lib. xxxij. cap. 16.

poor soul and reduce it to ashes. Or again, we should act in the same way as we would if a scorpion, or some other venomous insect, were to fall on our bare hands or feet. Certain is it that we should not wait to examine how it moves its claws or twists its tail, or whether it moves or remains still: but we should shake it off and crush it at once; for one instant would be enough for it to poison us with its venom. In like manner, then, should we at once drive away certain temptations, which are scorpions sprung from hell and which, if allowed to remain in the soul, though for never so short a time, would slay it by their deadly venom.

393 This was not the conduct of that unfortunate monk of whom we read in the Lives of the Fathers of the Desert.* Unable to overcome the temptations of the flesh which assailed him, he went to an aged solitary who enjoyed a great reputation for sanctity, and begged him, with tears in his eyes, to recommend him earnestly to God, as he was most grievously vexed by the spirit of fornication. The holy old man, taking pity on him, persevered in prayer day and night to obtain of God his deliverance from this misery; but in spite of this, the afflicted monk came back complaining that the temptation, far from diminishing, assailed him with greater violence than ever. He begged, therefore, that the hermit would increase the fervour of his intercession. On hearing this, the servant of God redoubled his prayers and supplications, shedding abundant tears in order to move heaven to pity. The monk, however, returned again to say that the devil still continued to molest him with the same violence as before. Now, one night when the holy solitary was quite sad and full of grief, wondering within himself how it came to pass that God refused to hearken to so just a prayer, the Lord revealed to him that his prayers had not availed because the youth was lazy, slow and irresolute, in rejecting his temptations. The revelation was made in the following manner:—The Saint beheld with the eyes of his mind this monk sitting listlessly in his cell, with the unclean spirit sporting about him, under the form sometimes of one woman, sometimes of another, and, instead of at

* Sec. 12.

once turning away his eyes from such objects, he kept gazing at them with a look of complacency. The Saint, moreover, saw the Angel-Guardian of the monk highly indignant with him because he did not at one reject these foul fancies, and because he did not forthwith prostrate himself in prayer and cry to God for aid. After a while, this monk returned once more with the same doleful tale; but the old man, being at length aware of the cause of the evil, said to him, "My Son, the whole of the mischief comes from yourself, because you will not help yourself, and are not prompt in rejecting your temptations. Just tell me, Brother, if a physician were as anxious as he could be about the health of his patient, were to watch his case with the greatest care, and prescribe for it the best remedies, while the patient on his side were to refuse to help himself, or to forego unwholesome food, or to take the requisite medicine, could he recover? Assuredly not. So in your own case, though others, through zeal for your eternal salvation, plead with God for you, you will never get rid of these filthy temptations, if you will not do your part by driving them away without dallying, by having instant recourse to prayer and by imploring the divine help." At these words the monk remained no less convinced than contrite; he followed the wise counsels of the servant of God, and in this way got rid of the unclean spirit of fornication. Hence we may conclude that the chief means of overcoming temptations and of not letting them get the better of us, are diligence and promptitude in shaking them off and rejecting them.

394. The second means is prayer and recourse to God. The reader must not be astonished if I put so important a means in the second rank only; for, in reality, it is already contained in that which I have placed first: because promptness in driving away temptation, of which I have just been speaking, is to be practised mainly by means of recourse to God. This is a weapon which Jesus Christ Himself puts into our hands for our defence against the assaults of our common foes. *Pray*, He says, *that ye enter not into temptation*;* meaning that we be not overcome by it. He has also inserted this petition in the Lord's Prayer, that we might

* Orate, ut non intretis in tentationem. Matt. xxvi. 41.

ever have it at hand, *And lead us not into temptation.*"* Wherefore it will suffice for us to know how to wield this instrument—that is, to avail ourselves of it when occasion requires—and we are sure to remain victorious over all our enemies.

395. We must bear in mind that this recourse to God in prayer is more than ever needed at the moment when the devil attacks us with some lewd suggestion ; as our danger of falling is then more imminent, and our want of help more pressing. St. Jerome gave his disciple Eustochium this warning, in order that she might preserve her virginal purity free from taint amid temptations : "As soon," he writes, "as you shall be aware of any suggestion contrary to holy purity, lift your mind, heart and voice to God ; cry out,—Lord, help me, succour me ; if Thou be with me, I shall not fear the wicked emotions which the devil and the flesh in league with him suggest."† And Cassian records that Abbot Isaias advised all tempted persons to turn at once to Almighty God, with the first verse of the sixty-ninth Psalm : *O God, come to my aid ! O Lord, make haste to help me !* ‡ And he added, that these words are a wall which the demons will never scale, a breastplate which they will never pierce, a shield of proof against all their weapons.§ But that these words may have this power to obtain God's help and to put the devil to flight, they must come not only from the lips but from the mind , they must shoot forth from the very bottom of the heart, as St. John Chrysostom observes in his comments on the words of the Psalmist, *Out of the depths I have cried to Thee, O Lord.*|| A prayer made thus cannot fail to touch the heart of God, and to urge Him to take our side with us against those who are His

* Et ne nos inducas in tentationem.

† Statim ut libido titillaverit sensum, aut blandum voluptatis incendium dulci nos calore perfuderit, erumpamus in vocem : *Dominus auxiliator meus, non timebo quid faciat mihi caro.* Ep. 22 ad Eustoch.

‡ *Deus in adjutorium meum intende : Domine, ad adjuvandum me festina.*

§ Hic versiculus omnibus infestatione dæmonum laborantibus inexpugnabilis murus est, et impenetrabilis lorica, et munitissimus clypeus. Collat. xix. cap. 9.

|| *De profundis clamavi ad te, Domine.* Non dixit solummodo ex ore, neque solummodo ex linguâ : nam errante etiam mente verba funduntur : sed ex corde profundissimo, cum magno studio, et magnâ alacritate, ex ipsis mentis penetralibus Hom. 101 super Psal. cxxix.

foes and our own. In a word, as St. Cyprian writes: "Even as a child, when alarmed by threatening words, or at the sight of any one whom he has cause to fear, runs at once to his mother's bosom, and there feels that he is safe; so we, when assailed by any of the devil's temptations, should run at once to cast ourselves on the bosom of Christ our Father, heartily imploring His help, and thus rest secure in the arms of His protection."*

396. St. Pachomius, the founder of so many monasteries, and the father of countless monks, used often to exhort his spiritual children to have prompt recourse to God in time of temptation for, as he told them, he had often heard the devils discoursing together as follows. One would say: "I have got a hard subject to deal with, for when I attack him with foul suggestions, he at once falls prostrate on the ground and implores God's help, so that I can go no further and am forced to retreat with confusion." And another would reply: "But my monk does not act in that way. When I suggest evil thoughts he cares not to turn to God, but listens to me, so that I often make him fall into acts of anger, and sometimes into sharp words and quarrels; or, again, into vainglorious thoughts, and into many similar faults." The holy Abbot ended his discourse with these words: "Hence, Brethren, it behoves you ever to watch over yourselves; and at every onslaught of temptation, or motion of passion, to delay not in calling upon the name of God and imploring His Almighty assistance."†

397. It will be well to join to this recourse to God the holy sign of the Cross, a weapon which is formidable to our hellish foes and puts them at once to flight; for, at the sight of this sacred sign, they are reminded of the crucified God Who hung thereupon; as St. Cyril observes.‡ And St. Augustine adds, that at the appearance of this saving sign, all their machinations come to

* Quemadmodum parvuli perterrefacti statim confugiunt ad sinum matris, sic nos cum aliquâ tentatione pulsamur, per preces confugiamus ad Deum. Lib. de Provid., cap. 3.

† Ideoque, fratres mei dilectissimi, semper oportet ut custodiatis sensum et animum vestrum, invocantes nomen Domini Dei nostri. Ex Lib. Sent. PP., § 33.

‡ Quando enim dæmones viderint crucem, recordantur crucifixi. Catech. 3.

nought, all their mines are exploded.* What St. Athanasius records in his Life of St. Antony is most worthy of note. While the fiends came in swarms to assail the holy Abbot, he said to them, arming himself with the sign of the Cross: "Now then, devour me, tear me to pieces, if God gives you leave. I am ready for every outrage, but if you cannot harm me, begone, cowards! for I know you to be such; the holy sign of the Cross and trust in God are, for me, an impregnable fortress against all your efforts."† So should we too, when set upon by the devils with their temptations, arm ourselves with the holy Cross and with recourse to God, and then we shall have no reason to fear all their endeavours; for, at the sight of this sacred sign, they all flee, even as darkness vanishes at day-dawn. Thus shall we be victorious over all the army of hell, even were it all to band together to attack us.

398. For my own part, I am deeply impressed by what St. Gregory of Nazianzus relates concerning Julian the Apostate. He, being terrified by the devils, defended himself against them with the sign of the Cross. And what is wonderful to relate, the very Cross that he persecuted became his defence against the assaults of the fiends of hell, who, alarmed at the sight of this holy sign, fled from his presence.‡ Now if the Cross was a weapon of such avail in the hands of one who hated it, and who was striving to destroy and to blot out every trace and all memory of it, how formidable to the devil will it not be when wielded by one who adores, venerates, and cherishes it, and places in it his whole confidence!

* Omnia dæmonum machinamenta virtute crucis ad nihilum redigi. Lib. de Symb., cap. I.

† Si quid valetis, si vobis in me potestatem Dominus dedit, ecce præsto sum, devorate concessum. Si vero non potestis, quid frustra nitimini? signum enim crucis, et fides in Dominum inexpugnabilis mihi murus est.

‡ Ad crucem confugit, eamque se adversus terrores consignat, eamque, quam persequebatur, in auxilium adscivit. Valuit signum: cedunt dæmones: pelluntur timores. Orat. I. in Julianum.

CHAPTER V.

OTHER MEANS FOR OVERCOMING TEMPTATIONS.

399. THERE can be no question but that a steady confidence in God is a most effectual means for overcoming every temptation, when joined to an entire distrust of ourselves; for God Himself has promised to protect such as put their trust in Him,* and to deliver them from the hands of their enemies.† He has promised to save them in the midst of every peril.‡ And in the Book of Daniel, He goes so far as to declare that those have never been confounded or put to shame who have placed their trust in Him.§ So that he who amid temptations has recourse to God, with a firm trust in His aid and protection, is as certain not to fall, as it is certain that God's word cannot fail nor His promises be made void.

400. The reason why this trust is so pleasing to God that He promises those who have it His holy help, is most obvious. For, on the one hand, the Lord is most jealous of His glory and, while declaring His readiness to share with us all His other good things, is tenacious of this alone, and will keep it all to Himself.|| On the other hand, God sees that a soul which, devoid of all reliance on self, has recourse to Him with a lively faith, will not take to itself, but ascribe to Him, the glory of the victories won over its foes, and of the good deeds which it performs. Hence, God cannot do less than shield it under the wings of His protection, so that each may truly say: *I shall be safe under the shadow of Thy wings.*¶ The truth of this may also be gathered from what St. Gregory the Great says in his Book of Morals: "The virtues we have acquired become more injurious than their absence would be, if they beget within us a vain reliance on self;

* Protector est omnium sperantium in se. Ps. xvii. 31.
† Quoniam in me speravit, liberabo eum. Ps. xc. 4.
‡ Qui salvos facis sperantes in te. Ps. xvi. 7.
§ Quoniam non est confusio confidentibus in te. Dan. iii. 40.
|| Honorem meum nemini dabo.
¶ Et in umbrâ alarum tuarum sperabo. Ps. lvi. 1.

for then virtue pierces the unwary soul with the sword of vanity, and though on one hand they strengthen and give it life, on the other they cause its ruin by unduly puffing it up.* Now, a soul that places trust not in itself but in God alone, is far removed from this danger; for the Lord seeing that, in giving to such a one His graces He leaves them in safe keeping, makes this person the recipient of His promise, and imparts gifts with a most liberal hand. Hence, no means can be found so effectual to obtain special aid in temptation, as recourse to God, full of confidence in His help and of distrust in our own powers.

401. Would the reader know how he is to act in order to awaken within himself, amid the assaults of the devil, this trust which is so mighty to prostrate the foe, my recommendation is that he gain a lively persuasion of the three truths from which this sentiment derives its origin, as from its proper source. First: That the devil, as St. Augustine observes, is a dog chained up; he can only approach us with his temptations so near as he is permitted by the length of chain allowed him by God. Secondly: That God, as St. Paul assures us, will never *allow us to be tempted above our strength.*† Thirdly: That God stands by us in our every struggle to supply strength sufficient—ay, and more than sufficient—to enable us to resist the advances of any temptation however violent, and even to find joy in the victory which we gain. With these truths of the Catholic Faith, deeply rooted in our minds, we shall be able to awaken within ourselves a great confidence in God, and great courage to withstand manfully every assault of this tempter.

402. St. Athanasius relates, in his life of his much-loved St. Antony, that the holy Patriarch, having one day sustained a fierce onslaught, Christ appeared to him to comfort him with His presence. On beholding his beloved Lord, the Saint began to

* Plerumque virtus habita deterius, quam si deesset, interficit: quia dum ad sui confidentiam mentem erigit, hanc elationis gladio transfigit: cumque eam, quasi roborando vivificat, elevando necat: ad interitum videlicet pertrahit, quam per spem propriam ab internâ fortitudine fiducia evellit. Moral., lib. vii. cap. 9.

† Fidelis autem Deus est, qui non patitur vos tentari supra id quod potestis. 1. ad Cor. x. 13.

exclaim: "Where wast Thou, Jesus, while I was so cruelly tormented and tempted by the devils?" * Our Lord replied: "I was here, Antony, giving thee help, and beholding with looks of pleasure the struggle thy unconquerable spirit sustained."† In like manner, let him who is tempted figure to himself that God is at his side, weakening the powers of the foe, and increasing the strength of His servant; that God takes delight in his resistance, applauds his victories, and is there with hands full of crowns and palms to give him an everlasting reward. Then, with a heart filled with trust, let him say: "Since my trust is in Thee, O my God, I fear not, and feel no alarm.‡ Though the devils should come in crowds to attack me, my heart shall not fear, resting as it does on Thee, my God, in fullest hope."§

403. By this lively trust in God did St. Antony set at nought those terrible attacks with which the fiends sought to subdue him; as may be seen in the life written of him by St. Ephrem of Syria. The devil began one day to shake the cell of the Saint, and having made a great breach in the wall called to his companions, saying: "Come along, come along, quicken your pace, an entrance is now made; go in, and strangle him."|| But the Saint, emboldened by his confidence, said: "Were you to let loose the whole of hell against me, still should I be the conqueror, in the name of the Lord."¶ At the sight of so much faith the fiends vanished forthwith, and the cell appeared as it had been before, entire and untouched, without any appearance of the opening. Another time, as he was chanting the Psalter, he saw the mat on which he was standing catch fire, but arming himself with a lively trust in God, he began to stamp out the flame, saying: "In the name of our Lord Jesus Christ, Who gives me help, I will over-

* Domine Jesu, ubi quæso eras, cum tam immanes plagas corpori meo exciperem?

† Eram præsens, O Antoni, et certamen, quod excelso, invictoque animo gessisti, spectabam.

‡ In Domino sperans non infirmabor. Ps xxv. 1.

§ Si consistant adversus me castra, non timebit cor meum. Si exsurgat adversum me prælium, in hoc ego sperabo.

|| Festinate, celeriter festinate, et introeuntes cito eum suffocate.

¶ Omnes gentes circumierunt me, es in nomine Domini ultus sum in eos.

come all the might of mine enemy."* At this expression of confidence, the phantom flames were extinguished, and the devils, discomfited and worsted, took to flight with cries and awful yells. Let us have the like trust, when tempted, and we need not be afraid of all the powers of hell being able to do us the smallest injury.

404. But that this ready and trustful recourse to God may fully avail to overcome temptation, it must further be joined with recourse and manifestation of ourself to our Spiritual Director. This means is no less effectual than important for weakening temptation, and for depriving the devils of their strength when they harass us. For this, two reasons may be assigned, which we have elsewhere alleged. First: God, in the present dispensation, does not commonly give His aid or guidance apart from the means of His ministers. We have therefore to recur to these, and to deal with them in all openness, if we would not go astray; especially in so perilous a matter as that of which we are now treating. Secondly: Because the devil, being a thief who wants to rob us of our spiritual store, like all other thieves takes to flight as soon as he is discovered. And experience shows that we have only to manifest a temptation to our Director, or indeed sometimes merely to make up our mind to do so, when the devil at once withdraws, and the temptation loses very much of its force even if it does not depart altogether.

405. It will be sufficient for our purpose to relate what St. Antoninus, Archbishop of Florence, tells of Brother Rufinus, a companion of St. Francis; for all those who are much tempted may take from the fact both a rule and a caution.† This servant of God was beset with a violent temptation to despair; his mind had received a vivid impression that he was not of the number of the Elect; that hence his prayers, fasts, toils, and privations in Religion, were all of no avail. But the most terrible part of this temptation was the shame and dread with which the fiend had inspired him, of discovering the diabolical suggestion to his Superior and Ghostly Father, St. Francis. Meanwhile, Satan, observing that he was not discovered, became more venturesome,

* Omnem potentiam inimici, in nomine Domini nostri Jesu Christi mihi auxiliantis, superabo.

† Part. iij., Titul. 24, § 7.

and renewed the assault with such violence as to cast Rufinus into an abyss of gloom and sadness. Then, adding to inner disturbances outward illusions, he appeared to him in the shape of the Crucified One, saying: "To what purpose, Brother Rufinus, do you wear yourself out in prayer and austerity, since your name is not entered on the list of those whom I have predestined to glory. I alone know whom I have chosen, and whom I have rejected Believe me, then, rather than Brother Francis: for I assure you that both you and he, with all his followers, are of the number of the reprobate." The phantom vanished, and the servant of God, doubly blinded by the temptation, instead of discovering it to his Director, kept it secret, giving it full credence, and was thus thrown into the utmost consternation and led to the very brink of the slough of desperation. God, being moved with pity at the danger of His servant, made known the whole matter to St. Francis, who sent Brother Matthew to call him. Rufinus made this insolent reply to the messenger: "What have I to do with Brother Francis?" so strong had the temptation grown from its long concealment, and so completely had it darkened his mind. He at length yielded to the prayers and entreaties of Brother Matthew, and betook himself to the cell of the Saint. On coming into his presence, the holy Father informed him in full detail of all that had passed within his soul, and of what had outwardly befallen him; giving him assurance that the whole was a deceit and suggestion of the devil. He commanded him to go to Confession, not to omit his usual pious exercises, and if the vision of the Crucified returned, he was to say to it: "Open thy mouth, and I will put filth into it." Brother Rufinus, seeing his innermost heart thus laid bare, burst into sobs, and fell at the feet of St. Francis, craving his pardon for the reserve with which he had treated him, in concealing his temptations; promised him to fulfil his orders, and returned calm and quiet to his cell. While he was here praying with abundance of tears, the devil returned under the accustomed figure of the Crucified, and rebuked him, saying: "Did I not warn you against giving credit to the son of Bernardone, as you are both of you damned?" But, Rufinus, now enlightened by the instructions of the Saint, spurned the phantom with the words which he had been instructed to use. Seeing himself discovered and despised, the devil took his departure in a fury, and in his flight stirred up on the mountain-side such a whirlwind, that pieces of rock were hurled about, accompanied with so much noise, that it seemed as if he was trying to overturn the whole mountain. St. Francis and his companions came forth at the noise, and saw that these fragments struck fire in falling one against the other, so that they were able to picture to themselves a lively image of the Last Judgment. Hereupon Jesus Christ Himself truly appeared to Rufinus, whom He comforted by His presence and kind words, and on whom He bestowed the gift of high contemplation, whereby, being freed from his former troubles, he lived ever after absorbed in God in unruffled calm. I would here ask any one who is much tried by temptation to make two reflections. First, let him consider what was the state of this great servant of God before he discovered his temptation to his Director. How harassed he was by the devil; how troubled, tossed about; how dejected; how unfitted for all good, and how near to being cast headlong into the abyss of all evils! Secondly, let him think of the entire change which took place after he had opened out his mind and allowed his holy guide to direct him. He became formidable to the fiends, secure against their delusions, calm, cheerful, disposed to prayer, and to everything else that is good and holy. We may infer from this how necessary it is for all persons, however spiritual and devout they may be, to declare their temptations with great sincerity to their Director, in order to break the strength of the devils who attack us, and to stand firm against the shock of their perverse suggestions.

406. But one who is tempted should take special heed not to expose himself to occasions of sin; because the devil deals with us as the general of an army deals with the places to which he lays siege. Satan sends forward a chosen band of occasions of sin, and by their help makes a breach in the fortress of our heart; after which he comes in person to take possession of it, by seducing us into sin. I shall do well if, on this point, I make the remark which Seneca made to his friend Lucilius: "We are

scarce able to meet the devil on level and dry ground, and yet we make bold to wrestle with him on that which is slippery."* We must needs lose our footing and be thrown. And as St. Basil says, "We ought to be forced to encounter the foes of our eternal salvation, against our will, and of sheer necessity; but of our own choice to go forth to meet them, and to expose ourselves to perils and the occasion of sin, is the height of folly. If in the former case we fall, we may claim some pity; not so in the latter, we deserve no pardon In such cases, our own foolhardiness is the sole cause of our misfortunes.†

CHAPTER VI.

PRACTICAL SUGGESTIONS TO DIRECTORS CONCERNING THE PRESENT ARTICLE.

407. FIRST suggestion. The Director must take care not to be harsh or severe with those who are tempted, as this would be to bruise the broken reed, and would be quite unlike the conduct of our most loving Saviour.‡ He should listen to such with patience, compassionate them tenderly, counsel them with charity, and encourage them to go to the encounter with great trust. In a word, he should deal with such as a father deals with his ailing child, whom he regards with the more pity, and for whose recovery he is the more anxious, in proportion as he sees his illness become more grievous. Above all, the Confessor must be on his guard not to feel surprise—and much more not to show it exteriorly—at any temptation which he may discover in his

* Quantum possumus, a lubrico recedamus: in sicco quoque parum firmiter stamus. Epist. 117.

† Etenim bellum, quod præter voluntatem nostram incidat, nobis excipere fortasse necessarium sit: ipsum vero aliquem sibi voluntarium creare, id vero summæ dementiæ est. Siquidem ignosci ei forsitan possit, qui in priore illo victus sit (nolim autem hoc omnino Christi athletis evenire). At qui in posteriore hoc superatus discedat, is præter quam quod rem admodum ridiculam facit, non meretur etiam ut sibi ignoscatur. Constit. Monast., cap. 4.

‡ Calamum quassatum non conteret. Isai. xlvij 3.

penitents; for he should be impressed with the maxim, which St. Bernard would have every one take to heart, that we cannot live in this world without trial, and that one temptation ceases only to give place to another.* The devil acts with us as a fowler, who observes what kind of food is the most acceptable with birds, and employs that as a bait to lure and trap them with. So, too, says St. Ambrose, the demon watches to find out our predominant passion, which he excites by his temptations; he seeks to know what bait is to us the most alluring, and sets it before us in order to bring us into his snares.† There is no single person upon earth who has not some passion, and may not be attracted by some one pleasure; it follows, then, that the enemy studies to know what bait is fittest to secure the ruin of each individual.

408. Satan showed as much to Abbot Macarius by a very marvellous apparition‡ This holy Abbot was living as a Solitary in a desert place, in the lower parts of which there dwelt other monks in separate hermitages. He was one day standing at the door of his cell, alone, and full of thought, when he saw, coming along the path, the devil clad in a white linen robe full of eyelet-holes, from each of which a phial was hanging. The holy solitary asked him where he was going. "I am going," replied the demon, "to tempt the monks who dwell in this desert." "But," asked Macarius, "what is the meaning of all those phials you have about you?" "These," answered the fiend, "are full of the baits by which I lure each one and draw him after me." He thereupon continued his journey, while the holy Abbot, curious to know what would be the upshot, stood awaiting his return. After a brief interval, he saw him coming, sad and gloomy, and inquired what success he had met with. "None," said the fiend; "no one will follow me, they are all saints. There is but one who is my friend, and who is lured by the sweet morsel which I cast in his way in order to win him." "What is his name?"

* Hoc enim præmunitos vos esse volo, neminem super terram absque tentatione victurum, ut cui forte tollitur una, alteram securus exspectet. In Psal. Qui habitat, Serm. 5.

† Tunc enim maxime insidiatur adversarius, quando videt nobis passiones aliquas generari, tunc fomites movet, laqueos parat.

‡ Ex Lib. Doct. PP., Lib. de Provid., n. 11.

asked Macarius. "Theopentus," was the answer. On hearing this, the Abbot betook himself to the lower part of the desert, and asked for shelter in the cell of Theopentus. He entered into conversation with him, and by skilful questions contrived to extract from him the avowal that he was sorely tempted and yielded to evil thoughts. Thereupon the holy Abbot admonished him, and giving him wise and suitable advice, by following which he might henceforth defend himself against such temptations, returned to his hermitage. After some days, he again saw the devil, in the shape in which he had first appeared, and asked him how he fared with the monks "Very badly, indeed," replied the fiend; "they are every one of them saints, and even he who used to be my friend has broken with me, and treats me worse than the others." Now, if the devil did not spare these saintly recluses, but kept for each of them a special dainty in a separate vessel, a particular gratification by which he might win each one of them, he will surely not spare the rest of mankind, from whom he has so much reason to hope for greater success with his temptations. The Director may then rest convinced that all men are liable to such weaknesses, and he should never marvel when he sees that it is so He must rather listen with kindness and charity to those who discover their temptations to him, and must give them fitting advice, suggesting suitable means for overcoming them.

409. Second suggestion. The Director should bear in mind that all temptations are not to be driven away by one and the same method. Some temptations are to be rejected by positive acts of the contrary virtue: others, by not caring for, and contemning them. I will explain my meaning. Some temptations are dangerous of their own nature, because they present objects most gratifying to human nature and most conformable to its propensities. Such are unchaste temptations which, by presenting an unlawful pleasure, incline the will to lay hold of it; such, too, are temptations to hatred, which stir up the will to take vengeance; of envy, which excite displeasure at the good fortune of others, as if it were an obstacle to our own good; of vanity, which spur on the will to take delight in our own excellence, to hanker after praise: and the same is true of vices of a like charac-

ter. These temptations are usually to be rejected by contrary acts; both because we thereby guard ourselves against all danger of a guilty consent and because, by means of these acts, the opposite virtue becomes grounded and deeply rooted within us. Thus he does a virtuous act who, when assailed by unclean temptations, declares that he would die rather than consent to such abominations; who, when moved to hatred, declares that he forgives the injury done to him, and that he is willing to do good to them that have used him ill; or who, when stirred up to envy, declares his satisfaction at his neighbour's good fortune, and that if this person were not in enjoyment of it, he would himself spare no pains in procuring it for him; or who, when tempted to vanity, gives to God the glory of his every good quality, and strips himself of all. Other temptations there are which are not dangerous, as they are abhorrent, not only to the rational, but even to the lower and animal part of our being, which finds in them no pleasure. Such are temptations to blasphemy, certain abominable thoughts and words against God, the saints, and holy images; temptations against faith, and others of the same kind, from which we naturally shrink. Now, with such temptations it is by no means prudent or wise to struggle or to enter on a hand-to-hand fight, saying, "I will not consent; I detest, I abhor them:" both because, on account of there being no danger of yielding them consent, there is no need to offer resistance and because, by resisting, the person subjects himself to a slavery, by conceiving such an intense abhorrence of them, as most frequently only stirs them to activity. and imprints them more deeply on the fancy: and, further, because we thereby expose ourselves to the danger of losing health and reason. It is far better, therefore, to deal with such temptations by despising and paying no heed to them. The Director must, consequently, tell the penitent, whom he sees to be troubled with such fancies, that he in nowise commits sin by having such thoughts, and thus must free him from all alarm. He must order him to abstain from making contrary acts, as they will prove a hindrance to his cure, but rather to despise these thoughts of blasphemy, impiety, or unbelief; and when they return to trouble him, to allow them to pass through his mind, without giving ear to them; and merely to fix his attention on what he is about—to go on praying, if at prayer—talking, if in conversation—working, if occupied. In a word, he has to deal with these fancies just as if an idiot were to whisper such wickedness in his ears: and just as, in this case, he would go on without noticing or giving heed to these ravings, so too, must he deal with these absurd suggestions. But let the Director take especial care, when his penitents confer with him upon such troubles, not to show any sign of dread or of attaching even the slightest importance to them; for he would only throw them into consternation, and aggravate their spiritual sickness beyond measure. He must answer clearly and without hesitation, that there is no sin, no harm (although it may seen otherwise to them) and that they must take no notice whatever of these fancies.

410. St. John Climacus relates that a certain monk was troubled by most horrible temptations to blasphemy for full twenty years.* He rejected them with abhorrence and vehemence, arming himself against them by fasts, watchings, and great austerities; but, because he adopted an unsuitable method, his temptation, far from showing any diminution, daily grew more harassing. At length, being quite at a loss to know what to do, he took counsel of a holy monk; and not venturing to tell him by word of mouth the wicked and detestable thoughts that swarmed in his mind, gave him to read a paper containing them, remaining meanwhile prostrate with his face upon the ground, deeming himself unworthy to raise his eyes to Heaven. The wise old monk read the paper, and, bursting into a fit of laughter, quietly spoke as follows:—"My Son, put your hand on my head.' The other did as was desired. The holy man then added, "I take upon myself all the sins which these temptations have led you, or may lead you, to commit: all I require of you is, that for the future you take no notice of them."† At these words the temptations vanished from the mind of the monk, who was never again troubled with them; simply because he was made free from the alarm which gave

* Grad. de Blasphem.

† Supra collum meum, O frater, sit hoc peccatum; et quæcumque olim fecisti, et facies: solùm id ulterius non habeas in mensuram.

occasion to all his fancies. The Director will follow the same course with his penitents whom he may find to be afflicted with similar temptations, and will say to them, "I take on my own conscience whatever sin you may commit in this point; I only want you to obey me by despising them and paying them no attention whatever."

411. Third suggestion. I have said that unclean thoughts, and images of objects which are gratifying to our passions, should be chased away and positively rejected by means of contrary acts; but I then spoke under a limitation, saying that this was the course *usually* to be adopted; because there are some persons whom it does not suit to take in hand a struggle with such thoughts, or strive to reject them by the effort of making contrary acts. For these it is more expedient to deal with such temptations by despising them; as we have observed with respect to those who are troubled with temptations to impiety. Not a few persons are timorous, and of so delicate a conscience, that they feel great abhorrence of all impurity, and of every action in which a grievous sin may lurk. When an image or a feeling contrary to purity presents itself to such as these, they fall into great fear and feel intense pain; they arm themselves against such thoughts by interior acts, and not seldom also even by exterior gestures, such as shaking their heads, pressing their hands upon their bosoms, rolling their eyes strangely, and making other efforts no less prejudicial to the mind than to the body. And what is the result? The more these thoughts are driven away the more they return to the mind. The more the feelings of delectation are checked, the more impression do they make upon the heart; and things come at times to such a pass, that these persons cannot speak to any one, cannot raise their eyes to look at any one, because there is nothing which might not act as a cause of temptation to them. Nor must the Director wonder at this; for, as I have already observed, nothing is so apt to awaken such thoughts, or to fix them in the mind, as excessive fear. The reason of which is obvious. Fear excites the fancy and impresses it with the dreaded object. Thus we see children afraid to pass, at night, through a dark room, because at one time they fancy that they see a black

shadow, at another they imagine that the devil is behind them. At every chance sound they start, at every slight noise their blood runs cold; while others who are not afraid can pass through dark places without having any of these painful fancies. Whence we may conclude that these poor souls, by being almost constantly in pain, and full of dread of these temptations, have impure objects continually in their imagination, and by the fear they feel of the temptations, awaken them and keep them in ceaseless activity. The same exactly may be said of those persons who seem to themselves to be judging rashly of their neighbours; and also of those to whom it seems that they are rejoicing at the evil which they may chance to discover in others; and again, in like manner, of those who, thinking that vanity is their main weakness, imagine that they give way to vanity in every word they say, and in every step they take. All these must get rid of such excessive, exorbitant, and indiscreet fears, which give rise to their temptations, to their trouble, and to their anguish. But in order to succeed in obtaining this end, there is no need to adopt a course of wrestling, struggling and repression; it is sufficient to despise, disregard and make no account of the temptation.

412. Hence the Director must start with instructing such penitents, impressing upon them that there is no sin, especially no grievous sin, in any thought, feeling of pleasure, or temptation, —though never so abominable—unless there be a full, free, and voluntary consent. For, as St. Bernard says, "There is no harm in the feeling when there is no wilful consent; but rather when we are tempted, in reward for the combat which we sustain and the annoyance that we have to bear, palms and starry crowns are laid up for us in heavenly glory."* He will next drive from their hearts all groundless alarm, by convincing them that, through God's grace, they are far from giving this guilty consent, since the pain and inward bitterness which they experience amid these temptations are a sure token that the will has no part therein; the anxiety wherewith they long to be rid of these suggestions

* Molesta est lucta, sed fructuosa: quia si habet pœnam, habet et coronam. Non nocet sensus, ubi non est consensus: immo quod resistentem fatigat, vincentem coronat. De Interiori Domo.

shows that the will is not in league with them; the indiscreet resistance which they practise is an unmistakable sign that their will is averse to such abominations. He must therefore order them, when such thoughts and temptations present themselves, to abstain from positive acts of rejection, since it will be enough to direct the attention to some other quarter, as if we were above such things and did not care for them, even as a wayfarer on a dusty road, who, when the wind blows, shuts his eyes and passes on. If, when the temptation comes, the persons can with peace and calm fix their mind on some holy object, making meanwhile acts of affection towards Christ or His most Blessed Mother, it is the best course, provided, however, that it be done without interruption of peace; but should the occupations they have in hand not allow them to make such acts, let them turn their minds to what they have before them, and to the matters on which they are engaged. But the Confessor must, above all, forbid them to reflect on the temptations when they have passed away, or to examine whether or not they have yielded consent; as this serves no purpose but to breed fresh scruples, which drive these timid souls to extremities; and by this retrospect the temptation is again awakened after it had been put to slumber. He may tell them to be quite calm, taking it on his word that they have not committed grievous sin.

413. Fourth suggestion. The Director must not forget that the method which we adopt to overcome temptations should vary with the temptations themselves. In the case of the harsh, unquiet, turbulent vices,—such as impatience, anger, indignation, envy, rancour, aversion,—the person tempted may laudably go forth to encounter them, and close with them in the hope of overcoming them. The reason is, that these passions do not gratify or delight us, nor are they such as our frail nature is attached to: so that the more we suffer from their attacks, the more fortunate we should be esteemed. If, further, the Director discovers his penitent to be a person of robust virtue, he may allow him, as an exercise of charity, to seek the company of rough, uncivil, and disagreeable persons, towards whom he feels an aversion; or to converse with those who by word or deed annoy him, in order to

exercise his patience and meekness; or he may be permitted to put himself under the obedience of some austere and strict person, in order to break his self-will. But, as we said above, there are other fascinating and attractive vices. Such are those which incline us to sins of the flesh, to excess in meat and drink, to over-freedom in dealing with others (especially with those of the opposite sex), to the pleasures of worldly amusements, and the like. The tempted person should ever flee these solicitations, for being most attractive, there is great danger that in the very acts of seeking to overcome them, we be overcome by them instead. It is of these temptations that the Holy Ghost speaks when He warns us how *He who loves the danger shall perish in it.** And St. John Chrysostom says expressly that such temptations should never be sought after.† To these did St. Philip Neri allude in his well-known adage, that in the war with our senses, "Cowards," that is, they who take to flight, "are victorious." Hence the Director will rigidly insist that persons who are inclined to these gratifications —whether by the instigation of the devil, or by natural character—should not trust to themselves, but should keep their distance, should retreat and take to flight; for to act otherwise would not be bravery, but foolhardiness, and the height of rashness. Cassian relates that a holy Hermit received a packet of letters which had been sent to him from home, from his friends and relatives. The holy man, feeling that affection awaking within him which nature instils into every breast, took these letters, and, without opening a single one, indeed without undoing the packet, threw them all into the fire, saying at the same time, "Away, thoughts of relatives and home; with these sheets do I commit you to the flames. I am resolved that your pleasing allurements shall not draw me back again to those affections to which I have long since bidden farewell."‡ This servant of God knew that there was question of entering on a struggle with a tender sentiment; hence he shrank from exposing himself to danger, and by

* Qui enim amat periculum, peribit in illo. Ecclus. iij. 27.

† Oramus, ne intremus in tentationem . quia eas quærere non debemus.

‡ Ite cogitationes patriæ, pariter concremamini, ne me ulterius ad illa, quæ fugi, revocare tentetis. Instit., lib. v, cap. 32.

this generous act put away every occasion that might have led him into sin.

414. Fifth suggestion. The Director must be attentive and quick in discerning the temptations of his penitents, when the devil covertly glides in under pretence of good; since, on the one hand, such temptations are with difficulty distinguished, and, on the other, they are the most dangerous of all; for, as St. Augustine says, "The devil is more to be feared when he comes in secret and in disguise to delude us, than when he assails us openly and rages against us with his evil suggestions."* At times, the fiend, transforming himself into an angel of light, proposes to devout persons things in themselves good and holy; and, having won their confidence, slips in something dangerous, and then something sinful, in order to draw them into open sin and to make them fall, before they are aware, down the precipice. Such temptations are most to be dreaded, because not being known to be temptations, we are put off our guard, and being attracted by their plausible appearance, are led on by them and at length fall into the snare, even as the bird drawn on by the decoy falls into the toils of the fowler. It is the duty of the Director—indeed, it is the main part of his duty—to discover these deceits, and to detect the devil, not only when he comes in his own person to tempt us, but when he approaches disguised under these devout appearances, and to warn his penitents, in order that, being made aware of the wiles of the enemy, they may be on their guard against them. The more so, as St. Bernard is of opinion that these are the temptations by which, for the most part, devout persons are assailed and undone. They who lead a good life are never seduced by the devil except under the appearance of good.† I will narrate an occurrence which will set forth my meaning more clearly.

415. St. Bonaventure relates,‡ that there lived in a monastery a certain Friar, who to all outward seeming led a most holy life, for he was given to prayer, and enjoyed such an abundance of spiritual consolations, that at the mention of God he could not

* Magis timendus est cum fallit, quam cum sævit. In Psalm xxxix.

† Bonus numquam, nisi boni simulatione deceptus est. Serm. 60 in Cant.

‡ In Vitâ S. Franc., cap. 10.

conceal the joy that filled his heart. So addicted was he to solitude and silence that he never uttered a syllable, and he came at last to such a point, that for fear of breaking silence even by sacramental confession, he made known his sins to the Priest by signs. Meanwhile, the great Patriarch St Francis of Assisi happened to pass by the monastery, and on the same occasion the Minister-General, who was present, conversing with the saint, gave a most favourable account of the sanctity of this particular Religious. St. Francis, being enlightened from above, said, "You are mistaken; he is under a delusion of the devil." "But how," rejoined the other, "is it possible that a man of so much prayer, so silent, exact and perfect, could be guided by the spirit of falsehood?" St. Francis answered, "Listen! Give him an order to confess twice a week, and you will soon discover that something is wrong." The Minister-General did so, and the unfortunate man, on hearing the command of his Superior, began to shake his head and to show by gestures that out of love of silence he was unwilling to do it. In a short time he afforded a more unmistakable proof of the falsehood of the spirit by which he was led, for he left his Order and returned to the world. Take notice how the devil, in this instance, transformed himself into an angel of light, in order to lead this poor Friar step by step to his ruin. He began by deluding him in his prayers with a multitude of sensible and false consolations. Next he beguiled him with an indiscreet love for silence; and seeing that he was caught by this bait, he induced him to deal in a most improper manner with the sacrament of Penance, afterwards to keep away from it as much as possible: then to be guilty of open disobedience to the orders of his Superiors, by which steps he at length withdrew him from Religion, and made him return to the Babylon of the world.

416. Of secret arts like these the enemy has a countless number for the seduction of poor souls. Thus, for instance, he will insinuate into the heart of a Priest a lively desire to lead some person of the other sex to high perfection; then at first he will excite in his heart an affection towards her which is wholly spiritual; later on he will bring about a great intimacy between the two, which will degenerate into familiarity, this, in its turn, will lead

on and on, even to taking improper liberties; and thus will he succeed at length in changing the Director of this unhappy woman into her seducer. Or, again, he will inspire a religious man or woman with an ardent zeal to make others exact in keeping the rule; so that, instead of taking heed to themselves and to their own progress, they will be all day prying into the doings of others, and will go about the Community spreading complaints and murmurings, with no other fruit than to disquiet both themselves and all the others who are in the house, provoking bitterness, rancour, and division in the monastery. However, to strive to count the arts whereby the devil deludes souls under pretence of good, would be like counting the grains of sand on the seashore. They are simply without number.

417. The Director should therefore make use of two means in order to detect the frauds and deceits of the evil spirit. First, he must crave light from above; for the snares of the devil are subtle, and can be discovered only by the all-searching light of God. Secondly, he must learn what are the tokens of the spirit of darkness; as by means of such knowledge he will easily be able to discern whether a given suggestion come from God for the salvation and advantage of a soul, or whether it proceed from the enemy of God with a view to its undoing.

418. Sixth suggestion. I would not have the Director to be of the number of those who lay the blame of everything on the evil propensities of nature, and who fancy that the devil crosses his arms and does nothing. Such a notion would be both false and ruinous. False; since holy Scripture teaches that our adversary ever goes about, is ever on the move, and never rests from inciting us to evil by his suggestions.* I do not say, mind, that our passions are not at times set in motion naturally of themselves; but I do say that when the devil sees that they are awakened, he comes forward and stimulates them by his temptations, making them more ardent and violent. Indeed, the greatest part of the sins committed, especially, by devout people, are seldom uninfluenced by some diabolical suggestion. Again, the idea is

* Adversarius vester diabolus tamquam leo rugiens circuit, quærens quem devoret.

ruinous; because when we are aware that we have a demon at our elbows, who suggests at one time a sinful thought, at another a bad feeling, we put ourselves on our guard; we take the defensive; we resist more courageously, and have more frequent and trustful recourse to God. A fact related by St. Gregory, Pope, will serve to illustrate this truth.* In a certain Benedictine monastery, one of the monks had resolved on leaving Religion and returning to the world, for monastic life appeared too hard to him, and far beyond his strength. He repeatedly expressed his determination to the holy Patriarch, from whom he received warning that he was under a temptation of the devil which he was bound to resist, and that he should have recourse to God. The monk, giving but little credence to these words, persisted in his determination to leave the monastery. As he set foot outside the gate, he beheld running towards him a hideous and frightful dragon, with its mouth open to devour him. Horrified at this sight, he began to cry out, "Help, Brothers, help!"† The monks hastened on hearing his cries, and found him trembling, pale and faint. They took him in their arms, and brought him back to the monastery, which he never again felt any inclination to abandon. The Director will take notice that, until he saw it with his own eyes, this monk could never be convinced that the instigation he felt to leave Religion came from the devil; as also the thought that he was wholly unable to overcome the temptation. The same holds good of most men. Hence it is very useful to convince them that their inward agitations proceed from the devil, as a general rule; in order that they may thus gain courage to arm themselves for their defence.

419. Seventh suggestion. The Director must insist on his penitents not leaving off their usual exercises of prayer, penance, mortification, and frequentation of the Sacraments in time of temptation, but that, on the contrary, far from diminishing, they rather add to these exercises, since they then stand in greater need of strength and vigour wherewith to fight against the enemies of their eternal welfare. Now this strength can be gained by no

* Dial., lib. ij., cap. 25.

† Succurrite, fratres! succurrite, fratres!

other means except that of such devout practices. He must also warn them not to make new resolutions in time of temptation, still less vows binding in conscience, because a soul under temptation is agitated by a diabolical spirit, so that it can hardly discern whether the impulses it then experiences come from a good or from an evil source. The mind is moreover clouded with darkness and the soul convulsed with passion; nor is it easy, amid this turmoil of thoughts and feelings, to discern what is expedient or to take wise and sensible resolutions. For which cause, before resolving upon any new measure, we should wait for times more quiet and tranquil.

420. I have spoken at sufficient length in the foregoing Chapters, of the motives which animate the soul under temptation to maintain its courage and constancy in the conflict without ever losing heart, and of the acts wherein it should exercise itself in order to come off victorious; and for this reason there is no occasion for me to give Directors any further instruction upon this matter.

ARTICLE XI.

The Hindrances which Scruples set to Christian Perfection.

CHAPTER I.

THE NATURE OF SCRUPLES EXPLAINED. THEIR CAUSES, AND THE SIGNS BY WHICH THEY MAY BE RECOGNISED.

421. AFTER having discoursed of the hindrances to Christian perfection that exist both within us and without us, some acting by enticement, others by direct opposition, there remains another obstacle to speak of, which at times takes its rise within us, at times comes from without; I mean scruples, which may have their origin from our characters, or, as we shall see, may proceed from

outward causes. But whatever their source, they are ever in their own nature a serious hindrance to perfection.

422. Imperfectly instructed persons fancy that a scruple comes from a certain delicacy of conscience, which takes alarm at real sin, and is careful to avoid it. Hence they give the name of scrupulous to persons of timorous conscience who guard themselves from certain faults which they themselves commit without compunction, and who flee those dangers and liberties which they themselves boldly go forth to meet. These are mistaken : for scruples are not a proof of delicacy of conscience in avoiding sin, as such imagine; but they are a vain apprehension, grounded on slight motives, and full of anxious fear lest there be sin in that which in truth is free from sin. The scrupulous person is like a horse that shies, rears, goes backward, and that will no longer obey the bridle or spurs of its rider on seeing the shadow of a tree, rock or post, lying along the road, as though it saw a lion or a tiger in front waiting to tear it to pieces; thus, by the groundless fear of a danger which does not exist, putting both itself and its rider in the real danger of a fatal fall. So too, a scrupulous person, through groundless alarm, by fearing lest there be grievous sin in this or that action which is of itself lawful and praiseworthy, becomes full of fear, anxiety, perplexity and disturbance; and being overcome by the agitation within him, no longer yields obedience to the Confessor under whose direction he has placed himself, nor to persons however able they may be who give him advice, nor even to friends who rebuke him. And hence, from the fear of what is sin only in seeming, he runs the risk of falling into real sins and, if his disease be not checked, of being brought to final ruin.

423. It will now be easy to distinguish the difference that exists between doubt and scruple; for doubt may be, and for the most part is, founded in reason; but scruple is not and cannot possibly be reasonable; for if it were reasonable it would cease to be a scruple. Doubt is a suspension of assent; the intellect hanging suspended between two extremes, the reasons for each of which seem alike to be of weight: just as the tongue of a balance, when the scales are equally weighted, does not incline either to the right or to the left, but remains in equilibrium. Just so, our mind,

when it perceives the reasons for the affirmative and the negative to be equal, does not incline to either side, but suspends its assent. Now this is wholly different from a scruple, which is not excited by reasons, but by appearances, fancies, and frivolous motives. Far from leaving our assent suspended, it inclines us to judge that there is grievous sin where in fact there is not the slightest fault. Besides which, scruples fill the mind with fears, anxiety, disquiet, harassing disturbance; none of which effects follow upon reasonable doubt.

424. Having thus examined into the nature of scruples, we are next to see what are the sources from which they originate. With some they have their root in character and disposition. Certain persons are naturally fearful, their cold and melancholy temperament is a soil well fitted for the production of these thorns; for, melancholy people are also timid and cowardly, and are easily alarmed at the slightest apprehension of sin, be it never so groundless. And this fear goes on increasing, heaping up in their minds many vain apprehensions of sin. Again, because these gloomy characters are obstinately attached to their own ideas, such unfounded apprehensions succeed in striking root so deeply that it needs the hand of God Almighty to pluck them out. And, at times, these fancies absorb their troubled imagination to such an extent as to make them think there is sin in everything, and wholly to rob them of their peace of mind, reducing them to live in continual turmoil and anguish.

425. Further, if persons of this melancholy complexion become addicted to immoderate fasts, watchings, and indiscreet austerities, then through a deficiency of animal strength their body and brain will both be so weakened that they will no longer be capable of distinguishing aright between good and evil, and will fancy grievous sin where there is not a shadow of a fault. Worse by far will it be should they retire into solitude, because in leisure and retirement these unquiet and scrupulous fancies grow apace. And if, added to all this, we suppose that the said persons be ill instructed, and have to deal with friends of narrow conscience, their brain will be filled with such a confusion of extravagant fancies, that if they go not mad themselves they will at least make their

Confessors go mad. We may then conclude that the first cause of scruples is a melancholy, gloomy, timid, and anxious character. Scruples which derive their origin from this source are with difficulty cured; for, just as we cannot get rid of our constitution, so we ever bear within us the source of these diseased fancies, these groundless alarms, anxieties, and the like extravagances.

426. The second cause of scruples is the devil. It is the peculiar course of this great enemy of mankind to relax the consciences of the dissolute by a presumptuous trust in God's mercy, and to contract the conscience of the good by excessive dread. He enters into the imagination of these latter, stirs up fancies, overclouds them with his darkness, and instils vain and gloomy apprehensions of sin, calculated to excite disquieting fears. Further, he stirs up humours in the sensitive appetite fitted to produce pusillanimity, anguish, bitterness and turmoil, so that the poor soul is tossed like a bark in a tempestuous sea. The person afflicted with scruples sees the heaven of his mind overcast; he is on all sides agitated by a storm of troubled emotions; he finds all his powers in confusion and indisposed to obey the guidance of reason, which is the pilot of this hapless vessel. The end at which the devil aims in thus narrowing the conscience is to render prayer irksome, the frequentation of the sacraments odious, the way of the Lord insupportable; so that the soul, being disgusted, may fall into want of trust and, if possible, into despair; may stray from the right path, and commit real sins by giving itself unbridled liberty, hurrying in this manner headlong to perdition. This is what St. Laurence Justinian assures us of.*

427. There are various marks by which this latter class of scruples can be distinguished from those which arise from natural temperament; since diabolical scruples are accompanied with a special darkening of the mind and a peculiar disquiet and bitterness of heart, and tend to lukewarmness and to the unnerving

* Plerumque enim, Deo disponente, ipsi spiritus nequam pusillorum conscientiam confundunt dubietate, ac multitudine stimulorum, ut neque, ut ita dicam, pedem valeant movere præ timore conscientiæ, qui sic tentantur; aguntque suis persuasionibus, et importunitatibus, ut quod minimum aut nullum peccatum est, mortale reddatur. De Discip. et Perf. Monast. Conver., cap 12.

of the spirit by distrust. the soul being made to imagine that God has withdrawn Himself, that there is no more peace to be had, no remedy for the evils endured: and thus the person is led to give way to the exhaustion which he feels. Moreover, these diabolical scruples are not always of the same intensity. Sometimes they press close upon us, sometimes they relax the pursuit, and sometimes cease altogether; just as Almighty God sees fit to lengthen or tighten the chain of the tempter. On the contrary, scruples founded on character occur almost invariably in the same degree, as nature ever proceeds in conformity with its own impulses; and it is well ascertained that persons who are scrupulous by character always behave in a timid and troubled manner.

428. The third cause of scruples is God Himself. Not indeed that He can cause them positively, as though He wished to infuse false and erroneous judgments, or really did produce them in scrupulous souls; but He is the negative cause, inasmuch as He withholds from the mind that divine light by which it is enabled to distinguish clearly between what is, and what is not, sinful; just as our hemisphere is involved in night by the sun's sinking beneath the horizon and withdrawing the brilliance of his rays. Thus we read of many saints who have been grievously tried by these inner perplexities: such as St. Bonaventure, who, being excessively alarmed by scruples, allowed many days to pass without approaching the Altar to offer the unbloody sacrifice of the Mass.* And St. Ignatius Loyola† was so sorely vexed by these inward agitations, that he determined not to taste food until God had freed him from so furious a storm; and he actually passed eight whole days without touching so much as a crumb of bread or a drop of water. Being, however, warned by his Confessor to employ more prudent means, he began to recruit his strength with food. Again, the Venerable Hippolytus Galantini, founder of the Congregation of Christian Doctrine,‡ suffered for a long time from the pricks of these troublesome thorns and briars. We read of St. Luitgarde§ that she was cruelly tormented with scruples in reciting the divine office. She often repeated

* Cons. Part I., Lib. iii., cap. 39.
† In Vitâ.
‡ In Vitâ, lib. iii., cap. 3.
§ Surius. In Vitâ, 16 Julii.

the same canonical hour two or three times in succession, because she did not believe that all the diligence that she had used had been in sufficient compliance with her obligation; and thus she was never at peace or contented. She determined at length to have recourse to God, in order to obtain deliverance from these anxieties. After many prayers, a shepherd, with whom she was wholly unacquainted, came one day to visit her and spoke to her thus: "God would have you know that your prayers are acceptable to Him: and hence, for the future, you are not to give way to the disquiet and the scruples that may arise within you while reciting the divine office." With these words, he departed, nor could it ever be discovered who he was, though no pains were spared in the search; so that he was taken to be an Angel under the form of a shepherd, sent by God to rid her mind of the turmoil of the scrupulous fancies which were agitating her. St. Augustine, too, at the beginning of his conversion, had some troublesome scruples about the use of food and drink, being greatly distressed on account of the natural and unavoidable gratification which results from both eating and drinking. We learn this from his own Confessions.*

429. The ends which the Almighty has in view in thus allowing souls to be tried by scruples are various. First, to cleanse the soul of past faults; for it is but just that souls should by an excessive and torturing fear pay the penalty of the criminal liberty they have allowed their thoughts, affections and appetites. Secondly, to ground the soul in a just fear of real sins, by means of an over-great dread of apparent faults; as it is obvious that one who trembles at the shadow of guilt will be much more on his guard in presence of real sin when it shows itself in its true aspect. Thirdly, to humble the soul by forcing it to form a lowly opinion of itself; because, of a truth, nothing so much lowers a person, especially if he be gifted with any remarkable degree of capacity, as to find himself all day long perplexed like a child by the merest trifles; and what is worse,

* Non ego immunditiam obsonii timeo, sed immunditiam cupiditatis. . . . . In his ergo tentationibus positus, certo quotidie adversus concupiscentiam manducandi et bibendi. Lib. x., cap. 31.

without knowing how to disentangle himself. He is then, indeed, able to see with open eyes and, as it were, to handle the greatness of his misery. Fourthly, as an exercise of obedience, of abnegation in our own views, of patience and other virtues: since if the scrupulous soul, amid these inner trials, wish to avoid going astray, it is compelled to follow blindly the guidance of another, to bear patiently with many troubles and distressing agitations, and to do much violence to itself in order to keep steady in the practice of virtue.

430. The tokens by which we may discern whether scruples come from a special permission of God for our purification, may be found in the good results which in that case they produce. For, as God intends this trial for the profit of the soul, He vouchsafes a special assistance of His grace. Hence the soul, despite the storms of scrupulosity, advances on its journey; and, though not sensible of it, draws near to the haven of perfection. Thus we see these souls shrink more and more from sin and its occasions, detaching themselves from both, and increasing their horror of offending God. We notice them to be really in earnest about making progress, and to be more amenable to obedience than others afflicted with the same disease, as well as to be more constant in prayer and pious exercises.

431. Such scruples as these are usually not permanent; for God has declared, that *He will not suffer the just to be for ever moved.** Hence, when these inner troubles have wrought that effect in souls which tempests bring about in the sea—that is, when they are cleansed of their defilements and well grounded in certain virtues—either the trial ceases forthwith, or it gradually becomes less intense, until at length undisturbed calm returns. I myself have met with a person who was incessantly tormented by scruples of every kind for the space of seven years. He determined at length to enter Religion, choosing an Order in which regular observance flourished, and which was ruled by the spirit of God. Wonderful to relate, scarce had he set foot in the Noviciate, where it would seem that his disease would have been aggravated beyond measure, by the mortification, solitude, and

* Ps. liv. 23.

silence prevailing there, and by continual meditation of the eternal truths (and still more by dealing with others whose conscience was contracted like his own) scarce, I say, had he entered, but his scruples vanished at once, and he suddenly became possessed of an interior peace of heart to which he had long since been a stranger. A clear token that these scruples had been sent by a special permission of God, either as a preservative, in order that, being thus hedged in on every side by thorns, he might not turn out of his path to cull any blossom of worldly pleasure; or, it may be, they had been permitted by God as a spur, in order that, being pricked by the thorns of these great troubles, he might more speedily run to take shelter in the secure harbour of religious life: for scarce had he reached this haven when he was rid of the distressing turmoil of his anxious thoughts and forebodings.

432 There are several symptoms by which a scrupulous person may be known. Of these I select a few, which appear to me of most importance. First, to be prone to doubt, and to fear without solid motives and reasonable foundation. Secondly, to be inconstant in such doubts and fears; to change opinion for every trivial reason that suggests itself; now thinking unlawful that which just before was reputed lawful, and then judging that to be lawful which lately was condemned as culpable. Thirdly, along with these doubts and hesitations, to experience disquiet, agitation, distress and trouble. Because, although the remorse which God awakens in the soul pricks the heart, it does not throw it into confusion or render it anxious Nor does remorse springing from the dictates of reason introduce anxiety and disquiet; this is the case only with the remorse that proceeds from a distorted and ill-formed judgment, such as abounds and prevails in the darkened minds of those who are scrupulous. Fourthly, a scrupulous person holds obstinately to his own opinion; does not rely on the advice of able men, nor even of his own Confessor; and after having consulted a multitude of advisers, ends at length, by doing what he himself thinks to be best. Fifthly, when questioned on the matters which are the cause of his perplexity, the scrupulous person will answer that he knows there is

no sin in the thing; but yet he remains full of fear about himself, and does not venture to act. Whoever discovers such signs in his own case or in that of others, may be assured that he is of the number of the scrupulous. In other words, he may be sure that he is in a condition which greatly interferes with the attainment of Christian perfection. This we shall now proceed to show.

CHAPTER II.

THE HINDRANCES SET BY SCRUPLES IN THE WAY OF PERFECTION.

433. SCRUPLES are the very canker of the soul, at which they gnaw by the disturbance they cause, spoiling the whole work of perfection. They are thorns which, growing in the inmost soul, choke the seeds of good thoughts and holy inspirations, and make the roots of every virtue dry up and wither. Let us now come to particulars.

434. Beyond all doubt the root from which the several branches of Christian perfection are to spring is prayer, which is the medium through which light comes from God. In prayer we see how worthy He is of our love, and by prayer His holy love is enkindled within us. It is by prayer that we discover the charms wherewith virtue is adorned, and by which we become enamoured of and stimulated in the practice of virtue, and in the mortification of those vices and passions which hinder our attainment of it. For, as St. John Chrysostom says, "Nothing contributes so much to make us grow in virtue as to converse with God in prayer."* And in another place he assures us, as of a thing perfectly manifest, that it is absolutely impossible to live a virtuous life without assiduity in prayer.† Now it is this fertile root of all spiritual good that is cut through by scruples and by the disturbance

* Nihil autem æque facit in virtute crescere, quam cum Deo assidue versari et colloqui. In Psal. vii.

† Arbitror cunctis esse manifestum, quod simpliciter impossibile sit absque precationis præsidio cum virtute degere. Lib. 1. De Orando Deum.

which they engender. The reason is obvious : God enlightens with His rays and His holy inspirations none but calm minds and peaceful hearts, for His abode is in peace, quiet, and tranquillity;* all which most assuredly cannot be predicated of the minds and hearts of the scrupulous, in whom darkness, perplexity, disquiet, turmoil, and care prevail. These hapless creatures being thus indisposed for prayer, are equally precluded from any advance in virtue or in Christian perfection.

435. As we all are aware, the holy sacraments are those springs and channels of Paradise by which God's grace is conveyed to our souls, to render them fruitful in good works. Now, these fountains and conduits are rendered less abundant by means of scruples, if not, indeed, wholly dried up and exhausted, for, when the scrupulous go to Confession, they approach the holy tribunal full of groundless alarms as to their actual dispositions and past sins; and, when they receive holy Communion, they go to the Altar all troubled and disquieted by foolish fancies; hence they cannot receive in these sacraments that fulness of grace which is usually found by other persons who are calm and at peace. If the scrupulous hear the word of God from the mouth of preachers, or read it written in the books of holy writers, or receive it in their private intercourse with their Directors, they ever mingle with the divine seed the tares of their sophisms, by which they choke it and prevent its bearing fruit. In a word, taken up as they are in combating against the phantoms of their scruples, they either neglect the use of the means necessary for their perfection, or if they do employ them, they render them of no avail by their unquiet fancies. What spiritual advancement, what progress in perfection, is to be looked for on the part of such as these?

436. There is another reason which clearly shows the great difficulty experienced by scrupulous persons in the practice of Christian virtue. The poor wretches either wholly lose the virtue of hope, in consequence of their scruples, or weaken it so much that it is no longer able to supply the energy which the practice of virtue requires. We must here observe that in hope it is that our

* Factus est in pace locus ejus.

souls find the strength, courage, and fortitude needed for virtuous action. As Isaias says, "They that trust in the Lord shall gather new strength, they shall walk, run, even fly like an eagle, along the path of perfection. They shall run and not grow weary, they shall go forward and shall not be faint."* On the other hand, take away hope, and at once energy, vigour, and strength must needs fail us:—we shall creep in the dust. Hence St. Ambrose might truly say, "A man may be inured to toil like an ox, may be firm and constant under persecution, may bear up against injustice like a rock; but, deprive him of hope, and his power of supporting fatigue will vanish, his patience in adversity will depart."† A little further on he gives the reason of this: "It is hope alone that affords us assurance, and it alone saves us from being baffled in our aspirations. Where there is hope, neither outward conflict nor inward fears can harm us."‡

437. Now hope which is, so to speak, the seed of every virtue, is choked or, at least, greatly weakened by scruples, which are ever accompanied by the passion most contrary to confidence; namely, excessive fear. And, indeed, you will always see that the scrupulous are timid, cowardly, sad, gloomy, full of alarm, of mistrust, of discouragement; and you will feel that St. Laurence Justinian spoke the simple truth, when he said of scrupulosity, that it is a cowardly habit of mind, which unnerves all the energies of the soul and unfits it for the practice of virtue §

438. But when scruples get beyond a certain point they not only enfeeble the virtue of hope, they destroy it and even deprive it of all germ of life; because, as they increase in extravagant proportions, they end by driving the soul to desperation. On this matter St. Bernard says: "The trial of scruples begets pusillanimity; this, in its turn, disturbs the peace of the soul: and the disquiet of the mind ends in despair, which leads the soul to its

* Qui sperant in Domino, mutabunt fortitudinem, assument pennas sicut aquilæ; current, et non laborabunt; ambulabunt, et non deficient. Isai. xl. 31.

† Esto sint aliqui duri ad labores, firmi ad injurias perferendas; si spem auferas, non potest perpetua esse patientia. In Ps. cxviii. Serm. 15.

‡ Spes est sola quæ nostrum non confundit affectum. Ubi est spes, apostolicum illud, *Foris pugnæ, intus timores*, nocere non possunt. Ibid.

§ Pusillanimitatem internam consumentem fortitudinem.

ruin."* The Cardinal de Vitry relates † that a Cistercian monk had foolishly made up his mind that he would actually attain the state of primitive innocence; but unable to compass his mad purpose, he fell into a very ocean of the most troublesome scruples. If in eating he found a relish in his food, he was distressed; at the first movement of a passion, he was downcast, if he fell into a slight fault, he thought it was a mortal sin, and he lost heart. Through these exaggerated scruples, he sank into a deep melancholy, and from this into the depth of despair; and having lost all hope of salvation, he utterly forsook the holy sacraments. His brethren, touched with pity, earnestly recommended him to God, gave him wise counsel, and began to reproach him with sharp rebukes; but nothing was effectual to bring him back to a proper state of mind, and if the Blessed Mary D'Oignies had not brought him to his senses by a miraculous grace, which she obtained for him from heaven, he would have died in this wretched state. I myself have known a person who, agitated by scruples, fell into such despair that he took a knife and stabbed himself repeatedly in the breast. Another with whom I was acquainted, for the same cause pointed a pistol at his own head, and drawing the trigger fell down dead upon the spot. So true is it that unless scruples be kept within bounds, they may lead into an abyss of utter despair.

439. But let us leave aside these cases, which are as terrible as they are rare, and turn to what is of daily occurrence. It is beyond question that when scruples get beyond a certain point, one or other of the following fatal effects will ensue: either the afflicted person, unable to bear up against so harassing a torture, will fall into a great laxity; or else, if he strain himself to make head against it, will go clean out of his mind. Human nature cannot stand an alarm which is so great and unceasing and so full of anxiety and disquiet: hence it must perforce shake off the yoke which bears it down, and from an extreme rigour pass to a no less extreme laxity. This was the case with that Franciscan

* Tribulatio parit pusillanimitatem, pusillanimitas perturbationem, perturbatio desperationem; et illa interimit. Epist. 32 ad Abb. S. Nich. de Remis.

† Lib. ii., cap. 3. Apud Surium.

friar, whose story was related in the concluding Chapter of the foregoing Article. The devil put into the unhappy man's head a scruple about speaking a single word, even in case of necessity, and even when approaching the tribunal of penance. But as he was unable to keep up so violent an effort, he returned to the world, where he not only recovered the use of his tongue, but took up a habit of useless swearing, to the great astonishment of some of his former brethren who, having heard him, rebuked him for it severely. If, on the other hand, the scrupulous person be a man of a strong character and, doing violence to himself, resist constantly the annoyance of excessive scruples, he cannot but go mad; since the continuous, or at least frequent, fixing of the mind on this multitude of extravagant fancies, the abundance of conflicting reflections, and the so many violent efforts of the understanding and imagination, must needs gradually weaken the brain, so as insensibly to paralyse the reason, and to incapacitate it from performing its functions aright. Moreover, these alarms, this disquiet, this agitation and distress, if continual, deteriorate beyond measure the humours of the body and undermine the constitution which, being injured, helps in its turn to weaken the brain, so that in the end the reason is overthrown. And daily experience is with us to prove that many, for not having known how to conduct themselves amid these scruples, have become unable to recite the divine Office: others have unfitted themselves for celebrating holy Mass: others again there are who have been judged incapable of receiving the sacraments: while not a few have had even to be put in chains and shut up in a madhouse, because they had gone quite out of their mind. And even granting that things will not come to such a pass as this, it is unquestionable that our frail bodies must at length sink under this constant worry and agitation of the soul, so that if reason be not lost, the health is ruined by these scruples, as is but too frequently the case with the majority of scrupulous persons. Hence Blosius might well say, that a spiritual person must keep away overweening fear, cowardice and gloom of soul, carking cares, the entanglements of anxiety, in a word, all scruples of conscience, by every means within his power. For there is nothing which can so hinder all spiritual progress and advancement in perfection; since, as we have shown, scruples succeed not seldom in rendering the soul either wholly incapable or, at least, little capable of progress.*

440 Before going any further, it is necessary for me to meet an objection which might here be raised against my doctrine. In the foregoing Chapter it was said that scruples are not unfrequently sent by God to cleanse and perfect virtuous souls which are well-pleasing in His sight. If, then, scruples are means aiding us in the acquirement of perfection, how can they be accounted hindrances to this same perfection? I answer, that scruples contribute to perfection in the same sense as temptations of the most loathsome, blasphemous, and horrible nature. Now, as such temptations help us to perfection, not in so far as they are admitted by the soul, but only in so far as we repel and drive them away without any parley, from the mind and heart; so, too, are scruples a means of perfection, not inasmuch as they are fostered, but in so far as we make use of suitable means to get rid of them. And just as it would be unlawful wilfully to entertain a temptation in our mind, although it may contribute to our perfection; neither is it lawful to dwell upon scrupulous thoughts and motions, even should they prove of use for our soul's advantage. In a word, all the good to be derived from temptations or scruples, consists in withholding from them our consent or adhesion, and in making use of fit means to rid ourselves of them. If, then, the reader wishes to know what pious practices and industries ought to be employed in order to root up these troublesome thorns—I mean scruples—let him go on to peruse what is found in the following Chapter.

* Nimium timorem, et inordinatam pusillanimitatem et tristitiam, superfluos conscientiæ scrupulos, inquietasque curas, et implexas sollicitudines, asceta semper devitet. Parad. Animæ, cap. 8.

CHAPTER III.

REMEDIES AGAINST SCRUPLES.

441. THE first remedy is prayer. This is a remedy against all sorts of evils, but it has a special efficacy against scruples, since the medicine which heals this dangerous disorder of the soul, is in God's hands alone. The first cause of scrupulosity is a want of light, by which the mind is left in darkness, unable to distinguish between leprosy and leprosy; that is to say, between grievous and venial sin, between what is lawful and not lawful. From which cause it follows that the soul gets perplexed and confused, and torments itself in countless ways. But this light none but God can bestow; He holds it within His hands. By opening them He sheds its beams on our minds; by closing them He withdraws it to Himself. The scrupulous person must then ever ask this light of God, in order that the darkness of his mind may be enlightened, and that he may gain discernment in judging without anxiety and disquiet what is sin and what is not sin. Let him, in all humility, acknowledge before Almighty God that he is blind. And, as the blind man in the Gospel, when asked by our Lord what he wanted, replied, *Lord, that I may see;** so, too, should the scrupulous man cry out in prayer, "Lord, I beg light for the eyes of my mind, in order that I may see and clearly discern what is and what is not evil, to the end that I may be able the better to serve Thee in calm of soul and peace of heart." Above all, a person afflicted with scruples should recommend himself to God, when the disturbance of his mind begins to set in, and he feels the first tokens of his soul being overcast and his heart agitated. He should, at such moments, lift up his voice to God, and call for help as did St. Peter when walking on the waves of the stormy sea. The Apostle began, little by little, to sink into the water and, affrighted at his danger, raised his voice, and cried out earnestly for help from our Saviour.† Thus should a

* Domine, ut videam.

† Cum cœpisset mergi, clamavit dicens: Domine salvum me fac. Matth. xiv. 30.

scrupulous person, amid the stormy billows of his heart, turn to God, and exclaim, *Lord, save me!**

442. A second remedy is to place ourselves in the hands of a spiritual director, and to obey him blindly. All moral theologians, and all masters of the spiritual life, are agreed that this is the main remedy to get rid of scruples, and the panacea for every form of the disease. The scrupulous person must be convinced of the important truth, that he cannot sin by acting in compliance with the advice or order of his Confessor; and the reason is, that our Blessed Lord has said, with His own lips, that the voice of His ministers is the same voice as His own: that whoever obeys their orders, renders himself conformable to God's most holy will.† Further, in order that the scrupulous person may banish from his heart every shadow of vain fear, he must print deeply in his mind that most comforting maxim: Whatever accusation may be brought against him, at the tribunal of the Divine Judge, he will be able to answer, "Lord, I have done this, or omitted that, in obedience to him who held Thy place." All will fall to the ground, nor can God condemn him on that head, nor punish him in any wise soever, because the Almighty cannot contradict Himself, nor can He punish us for having obeyed His ministers, after having enjoined us to obey them; otherwise He would be acting in opposition to His own most holy commands.

443. But that the scrupulous may be fully convinced of this truth, I will quote, for their instruction, a most impressive testimony. St. Teresa was, at certain times, most grievously tried and afflicted by her spiritual directors; some of whom, forming an incorrect notion of her most upright soul, considered that the extraordinary graces with which she was favoured by God were illusions of the devil.‡ One of these Directors commanded her, whenever our Saviour, or any visitor from heaven, should appear to her, to drive all away by the sign of the Cross, to treat all with scorn and contempt: and they assured her that it was not Christ, as she fancied, but the devil, who came to delude her under such

* Domine, salvum me fac. † Qui vos audit, me audit. Luc. x. 16.
‡ In Vitâ, cap. 29.

devout appearances. On the Saint betaking herself to prayer our Blessed Saviour came to comfort her with His loving presence; she, on her side, in obedience to her Confessor, strove to drive him away by signs of the Cross, and by such acts of contempt as were commanded her; but being meanwhile assured by a light from above that there was no illusion in this apparition, and not being any longer at liberty to doubt of the presence of her Divine Spouse, she humbly craved His pardon for her conduct, excusing herself by saying that she behaved thus in obedience to those whom He had set as His ministers in the Church. On hearing this, a scrupulous person may well wonder at the Saint's complying with such an order; he will think that Jesus Christ would have shown displeasure at being received so rudely and, having rebuked and threatened her, would have departed in great indignation. But this would be a mistake: for Jesus, looking at the Saint with a benevolent countenance, approved of her manner of acting; told her she was right to obey; and comforted her with the assurance that her spirit would become better known and appreciated before long.

444. Of what, then, have the scrupulous to be afraid? at what do they take alarm? since Jesus Christ is not offended at being rejected, at being sent away, at being so unhandsomely received, when this is done in obedience to one who holds His place. Is it possible that holy obedience, which has ever been for every one the sure road to bliss, will be, for the scrupulous alone, the way to perdition and the path of hell? Therefore let scrupulous persons rid themselves of their abominable pertinacity of mind and detestable obstinacy of heart, and determine to obey their Directors despite all apprehension, fear, or misgiving of conscience, which may persuade them to adopt a different course. Unless they do this, their cure is beyond hope; they will never, no, not for all eternity, be healed of their infirmity. On the contrary, by leaning on holy odedience, and allowing it to regulate them, they will easily get rid of their annoying perplexities and painful disquiet; as Blosius has observed.* The reason of this

* Qui si prudentum consiliis potiùs, quam proprio judicio prompte et intrepide acquiescere vellent, facile curarentur. Parad. Animæ, cap. 13

is plain. A person given to scruples has not a conscience which can guide him aright (I mean with reference to those matters about which he is scrupulous); for, overcast as it is with darkness, it is incapable of forming a correct judgment concerning his duty; hence no other course remains open to him, if he would act aright, than to submit his judgment to that of another who is free from the like infirmity. But whom can he take as his guide with more confidence than the Director given him by God to regulate all his doings? Let him say what he would do, were God to deprive him of his eyesight and to afflict him with total blindness. What would he do, in such case, when he wanted to go abroad without danger of stumbling and of falling at every step? Surely he would take a trusty guide and, being unable himself to see where to set his foot, he would follow the instructions of his faithful leader. Now, what he would do in order to walk in safety, as regards his bodily motions, he must also do in the spiritual path, wherein he must think himself blind, through the failure of supernatural light and the overclouding of his natural vision. He must, therefore, take his Confessor, or Director, as his guide; submit to his judgment, correct the distorted dictates of his own conscience, by rendering it conformable with that of his guide, and in all his doings set his foot in the path which has been pointed out to him. There is no other way by which he can possibly extricate himself from the labyrinth of his scrupulous fancies.

445. It was thus that St. Ignatius Loyola acted, when assailed by a storm of scruples. He put himself under the guidance of a good Confessor, who, like an able pilot, soon led him to the haven of a sweet calm. St. Antoninus tells us* of a Dominican friar, who, appearing after death to another of the same Order, that was greatly troubled with scruples, said to him: "Take counsel with wise and prudent persons, and acquiesce in their advice."† The same Saint relates that a disciple of St. Bernard was agitated with scruples to such a degree, that he durst no longer approach the Altar to offer the holy Sacrifice. He went

* Sum. p. prim., tit. 3, cap. 10. § 10.

† Consule discretos, et acquiesce eis.

to take counsel of his saintly master, who, having listened to him, said: "Say Mass on my authority." The latter bowed his head, yielded up his own opinion, set at nought all the inward contradictions of his scrupulous mind, and celebrated Mass. By this manly act of obedience he was cured, and finally got rid of all his distress.

446. Nor does it avail to object: "Ay, but my Director is not a St. Bernard." For we have not to obey our Director because he is a saint, but because he holds the place of God; and what assures us of doing the Lord's will when we follow his advice is, not his saintliness, but the declaration of Jesus Christ, that whatever His minister commands us is to be looked on as His own most holy will. I will add with a view to this same subject what Vercelli relates of a devout peasant.* This man had allowed his brains to be so far confused with scruples, as to have become convinced that his sole chance of salvation was to kill himself; fancying that such a death would be accounted as martyrdom by Almighty God, Who would at once receive him into heavenly glory. The poor wretch had, in consequence, frequently attempted his own life; sometimes by fire, sometimes by water. At length, the Blessed Virgin taking pity on him—as he was devout to her—appeared to Him clad in a snow-white mantle, and ordered him to open his mind to a Priest and to obey him faithfully. He complied with this command of the Queen of Heaven, and thus was delivered from his distress. As may now be seen, the saints themselves, and the very Queen of Saints, have no better remedy to prescribe for the healing of scruples than blind obedience to a Confessor. If persons confirmed in scrupulosity will not apply this remedy, we can only say that their case is desperate.

447. But I am well aware of the reply which the scrupulous will make, and of the reasons (or quibbles rather) by which they withdraw themselves from the yoke of holy obedience. They are in the habit of saying that if they really were scrupulous, they would be ready to obey a Director who believes them to be suffering from this disease, and who treats them accordingly.

* Quæst. Moral. Tract. 5, qu. 3, n. 12.

But, they add, here is the mistake; they are not scrupulous, their doubts are not unfounded, nor their fears vain; since what they doubt about, and what they are in fear of, are not apparent sins, but real. To this I answer, No madman thinks himself mad, hence, when rebuked and beaten for their antics, these poor creatures marvel at, and complain of, this harsh treatment: and in fact, an essential condition of madness is not to be conscious of one's derangement; for such consciousness is the first step to the recovery of reason. Just so, scrupulosity consists in being unconscious of the disease; for, if a person becomes aware that he is scrupulous, that his doubts are groundless and his alarms mere fancies, he will, from this time forward, make no account of them, and his conscience, which heretofore was scrupulous, will at once become a right and reasonable conscience. Therefore a person who is thus tormented must give credence to his Director, or to any other enlightened adviser, when he is pronounced to be scrupulous; for, according to the unanimous opinion of Divines, we are bound to give credit to our Confessors in what concerns our conscience. No one can be a fair judge of his own case, or be fit to pass sentence in his own cause; much less if agitated by scruples which render him wholly incapable of judging. To believe ourselves rather than our Director, especially in such matters, is an unbearable pride, worthy of the severest punishment.

448. Others will urge: "I would obey my Confessor if I had sufficiently explained to him my case, and if he understood me aright; but I cannot make myself known, especially under certain circumstances. He is in the wrong, not by his own fault, but by mine." To this I reply, that in laying ourselves open to our Directors, we are bound to a reasonable diligence, such as natural to man and is commonly used in matters of importance. Beyond this we are bound to nothing, neither can God require more of us. Hence we should believe that the Confessor has understood us; and granting that he does mistake in some particular instance we, at any rate, do not mistake in rendering him obedience. "But," replies the victim of scruples, "this diligence is

frightened heart. In the cure of diseases, contrary remedies are usually prescribed; now, nothing can be more contrary to the infirmity which we call scrupulosity than a firm hope, especially when it is accompanied by holy love.

450. To these remedies we may add a few others, which will avail much to the cure of this malady. First, to flee idleness; for the brains of scrupulous people are like a mill, which is always grinding, ever at work: and the grain which is ground in this mill is not any useful matter, but mere worthless tares of anxious and distressing misgivings. Hence such persons should keep themselves fully occupied, and divert their minds from being absorbed and racked by their groundless and distorted fancies. Secondly, to avoid dealing with persons of a narrow and straitened conscience; for scruples are a contagious disease, which is easily contracted in the company of those infected with the same sickness: and, for the same reason, not to read books containing rigid maxims or opinions which are over strict. Thirdly, not to speak of one's scruples, nor to go about talking of them indiscriminately; as is the fashion with some, of both sexes, who go from Confessor to Confessor, pouring out to each their doleful tale and, after having taken the opinion of a hundred, end by obeying none, but stick to their own way of thinking. Scruples are like paste or pitch; the more these are handled, the more they stick. The more that scrupulous people talk of their silly perplexities, the firmer hold do their diseased fancies take of their imagination; the deeper root do they strike in their minds. The best advice they can take is to lay open their distress to their own Confessor, and at the most, in some particular instance, they may have recourse to some other man of learning, with firm resolution to obey his directions. This is precisely the counsel which St. Augustine gave to St. Paulinus in one of his letters: "If these things make not on you the same impression that they make on me, confer about them with some experienced physician of souls, either in your place of residence—if you can find a fitting one there—or in Rome, when you go thither; and receive what he tells you or, better, what both he and I tell you, as coming from the mouth of God Himself: place an entire reliance upon what he

says, and acquaint me with the result."* It may be observed, that St. Augustine does not advise Paulinus to seek counsel in his doubts from the first Priest he may come across, either in his own country or in Rome; but only from some master of the spiritual life who is mild, that is to say, fit to give advice. Further, Paulinus is to take the decision, not as coming from man, but as inspired by God Himself; and this is just what scrupulous people refuse to do: whence it is that they lead a life full of trouble.

451. A fourth remedy is, not to speak of scruples, even with ourselves. I mean, not only not to mention them, but not so much as think of them; so as to get rid of the disquiet, misgivings and anxiety which they bring with them, and to persuade ourselves that there is no sin in what our fancy so baselessly represents to be sin; for by so doing, a scrupulous person will only get more deeply entangled, and will become more and more disturbed. I say again, that scruples are a kind of pitch; the more we handle them, by thinking and talking about them, the more they stick. Better is it not to take notice of them, but to despise them according to our Confessor's advice; and if they still trouble us, to bear it patiently, and to offer up the suffering to God. Fifthly, we must accustom ourselves to act just like persons of a good and timorous conscience, without fearing to find sin in what such are not afraid to find it. It would indeed be an insufferable pride to imagine that everybody does evil, and that we alone are right in what we do. Sixthly, we must habituate ourselves to follow mild opinions, as long as they are probable, in order to bring the conscience from excessive strictness to a state of reasonable freedom.

* Sin et te ita ut me moveant ista; confer ea cum aliquo mansueti cordis medico, sive illic inveneris, ubi degis; sive cum Romam toto anniversario pergis: et quod per illum tibi loquentem, seu nobis colloquentibus Dominus aperuerit, scribe mihi. Epist. 250 ad Paulin.

CHAPTER IV.

CERTAIN PRIVILEGES ENJOYED BY THE SCRUPULOUS, WHICH MAY BE OF GREAT HELP AGAINST THEIR SPIRITUAL AILMENT.

452. First privilege. A scrupulous person does not sin when acting under a nervous apprehension or fear of sin; in a word, when acting under the influence of his scrupulous conscience: provided he be made aware by his Confessor, or some other intelligent person, that he is scrupulous on this or that point, and provided also, that he despise the thoughts and groundless fears which trouble him and keep him in disquiet. Such is the common teaching of Divines.* Nor is it requisite that such contempt be always formally expressed, it suffices that the expression of it be virtual; in other words, it is enough that it proceeds from the good habit which one has formed of making no account of these empty alarms, and of acting in opposition to their unreasonable dictates. The reason of this is obvious; for scruples are not grounded on true reasons, as are the remorse and misgivings of a right conscience; but the reasons on which scruples rest are merely apparent. Consequently, to act in despite of them, and of the alarms and anxious repugnance which they stir up in the conscience, is not to act against reason but against a fantastic shadow; hence it cannot be said that such an action is unreasonable, and therefore it cannot possibly be sinful. Nay, more, it is necessary to act in this manner, else we could never get rid of these foolish fears and groundless anxieties; which, as was shown in the foregoing Chapter, are no less injurious to the body than to the soul. When a man first goes to sea, he is afraid of the violence of the waves, he fears the rocks and dreads the storms; on his next voyage he is less afraid; and if he con-

* Navar. in Sum, prol. 9: et in cap. 27, num 182.—Vasq. in 1, 2, disp. 67, cap 2—Azor. in 1 part, lib. ij., cap 2.—Castrop., tract 1, disp. 4, tit. 1.—Sanch. in Sum. supra Decalog.. lib. i., cap. 10.—S. Anton. in p. 1, Sum. tit. 4, cap. 10, sec 10.—Layman, lib i., tract 1, cap. 6.—Filliuc, tract. 21. cap. 18.—Valent. 1, 2, disp. 3, quæst. 14, p. 4.—Suarez in 1, 2, disp. 11, sec. ult.—Medina, Tabiena, Pellizz., Bardi, Sayro, et alii.

tinues to go to sea, he loses all fear, as, by acting against his alarms, he has conquered and overcome them. A raw recruit, at the first flash of the enemy's fire, trembles and shivers from head to foot; but by going frequently into action notwithstanding his fears, he cares no longer for lance or sword, but throws himself manfully amid bloodshed and wounds, wherever he sees the battle raging most furiously. So, too, the scrupulous man, if he act in contempt of his fears and whimsical notions, rises above them and at length conquers them, and by this means gets rid of the toils wherein his scruples, with their countless nonsensical fancies, had entangled him. But if, withheld by empty fears, he abstain from acting, they will begin to master him, to make him a very slave, and to leave him no longer the least liberty of following the dictates of right reason.

453. But I will go further, and I will say, with many theologians, that not only *should* a scrupulous person act despite the repugnance of his scruples,* but that he is *bound* so to do, under pain of sin. First, he will sin by pride, in not choosing to yield to the decision of his Director. And next, he will sin through refusing to obey this same Director when commanded expressly to do so. For, as the Prophet Samuel said to Saul, *It is like the sin of witchcraft to rebel: and like the crime of idolatry to refuse to obey.*† And the reason is, because, by disobedience, we set our own opinion and self-will above the will of God made known to us by holy obedience. Thirdly, he will sin on account of the grievous prejudice he does to his soul by unfitting it for making any progress in the way of perfection. Fourthly, he will sin by reason of the injury which he does to his bodily health, slowly consuming it and wasting it away, as though by the action of a file, with such ceaseless agitation and disquiet. Fifthly, he will sin through the hindrance that he puts in the way of the due and right discharge of his daily occupations, from which he disables himself by his quibbles. Hence, when the scrupulous person goes to Confession, instead of repeating for the hundredth time

* Laym., Castrop., et alii in locis citatis.

† Quasi peccatum ariolandi est repugnare; et quasi scelus idololatriæ, nolle acquiescere. I. Reg. xv 23.

the long and wearisome tale of his scruples, let him confess what is really sinful, let him say, "Father I accuse myself of stubbornness—of indocility—of having disobeyed your Reverence, by not despising the thoughts which you warned me were mere fancies and scruples: but, on the contrary, of stopping a long time disputing with them—of having consented to them, and allowed myself to be led into acting in conformity with my own false judgment, instead of acting against it. I accuse myself of the disquiet I have thus occasioned to my mind—of the injury I have thus done to my soul, to my body, and to my usual occupations." This is a right, a holy and profitable confession; not a wasting of the valuable time of the Priest with idle dreams, but setting forth real sins, of which an account will have to be rendered at the judgment-seat of Christ.

454. "But, Father," the scrupulous person may say, "I am afraid that I shall sin, and I do not want to run into the danger; for whoever puts himself in danger of sin, does in fact sin, according to the well-known words, *He that loves the danger shall perish in it.*"* To this I answer: This maxim applies not to scruples, which have no other foundation than silly notions and mere day-dreams, but only to solid doubts which have substantial reasons for their objects. Hence, a person who acts in opposition to the apprehension and fears occasioned by scruples runs no danger at all; I should rather say, he follows the opinion which is the most common among Divines—the opinion which is the most certain and the most safe; the only one, in a word, that can guide him aright in the spiritual path. "But, Father, as I am in such perplexity, I want to be on the safe side. Now, *in doubt, the safer side is to be taken.*"† Waiving for the present this maxim, which demands a long and careful analysis for its right understanding, I reply, that the safest course for a scrupulous person to adopt is to obey his Confessor, despise his scruples, and go against them. In acting according to the promptings of our scruples, not only is there no safety, but rather the height of danger, and even ruin. "But, Father, I should not

* Qui amat periculum, peribit in illo.

† In dubiis tutior pars est eligenda.

wish to act in this way if I were just going to die." I answer once more, that even at the point of death, every Christian should contemn scruples, and act contrary to them, if he would not be deluded by the devil at this last extremity and make a false step at that most awful point upon which eternity depends. "But, Father, St. Gregory does not speak at all like you. He says 'that it belongs to virtuous souls to discover faults where there are none,'* so that, in the mind of that holy Doctor, to be scrupulous was equivalent to being virtuous." To this my answer is, that the scrupulous aim too high, and that they should forbear doing this illustrious Saint the injustice of making him consider as praiseworthy the condition of those whose fancy is turned topsy-turvy, and who are full of false ideas; for in good sooth, these words were not spoken for such. Suarez says† that St. Gregory is not here speaking of scrupulous and foolish souls, but of peaceful, calm, humble, and cheerful persons who, fearing to offend God, proceed with caution even in matters which of themselves are not sinful. Navarrus,‡ Filliuccius,§ Bosius,‖ and others are of opinion that the Saint is here speaking of devout people (by no means, however, of a straitened conscience); such generally make acknowledgment of their sinfulness and many imperfections, and humble themselves before God, though they discover no notable fault in their particular actions. If, then, the scrupulous wish to be accounted of the number of good and virtuous souls, they must not encourage the worrying importunities of their scruples, but must despise them, and when they feel most annoyed by apprehensions and fears of sinning, they must call to mind the commands of their Directors, and adopt these as the rule of their conduct, in spite of their false conscience.

455. Second privilege. The scrupulous man who is anxious about the consent which he may think that he has given to interior acts, ought not to believe himself to have incurred mortal guilt by them, unless he be absolutely certain that he has given a con

* Bonarum mentium est etiam ibi aliquo modo culpas suas agnoscere, ubi culpa non est. Regist. lib. xij., Respons. 10. ad August.

† 1, 2, disp. 12, sec. ult.

‡ In Sum., cap. 27, n. 2, sec. 4.

§ Tract. 21, cap. 4, quæst 15.

‖ Tract. de Scrup., sec. 2.

sent with full advertence. Nay, more, if he be very scrupulous, he must not condemn himself as having consented, unless he can swear that his eyes were wide open to the malice of these interior thoughts and affections, and that with eyes thus open he gave them his full adhesion. Such is the teaching of grave authors.* And it is founded on the fact, that any one who has an immoderate fear of mortal sin (as is certainly the case with scrupulous people) could not change his will, and consent with full advertence to that which he heretofore dreaded with such horror, without being fully aware, and certain beyond the shadow of doubt, of so sensible and extraordinary a change of will. Hence, if the person do not know for certain whether he have yielded full consent, and if he only have fears on the point, it is a sure token that there has been no consent at all, or at least no full consent.

456. The signs enumerated by learned theologians whereby to discover whether a person, though not of a scrupulous conscience, have consented to a sinful thought, help further to confirm the view we have just given with regard to those of a timorous and straitened conscience.† Doctors say that the following may be taken as signs of a full consent not having been given:—First, if the person who is in doubt as to whether he has consented to an inward suggestion, have a hatred of sin, and be in the habitual disposition of preferring death to any grievous defilement of conscience; for in that case it is hard to suppose that a free and fully wilful consent, so out of keeping with this habitual disposition, could escape his knowledge. Secondly, if, as soon as any one becomes aware that he is dallying with an evil thought, he immediately shakes it off and rejects it; for this prompt and decisive action is a sure token that he was not adverting to the guilt and, therefore, that the advertence requisite for a deadly sin was wanting. Thirdly, if, on becoming aware of an evil suggestion, he does not follow it out into action, when this could be done without being held back by any human considera-

* Bon. De Pecc., d. 2, quæst. 2, par. 3, num. 19.—Sayr. in Clavi Reg., lib. viij., cap. 7, num. 6.—Herinc., De Pecc , d. 7, n. 41.—Bosi., De Pœnit., disp. 7, sec. 8, num. 104 et 107.

† La Croix, lib. i., De Conscient., cap. 3, num. 547.

tions but, on the contrary, abhors it; as this shows that, when the will is master of itself, it is quite averse to the suggestion. Fourthly, if the person doubts whether he was asleep or awake, whether, when he gave his consent, he was fully himself or absent in mind; for this proves that his knowledge was not completely free, in other words, that he had not full advertence; since, if it had been free and without hindrance, there could be no room for these doubts. Now every one of these signs, with many more that we could add, is to be met with, in a most marked manner, in scrupulous souls; whose dread of sin is excessive and beyond all due bounds, whose rejection of wrong is so violent as to break out in external acts, at times no less indiscreet than unbecoming, and who are most averse to taking measures to put any evil suggestions into practice. Hence, unless they know for certain that they have given consent to the interior sinful motions which they feel within them, they have every ground for believing and, indeed, they are bound to believe fully, that they have not consented. They must further be cautious not to delude themselves (as is but too often the case with persons in their state) and not to judge themselves guilty of sin, merely because, notwithstanding their earnestness in rejecting temptations, the inner feeling of delectation does not at once cease; for the sensitive appetite obeys the imagination rather than the will; nor does the imagination pay ready obedience to the commands of the will when this forbids it to dally with unlawful objects, or when it employs all due diligence in turning away the imagination. We may conclude with the doctrine generally received among Divines on this matter.* If the person who doubts as to his consent to an inward suggestion be of a loose conscience and in the habit of consenting, the presumption is against him and he must consider himself guilty. If, on the contrary, he be one of a delicate conscience, who habitually drives from his mind every unholy thought and emotion, the presumption is in his favour and, in general, he ought to account himself guiltless of all full and

* Castrop. in p. part, tract 2, disp. 2, n. 6.—Sayr. in Clavi Reg, lib. viij., cap. 7, num. 6.—Bar. Medina in p. part, quæst. 74, art. 8. - Trull. in Decal., lib. vij., cap. 1, dub. 13, et alii.

deliberate consent. If, further, the person be scrupulous, he is bound to believe, with moral certainty, that there has been no consent with full will, no deadly sin.

457. Third privilege. The scrupulous person is not obliged to the same self-examination or accuracy of self-inspection, which is required of those whose conscience is right; since, for such a one, self-examination would only be self-confusion.* Should he fear lest he have given consent, he must by no means search into the way and manner in which he has behaved under temptation. All he has to ask (as I said just now), is whether he is quite sure of his having consented with full deliberation and advertence? and unless he have such certainty, he must judge that there has been no mortal sin and must be at rest. As regards the fears of sinning which beset him, at one time in this, at another in that, action or circumstance, he has only to discover whether, according to the instructions he has received from his Director, these be scruples or no. In the former supposition he must waive all these inquiries and examinations, judge that such actions are lawful, and boldly step forward; but if he find himself in a labyrinth of perplexities, so as not to know what to do because he sees sin whichever way he turns, he may do as he likes, provided only it be not manifestly evident that the act he determines upon is sinful. Pursuing this course, he will not incur any guilt, as Vasquez rightly observes.† The other privileges belonging to the scrupulous will be set forth in the following Chapter, where we shall give to Directors the suggestions of which they may stand in need.

* La Croix, lib. i., De Conscient., cap. 3, n. 511.
† In 1, 2, d. 57, n. 1.

CHAPTER V.

PRACTICAL SUGGESTIONS TO DIRECTORS AS TO THE WAY IN WHICH THEY SHOULD DEAL WITH SCRUPULOUS PENITENTS.

458. THE care of scrupulous people is one of the most worrying and arduous tasks that can fall to the lot of a physician of souls. It is worrying; for as these poor creatures are ever tormenting themselves with the self-same scruples, they fail not to torment their Confessors with never-ending repetitions. It is arduous, because this malady is one from which few recover completely. But precisely because it is thus arduous, it makes the largest claims on the charity, patience, prudence, good sense, and powers of guidance of Directors, whom it is my purpose to assist with a few suggestions which, though they be not new, will yet prove useful to refresh their memory concerning various principles and precautions necessary for the due regulation of these unquiet spirits.

459. First, the Director must be decided in his tone with these timorous souls, taking care never to betray in his answers to them the slightest sign of doubt or perplexity; for otherwise their cure will be beyond hope, because his example would have more power to exaggerate their alarms than his words could have to enlarge their hearts. Secondly, in his answers, he should commonly abstain from assigning the reasons on which he founds his decisions, but he should proceed with authority, curtly telling such penitents what they must do, because, reasons in the puzzled and tangled brain of a scrupulous person are nothing but the seed from which fresh quibbles will spring. Thirdly, he must insist on their behaving towards him with full openness and sincerity; but, at the same time, he must warn them that as in Confession we may not conceal anything that is grievous, nor mention as doubtful that whereof we are certain, neither may we accuse ourselves as guilty of a mortal sin which we have not committed, nor can we bring forward as certain that which is doubtful, under the false pretext of being on the safe side; a rock

upon which these straitened and timorous consciences so often strike. Fourthly, he must treat this class of penitents with gentleness and charity, as it would be very ill-judged to add to the affliction of those who are already afflicted more than enough. He may, however, at times make use of a harsh tone of voice and may even, occasionally, send such persons away with a rebuke, in order to bend their stubbornness, when he finds them restive under the yoke of obedience, not amenable to his advice, and too much addicted to their own fancies. Fifthly, after having listened three or four times to their scruples, and laid down for them suitable rules of conduct, he must no longer give ear to them or allow them to repeat the same things, but must impose silence on them and insist upon their obeying his orders: both because the very talking about and dwelling upon their distorted fancies serves but to root these more deeply in such diseased minds, and because, when they see that their Confessor makes some account of them, they get confirmed in their whimsical notions. Better, then, is it that they should learn by the Director's example the contempt in which they ought themselves to hold such fancies. This is the advice given by most authors.* Sixthly, for the same reasons he must not allow them to confess scruples, but only such sins as they are sure of; and failing these, it is well to send them sometimes to Communion without absolution;† as this will be a great help to such for getting rid of their empty fears. Seventhly, he will not allow scrupulous persons any long self-examination, since they commonly stumble, fluctuate, oscillate, and distress themselves without cause in all their doings, fearing lest mortal sin lurk somewhere; but he will tell them that if at first sight there be no appearance of sin (especially grievous sin) they must judge that the action is lawful and set about it at once. The reasons for which most able theologians prescribe this rule are obvious, as experience shows that these alarms are groundless, and that such persons are incapable of finding this out by their long and tedious thinking; for to minds so confused as theirs, a long

* Bonac., Castrop., Sanch., Bosio, Busemb., in locis citat.

† Sanch. in Decal., lib. i., cap. 10, num. 81.—Castrop., tract. 1, disp. 4, part 2.

examination can serve no purpose whatever save to make confusion worse confounded. If, then, at first sight, they discover no sin—especially grievous sin—in what they are about to do, they may prudently believe that, being of an excessively timorous character, there is no real sin in the thing; and being incapable of any more accurate research, they must be satisfied with the knowledge of this truth, and act according to its dictates. Should they at times go astray and fall into some error, the Confessor must not look upon it as sinful, inasmuch as they acted with an upright intention, and for the best. Eighthly, the Director should take care not to dishearten a scrupulous person, by telling him that he despairs of his cure; for being already excessively timid and pusillanimous, the person may fall into utter dejection, and his disease become so aggravated as to drive him to some desperate step. The Confessor should rather make a point of always holding out the hope of cure; on the condition, however, that the patient be obedient, allow himself to be guided, submit his views to those of his Director, and act against his foolish fancies. He should further be told that he will obtain his deliverance from God, provided only he ask it perseveringly and with a lively faith. In this wise, the Director will keep up the penitent's spirits by hope, and dispose him to take the means requisite for his recovery. Ninthly, the Confessor should endeavour to keep his scrupulous penitent fully occupied; for, as we said above, idleness is the very well-spring of scruples. St. Antony complained to God as follows:—"Lord, I am resolved to save my soul, but these evil thoughts of mine will not allow me; for they are continually importuning me and throwing my soul into agitation." Whilst he was thus speaking, there appeared to him an Angel under the form of a working-man who, setting himself in front of the Saint, spent a certain time in work, then knelt down to pray; after which, having refreshed himself with food, he resumed his toil. At length, having completed this series of actions, turning to Antony, he addressed these words to him: "Do thou likewise, Antony, and thou shalt be saved"* This lesson was intended to teach that regular occupation overcomes the importunity of worrying

* Gerson, in part 4, Tract. cont. Tent. Blasph.

thoughts, and does away with the obstacles which these put to our salvation and perfection. Tenthly, though scrupulous people are usually of a timorous conscience, yet some are to be found whose conscience is in a deplorable state, and yet they have real scruples. As regards one description of sin, they are of a loose conscience, while they give way to excessive fears with respect to another. Their scruples usually turn either upon their past Confessions, or the vows they have made, or thoughts of unbelief or blasphemy. The cure of this latter class is more difficult as, though they have scruples, they cannot be said to be scrupulous. Yet they are not to be given over, and in the matters wherein they are scrupulous, any doubtful points should be settled in their favour. Their mind must be enlarged, and they should be dealt with in the same way as those of a straitened conscience. In those matters concerning which they are over free and lax, they must be drawn in, rebuked, put under restraint, and supplied with means of amendment, as is done with guilty and sinful souls. In a word, the two opposite excesses of laxity and rigour must be corrected, that they may be brought to that happy middle-path which is the sure road to heavenly bliss.

CHAPTER VI.

PRACTICAL SUGGESTIONS TO DIRECTORS CONCERNING CERTAIN CLASSES OF SCRUPLES.

460. THE suggestions set forth in the preceding Chapter may be called universal, as they will serve for the direction of all scrupulous persons, with whatever kind of scruples they may be afflicted. It has, however, seemed good to me to descend to particulars, and to lay down certain practical rules concerning points which are a frequent occasion of annoyance to numerous souls who, being detained in struggling with such scruples, are arrested in their course along the blessed road to perfection.

461. One great source of scruples for souls recently converted, and who have but lately begun to make profession of a spiritual and devout life, are the sins and Confessions of their former years. After having confessed them sufficiently, and more than sufficiently, they become much disquieted because they fancy that they have not told them all, or have omitted some circumstances which are necessary to be explained, so that they are ever urged to repeat the doleful history of their days of sin. Others are troubled by the thought that in their present Confessions they fall short of the necessary degree of sorrow; others, because they believe themselves now wanting, or to have once been wanting, in their purpose and firm resolution of never sinning again. Haunted as they are by these anxious thoughts, and worried by these empty fears, they can find no peace; hence they enjoy no calm in the good life which they have so happily begun.

462. For the relief of these afflicted souls, the Director will first recall to mind that converted sinners, who have already done their duty in the Tribunal of Penance, have no reason to go any more into the details of their past sins (to do which is very apt to excite scruples), but it is enough to think of them merely in general, as far as suffices to conceive a sorrow which shall be humble, calm, and full of trust in God's mercy. This is the teaching of St. Bernard.* To this does Cassian also allude in the twentieth Conference of Abbot Paphnutius in the following words: "We are not to dwell on our past sins, but should divert our minds from them when they recur to our memory." He means to warn us against that detailed review of the past which so often begets disquiet and scruples; but not against that general bringing to mind of our former sins, since this is fitted to awaken within us a lowly compunction and an enduring repentance.†

463. St. Laurence Justinian describes still more clearly the snares which the devil lays for beginners in the thought of their

* Ad Dominum conversos non nimis cruciet præteritorum conscientia delictorum; sed tantum humiliet vos, sicut et ipsum Paulum. Serm. 3 de SS. Petro et Paulo, cap. 9.

† Ceterum, quod paulo ante dixisti, te etiam de industrâ peccatorum præteritorum memoriam retractare, hoc fieri penitus non oportet: quin immo etiamsi violenter irrepserit, protinus extrudatur.

bygone transgressions. "How often," exclaims the Saint, "does not the devil, under pretence of compunction, delude inexperienced beginners and lure them to their ruin! Disguising himself as an angel of light, he persuades them to enter into themselves and to consider the grievousness of their faults, as a source of humility. While they do so without caution, the enemy exaggerates to them the heinousness of their past sins; stirs up within them a deep gloom; robs them of hope; and thus these hapless ones, before they are aware, fall into the abyss of despondency."* Take notice of the meaning of these words. The Saint says that an inexperienced person, from dwelling on his past sins, falls, through the deceit of the devil, into melancholy, distrust, and even into despair; all because he acts without observing due precautions. Here it is that the evil lurks; for to recall one's past sins—if duly done—is good, wholesome and most profitable. But what, will you ask, are the precautions required in calling to mind with a good result our former transgressions? They are the following:—To think of our past sins in general, without reflecting on individual acts and their accompanying circumstances, so that such consideration may serve to awaken a sorrow which is heartfelt, but at the same time humble, calm, and peaceful. Now the sorrow will certainly be such if we join with it a steady confidence in God; in such way that, while the soul is much grieved, it fails not to conceive an equal degree of trust in God's mercy. The memory of the sad past, when used in this manner, will help to cleanse the soul more thoroughly of all defilements and to make it advance to greater perfection; and hence Directors will do well to counsel it to their penitents.

464. Secondly, the Director will bear in mind, that for souls recently converted, a General Confession, though not always

* Oh, quoties sub specie boni, et sub imagine sanctæ compunctionis inexpertos, et ad spirituale certamen indoctos ludificat diabolus, et occidit! latenter namque invenit occasionem intrandi in ipsorum cor: et tamquam angelus lucis suadere conatur hujusmodi redire ad se, et humilitatis causâ suorum diligenter considerare sarcinam peccatorum. Hoc ipsis minus caute peragentibus, idem adversarius paulatim aggravat dolorem, accendit tristitiam, et aufert spem. Nec prius hi insidiatoris calliditatem agnoscunt, quam in foveam ruant desperationis. De Discipl. et Perfect. Monast. Convers., cap. 16.

necessary, is always of advantage; as, by means of a more exact accusation of all their faults and of a more lively sorrow, they are more thoroughly purified from all defilement, repair the omissions which may have crept into former Confessions, and, as far as may be amid the uncertainties of the present life, insure the pardon of all their sins. He may further allow them for a short time to confess some sin which they may have forgotten in their General Confession, as it easily happens that a grievous sin escapes the memory in the detail of so many faults. But when he finds that, having used all, ay, and more than all, the diligence required of them, they begin to repeat and, as it were, to dish up again the same things, to lose peace of mind and to get troubled at the notion that they have either not told everything, or not told it as they ought, he must bind them to a perpetual silence, and not let himself be persuaded to listen to any further confession of their past sins. If their scruples gain upon them, he must go on to acquaint them with the teaching of many grave Divines: that they are not bound to confess a sin unless they can swear that it is mortal, and that it has never been mentioned in a former Confession: and when they are about to recommence the recital of such faults, he should interrupt them with the question as to whether they are ready to take these two oaths, and if they hesitate, he should close their mouths and refuse to hear them.*

465. "But, Father," will some poor scrupulous person reply, "if I have not confessed, or not duly confessed this sin, what will become of me?" The Director will make answer: "You will come off very well: as far as this is concerned, you will be quite safe: for you are not bound to say any more." The reason of which is, that, while it is beyond question that the sin has been indirectly forgiven—supposing, of course, that the penitent has made his former Confessions with the requisite preparation and dispositions—on the other hand, he is in no manner bound to submit such a sin to the power of the keys; for, as the above-mentioned Divines teach, there is no obligation to insure the

* Sanch. in Declar., lib. 1, cap. 10, num. 8.—Castrop., tom. i., disp. 4, punct. 2.—Laym., lib. 1., tract. 5, cap. 6.—Sa, in Aphor. V. Dubium, n. 5 et alii.

material integrity of Confession at the cost of so much disturbance of the conscience and prejudice to the soul; as it is well known that less weighty reasons suffice in other cases to excuse us from material integrity. "But, Father," rejoins the scrupulous penitent, "allow me to make another examination; allow me for this once to mention some sins that are worrying me, and after that I will think no more of them." The Director must say, "No"; he must give no credence to such promises, nor allow himself to be deceived: as it is certain that, after a new examination and Confession, the penitent will be more troubled and agitated than ever. This is shown by daily experience; for, the more that scrupulous persons search and the more they talk, the more confused and troubled do they become. The remedy for them is, in subjection to obedience, not to confess, but to refrain from confessing the particular sin, and to make no account of their vain doubts. The Director will therefore insist on silence, requiring of them to obey; and if after all they feel trouble and remorse, let them offer all up to God, and bear all patiently for His sake; and, as Blosius says much to the purpose, great merit will be gained by his resignation.*

466. The Director will meet with others, again, who are always anxious about their Contrition, or about their Purpose of Amendment, fancying they are not doing, and never have done, what is required of them. In these cases, when the Confessor finds that the penitent is, or has been, careful to make an act of true sorrow, he must not allow him to repeat his Confessions; since the presumption is in his favour, and, until the contrary be clearly established, he is under no obligation to repeat them. On the other hand, the repetition is not advisable, on account of the spiritual injury which may easily result from these renewed accusations. Such penitents should be reminded that a sensible sorrow is not required for the validity of the Confession, but, as the holy Council of Trent says, the sorrow of the soul—of the will, that is—suffices; and when it says that the sorrow required for the Sacra-

* Si post Confessionem, ut oportet, peractam, remorsus adhuc remaneant, patienter cum humili resignatione ferendi sunt, et propter illos Confessio iteranda non est. In Confess. Animæ Fidelis, cap. 2.

ment should be *above all*, it means that it must be such in the appreciation of the intelligence, not in the sensibility or feeling of the affections. Whence it follows, that if he who confesses feel not a sorrowful heart, but acknowledging the evil which is contained in the offence against God, detests it above all other evil, and is determined to undergo anything rather than to repeat the offence against the Divine Goodness, he has a sufficient sorrow, and is duly prepared for Sacramental Absolution. Nor can any one justly complain that this sorrow is beyond his reach, because God is ever ready to grant it to all who will ask it of Him, and will do their part to stir it up in the will. Concerning the Purpose of Amendment, we may observe, that even relapses, however frequent they may be, are by no means an indisputable token of its having been wanting in past Confessions; for the will, driven on by passions within, and lured by the presence of agreeable objects without, and deprived of that light wherewith it was aided in approaching the Sacred Tribunal, may easily change. Hence, we must make no account of the anxiety of a scrupulous person—who is unduly troubled about his former Confessions from the experience he has had of his past inconstancy.

467. Some are greatly distressed in reciting vocal prayers, fancying they have omitted portions, or not pronounced the words plainly, so that they repeat again and again the same words, or frequently begin their prayers anew from the commencement; without, of course, ever gaining any peace or satisfaction from so doing. These should be commanded to go forward in their prayers, to despise the vain fear that straitens their heart and dries up in it all the sap of devotion, and they must be forbidden ever to repeat any portion. If they feel troubled about the attention which they fancy they fail in paying to their prayers, they must be told that there are three kinds of attention:—First, to the words; taking care to pronounce them without clipping the syllables, and in a becoming manner, and with the intention of praying. Secondly, we can attend to the sense of the words. Thirdly, attention may be given to God Himself, and this takes place whenever the soul is in any way recollected in Him. Any one of these kinds of attention suffices to render our prayers

availing and meritorious If, then, the penitent be seen to recite the Divine Office with the intention of praying, and of complying with the obligation laid upon him by Holy Church; and having his mind occupied in the correct pronunciation of the words, he do not admit any fully wilful distraction, the Director will never allow him to repeat any portion: because, although this kind of attention be less perfect than it might be, it is nevertheless sufficient. Enough has now been said on this point; for were I to undertake to go into the particulars of the several kinds of scruples that may be met with, the task would be the same as that of attempting to count all the distorted and mad fancies that can possibly be engendered in the human mind, or that the devil can manage to stir up in the soul for the destruction of man's peace and quiet.

END OF VOL. II

R. AND T. WASHBOURNE, 4 PATERNOSTER ROW, LONDON.

Lightning Source UK Ltd.
Milton Keynes UK
UKHW050045271021
392864UK00017B/540